LEVI ESHKOL

Levi Eshkol

From Pioneering Operator to Tragic Hero – A Doer

SHLOMO ARONSON

VALLENTINE MITCHELL
LONDON • CHICAGO

First published in paperback in 2023 by Vallentine Mitchell

Catalyst House, 720 Centennial Court
Centennial Park
Elstree, WD6 3SY, UK

814 N. Franklin Street
Chicago, Illinois
60610, USA

www.vmbooks.com

First published in cloth in 2011

British Library Cataloguing in Publication Data
An entry can be found on request

ISBN 978 1 80371 022 8 (paper)
ISBN 978 1 80371 023 5 (ebook)

Library of Congress Cataloging-in-Publication Data
An entry can be found on request

This book is dedicated to the memory of Ya'akov Amorai, a unique incarnation of the founding fathers of Israel, who educated generations of students in Judaic studies at Ha-Carmel Elementary School, Tel Aviv

Contents

List of Plates viii

Preface ix

List of Abbreviations xiii

1. A Practical Idealist in Ottoman and British Palestine 1
2. Eshkol, the Nazis, the Palestinians and the British 11
3. Eshkol during the Second World War, Trouble at Home and Abroad 19
4. Arch-Settler, Treasurer and Minister of Finance 35
5. Eshkol's Bid for Rescuing Mapai 53
6. Eshkol's New Era 89
7. Eshkol Response to a Stormy Period 133
8. Mr Eshkol's Tea and Coffee 149
9. Eshkol's Supreme Test 176
10. Levi Eshkol and the Lost Glory 197
11. Eshkol's Exploitation of a Problematic Victory 211
12. Eshkol's Last Acts 231

Epilogue 251

Bibliography 255

Index 264

Plates

1. British Mandate.
2. 1922: Separation of Transjordan.
3. 1947 UN Partition plan.
4. 1949 Armistice Lines.
5. Israel's armistice lines before and after June 1967.
6. Eshkol as a student in Vilnius High School, 1913.
7. Eshkol at a Negev water project, 1947.
8. Eshkol in a new moshav, 1955.
9. Eshkol with Yemenite settlers, mid-1950s.
10. Eshkol breaks the ground for a new moshav, late 1950s.
11. Eshkol launches the National Water Carrier, 1962.
12. Defence Minister Eshkol surveys a bombed kibbutz from the Syrian Golan Heights on the eve of the Six Day War, 1966.
13. Prime Minister Eshkol with his 'friend' President Johnson, Miriam Eshkol and Lady Bird Johnson, mid-1960s.
14. The Prime Minister is invited to visit the Wailing Wall, June 1967.

Preface

The memoirs of Dr Chaim Weizmann, legendary president of the World Zionist Organization and first President of the State of Israel, are titled *Massa' u-Ma'as* in Hebrew.[1] *Massa* is a play on words; the book is a treatise and a life struggle against all odds. *Ma'as*, in turn, means action – action rather than empty talk, based among other things on the following anecdote: As a young Zionist activist, while studying chemistry in Geneva in the early twentieth century, Weizmann heard a public debate on Zionism, in which a Jewish student excelled in debating the anti-Zionists Lenin and Plechanov. He approached the brilliant speaker and asked him whether his arguments could be extended and published. The orator responded that he first needed to visit the libraries in Paris. Weizmann invested much effort in raising the necessary funds and wished the promising author a successful trip. He never heard from him until much later, when he saw him by chance back in Geneva in the company of two young women. Weizmann asked him whether he had in fact gone to Paris and what he had done there.

> 'Oh', said he, 'I *talked* to everyone'.

The man touched upon a rather sensitive nerve among active Zionists: the utter passivity that, as they saw it, was so common among Jews in the European Diaspora when it came to far-reaching changes in their ways of life and the dangers awaiting them as problematic minorities, which made them talkers rather than doers.

> 'We', Weizmann retorted, 'have decided not just to talk – but to act'.

In a way, this was the life story of Levi Eshkol. It entailed relentless doing in Ottoman and British Palestine as a settler and the director of rural settlement and water resources, and in independent Israel as economic tsar, Minister of Finance, and finally Prime Minister and Minister of Defence.

Eshkol's pioneering efforts were sometimes criticized as though they were 'actionism', exertions for their own sake. Yet he was hailed as a cunning operator. His wisdom was a common wisdom among idealists, dreamers and far-sighted statesmen – solving enormous problems amid changing realities within the overall framework of Zionist social democracy and its partisan structure. Some saw contradictions among his and his peers' limitless efforts to transform socialist Zionism into reality, their partisan interests and loyalties, and the ideology of Social-Democratic Zionism itself – between short-term necessities and remote future demands, between the principles of good government and a state of law, and Eshkol's tough pragmatism. Here, for most of his life, his story is inseparable from that of David Ben-Gurion, his senior colleague and ultimately his nemesis. The issues that separated them, including the handling of the highly sensitive complex of Israel's quest for nuclear deterrence, conventional war doctrines, and – concurrently – necessary domestic rules of behaviour and government reform, finally attracted the attention of historians, especially because of his role in the lead up to the Six Day War and its ramifications to this day, thanks to the opening of archives and perspectives gained thereby. Eshkol himself, in most of his public life, skirted personal criticism in these matters by dint of his jovial, tremendously charming personality and his success in implementing an economic and social policy that proposed, as much as possible, to reconcile economic development with the prevention of socioeconomic disparities.[2] Such was the case until the tragic chapter in which he became the butt of mockery and parody due to the way the same personal qualities were construed in a new era, an era that he tried his best to welcome and shape but that suddenly seemed to be facing existential threats. Even then, as he tried to pave his own way, Eshkol's career was so strongly influenced by Ben-Gurion that this book will deal with Ben-Gurion and compare him with Eshkol through necessity rather than choice.

A trader, a fixer, an arbiter, and a highly experienced bureaucrat and machine politician, Eshkol was propelled to the offices of

Prime Minister and Minister of Defence of Israel after the political demise of his formidable predecessor Ben-Gurion, a demise to which Eshkol unintentionally contributed his share. Eshkol's loyal services to Ben-Gurion will preoccupy us here, as will the differences between the two men. Much of the discussion of Ben-Gurion's behaviour in this book is provided merely as essential background for an understanding of Eshkol's eventual deviation from it, not only in terms of the substance of policy decisions but also in terms of Eshkol's modus operandi in general. Once Eshkol assumed both portfolios, premiership and defence, he tried his best to modernize Israeli democracy amid constant conflict with Ben-Gurion. Later, he was expected to become a warlord on the eve of the 1967 Six Day War, a confrontation that he tried his best to avoid by counting on his personal ties with American President Lyndon Johnson and assuming that the latter would not leave him to fend for Israel as best he could, having his own view about the May 1967 crisis and its immediate outcome, while pursuing American, rather than Eshkol's interests. He was pushed out from the Defence Ministry before the war erupted, presided over a Government of National Unity shortly before, during and after the war, and died broken-hearted shortly after the war ended, even though it seemed to have been an enormous victory. The 'glory' went to others; Eshkol perceived himself as the architect of the triumphant Israel Defence Forces. In the time he had left, he contributed to changes in Israeli policy on the occupied territories that had ramifications of abiding importance, such as the unification of Jerusalem and demands for direct negotiations with the Arab states and territorial adjustments in Israel's favour. Presiding over a National Unity Government after the war, Eshkol authorized the first few Israeli settlements in the occupied territories. Concurrently, thanks to Israel's new stature among American Jews, he enjoyed relations with the White House that, under a new administration, not only exhibited greater balance but also evolved into a limited strategic alliance – an alliance that Eshkol had tried to forge beforehand without much success, although he planted a few of its seeds as best he could. Some of the decisions of Eshkol's post-1967 coalition prompted another war in 1973; others, under very different circumstances, led to peace with Egypt and Jordan but not yet with the Palestinians. Finally, Eshkol created the modern Israel Labour Party, which at the time of writing is en route to demise. Much abused in his last years, Eshkol's reputation now seems to have been restored, possibly in comparison with that of his successors. The reason his life story is worth telling from the perspective of the twenty-first century, however, while partly due to this factor is also due to newly opened archives. The story indeed needs to be told not only because it is the biography of an important figure that shaped Israeli history, but also because it may contribute new facts to, and illuminate the study of, some less-known dimensions of the Arab-Israeli conflict, United States foreign policy, and even Soviet behaviour at crucial historical junctures.

My intentions for this book were several. First to give a major actor in Israeli, regional, and finally in American-Israeli politics his due, particularly for the benefit of English readers who may be unaware of his achievements. Second, to discuss Prime Minister Eshkol's modus operandi on the road to the Six Day War of 1967, and the role played by Israel's nuclear programme on that road, which is usually missing from the conventional literature. Third, to discuss Eshkol's contribution to the results of the 1967 War, some of which that are of great importance to this day. Finally to illuminate Eshkol's domestic regime and its ramifications for our time and age.

There is a biography of Eshkol's life and achievements, a one-sided account in Hebrew, based on Israeli sources only.[3] The retelling that follows, in contrast, makes use of available sources, old and new, including a variety of foreign records and foreign observations of Eshkol's behaviour at the most important junctures of his career. I also draw on my own forthcoming book on David Ben-Gurion and a variety of research articles pertaining to both Ben-Gurion and Eshkol.[4]

NOTES

1. In English: *Trial and Error: The Autobiography of Chaim Weizmann* (New York: Harper & Bros., 1949).
2. See Moshe Lissak, chief editor, *The History of the Jewish Community in Eretz Israel since 1882, Israel, the First Decade,* in Hebrew (Jerusalem: The Israel Academy of Sciences and Humanities, 2009), pp.207–32. See also Fanny Ginor, *Socio-Economic Disparities in Israel* (Tel Aviv: Tel Aviv University; Transaction Books, 1979), pp.101–20.
3. Yossi Goldstein, *Eshkol, Biography*, in Hebrew (Jerusalem: Keter Publishers, 2003).
4. See Shlomo Aronson, 'David Ben-Gurion, Levi Eshkol and the Struggle over Dimona: A Prologue to the Six-Day War and its (Un) Anticipated Results', *Israel Affairs*, 15, 2 (April 2009), pp.114–34; 'Israel Security and the Holocaust: Lessons Learned, but Existential Fears Continue', *Israel Studies*, 14, 1 (Spring 2009), pp.65–93; 'David Ben-Gurion and the British Constitutional Model', *Israel Studies*, 3, 2 (Autumn 1998), pp.193–214; and *David Ben-Gurion and the Jewish Renaissance* (New York: Cambridge University Press, 2010, in press). Parts of these publications have been incorporated into this book.

Abbreviations

COGS	Chief of the [IDF] General Staff
DP	Displaced Persons
Deptel	Diplomatic telegram [US]
FADC	Foreign Affairs and Defence Committee of the Knesset
FAEC	French Atomic Energy Commission
FRUS	*Foreign Relations of the United States*
GHQ	General Headquarters [IDF]
GOC	General Officer in Command
GOI	Government of Israel
HMG	His Majesty's Government
IAEA	International Atomic Energy Agency
IAEC	Israel Atomic Energy Commission
IAF	Israel Air Force
IDF	Israel Defence Forces
IRBM	Intermediate Range Ballistic Missile
IZL	[Irgun Tsva'i Leummi] National Military Organization or 'Irgun'
MI	Military Intelligence
MOD	[Israel] Ministry of Defence
NMO	National Military Organization, aka IZL or 'Irgun'
NPT	Non-Proliferation Treaty
NRP	National Religious Party
NSC	National Security Council [US]
PM	Prime Minister
PMO	Prime Minister's Office [Israel]
PRO	Public Records Office [British]
UAR	United Arab Republic [Egypt]
USG	United States Government

Chapter One

A Practical Idealist in Ottoman and British Palestine

PROVENANCE

Levi, son of Deborah (as he called himself all his life), Shkolnik-Eshkol[1] was born on 25 October 1895, in Oratovo, a small town in the Ukraine, to a relatively affluent but declining Jewish family rooted in the surrounding nature.[2] Later, as 'tsar' of the Zionist settlement effort in British Palestine and independent Israel, Eshkol referred to his Ukrainian birth place as the source of his love of nature and agricultural labour. His future as a young Jew in this habitat, however, was rather grim. In his early years, the discrimination that was applied against Jews in Tsarist Russia; the limitations imposed on them in education, future employment and political emancipation; and their victimization in government-supported pogroms, created much accumulated latent energy in some Jews that resulted in an explosion of hectic activity once they were given a chance. Other Jews were unable to find their way in the rapidly changing world of early twentieth-century Russia or sought refuge in the west until Great Britain and the United States closed their gates to Jewish immigration in 1905–19 and 1921–24, respectively. During the years of Eshkol's youth, the process of secularization drove many East European Jews in various directions such as revolutionary activities at home, a quest for Jewish autonomy in Tsarist Russia, or emigration to the west.

Eshkol, after receiving a traditional Jewish and general education at primary level, graduated from a secular, Zionist-inspired high school in Vilnius, joined a non-Marxist Labour Zionist movement, and stepped ashore in Ottoman Palestine on 19 February 1914. Before doing so, Eshkol had absorbed traditional Jewish and Russian literature – as he would continue to do later on – and had been exposed to the process of the proletarization of the Jewish middle class, which gave rise to a range of secular partisan Jewish national organizations, a wide range of cultural activities, the revival of the Hebrew language, and widespread teaching activities that transcended partisanship.[3] Due to all these factors, the Tsarist government's economic siege on the Jewish population had begun to create a Jewish proletariat, which distinguished itself by a separate identity in terms of culture, language and social and mental habits, from the Russian, Ukrainian and Polish masses, most of which emerged from the ranks of the anti-Semitic peasantry and the new urban working class. Eshkol was neither here nor there; he was the product of a Jewish middle class that was facing decline and ruin. Nor could he find a home in the non-Jewish socialist parties, for these entities perceived the masses of impoverished Jews as unwanted aliens or even as a political burden for reasons that had to do, among other things, with the radical anti-Semitic doctrines of Karl Marx. In this turgid environment, many Jews maintained their own identity or at least tried to create new-old identities of their own. Among the Jewish masses, Professor Eliezer Schweid draws our attention to the growing tension between the small, wealthy Jewish financial elite and the Jewish masses, against the background of the scanty investments by the former in alleviating the grinding poverty of the latter.

FIRST CAREER STEPS IN OTTOMAN PALESTINE

Young Levi Eshkol, then, set his political sights on a Jewish national social democratic party and eschewed other Jewish socialist organizations that adopted Marxism for their diverse Zionist and anti-Zionist purposes and recruited large numbers of Jews at the time, for example, the large anti-Zionist Bund.[4] Eshkol made his choice as a man of action. Unlike others who embraced the ideology of the Jewish renaissance in Zion but failed to follow through on the idea – at least at that time – he joined the handful who eventually formed the group of Israel's founding fathers as a practicing, moderate socialist. Remaining loyal to his small group, called Ha-po'el ha-Tsa'ir (the Young Worker) for decades to come, Eshkol proved to be a hard-working pioneer under challenging conditions, an organizer of idealistic Zionist agricultural workers like himself and of communal settlement efforts that required constant negotiations and pleading with Zionist organizations for minimal financial support. For these reasons, he was drawn at a rather early stage to public economic activities, which he combined with his own physical labour, in which he excelled, and his partisan affiliations. As such, Eshkol quickly earned the Yiddish nickname of *makher* – a doer – whose energy, good humour and persistence yielded maximum results under difficult conditions. Over the years, Eshkol, like many other leading pioneers, became a prolific contributor to his party's publications and those of other factions of the Zionist Labour Movement. He also delivered lengthy speeches at their assemblies and wrote detailed reports to his colleagues, wives and lovers, and superiors, mostly dealing with nitty-gritty hardships and how to deal with them while searching for immediate resolutions within the treatises like Ben-Gurion's, they are an important source in understanding the almost insurmountable obstacles that he and the other founding fathers of Israel confronted. They also shed light on the workings of the mind of a socialist pioneer who, under changed circumstances, had been transformed into a socialist operator and a political bureaucrat.

Eshkol, like other Zionist activists at the time, tried to work within the Ottoman system in the hope of acquiring official minority status for the Jews in this multinational empire. He was atypical among the pioneers of the Second Aliya[5] (the second wave of Zionist immigration to Palestine, the first having arrived in the early 1880s). Although many participants in the Second Aliya either died or left the backward, desolate country shortly after reaching it, these pioneers were an austere, tough, deadly serious, humourlessly puritanical bunch, many of whom divided their loyalties among various ideological groupings in spite of their very small numbers. Eshkol, in contrast, was as fun-loving as the circumstances permitted, far from Puritanism, and physically capable of distinguishing himself by performing the hardest labour.

During the First World War, Eshkol tried his best to support the Jewish agricultural workers, whose living conditions had become almost untenable under the harsh realities of the war and the growing Turkish-Muslim enmity.[6] As the British closed in, he joined the Jewish battalions that served the British Army in the process of occupying Palestine. Concurrently, he remained politically active and became increasingly doubtful about the possibility of Jewish–Arab coexistence in view of Muslim loyalty to the Ottomans and various acts of Arab violence against Jews immediately after the war. The issue was not only the yawning mental gap between Muslims and non-believers but also the cultural gap that transformed the Zionist women pioneers, who dressed in shorts and worked in the fields with those strange 'new Jews' – so different from the humble Orthodox who inhabited the Old City of Jerusalem – into 'Communist sinners' in Arab eyes, and that rendered the kibbutzim into 'Bolshevik endeavours'. Eshkol also noted the role of violence among the Arabs in settling feuds at all levels: within the family or the clan, between families and clans, and between those who harboured repressed hate to those who could transform hidden danger to action, prescribed by tradition, power struggle and missing defences. It was a highly political culture, Eshkol thought, in the sense that it taught people to hide their own feelings and use a rich, complicated and politically correct language to avoid trouble with the mighty, the cunning and those who harboured repressed hate – a humourless culture that was nevertheless capable of kindness and warmth, a culture that allowed split-second transitions from gracious hospitability to terrible outbursts of rage and violence.

Over the years, such generalizations became impossible to enunciate publicly for a progressive social democrat like Eshkol. Therefore, the actual outcome was an ambivalence and suspicion that impelled Eshkol to seek and obtain important positions in the defence entities that preceded and shortly followed the attainment of statehood – which we discuss briefly below – and that led, later on, to his views about the Palestinian refugee question combined with his domestic priorities, which we discuss in greater detail in the continuation of this account.

Intellectually, Eshkol was a practical man, a negotiator and a compromiser who would abolish the military government that Israel initially imposed on its Arab population. For most of his life he concentrated on the positive, that is, the Zionist settlement effort in a country that he simply believed to be his Jewish homeland. Emotionally, however, he was ambivalent about Arabs and especially suspicious of their leaders and their dialectical relations with their own masses – and so he would be to his dying day. By drawing dialectical associations, Eshkol understood the agitation from above and the anti-Jewish sentiment among the masses as feeding each other. He encountered it every now and then, especially during the tenure of the Palestinian leader Hajj Amin al-Husaini as Mufti of Jerusalem and the extremely violent war that Husaini waged against moderate Palestinian leaders and the Jews of Palestine during the 1930s culminating in an alliance with Hitler.[7] Finally, during his last two years, Eshkol refused to trust Arab leaders both emotionally and intellectually. As a man who was devoted at the practical level to the great victory that Israel won in a war that he had initially opposed, Eshkol refused to barter the triumph for nothing but entertained grave doubts about his own and others' post-1967 policies – which he carried out anyway, as if the gods had made him into a triumphant but neglected hero and the tragic tool of a hazardous future.

Eshkol developed his settlement activities in a country where pre-Zionist and early Zionist efforts had preceded his own.[8] The pre-Zionist endeavour was largely financed by philanthropists such as the Baron Edmond de Rothschild of France, who established several farming settlements based on capitalist principles and ruled them rather strictly by means of his representatives. As Penslar describes it, the early Zionist enterprise was created by an international organization that attempted to settle people in a barren land by importing modern agricultural technologies instead of exploiting the treasures of a colonial endeavour, which were absent in the country at issue. By the time Eshkol arrived, in contrast, modern Zionist efforts had already created a number of settlements, agricultural enterprises and privately owned colonies, and the seeds of communal work were already planted in the first kibbutz. This form of collective enterprise was born as an idealistic scheme and an incorporated legal entity that could, as such, guarantee the loans granted to it by the local representative of the World Zionist Organization, a tough entity run by German Jews.

Most of Palestine, to Eshkol's mind, was a neglected desert, some of it infested with malaria, which he contracted in due course. Zionist individuals and agencies were buying land, but the real effort, he believed, had to be invested in 'making the desert bloom' by dint of Jewish physical labour, community-building and the return to nature, which Eshkol hoped to promote by virtue of the November 1917 Balfour Declaration.[9] From the outset, Eshkol and his peers were determined to advance their venture within the framework of Jewish communes, based on Jewish labour, as opposed to the First Aliya farmers, who hired cheap Arab labour and subjected socialist pioneers who worked for them to conditions of misery and exploitation in view of their small-minded profit calculations. It was due to this exploitation that the socialist pioneers consecrated the goal of 'Hebrew labour' and organized Hebrew labourers in regional and later countrywide settings, in which Eshkol quickly surfaced in a leading role.

BRITAIN AND ESHKOL SHARE A MANDATE

In the meantime, Palestine lacked even the most rudimentary infrastructure for modern enterprise. The British, however, started to create such an infrastructure by the sweat of Jewish pioneer labour, and thanks to Jewish tax payers, alongside the development of the existing communal settlements, most of which – like Eshkol himself – rejected Marxism in favour of various social-democratic forms.

Manoeuvring in the fragmented Labour Zionist camp, Eshkol quickly demonstrated his qualities as a pragmatic social-democrat, a man of relentless action, but a compromiser when necessary, always seeking a measure of unity among the diverse labour parties and groupings, many of which arrived after the First World War (in the Third Aliya) and acting in the service of the voluntary Federation of Jewish Labour in Palestine, which had been established in 1920. Known as the Histadrut[10] in Hebrew (*histadrut* denoting a federation), its task was not only to serve as an umbrella organization for the few existing labour unions and to create new ones, especially in the construction and manufacturing industries, but also to spearhead economic development and settlement throughout the area mandated to Britain.[11] To attain the latter goal, the Histadrut proposed to invoke an expansionist economic policy in general disregard of profit and even the rules of economic efficiency. The Histadrut would create jobs and provide healthcare, education, cultural and identity services in a country that lacked basic public facilities. The services would be paid for by the membership on a voluntary basis, with help in the form of capital imports, especially from American sources. These activities, aimed at gaining control of the country's non-existent economy and thickening the Jewish fabric of Palestine, were unique in the sense that socialists of various complexions were operating in a reality devoid of any resemblance to the European nations in which an industrial proletariat honed various tools to deal with well established middle classes and traditional elites. The reality of British Palestine and that of the post-First World War era demanded different tools and innovative ideas that would accompany the idealism of those who had managed to leave behind the civil-war-torn Soviet Union, Poland's birth problems and the emergence of volatile nation-states across Europe.

At that time (1920), Eshkol and other pioneers established one of the first collective settlements, Kibbutz Degania Bet, to which he formally belonged all his life.[12] However, other forms of settlement conceived the early 1920s, foremost the moshav (smallholders' cooperative) attracted his attention and support.[13] Initially Eshkol invested much personal effort in making his kibbutz a success while continuing his activities as a member, and later the director, of the Histadrut Agricultural Center. He also became the Center's water expert, but in practice he had the sense to hire professional hydrologists, especially the innovative water engineer Simcha Blas, to develop the country's water resources.[14]

In the face of the Arab riots in April 1920 and in 1921, the Zionists began to create a semi-legal militia known as Hagana ('defence'). Eshkol joined its directorate, in which he was mainly in charge of weapons and equipment procurement and recruitment until 1923. He would return to this office in 1940 and retain it until 1948. During the 1920s, Eshkol also contributed an important share to the creation and development of the Histadrut's corporative tools.

Eshkol's main characteristics had matured by now. He was indeed a doer, and a grand doer at that. He displayed a finely developed sense of humour, flashing the Yiddish anecdotes and puns that became his trademark. A man of endless wit as a conversationalist among small circles of friends and foes, he was, however, a poor and less-than-charismatic public speaker then and forever. He was also a rather successful womanizer at a time when the pioneers' official Puritanism often served as a mere fig leaf for romanticism and release from traditional Jewish restrictions. It was another habit that Eshkol would keep up until old age.

His activities at the Histadrut focused on the integration of waves of immigrants, mainly from Poland, who were settling in cities such as Tel Aviv in the mid-1920s (the Fourth Aliya) rather than the countryside – people who were hardly motivated by the communal pioneering spirit that drove Eshkol.[15] The expansionist economic policy that extensive urban settlement entailed, however – including investments in construction and other embryonic industrial efforts – proved so problematic that Eshkol turned his main attention to various forms of collective agricultural effort that eschewed the highly demanding kibbutz way of life.[16] At the same time, he became a fully fledged Labour politician, representing his rather small anti-Marxist party in the Histadrut organs but maintaining acquaintance with, and being appreciated by, mainstream labour-movement leaders such as David Ben-Gurion. Ben-Gurion was drawn to Eshkol by the latter's quest for a Labour Movement unity that was still unacceptable to his own party colleagues and rejected by the radical Marxists who populated the far Left. As a moderate socialist, Eshkol travelled extensively in his quest for unity among the various labour factions abroad, and contributed importantly to the creation of the Palestine Labour Party (Mapai) in 1930.[17] This body, however, never attained the full unity that was advertised for it, and much effort had to be invested by David Ben-Gurion and Berl Katznelson, its primary leaders, and by secondary leaders such as Eshkol, to keep it from falling apart until the inevitable fracture in 1944, discussed below. Much later, Eshkol would become the 'boss' of Mapai, in which capacity he would attempt to reunite the labour bloc, with unforeseeable ramifications for Israel's future polity.

NOTES

1. The subject of our study adopted his Hebrew surname Eshkol, denoting a bunch or a cluster of grapes, during Israel's War of Independence. For the reader's convenience,

we refer to him by this surname throughout.

2. The primary sources on Eshkol's background and early and later career are culled from the official history published by the Israel State Archives, *Levi Eshkol, the Third Prime Minister of Israel, Selected Documents on Chapters in His Life*, in Hebrew (Jerusalem: Israel State Archives, 2002), and verified by comparison with other primary sources now available at the Archive and matched by others, such as various volumes of *Foreign Relations of the United States* (FRUS) and British primary sources obtained at the National Archive, Kew, where Eshkol's roles as Prime Minister and Minister of Defence are concerned. Other collections of records, updated scholarly works unknown to the English reader, and interviews with qualified Israeli scholars and witnesses are quoted separately. I augmented the written sources by interviewing major figures who played various roles at the time of Eshkol's activities. I also took the liberty to use my own reminiscences from Eshkol's times as an active observer. There is also a biography in Hebrew by Yossi Goldstein, *Eshkol – A Biography* (Jerusalem: Keter, 2003), Goldstein's biography is uncritical if not biased and contains in various cases factual mistakes; thus, it is unreliable as a source on Eshkol's career as a major player in Israel's foreign and security policies. Hence I quote it only on the basis of verifiable primary sources used by its author. *Levi Eshkol, on the Steps of the Mission* (Tel Aviv: Massada Publishers, 1969) in Hebrew, by Yosef Shapira, is in fact a collection of parts of Eshkol's own speeches and interviews.
3. See Eliezer Schweid, *A History of Modern Jewish Religious Philosophy,* Part III, vol. I, *The Historical Crossroads*, in Hebrew (Tel Aviv: Am Oved, 2003), pp.255–7. See also Moshe Mishkinski, *Studies in Jewish Socialism*, in Hebrew (Sede Boqer and Tel Aviv: Ben-Gurion and Tel Aviv University Press, 2004).
4. See Mishkinski, *Studies in Jewish Socialism*, pp.24–39.
5. See Mordechai Naor (ed.), *The Second Aliya 1903–1914, Sources, Summaries, Selected Issues and Supplementary Material*, in Hebrew (Jerusalem: Yad Izhak Ben-Zvi, 1984).
6. Israel State Archives, *Levi Eshkol*, pp.4–5.
7. For an updated biography of Hajj Amin al-Husaini, see Klaus Gensicke, *Der Mufti von Jerusalem und die Nationalsozialisten. Eine politische Biographie Amin el-Husseinis*, ed. Klaus-Michael Mallmann (Ludwigsburg: Ludwigsburg Series of Publications, 2007). For an English version based on newly available German records, see Klaus Gensicke, *The Mufti of Jerusalem and the Nazis. Amin al-Husaini: The Berlin Years 1941–1945* (London and Portland, OR: Vallentine Mitchell, 2010). See further Efraim Karsh, *Palestine Betrayed* (New Haven, CT: Yale University Press, 2010), especially chapter 3.
8. See Derek J. Penslar, *Zionism and Technocracy: The Engineering of Jewish Settlement in Palestine, 1870–1918* (Bloomington and Indianapolis, IN: Indiana University Press, 1991); see also Margalit Shiloh, *Experiments in Settlements. The Palestine Office 1908–1914*, in Hebrew (Jerusalem: Yad Izhak Ben-Zvi, 1988).
9. The Balfour Declaration was an official British letter of intent to create a Jewish National Home in Palestine, provided that the rights of the indigenous population not be compromised; as such it was incorporated into the mandate that the League of Nations granted the British Government in June 1922.
10. This section and subsequent chapters that discuss the Histadrut and its roles in the history of the Yishuv and independent Israel are based on Yosef Gorny, Avi Bareli and Yitzhak Greenberg (eds), *From a Labour Society to a Labour Organization. Articles on the Histadrut during the Yishuv and the Statehood Periods*, in Hebrew (Sede Boqer: Ben-Gurion Heritage Center and Tel Aviv University, 2000).
11. Israel State Archives, *Levi Eshkol*, pp.22–3; cf. official website of the Prime Minister's Office, http://www.pmo.gov.il/ PMO/History/FormerPrimeMinister/eskol.htm.
12. See Henry Near, *The Kibbutz Movement: A History*, in Hebrew (Jerusalem, Tel Aviv and Sede Boqer: Ben-Gurion University Press, 2008).
13. See Abigail Paz-Yeshaiahu and Yosef Gorny (eds), *A Historical Achievement and Its Evolution, the Kibbutz and Moshav Settlement Movements, 1910–1990*, in Hebrew (Sede Boqer and Tel Aviv: Ben-Gurion University Press, 2006).
14. Indeed, it was through Blas' recommendation that the National Water Carrier, which

would feed especially arid parts of Israel using the water of the Sea of Galilee, would be built.

15. Israel State Archives, *Levi Eshkol*, pp.55–60.
16. Ibid. The depression of the mid-1920s was alleviated by large public works such as the construction of Haifa port, development of the electricity grid and the establishment of potash works at the Dead Sea. Apart from the port, where the Anglo-Iraqi oil pipeline terminated, the other projects were chartered by the British Government to public corporations.
17. Israel State Archives, *Levi Eshkol*, pp.80–3.

Chapter Two

Eshkol, the Nazis, the Palestinians and the British

NEGOTIATING WITH NAZI GERMANY

Following Hitler's rise to power, an initiative by the German Consul General in Jerusalem and a local Israeli businessman, representing a private enterprise that wished to transfer German-Jewish assets to Palestine, was transformed by Eshkol into a Labour-controlled operation.[1] The endeavour itself was connected with German deliberations aimed at avoiding Jewish-inspired boycott, or counter-boycott, of Nazi Germany as a reaction to anti-Jewish measures taken by the regime, and could be justified by it in terms of the official Nazi policy of forced Jewish emigration, including to the 'Jewish homeland' in Palestine. At that time, the British Mandatory authorities were willing to increase Jewish immigration into Palestine if employment for the newly arrived could be found. This required capital investment, and German-Jewish immigrants – few of whom had identified with the Zionists before Hitler's rise to power and, even if they had, had never seriously thought of leaving Germany for Palestine – would make a much greater contribution to the country's Jewish population (about 280,000 in 1932) and its economy in general, including Arabs who profited from Jewish economic activities, than the previous waves of poor immigrants from Poland and Romania.

Representing the Jewish Agency for Palestine, the newly created governing body of the World Zionist Movement, Chaim Arlosoroff, director of the Agency's Political Department, and Levi Eshkol, by now a leading investment expert for the

Histadrut, negotiated a rather complex deal with the German Ministry of Economic Affairs. In the Ha'avara (Transfer) Agreement, signed in August 1933, German Jews with capital at their disposal were permitted to buy German industrial goods, mainly consisting of means of production such as machinery, cement mixers and irrigation equipment, that Eshkol and his colleagues specified according to the needs and development plans in Palestine. The Anglo-Palestine Bank, the financial arm of the Jewish Agency, collaborated with buyers in the country who were interested in the German goods. In Germany, a Jewish financial institution was established to receive money from Jewish individuals and order the required goods from German suppliers, after paying 'what in effect were ransom taxes to the German government'.[2] The goods were shipped to Palestine, and when the German-Jewish investors reached that destination, they received their money back in pounds sterling less deductions for Zionist endeavours that the Agency and Eshkol and his colleagues specified. This arrangement had the further advantage of facilitating the immigration to Palestine of other Jews who had no funds of their own. The flow of capital to the poor Yishuv became a major turning point in its development, along with the qualities of the German immigrants, who transformed the landscape of Palestine not only in physical, but in cultural, educational, industrial and financial terms.

As for the Germans' interest in the Transfer Agreement, the accord did prohibit preparations for an anti-Nazi boycott campaign that were being made by American Jewish organizations and yet allowed Jews to leave Germany with some means for their absorption in Palestine. It also fractured Zionist unity because the scuttling of the boycott touched off a bitter controversy, followed by sharp criticism of the deal by right-wing Zionists organized under Ze'ev Jabotinsky's Revisionist (radical right-wing) Zionist Movement, several of whose most extreme followers were accused of murdering Arlosoroff later in 1933. The resulting feud between Labour Zionists and the Revisionists would only intensify and acquire violent characteristics during the Second World War and the peak of the Holocaust. Only after assuming power as Prime Minister of Israel was Eshkol able and ready to allow Jabotinsky's remains to be buried in Jerusalem (Jabotinsky died in New York in 1940), as the latter's will requested. This gesture on Eshkol's part – a typical departure by

Eshkol from the previous schism between the Left and far-Right wings of the Zionist Movement, which Ben-Gurion had tried unsuccessfully to bridge in the mid-1930s[3] – culminated in Eshkol's invitation to Menachem Begin, Jabotinsky's self-proclaimed heir, to join Eshkol's national emergency coalition on the eve of the 1967 Six Day War. By so doing, Eshkol legitimized Begin's radical ideology to a growing degree in the context of the outcome of the war, as I discuss below.

ESHKOL AND THE RESTRAINT POLICY

The inflow of German Jews to Palestine and the rise of Nazi Germany and Fascist Italy seemed to combine later in the 1930s to allow the Palestinian leader Hajj Amin al-Husaini, the Mufti of Jerusalem, to adopt a policy against the British that began with passive resistance (general strike) and soon evolved into an open revolt against the Mandatory Government and a protracted all-out war on the Jews of Palestine.[4]

Since the very beginning of Zionist activities in British Palestine, the Mufti had been trying, rather successfully, to portray the country's growing Jewish presence not just as a political challenge or a British-supported colonial endeavour, as some describe it today, but as an unacceptable religious affront under any circumstances whatsoever. The revival of the Jewish presence in the Holy Land, especially in Jerusalem – the third-holiest place in Islam – with its ultimate goal of political sovereignty, was described by the Mufti as an act of rewriting history. Plainly deeming Islam to be the one and only true faith, he construed any other religious or cultural challenge to its exclusive predominance in Arab lands as the resurrection of an alternative to Islam that was not only illicit but dead, having been destroyed by the Prophet himself.[5] Instigating the first major riots against the Jews in Palestine in 1920 and another, more intensive round of the same in 1929, Hajj Amin was able to greatly enhance the status of Jerusalem in the Arab and Muslim worlds, which had been half-forgotten and neglected for many generations, by restoring the two Temple Mount mosques, al-Aqsa and the Dome of the Rock – having the latter gold-plated with funds that he raised abroad.

Waged by the Mufti and his supporters, who forcibly quelled

more moderate Palestinian voices, the no-holds-barred uprising started in 1936 and lasted until 1939, when the British finally quashed it with the help of massive regular forces and RAF warplanes, in so doing revising its stance on the political ownership of Palestine by dropping the Jews in favour of the Arabs while preparing to fight the Germans. Much earlier, in 1933, the Mufti had tried to enlist the support of Nazi Germany against the British, but Berlin deflected this appeal due to Hitler's refusal to intimidate the British for the time being.[6] Now that a violent Arab offensive was under way and given its steep cost in Jewish lives and property, the Jewish Agency, chaired by Ben-Gurion since 1935, opted for two responses:[7] the eschewing of counter-violence, a policy known in Hebrew as *havlaga* (self-restraint), and enhanced rural-settlement efforts using, in part, equipment and capital that the Yishuv possessed thanks to the Ha'avara Agreement. The latter policy was strongly supported and managed by Eshkol,[8] among other leaders.

In regard to the self-restraint policy, however, the two men differed. Ben-Gurion justified *havlaga* as a strategic necessity; in its absence, the Arab revolt would become a civil war that would inevitably evolve into an unmanageable exchange of tit-for-tat terror. If confined to its current dimensions, Ben-Gurion thought correctly, the Mandatory Government would crush the uprising, even if reluctantly at first. Eshkol, in contrast, was ready after a while to take counter-action against the Arabs. However firm his patience was, it had its limits, which the Palestinians crossed with much room to spare at the instigation of the Mufti, who in the meantime had gone into exile to avoid prosecution by the British in 1937. This pattern of behaviour would repeat itself in 1966–67, fuelled by the accumulated enmity between the sides since the revolt of 1936, the Mufti's alliance with Hitler and, finally, the Palestinian rejection of the UN's Palestine partition resolution of November 1947 and the war waged by the Palestinian leadership and rank and file to destroy the Jewish state upon its birth.

THE PEEL PARTITION CHALLENGE

Above we noted *en passant* a British policy change that coincided with the repression of the Arab revolt. So it was: amid their military counter measures, HMG appointed a Royal Commission to investigate the roots of the Arab–Jewish conflict in Palestine and tender recommendations about its future. The commission, headed by Lord Robert Peel, invited a large number of representatives of both sides to its hearings. Noting the total rejection by the Mufti's camp of any Jewish presence in Palestine after the Balfour Declaration had spoken in favour of a Jewish National Home there in November 1917,[9] the Peel Commission saw no way to reconcile the demands of the Arabs of Palestine – largely under the Mufti's control – with those of the Jews. Thus, the commission recommended in July 1937 that the country be partitioned, that the Mandate be limited to a narrow zone between Jaffa and Jerusalem along with a form of international supervision, and that land exchanges be made concurrent with the transfer of population from one state to the other, the demarcation of exact borders being left to a technical partition committee.

Thus the idea of a two-state solution to the conflict was born, as was the idea of transferring Arabs out of the Jewish state – both bruited by the British. The Jewish state would be comprised of a coastal strip from Mount Carmel in the north to Be'er Toviyya in the south, plus the Jezreel Valley and the Galilee. The entire upland area in the heart of the country, plus the Negev, was apportioned to the Arabs; Jews would be enjoined against buying land there. Thus the Arabs would receive more than two-thirds of western Palestine (Cisjordan); the entire eastern part (Transjordan) had become a British-backed Hashemite Arab emirate in the early 1920s. As the British mulled, Eshkol and his colleagues hurriedly created 'facts on the ground' by initiating and supporting a clutch of new Jewish settlements. The embryonic localities were meant not only to absorb groups of immigrants who had received agricultural training in Nazi Germany and elsewhere in Central Europe under Zionist guidance, but also to establish a claim to various parts of the country should the British go ahead with partition. 'Creating facts on the ground' has been part of the Zionist legacy ever since, and Levi Eshkol was one of its architects.

Just the same, Eshkol, joined by a few others such as Ben-Gurion, endorsed the partition plan, at least at the level of appearances. However tiny the parcel earmarked for the Jews was, it would be sovereign, free of British control, absolved of the

Mandatory Government's restrictions on Jewish immigration, and economically viable due in part to the immigrants' capital imports and occupational skills. Still, the issue sparked a huge controversy in the Yishuv. The Zionists, having lost Transjordan,[10] would be confined to a sliver of western Palestine, excluding Jerusalem, where Jews had been a majority for generations; the city was to remain under British control along with a vague form of international supervision. They would also be deprived of Jewish holy places such as Hebron, where the Jewish population had been massacred by Arabs in the riots of 1929.[11] An ensuing referendum among members of the Histadrut defeated the partition proposal. This taught Ben-Gurion a lesson about the problems of direct democracy but had less of an effect insofar as Eshkol, not exactly a constitutional expert, was concerned. He continued to pursue his settlement drive vigorously, concentrating on the acquisition and development of land and the assurance of water supplies.

In the meantime, the British moved on. They shelved the Peel plan due to Arab refusal to even discuss it and granted semi-independence to Egypt and Iraq. The Zionists' influence in London declined for reasons including the growing Nazi and Fascist power and the fear of importing anti-Semitism to Britain itself by allowing Jewish refugees to emigrate there. For the British, these developments also demanded a new approach to the Zionists. For Eshkol, they created an emergency situation that dictated increased recruitment, training and resettlement of Jews from Austria, annexed now by Hitler; Czechoslovakia, the victim of Neville Chamberlain's appeasement policy; and Germany itself. Paradoxically, Hitler's forced-emigration policy made the attainment of these goals all the more difficult, for Nazi Germany now imposed increasingly stiff financial limitations and dispossession of property on would-be immigrants. Thus, the absorption of Jewish refugees in foreign countries became harder and harder, except for Zionist pioneers who had been trained in essential farm labour. Hitler's policy in this regard was a kind of contradiction in terms: on the one hand, he overruled objections from his subordinates, who feared that a sovereign Jewish state as suggested by the Peel Commission, or otherwise built by refugees from German-controlled areas, would become an independent anti-Nazi centre of power. On the other hand, he claimed[12] that

Jewish property in German-controlled areas had been robbed from Germans and hence should be 'Aryanized'.[13] In both cases, he may have hoped that the ostensibly omnipotent Jews in the west would impose themselves on their respective governments in order to make his forced-emigration policy a success, thereby fomenting an increase in western anti-Semitism, alienating the masses and offending the Arabs. Thus his policy would serve as a cheap tool of the riddance of the Jews and might even drive a wedge between the western elites and their masses, thereby limiting western freedom of action against him.[14]

NOTES

1. This section is based on Yehuda Bauer, *Jews for Sale? Nazi Jewish Negotiations 1933–1945* (New Haven, CT and London: Yale University Press, 1994), Chapter 1, 'Deliverance through Property Transfer', pp.8–29. Cf. Israel State Archives, *Levi Eshkol, the Third Prime Minister of Israel, Selected Documents on Chapters in His Life*, in Hebrew (Jerusalem: Israel State Archives, 2002), pp.102–70.
2. Bauer, *Jews for Sale?*, pp.5–29.
3. Ben-Gurion negotiated an agreement with Jabotinsky aimed at preventing a formal split among the members of the World Zionist Organization in 1934, supported by Eshkol. The agreement was rejected by the majority of the members of the Histadrut in 1935. See Shabtai Teveth, *David's Zeal, The Burning Ground, The Life of David Ben-Gurion*, in Hebrew (Jerusalem and Tel Aviv: Schocken, 1987), Vol. III, pp.102–12. Ben-Gurion's attitude toward Jabotinsky profoundly changed after the latter's decision to split the World Zionist Organization and when Jabotinsky's political movement adopted profound paramilitary, Fascist-like characteristics, including those of a minority aspiring to dictate policy to the majority. See Dan Horowitz and Moshe Lissak, *From Yishuv to State, The Jews of Eretz Yisrael during the British Mandate as a Political Community*, in Hebrew (Tel Aviv: Am Oved, 1977) p.412.
4. See Yigal Eyal, *The First Intifada, The Repression of the Arab Revolt by the British Army 1936–1939*, in Hebrew (Tel Aviv: Ministry of Defence, 1999).
5. This interpretation of the Qur'an, although deliberately misleading, has taken root since then and gone all the way to contemporaneous Hamas and Islamic Jihad doctrines. For a balanced study of the development of Palestinian nationalism, see Yehoshua Porath, *The Palestinian-Arab National Movement, 1918–1929* (London: Frank Cass, 1974) and Porath, *The Palestinian-Arab National Movement, 1929–1939: From Riots to Rebellion*, Volume II (London: Frank Cass, 1977). See also Daniel Karpy, 'The Mufti's Plan to Poison the Waters of Tel Aviv', in Hebrew, *Ha-umma* (The Nation), 1, 2 (Summer 2003), pp.37–41, and Karpy, 'The Mufti of Jerusalem, Amin el Husseini, and His Political Activities during World War II (October 1941–July 1943)', in Hebrew, *Ha-tsiyyonut* (Zionism) 9 (1971), pp.285–316.
6. See Michael Wildt, 'The SD and Palestine: New Evidence from Captured German Documents in Moscow', in Shlomo Aronson (ed.), *New Records–New Perspectives* (Sede Boqer: Ben-Gurion Research Institute, 2002), pp.64–77.
7. See Meir Avizohar, 'Fighting Zionism', introduction to the scholarly edition of David Ben-Gurion, *Left Behind (Post-Mortem) Memoirs,* Volume VI, January–August 1939, edited and annotated by Meir Avizohar, in Hebrew (Tel Aviv: Am Oved, 1987), pp.18–21. See also Avizohar's full-scale work, *National and Social Ideals as Reflected in Mapai – The Israeli Labour Party – 1930–1942*, in Hebrew (Tel Aviv: Am-Oved, 1990); and Yosef Gorny, *From Binational Society to Jewish State. Federal Concepts in Zionist Political Thought, 1920–1990, and the Jewish People* (Leiden and Boston, MA: Brill, 2006).

8. For details, see Mordechai Naor (ed.), *Stockade and Tower 1936–1939,* in Hebrew (Jerusalem: Yad Izhak Ben-Zvi, 1987).
9. See Ben-Gurion's conversation with Mussa Husseini, representative of the Supreme Arab Committee, in talks with Lord Peel's commission, reprinted in Joseph Heller, *The Struggle for the Jewish State, Zionist Politics, 1936–1939*, in Hebrew (Jerusalem: The Zalman Shazar Centre for the Furtherance of the Study of Jewish History, 1984), pp.228–9.
10. There exists a vast literature on the subject, but Roy Jenkins summarizes in two well-written pages the decisions made by the Secretary of the Colonies at the time, Winston Churchill, on post-First World War British policy in the Middle East, including the haphazard birth of today's Hashemite Kingdom of Jordan. See Jenkins, *Churchill: A Biography* (New York: Ferrar, Straus and Giroux, 2001), pp.359–60.
11. About 60 per cent of Jewish quarters and settlements across the country were affected by the riots. Hundreds of Jews were killed and wounded. See Eyal, *The First Intifada*, pp.21–32.
12. See Shlomo Aronson, *Hitler, the Allies, and the Jews* (New York: Cambridge University Press, 2006), p.16 and its sources.
13. Ibid., pp.6–8.
14. Ibid.

Chapter Three

Eshkol during the Second World War, Trouble at Home and Abroad

BUILDING AMIDST RESISTANCE AND DIALECTICS

When Great Britain abandoned its policy of appeasing Hitler and extended its guarantee to Poland in order to check Hitler's advances in Europe, war was portended and thus required adequate preparation. One preparatory step considered was an attempt to appease the Arabs of Palestine after crushing their revolt by force. After trying one last time to invite the Jews and the Arabs of Palestine to negotiate a compromise and finding the latter resistant to any such deal, the Chamberlain Government decided to drop the Jews. In May 1939, the British announced a 'White Paper on Palestine', a new official policy that abandoned the Balfour Declaration, subsequently mandated by the League of Nations, in favour of the Palestinian Arabs. The new policy placed Jewish immigration to Palestine, practically the only outlet for refugees whom Hitler continued to deport from Europe, under severe restrictions. Only 75,000 certificates of entry would be issued during the next five years, after which no further immigration of Jews into the quondam Jewish National Home would be allowed. Thus guaranteed a majority in the population, the Palestinian Arabs would decide the future of the country in due course. Furthermore, no further purchase of land by Jews in Palestine would be allowed. At this time, the dismayed Yishuv leadership was also confronted by Hitler's pact with Stalin and the ensuing eruption of the Second World War, the partitioning of Poland – the most important centre of Jewish life in interwar Europe – between Nazi Germany and the Soviet Union, and the onset of the 'Phony War' in the west.

The Labour leadership of the Yishuv under Ben-Gurion, Eshkol included, adopted a rather contradictory policy of 'fighting the Nazis as if there were no White Paper and fighting the White Paper as if there were no Nazis'.[1] In practical terms, this meant mobilization for service in the British Army, combined with the demand – rejected by the British until 1944 – to create Jewish units or, rather, a Jewish military presence in the army, coupled with efforts to bring Jewish refugees to Palestine illegally from the British standpoint, that is, outside the White Paper quota. These efforts faced an additional obstacle: the alarming economic reality of Palestine in the late 1930s and early 1940. The outbreak of the war and its side effects – the decline of traditional exports such as citrus fruit and wartime economic regulations imposed by the British – plunged the Jewish sector into a major recession. Eshkol, believing that the British had adopted the White Paper policy due to particular circumstances, hoped that a change in circumstances would soon reverse the policy.[2] In the meantime, he did his best to acquire land in southern Palestine despite the British prohibition and to concentrate the settlement effort instead of dispersing it.

Indeed, the economic crisis quickly passed as the British military began investing huge sums in infrastructure and facilities around the country as were needed to sustain the fighting in the North African desert. At the same time, Britain employed Jewish volunteers in auxiliary army units instead of allowing them to fight under their own flag. Although the Jewish Agency's recruitment campaign proved a relative failure, the mass unemployment that had bedevilled the Yishuv was over. Thus, Eshkol turned his attention and actions to the war situation and a new and grave domestic by-product of the same. The trouble began when a small group of followers of Ze'ev Jabotinsky, organized under the illegal anti-British group IZL (Irgun Tsva'i Leummi, National Military Organization [NMO] or 'Irgun'), broke away from IZL due to its refusal to follow Jabotinsky's order, upon the outbreak of the Second World War, to fight the Nazis. The leader of the breakaway faction, Avraham 'Yair' Stern (hence the sobriquet of the group, the 'Stern Gang') perceived the British as the Jews' real enemies following the adoption of the White Paper, and perceived Fascist Italy and even Nazi Germany as potential allies. The majority of members of the IZL, commanded by David Raziel, followed Jabotinsky's order (he died in 1940 in New York) and aided the British, among other things, by quelling a pro-Nazi takeover in Iraq, during which Raziel lost his life. Stern, in contrast, instigated terrorist activities against the British inside Palestine, tried to contact the Fascist Italians, and later offered 'Mr Hitler' a political, military and ideological alliance[3] after which he would usurp the Yishuv's leadership by force following an Axis occupation of the Middle East.[4] The result was a concerted IZL-Hagana campaign to betray the Sternists to the British, who captured Stern himself and shot him without trial.[5]

FIRST INVOLVEMENT IN MILITARY AFFAIRS

Eshkol became involved in Hagana affairs in 1940 as the representative of his party and of the Histadrut in the militia's command; subsequently, he also became its treasurer. As such, he was privy to various plans to expand the Hagana's infrastructure and illegal weapons procurement, which he opposed for lack of funds. It was at this time that, as an adjunct to his pioneering zeal, Eshkol developed the consciousness of a treasurer, which would be his alter ego later on. Despite his financial misgivings, the decision was made to create the Palmach (an abbreviation of *pelugot mahats*, strike forces), the Hagana's first mobilized unit, which would support itself by working on kibbutzim while training to confront the German-Italian invasion that was feared after the Axis advance into Egypt in 1942.

By itself, this force and other preparations – which the British supported until they defeated the Axis in northern Africa in 1943 – were wholly inadequate. The Palmach, however, took on a life of its own and embraced the spirit of a left-wing faction in Mapai. This faction, led by Yitzhak Tabenkin, a Marxist guru of great influence in years to come, especially after the Six Day War, opposed Ben-Gurion's mainstream Mapai leadership because of its relatively pragmatic social-democratic embrace of different and less rigid forms of collective enterprise than the kibbutz, and due to Ben-Gurion's adoption of Lord Peel's partition plan. Thus a Left-nationalist faction came into being within Mapai, demanded democratic rights and, in fact, claimed minority independence from the party majority by adopting anti-majority planks in the Histadrut institutions with the support of Marxist groups outside Mapai. This development, coupled with the faction's increasingly pro-Soviet spirit, led to the partitioning of Mapai in 1944 and the abolition of the Palmach command by Ben-Gurion in his capacity as Israel's first Prime Minister and Minister of Defence. These developments are crucial to understanding Eshkol's behaviour when he succeeded Ben-Gurion as Prime Minister and Minister of Defence in 1963: his appointment of Yitzhak Rabin, a former Palmach commander as IDF Chief of Staff, his creation of a parliamentary alliance with the nationalist Left, all the way to the Six Day War and up to his death in 1969.

In the early 1940s, Eshkol opposed various proposed preparations to meet the Germans if they were to defeat the British in northern Africa, terming them unrealistic. Instead, he strongly supported the continuation of efforts to mobilize the Yishuv for service in the ranks of the British 8th Army. This, he reasoned, would create a growing nucleus of regular troops in anticipation of the end of the British Mandate, when the Jews would face Arab aggression.[6] The birth of a Jewish Brigade Group under the British Army standard would have to wait until November 1944; in the meantime, Eshkol returned to his settlement and water-supply efforts.

ARCHITECT OF CONSENSUS

At this juncture, however, he found himself embroiled as a mediator between the leftist parties and the Mapai leadership after Ben-Gurion and his supporters adopted the Biltmore Programme in May 1942. This programme, submitted by Ben-Gurion and endorsed by the American Zionists in a conference held at the Biltmore Hotel in New York, called for the immediate end of the British Mandate, the summary creation of a 'Jewish Commonwealth', and unrestricted Jewish immigration not to a partitioned western Palestine but to all of it. At that time, the Jewish leadership in the free world was unaware of the dimensions and intentions of the Holocaust. It assumed that millions would suffer very badly but that many would survive, especially in German-allied countries such as Slovakia, Romania and Hungary, and possibly even in the ghettos of Poland. The immediate mass immigration of European Jews to Palestine made possible by the embryonic state that the Zionists proposed to create there, and in some, crucial socio-economic and institutional ways had already created, would do more than rescue these Jews from Nazi-dominated Europe. Their arrival would transform the Palestinian Arabs into a minority in the non-partitioned country; since they would receive full civil rights, the population transfer proposed by the Peel Commission would not be necessary. Ben-Gurion's next step was to line up his own party's support of the Biltmore Plan. Here, however, he was confronted by his intraparty nationalist-Left rivals, led by Tabenkin, who joined forces with the Marxist Ha-Shomer ha-Tsa'ir (Young Guard) under Meir Ya'ari and Ya'akov Hazan and an additional Marxist group. This opposition was divided between Tabenkin, who feared that the coupling of an immediate end to the Mandate and a mere trickle of immigrants – a conceivable prospect at that stage – would force the notion of partition back onto the agenda, and Ya'ari. Committed to the idea of an unpartitioned Palestine, the opposition opted for the continuation of the Mandate or its replacement by a joint Soviet-American mandate that would allow unrestricted Jewish immigration. Ben-Gurion envisioned the outcome of this scheme, which he perceived as a typical excursion into fantasy on his opponents' part, as either aiming at a binational Jewish-Arab state of the sort endorsed by Ha-Shomer ha-Tsa'ir, or as a pipe dream endorsed by Tabenkin as against the 'Jewish Commonwealth' idea proclaimed at the Biltmore conference. In response, Ben-Gurion and Berl Katznelson, the main moral-ideological leader of Mapai until his death early in 1944, launched an immediate bid to split Mapai or, rather, to push Tabenkin's group out of it.

Eshkol, as noted, tried to intervene and mediate between the rivals. As the representative of his small party in the Mapai institutions, he wished to preserve a modicum of autonomy in these institutions for minorities at large. Tabenkin's faction, however, rejected Eshkol's compromises and opted in May 1944 for splitting the party.[7] Thus Mapai, under Ben-Gurion's leadership, was freed of its leftist wing ahead of elections later in 1944 and was able to maintain its pivotal position in the Yishuv's representative body and a majority in the Histadrut Executive Council, the democratic bases for future decisions.[8]

In the meantime, Eshkol, at Mapai's behest, took over the chairmanship of the Tel Aviv Workers Council in lieu of its incumbent leftist chair. This position gave him much political clout and, in fact, made him a labour 'boss' as an extension of Mapai's control of the Histadrut. Now turning his attention to urban workers and salaried employees in the country's largest city, Eshkol was able to negotiate better wages, deal with endless troubles of individuals, and reject unfounded or exaggerated demands by invoking his sense of humour and quest for compromise.[9] At the same time, Eshkol was conscious of the power of the organized unions such as the electricity and water workers, who acquired for their members preferential wages and tenured positions. Yet their power was needed to maintain Mapai's control over the Histadrut in competition with the parties of the Left for years to come.

Later in 1944, Eshkol, who remained a member of the Hagana Command, came out unequivocally against the Jewish terror operations that resumed soon after the arrival in Palestine of Menachem Begin and the latter's appointment as commander of IZL. IZL had gone through a passive, practically leaderless period after the death of David Raziel in the service of the British, but under the influence of the Holocaust, the continued British restriction of Jewish immigration under Arab pressure,[10] and the resumption of Sternist anti-British terror, Begin proclaimed his own 'revolt' against the Mandatory Government early in 1944.[11] Begin's act and the Sternists' terror campaign were pointless because in late 1940 the Nazis had closed the gates of Europe to Jewish emigration en route to the 'Final Solution'. Thus, not only did the IZL and Sternist actions not affect the British immigration restrictions, the restrictions themselves had become irrelevant. Hence the killing of British soldiers or policemen, the blowing up of British installations, and similar operations while Britain haemorrhaged blood in its war against the Nazis were an unacceptable moral-political blunder as far as the elected leadership of the Yishuv, Eshkol included, was concerned. Moreover, the terror campaign, culminating in the Sternists' murder of Walter Edward Guinness, 1st Baron Moyne, the British Minister Resident in the Middle East, in November 1944 in Cairo, was an unacceptable act of defiance, in fact a rebellion, against the elected leadership.[12] Having just won the 1944 elections, Ben-Gurion ordered a massive campaign against IZL and the Sternists. With strong supported from Eshkol, other members of the Mapai leadership and Tabenkin's now-independent party, IZL and members of the Stern group were handed over to the British authorities, who exiled them to Africa, thereby bringing their activities to a halt until after the war.

BACK TO PEACETIME, ON TO WAR PREPARATIONS

Once the Second World War in Europe was over and the British Labour Party won the ensuing general elections, the new Labour Government persisted with the White Paper policy of 1939 even though it had endorsed a Zionist plank in its 1944 convention, including a bid to transfer the Palestinian Arabs from the recommended Jewish state to Arab locations. Faced with this change, which prohibited the departure of Holocaust survivors from DP camps in Europe to Palestine following Whitehall's decision to adopt an Arab-oriented foreign and security policy, Ben-Gurion instigated a policy of active resistance against the Mandatory Government in cooperation with Hagana, IZL and the Sternists. At the same time, he concentrated on political action in the United States in an attempt to drive a wedge between Washington and London in regard to the future of Palestine.[13] Eshkol, ignoring the more moderate opinion of his colleagues in his small party, backed Ben-Gurion's policy of active resistance in cooperation with the revived IZL and the Stern group.[14] He joined the multipartisan 'X-Committee', the body in charge of the actual operations against the British, which were given final approval by the Executive Committee of the Jewish Agency. The resulting operations, carried out over an eight-month period, targeted British installations such as a radar station, railroads and bridges, and military camps and airfields. Their purpose was to isolate Palestine from its British-dominated Arab neighbours and neutralize the infrastructure that the British had erected to block the Hagana-commanded vessels that carried illegal Jewish immigrants to the Promised Land.

US President Harry S. Truman intervened at this stage, for various reasons, one of which was the problem of the Jewish DPs, most of whom had congregated in the American occupation zone in Germany and many of whom had undergone a process of 'Zionization' due to their experiences during the Holocaust. Another was a pro-Zionist American-Jewish campaign led by Rabbi Abba Hillel Silver, also very much a result of the Holocaust experience of American Jews and its lessons.[15] Thus, Truman suggested that the British allow the entry to Palestine of 100,000 DPs; the British rejected this intervention, proposing instead the appointment of a joint British-American commission to discuss the future of the Middle East, hoping to turn the United States away from the Zionists. The ensuing political process ultimately led to the well known chain of events: the British decision to return its Mandate for Palestine to the United Nations and withdraw from the country, thereby paving the way to the November 1947 UN partition resolution (a recommendation that finalized the departure of the British), which was immediately rejected by the exiled Mufti and then by the Arab states. These developments overstep the boundaries of this work except insofar as Eshkol was involved in their various stages.[16]

Eshkol continued his activities in the 'X-Committee', endorsing several major operations before and after the arrival of the Anglo-American Commission. But he agreed to a cease-fire due to the intervention of Dr Chaim Weizmann, the Anglophile president of the World Zionist Organization. Weizmann hoped the British would change their attitude in the aftermath of the Commission's report and as a result of harsh British counter measures against the Yishuv's leadership and military infrastructure on 29 June 1946, which endangered the Yishuv without much effect on the ongoing political struggle against the British in America. IZL and the Sternists rejected the cease-fire and went about their operations, which culminated in the bombing of the British headquarters in Palestine at the King David Hotel in Jerusalem on 22 July. Horrified by the resulting large number of civilian and military casualties and concerned that the question of the Yishuv majority's control over renegade minorities would be reopened, Eshkol condemned the separate war waged by IZL and the Sternists and accepted Weizmann's demand to dissolve the 'X Committee' altogether.

The mainstream Zionist leadership turned its attention to the escalation of illegal immigration – demonstrating the plight of the

DPs in Europe – and the enhancement of settlement efforts, especially in the Negev, in order to create 'facts on the ground'. Eshkol and his colleagues pushed hard for the settlement effort in the Negev; Eshkol himself pledged his full energy to it immediately because this part of the country was largely empty and much less politically sensitive than what is known today as the West Bank, with its huge Arab population. Thus, a large number of Jewish settlements were established in the northern Negev in an overnight operation that included the provision of water supplies, an act in which Eshkol was involved throughout. In the meantime, IZL and the Sternists continued to raid British facilities and acquired a few martyrs by doing so.

Concurrently, Ben-Gurion dropped the Biltmore Plan and prepared for war. The Plan had envisioned the settlement of millions of Jews in a non-partitioned Land of Israel – millions who had by now gone up in the flames of the Holocaust. Those who could have fled before the 'Final Solution' was decided upon in 1941 had been left to their fate due to Palestinian and Arab pressure on the British, which the British accepted, to pursue the White Paper policy regardless of the fate of the European Jews. The Palestinian Arabs' leader and Hitler's ally, Hajj Amin al-Husaini, remained in control of the Palestinians after the war from his places of exile in France and, later, in Beirut and Cairo. The Yishuv had to prepare for an inevitable assault by the Palestinians and, if a Jewish state were born per UN resolution even in a partitioned country, by the Arab states. Thus Ben-Gurion, as Chairman of the Jewish Agency Executive, was named by the Congress of the World Zionist Organization to an additional defence portfolio in 1946 and began to examine in depth the preparations already made and those that must follow.[17] He chose Eshkol as his senior, salaried aide.[18]

The difference between the two men should be examined at this stage and will help to explain the rupture between them years later. During this highly critical time – between 1946 and late 1947 – as the future of the Zionist endeavour rested in the hands of the Truman Administration, the British, a United Nations committee, and finally the UN General Assembly after the Soviet Union suddenly dropped its traditional anti-Zionist policy and supported the UN partition plan, Ben-Gurion devoted much time, along with his quotidian involvement in this political battle abroad, to what became known as his strategic-military 'seminar'.[19] By reading and interviewing Arab experts, he learned as much as he could about the positions of the other sides, attempting to put himself in their shoes and in fact justifying their positions from their point of view while preparing the necessary counter-measures from the Zionist perspective. He then immersed himself in the study of the Hagana's structure, operational history and actual behaviour in order to transform this civil militia into a regular army as expeditiously as possible. He needed Eshkol to organize the recruitment effort, attend to subsequent financial issues and manage ongoing political frictions. In these capacities, Eshkol rendered invaluable services to the embryonic army.[20]

In Ben-Gurion's service, Eshkol was neither a strategist nor a military statesman, as Ben-Gurion would prove to be in Israel's wars, but a doer as before. To discharge this function, however, the political and organizational base had to be streamlined in order to implement the leader's mid-war and post-war decisions.[21] This difference between the two ultimately explains not only the rift between them from 1964 onward but also their tragic relations in the run-up to the Six Day War in 1967.[22] Ben-Gurion, unlike Eshkol, invested much of his time in studying the historical forces at work in and around Israel, the global forces and the would-be powers. In short, Ben-Gurion gathered and analysed comparative-historical knowledge; strove at length to understand the workings of regional and global politics and the realities of Palestinian politics (still very much under the control of the erstwhile Mufti of Jerusalem); and drew the necessary conclusions for himself and the public, including the decision to proclaim independence on 14 May 1948, which he pushed through despite grave doubts among his colleagues, who knew that it would make war unavoidable.[23] For him, the timing of the right decision with its related inevitable risks was a matter of the utmost importance. Thus, he created an efficient – insofar as possible at first – political-partisan military staff under his own civilian authority. In due course, he eliminated positions and people who not only disagreed with him but represented political and ideological views that he considered provincial and/or divorced from reality, as well as minority interests within the Labour camp such as those of the nationalist Left and their anti-partition, pro-Soviet doctrine.[24] In this sense, Ben-Gurion was a founding, mobilizing statesman, who insisted on an order of priorities derived from his analytical approach to Israel's problems. Since the United States withdrew its support for the UN Palestine partition plan at this time, Israel created itself and became a fact on the ground by virtue of Ben-Gurion's own decision[25] and assessment of the related risks, using a rough-and-tough style aimed at making the choices clear-cut, and threatening many times to resign from his posts as Prime Minister and Minister of Defence.

Eshkol largely followed Ben-Gurion against his own party's leading members, who opposed the declaration of independence, thus becoming a political asset to Ben-Gurion despite his reservations about the latter's style. Perceiving the Arab-Israeli conflict as a given since the 1920s and ready to fight the Arabs since that time, Eshkol suggested his own, political style in due course, as an alternative to Ben-Gurion's manners. But in fact he became a 'Responsive Leader' later on, paying much attention to partisan domestic realities as he saw them as givens, rather than moulding them toward clear-cut priorities formulated by him. Thus he diluted his own political base twice over: first by reintroducing the nationalist Left into the body that made decisions on vital foreign and security affairs without paying much attention to their possible input, and later by allowing Mr Begin's nationalist Right to join his coalition on the eve of the Six Day War. At the same time, his responses to what he deemed Arab provocations, unilateral changes of the status quo or other infringements on Israeli rights were initially none or measured, but later became rather tough – tougher than Ben-Gurion's sometimes and weaker at others. In other words, Ben-Gurion was quick to act under circumstances while Eshkol was not, and Ben-Gurion was ready to refrain from action while Eshkol was forced into actions despite his grave doubts about them.

PERSPECTIVES ON ISRAEL'S WAR OF INDEPENDENCE

As far as Israel's War of Independence itself is concerned, one needs to compare this conflict with other wars of independence, *mutatis mutandis*, for historical and geo-strategic differences. The right comparison to make, I would say, is not between the IDF, established on the eve of the War of Independence, and the

American Army in the Revolution as some scholars have suggested, but between the IDF and the army of the North in the American Civil War, almost a century later. Such comparisons were made by the Israeli military historian Colonel (Res.) Professor Yehuda Wallach,[26] who availed himself, on the one hand, of Zahava Ostfeld's important study[27] and studies by his Israeli pupils, Elhanan Oren and Meir Pa'il. Systematically comparing all aspects of the almost *ex nihilo* establishment of an army in the midst of a lengthy and blood-drenched war in the United States with the establishment of the Israel Defence Forces, Wallach explicitly shows the superiority of the fledgling Israeli army in many respects, from total mobilization – which did not work properly in the American North until the end of the war – to the training of commanders during the Hagana era, procurements (in which Eshkol excelled), communications, tactics and strategic conduct of the war, which both countries entrusted to the head of the political echelon. The secessionist Confederate states had risen to fight a life-or-death war – as they construed it – and viewed the conflict in this respect as a war of the many (the industrialized North) against the few (the agrarian South). The results of the war hinged largely on the involvement or assistance of foreign powers (Britain and France), which, the Confederacy hoped, might deem the independent South to be a *fait accompli* after observing developments on the ground, and for economic and political reasons of their own. In other words, the correct comparison is with the South – which Wallach overlooks – and not with the wealthy, righteous, flabby and rather corrupt industrial North, which was headed by an outstanding statesman. The correct comparison is with the intrepid but wrong South, fighting for its very existence as it perceived it under its talented commanders Robert E. Lee, 'Stonewall' Jackson and Nathan Bedford Forrest, the likes of whom the victorious North did not have until the emergence of Grant, Sherman, Thomas and Sheridan. The North also triumphed because the Southern political echelon fell immeasurably short of Lincoln's stature and made too many strategic mistakes.

The winning side in Israel's War of Independence was the one that, while being the weaker and the poorer, had technological, tactical and strategic advantages and enjoyed outside assistance that was withheld from the Arabs during the war. Due to the

Arabs' dependence at the time on western arms supplies, the west's embargo against both sides stymied them while Israel was able to secure Soviet-authorized supplies due to Stalin's interest in weakening western influence in the region. The question that arises here is this: from whom should we learn the lessons of the victory in the 1948 war, a victory attained at steep cost and under special conditions that could not persist for long, even in the realm of hope? The IDF and its commanders had to be taught not to rest on their laurels.[28] The American Civil War had a 'final' outcome: once the South's ability to secede had been broken, the United States of America would remain one political entity. In contrast, it was not at all clear to Ben-Gurion that the War of Independence had attained a similar finality, given the geopolitical and strategic realities at the regional and global levels.

We shall return to these realities later; for the time being, we should mention foreseeable changes in the Arab world and in the quantitative balance of forces that would steadily turn in the Arabs' favour.[29] On the basis of his rather early analysis, Ben-Gurion would search for nuclear weapons while maintaining the partition of the country. Eshkol's view and handling of the nuclear issue as Ben-Gurion's successor took a different turn in various respects under American pressure, while his most important allies on the nationalist Left rejected the bomb and the partitioning of the country as well. The issue of the Arab-populated West Bank and Gaza, that is, the area that was occupied and annexed by Jordan – including Jordanian controlled eastern Jerusalem and its enormous political-religious sensitivity – and the area in Gaza occupied by Egypt in the 1948 war, remained a topic for discussion during Ben-Gurion's times, but the 'old man' was extremely careful not to make the West Bank the target of Israeli expansionism and settlement efforts, and established the state's power to make decisions in this regard by force, when necessary.[30] The West Bank (including eastern Jerusalem and its annexation to Israel) and Gaza would be occupied by Eshkol's National Emergency Government in 1967 and his decisions in this regard will be discussed in due course.

During and immediately after Israel's War of Independence, Ben-Gurion made two crucial decisions that would ensure the emergence of the IDF as the sole and unified arm of the elected civilian leadership. The first was to fully disband Mr Begin's IZL and incorporate it into the Israeli Army.[31] The second was to disband the Palmach's separate command and fuse it with the IDF General Staff, much to the dismay of the Palmach's civilian leaders such as Yisrael Galili and military commanders such as Yigal Allon, who had hoped to retain strong influence, in the spirit of the nationalist pro-Soviet Left, over the Palmach as a semi-independent formation within the Israeli Army.[32] Eshkol supported both measures, but not before making serious efforts to bridge the differences between the Minister of Defence and the representatives of the nationalist Left in the defence establishment. The differences proved unbridgeable and the national Leftists' forced retirement from the active defence establishment, imposed by Ben-Gurion, triggered a short-lived protest against him by previous Palmach officers.[33] In due course, Prime Minister and Defence Minister Eshkol would also have difficulties in controlling his Generals, even if he did not have to face quite the same sort of protest, preceded by an outright rebellion as described above.

NOTES

1. Israel State Archives, *Levi Eshkol, the Third Prime Minister of Israel, Selected Documents on Chapters in His Life*, in Hebrew (Jerusalem: Israel State Archives, 2002), pp.172–3.
2. Ibid.
3. See Joseph Heller, *LEHI – Ideology and Politics, 1940–1949,* in Hebrew (Jerusalem: Shazar Centre and Keter, 1989), Vol. I, pp.128–45.
4. Ibid.
5. See Shlomo Aronson, *Hitler, the Allies, and the Jews* (New York: Cambridge University Press, 2006), p.94, and related British sources pertaining to Stern's terrorist activities, Hagana Archive, Tel Aviv (Record Group 47, Criminal Investigation Department, Government of Palestine).
6. Israel State Archives, *Levi Eshkol*.
7. Ibid., pp.181–8.
8. Aronson, *Hitler*, pp.298–9.
9. Affidavit Ya'akov Aharonson, the author's father and an executive with the Palestine Electricity Corporation at the time. My father used to complain about the growing power of unionized workers, which they had acquired with Eshkol's support. Eshkol, in turn, argued that their jobs entailed extra labour and, from November 1947 on, became quite dangerous due to Palestinian-Arab attacks.
10. See Aronson, *Hitler*.
11. On Begin and his social entourage, see Dan Horowitz and Moshe Lissak, *From Yishuv to State, The Jews of Eretz Yisrael during the British Mandate as a Political Community,* in Hebrew (Tel Aviv: Am Oved, 1977), p.178, p.412.
12. Joseph Heller, *LEHI – Ideology and Politics, 1940–1949*, Vol. I, in Hebrew (Jerusalem: Shazar Centre and Keter, 1989), pp.185*ff*.
13. See primary sources quoted by Joseph Heller, *The Struggle for the Jewish State, Zionist*

Politics, 1936–1939, in Hebrew (Jerusalem, The Zalman Shazar Centre for the Furtherance of the Study of Jewish History, 1984), pp.421–9.

14. On the so-called 'Hebrew Resistance Movement' and Eshkol's involvement in it, see Israel State Archives, *Levi Eshkol*, pp.206–8.
15. See Eliahu Elath, *The Struggle for Statehood, Washington: 1945–1948*, Vol. I, 1945–1946, in Hebrew (Tel Aviv: Am Oved, 1979), pp.9–138. See also Ariel L. Feldstein, Introduction, *Gordian Knot: David Ben-Gurion. The Zionist Organization and American Jewry 1948–1963*, in Hebrew (Jerusalem and Sede Boqer: The Hebrew University of Jerusalem, 2005).
16. Heller, *The Struggle for the Jewish State*, pp.493–510; and Alon Kadish (ed.), *Israel's War of Independence 1948–1949*, in Hebrew (Tel Aviv: Ministry of Defence, 2005), pp.13–76; Efraim Karsh, *Palestine Betrayed* (New Haven, CT: Yale University Press, 2010), chapters 5–12.
17. Michael Bar-Zohar, *Ben-Gurion, A Political Biography*, Part II, in Hebrew (Tel Aviv: Am Oved, 1977), pp.645–65.
18. Ibid.
19. Kadish, *Israel's War of Independence*, pp.723–35.
20. At the outset of the War of Independence, Ben-Gurion encountered a mutiny among members of the newly born IDF GHQ when he decided to dismiss Yisrael Galili, the civilian chief of territorial defence under Ben-Gurion's own overall command. After a brief showdown with the generals, however, Ben-Gurion reasserted his control as the supreme civilian authority. Galili was a popular figure among the generals but a representative of Ahdut ha-'Avoda, a pro-Soviet party that favoured a special status for the Palmach inside the IDF; his removal left him and his party frustrated and seeking to regain their position, which they eventually did, to an important extent, under PM Eshkol (see below). Professor Anita Shapira likened Ben-Gurion's behaviour at the time to a dictatorial act similar to the behaviour of Third World leaders; she overlooked the British model of relations between the elected minister of defence and his subordinates, pursued by Ben-Gurion. See Shapira, *From the Dismissal of the Chief of Territorial Defence to the Abolition of the Palmach, Issues in the Struggle for Security Leadership*, in Hebrew (Tel Aviv: Hakibbutz Hameuchad, 1985).
21. See Shlomo Aronson, 'David Ben-Gurion and the British Constitutional Model', *Israel Studies*, 3, 2 (Autumn 1998), pp.193–214.
22. Kadish, *Israel's War of Independence*, pp.85–6.
23. The anti-partition plank plus the quest for a binational Jewish–Arab state constituted the official programme of the Marxist group Ha-Shomer ha-Tsa'ir, which joined Ahdut ha-'Avoda to create the Mapam, the United Workers Party, in January 1948. Many senior IDF officers belonged to Mapam and the Palmach and most served with distinction – or were killed – in the War of Independence. Those who survived attempted to influence the IDF by maintaining the Palmach as an autonomous body after the war, whereupon Ben-Gurion disbanded it.
24. Heller, *The Struggle for the Jewish State*, pp.535–50.
25. Israel State Archives, *Levi Eshkol*, pp.221–2.
26. Y. Wallach, *To the Flag: The Establishment of a People's Army in the Midst of Combat*, in Hebrew (Tel Aviv: Ministry of Defense, 1997). For a detailed discussion of the Israeli war story, see Moshe Lissak, chief editor, *The History of the Jewish Community in Eretz Israel since 1882, Israel, the First Decade*, in Hebrew (Jerusalem: The Israel Academy of Sciences and Humanities, 2009), pp.1–105.
27. Zahava Ostfeld, *An Army is Born*, in Hebrew (Tel Aviv: Ministry of Defense, 1994, two volumes).
28. See Ben-Gurion lecture in November 1948 to senior IDF commanders, reprinted in his *War Diary, The War of Independence 1948–1949*, in Hebrew (Tel Aviv: Ministry of Defense, 1982), p.901.
29. See Ben-Gurion speech, 14 January 1951, to IDF high command, Ben-Gurion Archive

(BGA), Sede Boqer, doc. 88/1162/81.
30. See article by Pinchas Meding in Lissak (ed.), *The History of the Jewish Community*, pp.457–60.
31. See Shlomo Aronson, *David Ben-Gurion, Renaissance Leader and the Waning of an Age*, in Hebrew (Sede Boqer and Beersheva: Ben-Gurion Research Institute, 1999), pp.269–71. English translation forthcoming in September 2010.
32. Galili regularly consulted with Yitzhak Tabenkin who, while outside the decision-making bodies of the young state, was the guru of Ahdut ha-'Avoda. Ha-Shomer ha-Tsa'ir adopted a far reaching pro-Soviet plank in early 1948. See Elie Zur (ed.), *'Can't Do Without Us', Mapam's Views on Security and Foreign Policy 1948–1950*, in Hebrew (Kibbutz Dalia: Yad Yaari and Yad Tabenkin, 2000), pp.175–248.
33. Israel State Archives, *Levi Eshkol*, pp.240–65.

Chapter Four

Arch-Settler, Treasurer and Minister of Finance[1]

RESETTLEMENT, ABSORPTION, INTEGRATION

Leaving his job as assistant to the Minister of Defence after Israel won its war of independence, Eshkol turned his efforts in two directions: settling the territories acquired during and immediately after the war[2] and absorbing mass immigration that more than doubled the country's population within three to four years. Both causes combined to justify the Israeli Government's decision, very much adopted and carried out by Eshkol, to settle immigrants in deserted Arab villages and towns. The mass departure of Arabs from the Jewish state once they lost their leaders' initial bid, following the UN partition resolution, to destroy it, took the victorious Israelis by surprise at first. Palestinian deportees, or refugees, numbering around 700,000, left on their own in order to wait elsewhere for the invading Arab armies to restore the whole country to their control. Some were left to their fate by leaderless local chieftains and foreign volunteers, as happened in Jaffa, to fight the Jews as Hajj Amin al-Husaini, their supreme commander, promised them an assured victory from his post in faraway Cairo. But others were forced to leave, especially from strategic areas, and yet others left because their local and country-wide social structure had collapsed upon the departure of the well-to-do. Still others left when, on top of the absence of the ex-Mufti who tried to make them fight while residing abroad, they fell victim to inner divisions among other leaders and commanders of the Arab volunteers who joined the Palestinians in their armed struggles.[3]

The formation of an official Israeli policy regarding the refugees went through several stages. At first, people such as Eshkol, tasked with settling hundreds of thousands of Jewish refugees from Europe and from the Arab countries, were not sure whether the departure of Arab civilians to neighbouring Arab countries from territories that Israel had occupied in and beyond the UN-allotted boundaries after the initial Arab aggression would be permanent; these civilians might, after all, be allowed to return under conditions of peace treaties to be negotiated pursuant to the Armistice Agreements negotiated with Arab states in 1949. The prevailing hope was initially formulated in terms of peaceful co-existence and cooperation between Arabs and Jews, based on a distinction between the Arab people, their governments and leaders and British Imperial pro-Arab interests, which soon enough proved to be divorced from reality. For one thing, the return of Arab refugees to Jaffa, right up against the heart of Tel Aviv, was out of the question in view of their attacks on the Jewish city after the UN adopted the partition resolution in November 1947. Eshkol and his aides did think, however, that at least some abandoned Arab villages should be kept empty for refugees who might return. After all, the official Israeli policy toward Arab civilians in Israel territory, including that acquired during and after the war, was coined in terms of asking them to stay and ruling out their departure by force once strategic towns such as Lydda and Ramle – about ten miles from Tel Aviv, controlling Israel's major international airport to this day – were forcibly evacuated.[4] On the ground, this policy was not always implemented due to military efforts by inhabitants who, refusing to recognize partition, blocked highways leading from central Israel to the north in a way that could serve invading regular Arab armies at that time and some future time if the war were restarted. The Arabs residing in West Bank territories that were annexed to Israel as a result of the armistice negotiations with Jordan became Israeli citizens against their wishes, while the question of Palestinian refugees who left, voluntarily or otherwise, continued to preoccupy the Israeli leadership intermittently and seemed to weigh on them as a moral burden.[5]

After the armistice agreements were followed not by peace but by official Arab belligerence, however, the empty towns and villages left behind by most refugees quickly became the objects of a formal Israeli decision to keep the refugees out, except for the unification of some families that the war had torn apart and Arab rejection of Israel's offer to take back 100,000 refugees. Hence the decision to settle Jewish immigrants in erstwhile Arab dwellings. The process leading to this decision was not simple; in fact, it was influenced by the enormous rage that had accumulated among the Jews of British Palestine due to the Arab riots of 1920 and 1929 and, above all, the 1936–39 rebellion and the ensuing May 1939 White Paper, which closed the gates of the Jewish National Home in Jewish refugees' faces as a result of Palestinian Arab pressure. Thus, hundreds of thousands of Jews who could have been rescued from Hitler's Final Solution during the Second World War, when Hitler was still deporting the Jews, were murdered. Later on his decision to kill them all, actively supported by the Mufti in Berlin, was decisive in preventing rescue. The Arab refugees of 1948 were – and are, biology permitting – alive; Jewish refugees expelled from Arab countries, along with Holocaust survivors, replaced them. Ben-Gurion explained the dual démarche in the following terms:

> When World War II was over and the hostile policy of the British Government [the 'White Paper' policy and its Arab-inspired ban on Jewish immigration] did not change, it became clear that sooner or later we would face a confrontation with the Arab world. *Hitler's lesson was not lost on them. Among Hitler's allies the Mufti and his friends were to be found* [i.e., the recognized leadership of the Palestinians]. The rulers of Egypt, Syria, and Iraq were all pro-Nazi, and it was plainly clear to them that they should do in Eretz Yisrael [Palestine] what Hitler did in Europe: to annihilate the Yishuv to the ground. [Italics added.][6]

Hence, the possibility of allowing Palestinian refugees to return became increasingly a matter of admitting Palestinians whose attitude toward Israel must have been considered as uncompromising, inspired by the still-active Mufti in Cairo or Beirut and by hostile Arab governments. The lessons of the Second World War reinforced this perception, that is, the post-war forced evacuation of millions of Germans from their historical homelands by the Czech, Polish and Soviet authorities after the pre-war presence of Germans in foreign countries was construed as the source of much trouble to the host nations. This affair, as well as Mustafa Kemal Atatürk's eradication of the Greek presence in modern Turkey, is missing in Goldstein's discussion of the refugee question in his biography of Eshkol. To Ben-Gurion, Eshkol and others, the Palestine shake-up seemed to constitute an exchange of Palestinian refugees for the dispossessed Jewish population in the Arab countries. It worked in Europe: the massive movement of populations after the Second World War, including the immigration of most surviving Jews to Israel, transformed the continent into ethnic nation-states and eliminated the pre-war minority problems.[7] The Greek precedents also aroused Israeli expectations that the neighbouring Arab states would absorb the Palestinian refugees, as was happening at that very time in India and Pakistan without similar bloodshed. It is not surprising that Eshkol also tried to learn some practical lessons from the Greek precedent; when the waves of immigrants from Europe and the Muslim countries began to come ashore in Israel, he travelled to Greece to familiarize himself with methods of absorbing very large numbers of refugees in a short period of time.[8]

According to Goldstein, a major contribution to the Israeli decision to oppose the return of the Arab refugees was UN General Assembly Resolution 194 of 11 December 1948, which – among other issues pertaining to the 1948 war – recommended that the Palestinian refugees be allowed to return to their homes 'at the earliest practicable date', provided that they be willing to 'live at peace with their neighbors', and, if choosing not to do so, be compensated for their property. The problem here, which persists to this day, is the freedom of choice that the relevant Arab governments hardly gave the refugees, instead keeping them in refugee camps on Israel's borders and helping to force their return in due course. By keeping the refugee problem alive, the Arab governments would keep their conflict with Israel alive. Indeed, having refused to transform the armistice agreements of 1949 into peace treaties, they soon applied this policy in a more aggressive fashion by trying to isolate Israel economically and politically.[9] UN agencies made various attempts to reconcile the Arab parties and Israel afterwards and Ben-Gurion hoped that they might bear fruit, believing that a major reason for the Arab intransigence was British imperial interest, along with his analysis of their own motives and Hajj Amin's role.

Since Eshkol was not involved in these deliberations, I leave them aside, including Ben-Gurion's decision not to occupy the West Bank even though this was militarily possible – partly due to the British-Jordanian Defence Treaty and also, mainly, due to the threat of annexing and ruling over masses of alien Palestinians combined with the pressing task of absorbing Jewish mass immigration. Later on, UN Resolution 194 became a legal basis, in the eyes of the refugees and the Arab states, for the Palestinian 'right of return' to pre-1967 Israel, and as such remains so firmly enshrined in the ethos of the Palestinians and the Arab states that it prevents progress in the Israeli-Palestinian peace negotiations that have taken place since the early 1990s.[10]

Ben-Gurion's decision to maintain the improved post-1948 frontiers, use the old and newly acquired territory for Jewish settlement, and prohibit the return of Palestinian refugees became Eshkol's new challenge. Eshkol had always perceived settlement as the most important key to Israel's security and its final boundaries in a hostile environment, where Arab inhabitants would have become a source of permanent friction with the slender Jewish majority in the partitioned country. Now that some 700,000 Palestinian Arabs had eliminated this threat by leaving the Jewish state, the enormous pressure created by the arrival of the Jewish refugees could be alleviated by settling the newcomers in former Arab towns and villages from Jaffa to the approaches to Jerusalem, in the northern Negev, and in other parts of the country. New settlements in strategically sensitive areas such as the bottleneck between central Israel and the north, where the country between the Mediterranean and the Jordanian-occupied West Bank was about twelve miles wide, were perceived by Eshkol as fortresses or necessary human shields against renewed Arab aggression. He had learned these lessons from the war, during which Jewish settlements had played a vital role in blocking the advance of the invading Egyptian and Syrian armies.

Thus, the initial moral qualms about the former Arab presence in the country and its dispossession were ignored not only by Ben-Gurion and Eshkol but also by the moderate Moshe Sharett, Israel's first foreign minister. They were, however, adopted by intellectuals such as Martin Buber,[11] who entertained an anarchistic view of the Jewish state and of nation-states in general, and by other intellectuals and politicians on the far Left. At the present, such perspectives have been revived under the slogan that Israel was born in sin, the 'sin' being the *nakba*, the ostensibly Holocaust-like disaster that befell the innocent Palestinian refugees as a result of a deliberate Jewish conspiracy aimed in advance to uproot them.

As for the permanence of partition, it was Ben-Gurion's policy to maintain the partition and refrain from occupying the West Bank for reasons including fear of British intervention in favour of the Jordanians, who had invaded and later annexed what became the West Bank of their kingdom. Above all, however, Ben-Gurion rejected the idea of controlling the vast Arab population of the West Bank, for such control would foist a strategic and ideological burden on Israel – a large Palestinian population group under Israeli occupation rule – that might challenge Israel's very legitimacy. Since Eshkol was as aware as Ben-Gurion of the ramifications of such a development, it remains to be seen how and when he departed, at least partially and in stages, from this traditional policy.

For some time after the 1948 war, Eshkol and his aides busied themselves transforming vacant Arab villages into Israeli settlements, surmounting innumerable difficulties in making them hospitable to newcomers whose background offered little entrée to rural life. The financial resources available were, at best, meagre. Ben-Gurion's and Eshkol's hopes that the various kibbutz movements would play a leading role in the absorption campaign were dashed[12] by the elitist nature of the movements, especially their leftist groups.[13] This prompted public condemnation of the movements by Ben-Gurion,[14] after which – among other reasons – the kibbutzim began to lose their role as major players if not a cherished social avant-garde due to their leading role in the pre-independence settlement effort and their major contributions in the 1948 war.[15]

Salvation came from the moshav movement. A moshav is a smallholders' cooperative village; settlements following this structure were organized nationwide under the auspices of a separate movement. In the 1920s, moshav settlers had created with Eshkol's help a much less idealistic and less communal form of collective life than the kibbutz paradigm. In such cooperatives, private property is maintained; only means of production such as machinery, water resources and marketing of agricultural produce are shared by members. During the time at issue, these common assets were organized under mechanisms controlled by the Histadrut and the Jewish Agency. While willing to mobilize for the purpose of absorbing immigrants, the veteran 'Moshavniks' preferred to help them create new settlements of their own rather than invite them to join existing cooperatives. The new settlements would then be run as economic units that would go about their business under the control of Eshkol's Rural Settlement Department at the Jewish Agency and be obliged to individual members, elected local councils, and, by contract, the Histadrut's marketing apparatus. The moshav residents who volunteered to help the immigrants sink roots in their new surroundings were motivated by a sense of mission and the quality of their instructors, supported by Eshkol's efforts and personal involvement in the absorption campaign.

The dimensions of this settlement effort exceeded everything that Eshkol had done before and seemed to be successful. In reality, however, cultural complications bedevilled the enterprise on top of the missing funds. The immigrants from Muslim countries began life in Israel with lengthy stays in transit camps; what is more, many of them had been merchants, artisans or jewellers in their former countries of residence and had for generations supported their families in the manner of patriarchs. Their transformation into cooperative rural farmers proved difficult and in some cases tragic or impossible. They found Eshkol's distinct East European Jewish style, peppered with Yiddish stories and jokes, alien and patronizing. Ben-Gurion made quite a different impression on them; he courted them, using the Bible and its language to establish common ground. His tactic was quite successful because this language not only appealed to their Jewish tradition but was neutral in the sense of being free of the East European contents of Eshkol's style, notwithstanding Ben-Gurion's heavy Polish accent. Furthermore, these immigrants hailed Ben-Gurion as the great saviour who had personally delivered them from exile, and as the incarnation of their Jewish emancipation thanks to his strong, towering persona, which fit well with their traditional respect for authority.

Differences aside, the founding fathers including Eshkol adhered to the idea of a melting pot that was supposed to mould masses of immigrants from more than a hundred counties into 'new Jews' or, rather, into independent, proud, Hebrew-speaking Israelis. The results were mixed. There was much success, thanks to military service and the abilities of the largely secular newcomers who had survived the Holocaust or immigrated from Romania, Bulgaria and Poland. The traditional-minded immigrants from Muslim countries, mainly northern Africa, responded differently and evolved into what soon became known as 'the Second Israel'. Many of them quickly left the localities that had been established for them – rural settlements and, later on, 'development towns' (discussed below) – for the major cities, where they became an urban sub-proletariat of sorts. As such, they were targeted by Mr Begin's right-wing opposition, which weaned them from their initial Mapai sympathies due to the aforementioned socioeconomic problems. The process that ultimately turned them into loyal supporters of Begin's Likud (Unity) Bloc, despite their personal devotion to the towering personality of Ben-Gurion, which they perceived as sympathetic to their own traditional Judaism – and Eshkol's role in it, will require our attention in due course.

NATIONAL PENURY AND DOMESTIC DISARRAY

At this stage, however, having presided over an enormous rural-settlement effort, Eshkol became treasurer of the Jewish Agency, the vehicle of all forms of immigrant absorption due to its new role in independent Israel as the link between the government and Jewish fundraising institutions abroad, mainly in the United States. By now experienced in the treasurer's craft, Eshkol was very much aware of the dire financial difficulties that accompanied the settlement effort: a ruined wartime economy that had depleted its resources, its exports barely above zero, its foreign-currency reserves nil. Its vital imports, from food to oil to weapons to basic construction materials for the settlement effort, required financing without risking hyperinflation. Eshkol, quondam secretary of the Tel Aviv Workers Council, was also well acquainted with the powerful unions that were represented in councils of this kind across the country, some of which controlled vital parts of the economy. Indeed, he had helped to create a few of them, such as the Mekorot water company ('sources' in Hebrew). The unions chose this juncture in history to exploit their monopolies in pursuit of higher wages, sometimes without offering higher productivity in return. In fledgling Israel, as in European social democracies, the right to strike was enshrined in the unions' ethos and was brandished, either as a threat or for real, whenever wage demands were unfulfilled, with the support of the Histadrut Trade Union Department. Firing was impossible due to the tenured members' status, anchored in collective labour agreements negotiated by their leaders and the employers, who also paid for the leaders' union jobs. The resulting system might function rather smoothly as long as Mapai controlled the Histadrut and the Government and as long as a reasonable degree of equality was maintained between the various employees. At this time, however, the parties on the Left exercised much pressure on the unions and dictated policy to public-sector employers, including the state bureaucracy and government-owned businesses such as the Israel Electric Corporation, to such a degree that decisions could hardly be made without their consent. The same occurred among the various teachers' unions, whose members eventually slipped into mediocrity but retained their jobs due to seniority, crowding out the earlier generations of idealistic teachers – a problem that persists to this day. This turgid reality overshadowed Eshkol's policies so severely that he considered making union representatives official members of the directorates of state enterprises. The unions, however, divided along regional lines and fractured by conflicting interests, could agree only on issues such as wages or the improvement of collective labour agreements as driven by left-wing parties' activists. As time passed, Eshkol allowed these circumstances to dictate several fateful political decisions that, he thought, would accommodate the left-wing parties that were backing the irresponsible wage demands.

In the meantime, the Government, following the British post-war example, imposed a strict policy of economic austerity, which soon proved to be a complete failure. Eliezer Kaplan, Israel's first Minister of Finance, and David Horowitz, director general of the ministry, now became crucial players in staving off national bankruptcy.[16] Resisting them was Ben-Gurion, who believed that economic development and settlement efforts could and should be dictated by human will rather than by objective rules of economics. Ben-Gurion's sidekick, Eshkol, had been engaged mainly in microeconomic issues; such were his settlement efforts, however large in scale they were. Now, however, he received an introduction to macroeconomics and would do his best to bridge his political superiors' utopian expectations with the unions' relentless wage demands, the newcomers' misery, and the quest for food aid and financial support from abroad.

In this regard, Israel enjoyed an unexpected stream of financial aid from three sources: the British, who released the Yishuv's sterling assets thanks to Horowitz's exertions in London, financial and food aid from the Truman Administration,[17] and, later, a fundraising campaign among American Jews and Zionist supporters in the United States, many of whom were readily mobilizable due to the lessons that they had learned from the Holocaust. An example is Henry Morgenthau, Jr., who proved strong enough to stand up to the oil lobby and the firm objections of the State Department and major figures at the Pentagon to America's recognition of Israel and, in fact, the country's very birth.[18] The idea that the creation and consolidation of a sovereign Jewish state was vital for the restoration of Jewish honour and standing among the nations, following the poisonous Nazi anti-Semitic crusade against all of Jewry, proved very helpful in mobilizing American Jewish support and financial aid. It would lead to the sale of Israel Bonds in the United States – an initiative of Golda Meir as Minister of Labour, Levi Eshkol and Moshe Sharett – despite ongoing difficulties in the fundraising system itself.[19]

The influx of foreign aid seemed to have justified Ben-Gurion's utopianism, but Kaplan and Horowitz knew better; once Eshkol's transit camps became overcrowded and hardly able to absorb more newcomers, they tried in vain to stem the ongoing influx of immigrants, especially from Arab countries.[20] The camps were a stopgap solution that Eshkol devised after previous waves of immigrants had filled up the deserted Arab villages and towns. Facing even larger waves of Jews who sought to reach Israel from Iraq, Yemen, Libya and other countries, above all Morocco, either as expellees or in an attempt to transform their thousand-year dream of returning to the Holy Land into reality, Eshkol hoped that his interim housing system, located not far from the country's urban centres, could also supply the newly arrived with work. Alternatively, he thought the government should become their employer in manual, unskilled jobs. Since there was no money for this – much of it claimed by the rising standard of living outside the transit camps and the constant wage demands of the established Israeli public sector – additional sources from abroad had to be sought. Although Eshkol shared Kaplan's and Horowitz's belief that immigration had to be limited, the efforts made in this direction failed badly. Horowitz saved the day by finding a new potential source, West Germany – a story outside our purview.[21]

One should not confuse Ben-Gurion's utopianism with pie-in-the-sky fantasy. Rather, it was a thick stew composed of the pioneering spirit that he and others exuded, their enormous energy and devotion to the secular, social-democratic vision of Judaism, the transformation into reality of the Biblical commitment to become the 'chosen people', and the tools that they created to implement this vision such as the Histadrut, its cooperative enterprises, and the vast array of services that it provided, such as healthcare, jobs and psychological hospitability. All of these had been advanced by the creation of party machines, which translated the services rendered into votes in general elections for the Knesset, Israel's parliament. Mapai cemented a pivotal role for itself in the Knesset even though it never won much more than one-third per cent of votes cast; it owed this to the proportional ballot system that Israel had inherited from the Yishuv era, which encouraged, if not dictated, a proliferation of political parties. Its plurality sufficed to maintain control over the house and over the Histadrut. Eshkol was a leading member in both institutions and remained loyal to this double-edged control mechanism created by Mapai, despite the inherent conflicts of interest among a powerful and privileged General Federation of Labour, its leading unions' continued quest for a higher standard of living, constant friction with the doctrinaire but power-seeking leftist parties, and the needs of the state.

The result was brisk economic growth coupled with chronic penury. Israel in the early 1950s lived hand-to-mouth on American financial gifts, grants and loans, and flirted with hyperinflation and bankruptcy. Instead of seeking necessary economic reforms, Eshkol angrily demanded that the Finance Ministry work for the expansion of capital imports.[22] What he got, and finally accepted, was a new economic programme, devised by the Finance Ministry, that helped to bring the economy under control by subjecting all budgets including defence to drastic cuts.

Although this led to the departure of the IDF Chief of Staff, General Yigael Yadin, it established a new order of priorities that positioned immigration and settlement efforts at the top, surpassing even the military. The new order prevailed; after all, it was enforced by Defence Minister Ben-Gurion himself. A story by itself, discussed below, was the planning of 'garden towns' or 'development towns' across the country by Ben-Gurion's PMO (Prime Minister's Office). This policy proved successful in some cases (Beersheva, Ashdod and Eilat) and tragically unsuccessful in other cases on the national periphery; these would be taken over by Eshkol as Finance Minister and by his close aide, Pinchas Sapir.

The combination of imported capital and goods from West Germany, additional aid from American Jews and the American Administration, the waning of mass immigration and the Horowitz and Kaplan reforms gave the country a semblance of economic stability.[23] It was the last act of the Horowitz and Kaplan duo at Finance. Kaplan died soon afterward and Horowitz – tired of trying to impose a restrictive economic programme – resigned, only to be appointed several years later as the first governor of the Bank of Israel. The man who made the appointment was Levi Eshkol, who assumed the office of Minister of Finance in June 1952[24] after a term as Minister of Agriculture and Development in 1951–52, without relinquishing his control of the Jewish Agency's Rural Settlement Department.

PROTÉGÉS AND THE PARTY BOSS

To consolidate his 'empire', Eshkol promoted Pinchas Sapir, his deputy at Mekorot and later Director General of the Ministry of Defence (mainly in charge of procurement), to second-in-command at Agriculture and Development, thereby placing him within the highest echelon of Israeli economic decision-makers. Subsequently Sapir would become one of the most important Mapai bosses and, as such, responsible together with Eshkol for the party's future. The two continued to collaborate when Eshkol became Finance Minister. In 1955, Eshkol arranged Sapir's appointment as Minister of Industry and Trade, paving the way to vigorous economic growth and the abandonment of Israel's pursuit of strict social democracy, especially in creating a complete welfare state based on communal principles as envisioned by the parties of the Left.

Indeed, both men, Eshkol and Sapir, were 'doers' who eschewed enslavement to doctrines of the past and created greater room for private enterprise and private investment from abroad. Still, they tried to maintain state and Histadrut control over the growing economy. Histadrut-owned enterprises such as Mekorot, Bank Hapoalim ('Workers Bank'), the controlled rural-settlement and housing mechanisms, industrial operations, and the consumer-goods supply system played important roles in expanding the economy and the infrastructure for the Jewish population countrywide. The Histadrut's institutions and enterprises maintained a high level of equality,[25] outperformed the rest of the economy, and financed Mapai's political machine. Some, however, were more equal than others. Public control over this praxis and transparency in this regard were lax, and the 'bosses', Eshkol and Sapir, ignored required rules of behaviour regarding clean and transparent use of public finances provided that such shortcuts would yield quick results. When Dr Emil Schmorak, comptroller general of the Jewish Agency, criticized Eshkol's ways, the latter brushed him aside in a typical way, by quoting the Bible: 'You shall not muzzle the ox as it treads out the corn'. Eshkol was referring to shortcuts, in his view, that were applied by him without waiting for formal approval by the Knesset and by the Jewish Agency in order to deal with urgent settlement efforts. Yet in one case he made government property under his control available to his daughter, helped a renowned actress to own a flat for herself in old age, and ordered similar actions which bordered with political or personal favouritism, known in Israel as 'Protektsia'. The long range result would be a rather tough legislation aimed against such cases, which landed Israeli cabinet ministers in jail, possibly also a former PM.

In the rural-settlement domain, it took Eshkol some time to gather the reins. Among his colleagues and aides, he chose two members of one pioneering family – the father and son Yosef and Ra'anan Weitz – as his collaborators. Yosef Weitz had arrived in Ottoman Palestine in 1908 and started out as Eshkol did, as an agricultural worker who joined Eshkol's anti-Marxist, social democratic political party. He studied agriculture, mastered a variety of foreign languages and became a prolific writer. By 1932, he had become an expert in purchasing land; following the Arab revolt of 1936–39 he spearheaded its speedy settlement and development. He was able to initiate an all-out settlement effort to 'create facts' on the ground even when the economic preconditions for further success were missing, thanks to his independent role as an executive with the Jewish National Fund, an arm of the Jewish Agency. Later on, he concentrated on afforesting the barren hilly parts of the country. Weitz's afforestation campaign supplied unskilled immigrants with work and did much to reclaim the countryside, but his efforts to settle the hill country on the basis of individual immigrant moshavim that would also serve as obstacles to a renewed Arab invasion proved to be a failure. This may have been one of the reasons for Eshkol's concentration of the whole settlement effort in his own hands later on. Later in the 1950s and in the early 1960s, directly under Eshkol and in cooperation with Professor Emmanuel Vilensky-Yallan,[26] Yosef's son Ra'anan would introduce a new regional-settlement scheme that proved a resounding success.[27]

Ra'anan Weitz was born in Ottoman Palestine in 1913 and studied agronomy in Italy (1932–37). Yallan-Vilensky was a Russian-born architect and later an agricultural engineer whose cooperation with Weitz *fils* would yield innovative but practical ideas that, once implemented due to Eshkol's ongoing interest and decisive support, earned Israel global fame in these spheres. The basic idea was to create not scattered individual moshavim, each with small membership comprised of ethnically diverse populations, but a cluster of many moshavim in a carefully planned and executed fashion. The most appropriate parts of the country were selected; they were the ones that offered fertile soil and were neither in the central and southern Negev nor in the Galilee, where water-supply and pricing problems would prompt Eshkol to seek American desalination technology and its requisite nuclear reactors later on. Once the locations were chosen, the infrastructure was created and the population – comprised as before from new immigrants from the Muslim world – became ethnically homogeneous. Finally, the necessary investment in agricultural specializations was made thanks to much effort rendered by Eshkol himself and seasoned volunteers, American aid and Jewish funding from abroad. The moshavim in the clusters remain successful to this day. Concurrent initiatives to move middle-class population from the major cities to an extended cluster were rejected by Eshkol because the potential settlers were politically alien to Mapai.[28]

A story in itself was the effort to establish 'development towns', begun under Ben-Gurion but later heavily dependent on Eshkol's involvement as Minister of Finance and on the initiatives of Pinchas Sapir, his aide and close colleague.[29] The very idea and the planning of a large number of new urban centres countrywide deviated from the traditional emphasis on agricultural settlement as pursued by Eshkol and his aides before independence. These officials, while conscious of the objective limitations of the agrarian sector in terms of water and land resources, left the urban sector to the workings of market forces until 1943, when a planning committee set up by Ben-Gurion as chairman of the Jewish Agency attempted to develop a countrywide urban scheme on the basis of the British experience in planning 'new towns'. The actual planning work was carried out by the architect Arieh Sharon, who moved with Ben-Gurion from the Jewish Agency to the Prime Minister's Office after independence. The 'Sharon Plan' envisaged the establishment of twenty-four regional urban centres across the country, each with 10,000–60,000 inhabitants. Soon enough, however, the political 'system', that is, the multiparty coalitions dictated by the proportional electoral method, divided responsibility for the new localities – the development towns – among various government ministries and the Jewish Agency, where Eshkol controlled land and water. Furthermore, the whole ambitious plan was very poorly financed due to funding shortfalls and competing priorities. Consequently, several development towns, such as Kiryat Shemona in the north and Kiryat Malachi in the south, evolved into impoverished, dreary places that served for many years as way-stations for immigrants who came and left. Other towns, such as Beersheva, Eilat, Acre, Ashqelon and Ashdod, were closer to existing economic hubs or otherwise strategically located.

The politics of these towns quickly assumed the characteristics of give-and-take by voters in exchange for services rendered by political parties that took 'possession' of various benefits in one town or another. The established centres of economic power, foremost unionized key services such as electricity and water, continued to support a steadily rising standard of living. From

Mapai's standpoint, however, these centres, embodied in the Histadrut, assured the control of crucial services such as healthcare and jobs – especially in parts of the country where private investors could not expect to make a profit for the time being. This control translated into votes. In Ben-Gurion's eyes, this 'system' had to be overhauled from the ground up, that is, replaced by a two- or three-party political regime after the British model. Ben-Gurion resigned from both offices – the premiership and the Defence Ministry – in 1953 to pursue this reform. However, Mapai's secondary leadership, Eshkol included, considered the existing method, the pivotal role of Mapai in the Knesset and its control of the Histadrut and the Jewish Agency's settlement apparatus, would suffice to develop the country optimally.

It was seemingly the heyday of the Mapai doers. Mapai controlled, if not fully, every centre of power in the country. Eshkol was now in charge of the nation's economic and settlement efforts, and very much of its party machine. The party's founding father, David Ben-Gurion, did not share the sense of hubris. In reality, Mapai depended on small coalition parties and had to concede to them in various areas such as religion and state, education and the division of the government ministries in charge of the development towns to competing bureaucracies. The resulting hodgepodge encouraged dissent and polemics inside the coalition and out, allowed other parties to pursue short-term sectarian goals, and prevented Mapai from ever achieving a decisive majority in national elections. It could use its pivotal stance in the Knesset (around one-third of the seats) and the Histadrut as long as the rest of the electorate, the majority, was divided between Left and Right.[30]

Now, however, Eshkol had to face an upcoming storm inside Mapai itself, following Ben-Gurion's decision in 1953 to resign his two portfolios.

NOTES

1. This chapter is partly based on Arnon Golan, *Wartime Spatial Changes, Former Arab Territories within the State of Israel, 1948–1950*, in Hebrew (Sede Boqer: Ben-Gurion Research Center, Ben-Gurion University of the Negev Press, 2001); David Ben-Gurion, *War Diary, the War of Independence 1948–1949*, in Hebrew (Tel Aviv: Ministry of Defense, 1982); Alon Kadish (ed.), *Israel's War of Independence 1948–1949*, in Hebrew (Tel Aviv: Ministry of Defense, 2005); and verified primary sources in Yossi Goldstein, *Eshkol – A Biography* (Jerusalem: Keter, 2003), Chapter 23, 'Director of the [Rural] Settlement Department', pp.288–302.

2. This pertains to territories designated by the UN Partition Commission to be included in the Palestinian state that was supposed to be established alongside Israel, but mostly occupied by Jordan, and thus became the 'West Bank' of the Hashemite Kingdom.
3. See Golan, *Wartime Spatial Changes*, and Goldstein, *Eshkol – A Biography*, p.289.
4. No further evictions were allowed without explicit permission from the Minister of Defence, David Ben-Gurion. When local commanders such as Moshe Carmel ordered the eviction of the Arab inhabitants of Nazareth in July 1948, Ben-Gurion ordered their immediate repatriation. See Ben-Gurion, *War Diary*, Vol.II, p.599.
5. Early in the war, a 'Transfer Committee', chaired by Yosef Weitz, was created to recommend alternatives relating to the resettlement of Palestinian refugees in Arab countries and the transfer of Jews from these countries to Israel. See Ben-Gurion, *War Diary*, Vol.III, pp.776–7.
6. Ibid., Vol.II, p.620.
7. See Tony Judt, *Post War, A History of Europe since 1945* (New York: Penguin, 2006), pp.13ff.
8. See Joseph Rubin (ed.), *Workers' Moshavim, an Anthology*, Vol. 1, in Hebrew (Moshavim + Workers Movement Publishing House, 1969, no further publication data available), p.370.
9. See Ben-Gurion's diary entry of 19 March 1949, on the emergence among Palestinians of the pan-Arab, fascist Ba'ath Party, *War Diary*, Vol.III, pp.964–5. Eventually the party took over Syria and as such played a major role in instigating the 1967 war. Saddam Hussein's Iraq was also ruled by his version of Ba'athism.
10. This remark pertains to the August 1993 Oslo accords, which go beyond the scope of this book. This book, however, may join other works in serving as an introduction to the study of the roads leading to the Oslo accords.
11. See Goldstein, *Eshkol – A Biography*, p.293, note. Buber and several of his colleagues at the Hebrew University, who had preached for limitations on Jewish immigration before independence, offered a moralistic criticism of the refugee issue. Buber, born to a Polish-Jewish family in Vienna, was an early German Zionist but resigned his office as editor of the Zionist publication *Die Welt* in order 'to be in the opposition'. During the First World War, he took a highly nationalistic stance in support of the Imperial German Army as 'the carrier of German civilization', to the dismay of Albert Einstein. After the First World War, he became a 'utopian Socialist', but when Israel was born he hailed its soldiers in a rather utopian fashion that he later abandoned in favour of moralistic opposition to Ben-Gurion's policies across the board, especially regarding the 'Lavon Affair'. See below in the text and Shlomo Aronson, *David Ben-Gurion, Renaissance Leader and the Waning of an Age,* in Hebrew (Sede Boqer and Beersheva: Ben-Gurion Research Institute, 1999), pp.345–8.
12. The issue here was the refusal of most kibbutzim to hire outside labourers, such as immigrants who had been housed next door to them, since according to kibbutz principles the work – especially hard physical jobs – should be done by members themselves for free. Hiring 'outsiders' meant cheap labour and signified a betrayal of the kibbutz mission and the introduction of non-members into the kibbutz social fabric. The immigrants' financial needs were of consequence. Eventually, several kibbutzim did hire immigrants as 'external labourers', maintaining their own higher standard of living compared with that of the immigrants in neighbouring 'development towns' and rural cooperatives – an experience not forgotten by the immigrants and exploited by Mr Begin's political party in due course.
13. See Ofra Keinan, 'The Kibbutzim and Moshavim Movements and Mass Immigration to Israel during the First Decade of the State', in Hebrew, *Cathedra, Quarterly for the History of Eretz-Israel and its Yishuv*, June (2004), pp.113–36.
14. There were exceptions. One major immigration-absorption effort undertaken by kibbutzim before and after independence was the acculturation of youngsters, whom they organized in youth communes and who eventually could, if accepted, join the kibbutz on an individual basis. Many members who did join, and others who did not, integrated successfully into Israeli society. The basic idea was that while the young could be educated under the premises of the Israeli melting pot, the elderly could not. Another rather successful effort to absorb young immigrants was undertaken by the Youth

Aliyah organization, which via its boarding schools educated a large number of immigrant youngsters and non-immigrant youth from the lower urban strata with funding by the Jewish Agency.

15. Keinan, 'The Kibbutzim and Moshavim Movements', p.134.
16. See Horowitz's memoirs, *In the Heart of Events*, in Hebrew (Ramat Gan: Massada, 1975), especially pp.13–78.
17. Eshkol was told once that a drought was expected soon. He responded by asking 'Where?' 'Here, of course'. 'Well, I was afraid that you were talking about a drought in the US'. Eshkol's American orientation was born at the time, thanks to the vital aid rendered by the Administration and American Jewry.
18. Eliahu Elath, *The Struggle for Statehood, Washington: 1945–1948*, in Hebrew, Vol. I, 1945–1946 (Tel Aviv: Am Oved, 1979), on American anti-Zionists at State, oil and strategic interests, the role of British Government in the run-up to Israel's declaration of independence and after, pp.322ff.
19. Goldstein, *Eshkol – A Biography*, pp.303ff.
20. Israel State Archives, *Levi Eshkol, the Third Prime Minister of Israel, Selected Documents on Chapters in His Life*, in Hebrew (Jerusalem: Israel State Archives, 2002), pp.240–70.
21. Horowitz, *In the Heart of Events*, pp.79ff.
22. Goldstein, *Eshkol – A Biography*, p.306.
23. Horowitz, *In the Heart of Events*, pp.115ff.
24. Israel State Archives, *Levi Eshkol*, pp.280ff.
25. See Yosef Gorny, Avi Bareli and Yitzhak Greenberg (eds), *From a Labour Society to a Labour Organization, Articles on the Histadrut during the Yishuv and the Statehood Periods*, in Hebrew (Sede Boqer: Ben-Gurion Heritage Center and Tel Aviv University, 2000), p.623.
26. During the Second World War Vilensky established an interrogation centre under Jewish Agency auspices for Allied Military Intelligence; its task was to obtain information from Jewish refugees about Axis activities and bombing targets. See Shlomo Aronson, *Hitler, the Allies, and the Jews* (New York: Cambridge University Press, 2006), p.80.
27. See Ofra Keinan, 'Immigrants as Implementers of Zionist Ideals: The Impact of Immigrant Settlements on Environmental Change in the Ta'anach Region 1948–1967', in Hebrew (Ph.D. Dissertation, Bar-Ilan University, 1989).
28. Interview with Ofra Keinan, quoted above, note 13. See Rubin (ed.), *Workers' Moshavim, an Anthology*.
29. See most recent collection of research papers: Zvi Zameret, Aviva Halamish and Esther Meir-Glitzenstein (eds), *The Development Towns*, in Hebrew (Jerusalem: Yad Izhak Ben-Zvi, 2009).
30. See Moshe Lissak, chief editor, *The History of the Jewish Community in Eretz Israel since 1882, Israel, the First Decade*, in Hebrew (Jerusalem: The Israel Academy of Sciences and Humanities, 2009), pp.481–511.

Chapter Five

Eshkol's Bid for Rescuing Mapai

STORMY SUCCESSION

As Eshkol strove desperately to absorb the waves of immigrants in the early 1950s using every means available, Ben-Gurion, in direct control of the Ministry of Defence (MOD), used the IDF as an emergency agency of the state to alleviate immediate problems such as food supplies in the transit camps, interim housing for immigrants, flood control and other practical deficiencies that made life in the camps miserable. He also employed the IDF as an educational agency by employing women soldiers as Hebrew teachers and by using conscription (two and a half years for men, less for women) and subsequent reserve service to create a huge melting pot, with conscript-commanders providing *esprit de corps* and serving as role models. Thus, the IDF became a great immigrant-absorption agency in terms of imparting language skills, elevating commanders to the role of paragons in their treatment of soldiers and their families, and assisting in transit camps and frontier localities.

In 1953, however, resigning his dual portfolios and heading to the non-partisan Kibbutz Sede Boqer, Ben-Gurion seems to have been convinced that he had failed to bring on the requisite changes in the lives of Jews in the Zionist state, be it in respect of the institutionalized, reformed self-rule that the Jews must adopt and internalize due to the principle of their return to history as a sovereign nation, and in the challenges of absorbing the immigrants and settling the empty Negev and the Galilee. The young were being drawn into the wake of Left-leaning parties and youth movements, adopting the elitist attitude of aboriginal inhabitants vis-à-vis the new immigrants, or searched for personal achievements; the Mapai-affiliated movements responded to the challenges of that kind by going on the intellectual defensive. Reaching Sede Boqer in December of that year, Ben-Gurion occupied himself more with the question of youth than with anything else. Shortly afterwards, however, he was 'reoccupied' by something that had troubled him since the outset of statehood: regime change of a sort that would help the Jews to become a sovereign nation that would take charge of its fate. Addressing the Second Knesset on 8 June 1953, before his resignation, he heatedly accused the pantheon of political parties of 'being not parties but sects' that looked out for their short-term interests instead of the public's welfare. Shortly after his resignation, Ben-Gurion launched his public campaign for fundamental regime change, that is, the introduction of a district-majority electoral method and a two-party parliamentary system after the British model, which he considered prerequisites for the creation of a 'sound regime'[1] that would allow the masses direct representation instead of the machine politics controlled by his own party.

Thus far Ben-Gurion had created an infrastructure for the defence system, paying strict attention to the separation of the army, which concerned itself mainly with preparing for and engaging in combat but actually functioned as an immigration-absorption agency, and the MOD, which dealt with sensitive political and financial matters related to defence procurement, both at home and abroad. The MOD was also charged with the other interfaces of army and civilian society, including the draft, the paramilitary training of youth, and the mobilization of soldiers for work in rural and frontier settlements. The practical performance of the army in those early years, when it had become an immigrant-absorption agency, was unsatisfactory. The second Chief of General Staff (COGS), Lt Gen. Yigael Yadin, resigned or – truth to tell – was dismissed by Ben-Gurion when he objected to the slashing of his budget and its subordination to Israeli society's higher priorities in those times of mass immigration. The third COGS, Mordechai Makleff, a British Army veteran, was swiftly replaced by Moshe Dayan. Dayan himself had certainly been angling for this post and did not make Makleff's life easy.

The appointment of Dayan, however, seemed to strike the right blend of originality and due caution, the yoke of the political echelon and the display of initiative, the restoration of the fighting spirit that the IDF had displayed in the War of Independence, and the engagement of young people's imagination so that they would regard the army as an enterprise worthy of their commitment. When he headed off to Sede Boqer, Ben-Gurion could assume that the army was in good hands. At the MOD, too, the swift replacement of Ze'ev Schind with Shimon Peres as director general made it seem as if the stability and proper subordination of the IDF to the political echelon had been achieved. It was the appointment of Pinchas Lavon to the defence portfolio that destabilized the defence system so badly – a point to which we will return presently.

Ben-Gurion's successor as prime minister was Moshe Sharett, a senior veteran diplomat, Israel's Foreign Minister since its birth, and the director of the Jewish Agency Political Department (the 'foreign ministry' of the state in the making) since 1933. For Ben-Gurion, Sharett was a weak and intellectually less serious politician. Eshkol would have been a much better choice, he thought. Ben-Gurion appreciated Eshkol's support of the declaration of independence in 1948, a stance that countered the views of the leading members of Eshkol's own original party. He deemed Eshkol strong enough and popular enough among the Mapai's secondary leadership to continue to support Ben-Gurion's foreign and defence policies as he had so far. In his vision of semi-retirement, Ben-Gurion would concentrate on domestic priorities and expect nothing alarming in the foreign and security fields. Sharett, in turn, in the judgment of the 'old man', had never enjoyed the appreciation of most of the secondary echelon and would not now, either. In this he proved to be wrong or, at least, unaware of the seniority system that politicians cherish and that Eshkol himself honoured.

Pinchas Lavon, a major socialist theoretician and an outspoken dove who had opposed Ben-Gurion's declaration of independence until Ben-Gurion delivered it, was chosen by Ben-Gurion as the next Minister of Defence, and Mapai's secondary leadership named Sharett Ben-Gurion's successor in the premiership. Lavon seemed a promising choice for defence thanks to his bright mind, his party seniority and his oratory, which signalled not only a move to the centre – against Right and Left – but also an eloquent voice in Knesset debates. Lt Gen. Dayan remained COGS and Mr Peres remained Director General of the MOD. Very soon all three – including Prime Minister Sharett – found themselves embroiled in hopeless battles related, among other things, to Lavon's sudden outburst of radical, militarily risky operational planning, his personality problems and his drinking habits. 'A shining mind in a dark soul' was an expression that Mapai's spiritual leader Berl Katznelson had used to characterize Pinchas Lavon's problematic character.[2]

THE ULTIMATE DETERRENT

In the mean time, some Arab leaders were steadily embroiling themselves in policies that weighed on Israel (economic boycott, isolation from key countries in the Third World, blocking the Suez Canal and the waterway to Eilat to Israeli shipping, terror attacks in Israeli territory), giving the Israeli public a sense of siege and strangulation. Others busied themselves in domestic turmoil, but Ben-Gurion assumed that they might unite against Israel sooner or later due to the logic of modern pan-Arabism and the Arab world's enormous potential advantages in manpower, resources and East vs. West strategic positions over the tiny and, to their minds, 'illegal' Jewish island in their ocean.

All these circumstances, which Ben-Gurion considered axiomatic, coupled with the main lesson that he had learned from the Holocaust – the 'trap' in which the Jewish people found themselves during the Second World War, as the Allies ignored the Nazis' unprecedented carnage on the grounds of the political nuisance that countering it would cause them[3] – justified an effort to acquire an 'ultimate' weapon that would nip the conflict in the bud, even if recognition of the legitimacy of this weapon would have to be struggled for. The struggle at issue lies beyond the concern of this chapter; what remains is the field of concern to Ben-Gurion: a historical reality that had largely ignored the fate of the Jews while favouring Arab interests and claims during the Second World War and that continued to play an important role in Western and Soviet activities afterwards. The lessons of that war were as pointed and permanent in people's minds as other values are today. Therefore, members of that generation thought in terms of total war and its prevention by any means, including those that would have stopped Hitler himself had they been taken in time. Specifically, had the West armed itself properly before allowing Nazi Germany to abrogate the prohibitions of the Versailles Treaty, and had Hitler been shown clearly that he had no chance of attaining his goals by force, the Second World War might have been precluded, as Churchill repeatedly claimed in the highly influential memoirs that he published in the early 1950s.

In the Israeli case, the Arabs had proclaimed publicly that it was their duty to annihilate an existing state that had been born in the tumult of a war that they had instigated. By implication, they would attempt to destroy it by any means, be it the might of their armies or through unconventional means – if Israel allowed them to obtain these means before it did. How the Arabs would destroy Israel was immaterial to Israel. However, if Israel beat the Arabs in the race for nuclear capability, it could counter their existential threats by posing its own existential threat to them and their regimes. This capability would give the Arabs the option – which did not exist in the conventional era – of recognizing Israel's existence and suspending, if not terminating, the conflict. And even if the Arabs eventually obtained unconventional weapons and intended to use them against Israel, the result would be so catastrophic that the destruction of Israel would be poor compensation.

In this respect, the issue of the Second World War refugees – the millions of Germans who were uprooted in the aftermath of the Nazi aggression and crimes, and the many thousands of Japanese who were forced to leave Korea, Manchuria and other territories – seemed to have justified the departure or forced exile of Palestinians after their war against the Jews in 1936–39, the role of Palestinian leaders in preventing the rescue of Jews during the Holocaust, and their war against the 1947 UN partition resolution all the way to the continued quest to undo the Jewish state.

In the 1950s, the United States leadership had not yet settled into the role of a power willing to risk itself in a nuclear war on behalf of its allies; consensual behavioural norms in this respect had not yet been determined and imposed. The very meaning of nuclear arms – were they instruments of combat or of its prevention? – had been debated in the US since the days of Hiroshima. Amazingly, it took America until the late 1950s to develop a systematic theory of nuclear deterrence. From the outset, of course, there were important theoreticians in this field, including some who believed that nuclear weapons had ended an era in human history and would henceforth prevent the resolution of matters by war. The US Air Force, contrarily, regarded nuclear weaponry as a perfect instrument of victory as long as the American nuclear monopoly lasted. After the USSR breached this monopoly, a debate erupted over maintaining the American quantitative and qualitative edge by shifting from atom bombs to hydrogen bombs, the power of which was theoretically unlimited. The possession of this power generated horrific fear in various American circles, prompting some to embrace the 'better Red than dead' outlook, take their country's military-industrial complex to be a pack of irresponsible risk-takers, and treat those abroad who wished to follow their lead – even if only for defensive purposes – with a mixture of fear and loathing. Others could see the case of Israel – given the Holocaust and the Arabs' current threats of annihilation – as an outlier that justified nuclear deterrence. This, at least, was the conviction of a certain group of French *responsables* who wished to help Israel – and France – in this respect.[4] The British chiefs of staff, in contrast to the Americans, had developed an explicit defensive concept very early in this era and even before they had their own A-bomb. From their standpoint, a Soviet threat to the homeland islands (or any other threat to the British Isles, given Germany's recent past) would trigger a British atomic threat against the Soviet Union (or against Germany). Eventually, the hydrogen bomb prompted the British to rethink the maintenance of foreign bases that could be obliterated with one bomb, such as those in the Suez Canal area.

As these debates ebbed and flowed in the West, Israel was busy being born and hunting for uranium in the Negev by means of Hemed C, a special division of the IDF's Science Corps commanded by Shlomo Gur (Grazofsky) and two scientific authorities, the brothers Aharon and Efraim Katchalsky-Katsir. While on a mission to the United States, Gur made the acquaintance of Jewish scientists who were working on the atomic bomb. Evidently Professor Ernst David Bergmann (Ben-Gurion's scientific advisor and, at an earlier time, founder of the Israel

Biological Institute, part of the defence administration) the Katchalskys and Gur were the patriarchs of an idea that Ben-Gurion had adopted even before the war was over. In his *Yoman ha-Milhama* (War Diary) 1948/49, Ben-Gurion made the following entry on 25 December 1948, titled 'Hanukkah reflections':

> We are facing the greatest upheaval in human life – the discovery of atomic energy – and its exploitation in the global economy. Our participation in readying this revolution and using its fruits is the scientific role of our generation. *The adoption of science for the betterment of security* and production. [Emphasis added.]

Ben-Gurion penned these reflections after his meetings with Professors Bergmann and Joel (Giulio) Rackah, a major nuclear physicist and later the rector of Hebrew University of Jerusalem, who alerted him during the War of Independence to the gravitas and significance of the atomic revolution and even put him in touch with Jewish nuclear experts abroad at that time.[5]

Bergmann – an organic chemist by training – had relations with French nuclear scientists, some of them Jewish, working in Canada on behalf of the American Manhattan Project. He himself had worked in France after its liberation. These French scientists – like Bergmann when he approached Ben-Gurion – called General de Gaulle's attention to the atomic bomb and helped de Gaulle establish the French Atomic Energy Commission (FAEC) during the latter's tenure as prime minister of liberated France. The FAEC was at once a typical product of traditional French bureaucracy, pioneering creativity, and learning from the past, and Bergmann was associated with personalities in its administration from its inception.

In the middle of 1952, Defence Minister Ben-Gurion established the Israel Atomic Energy Commission (IAEC) – the 'Umbrella Division', as one of its members, Professor Yisrael Dostrovsky, called it[6] – and appointed Bergmann as its chair. The IAEC was formed after Hemed's probes in the Negev turned up phosphate deposits that contained small amounts of uranium. In 1950–51, the Science Corps was civilianized and efforts began to develop patents for the extraction of uranium from phosphates and the manufacture of the heavy water that nuclear reactors need. Patents for both processes were acquired and sold to France and Britain several years later. When it came to implementing the idea of creating a nuclear reactor in Israel, however, the debates that erupted were reminiscent of the term 'wars of the Jews', which members of the Israeli elite were fighting behind closed doors at the time. One ostensible possibility was for Israel to build a nuclear reactor by its own efforts, thanks to the aforementioned developments, Jewish genius abroad and in Israel itself, the establishment of a steelmaking infrastructure in Acre using German reparations funds, and the hopes that Ben-Gurion and Bergmann evidently pinned on the Jewish and Israeli scientific community. Indeed, talented physicists who had been sent abroad to study nuclear physics at the end of the War of Independence began to return to Israel at this time. They of all people, however, along with the heads of the Israeli scientific community, opposed the home-manufacture project for various reasons. One was their concern that the vast endeavour would consume all of Israel's scientific potential and capital amid the absence of the industrial infrastructure that the implementation of such a venture required. Furthermore, moral considerations were already being expressed at this time – and would be voiced with greater intensity in the next phase – as the bombing of Hiroshima and the fear of inter-bloc nuclear war plunged the Western scientific world into horror and remorse. Responding to the principled problems of scientists' retention of control over their handiwork, Ernst Bergmann's working methods, and the zeal of the Director-General of the Ministry of Defence, Shimon Peres, to put the idea into practice at almost any price, the entire Commission resigned with the sole exception of its chair, Bergmann.[7]

Absent any chance of American or British assistance in this sensitive matter and as long as the French nuclear infrastructure had not yet jelled, the implementation of the idea had to take a time-out. The idea itself, however, remained alive and continued to occupy Ben-Gurion even after he had resigned his portfolios and relocated to Sede Boqer. His successor at the MOD, Pinchas Lavon, displayed no interest in the nuclear topic, as one may gather from Bergmann's direct contact with Prime Minister Sharett on this issue.[8] Sharett, considering Bergmann overly ardent on the topic, sought conventional solutions to the conventional problems that concerned him, for example, solving the water problem in northern Israel and exploring the possibility of a settlement of sorts – formal peace was unattainable as far as the Arabs were concerned; what is more, it was linked to the Palestinian refugee question – with Egypt via American mediation.[9] He thought it might be possible to solve the water problem by buying an American nuclear reactor for desalination. Nevertheless, Sharett thought it ill-advised to enrage Washington and, perhaps, elicit an undesired Egyptian response by developing a made-in-Israel reactor. After all, Egyptian President Nasser had become a personality of international importance during Sharett's tenure. In 1955, the Bandung conference of 'non-aligned' states – which challenged the leadership of the nuclear superpowers – catapulted Nasser to the centre of the global stage and transformed him into the leader of modern pan-Arabism. Concurrently, Nasser ordered from the USSR, and received, a small research reactor.

Prime Minister Sharett and Defence Minister Lavon seemed unimpressed by this, each in his own way. By then, Lavon had ensnared himself in disputes both with COGS Dayan, for various reasons including extreme reprisals against Palestinian infiltrators that Lavon had initiated and Dayan ruled out, and with MOD Director General Peres, by attempting to crimp the latter's steps in the procurement of conventional weapons in France, viewing them as circumventions of his authority. We do not know whether at this stage Lavon actively opposed the nuclear option as well or, perhaps, thought of it as pie in the sky. At this time, Bergmann visited Ben-Gurion in Sede Boqer and spoke with him about the nuclear option. Ben-Gurion described it as a goal toward which no effort should be spared and expressed confidence that 'we shall have the bomb within ten years'.

Some time later, Defence Minister Lavon was forced to resign from Sharett's Government due to a futile attempt to thwart the British departure from the Suez Canal area in what became known as the 'Lavon Affair'. Lavon would try to reopen the case in 1960 so in order to avoid confusion the two stages of the affair will be referred to as the '1954 Affair' and the '1960 Affair'. What matters here, however, is that Lavon's resignation brought Ben-Gurion back to the MOD as his successor and, after the 1955 elections, back to the Prime Minister's Office (PMO) as well.

In the mean time, the French nuclear infrastructure was nearly complete and the political echelons in Paris had to decide what to do with it: should it be used to generate electricity for peaceful purposes only, or to make bombs for strategic and political ends? Prime Minister Pierre Mendès-France had already made an initial decision in favour of the military-political calculus (the idea being to maintain a decisive French edge over West Germany) in his decision to extract France from Indo-China. No one at the time was able to make a similar decision on the Algerian question, where an armed uprising against France's grip on this 'district' of the homeland was swiftly developing with Nasser's assistance and Soviet support. This paved the way to Israeli–French cooperation against a common foe, Nasser, which in turn engendered nuclear collaboration as well. Such a partnership solved the problem of home manufacture of an Israeli atomic infrastructure – there would be none – and could justify conventional military collaboration between Israel and France for the dual purpose of occupying the Suez Canal zone and toppling Nasser.

Ben-Gurion's defence doctrine since 1949 was basically defensive, at least insofar as full-fledged preventive wars at Israel's initiative were concerned.[10] He rejected the drive proposed by Lt Gen. Moshe Dayan – his COGS – for a preventive war in 1956, despite Egypt's open acts of aggression and its threatening acquisition of modern Soviet weapons. His reasoning was twofold: the price to Israel in lives and materiel, and his expectation that the Egyptian army would quickly rebound from any damage Israel might inflict. 'Our problem', he cautioned Dayan, 'is that we cannot destroy them. We push Egypt down ten times, this would be nothing. If they win once, it'll be the end.' Ben-Gurion added that every Israeli-initiated, successful war would not be accepted by the Arabs as final, since they would recover and get ready for a new round again and again 'with no end to it', so even if Israel should win them all, the accumulated victories may become pyrrhic.[11] If Israel should nevertheless resort to war, it should do so not alone but in cooperation with allies or one worthy ally, and even then only in the presence of an appropriate *casus belli*.[12] These maxims must be borne in mind and compared with Eshkol's behaviour during the crisis of May 1967 onwards. The long-term solution to Israel's security problem, in Ben-Gurion's opinion, should be sought in the acquisition of a nuclear deterrent which, while not necessarily preventing limited acts of aggression that would entail limited conventional responses, may avert a war of annihilation of 1948 dimensions. When Ben-Gurion resorted to what seems to have been a preventive war in 1956 against Nasser's Egypt, he did so for the purpose of cementing an alliance – albeit informal – with France involving nuclear cooperation.[13] Eshkol was not privy to the preparations for what later became known as Operation Kadesh – the Israeli part of the French-British campaign against Egypt in late 1956. However, he supported it wholeheartedly once Ben-Gurion introduced him to the conventional aspects of what sounded like a necessary action to restore Israel's deterrence in view of Egypt's growing acts of belligerence, which thus far had been answered inadequately, if at all. We do not know the extent to which Eshkol was apprised of the unconventional part of the preparations – the acquisition of a nuclear infrastructure from France, which was so costly that he was subsequently badly troubled by that aspect of the project. Ben-Gurion tried hard to mobilize him in support of the operation itself,[14] expecting him to oppose it in view of the stance of Eshkol's influential, dovish colleague Pinchas Sapir and Minister of Education Zalman Aranne. Instead, the Mapai boss followed Ben-Gurion's lead even in regard to the less important, conventional goals of the campaign, that is, stopping terror attacks from Egyptian-controlled Gaza, lifting the Egyptian blockade on Eilat, and inflicting a considerable blow on the Egyptian army and, possibly, on Nasser's regime. Eshkol also supported Ben-Gurion's decision after the operation to withdraw from Sinai, the Straits of Tiran and the Gaza Strip under combined Soviet-American pressure, in exchange for the deployment of UN peacekeepers in the Straits and along the Strip and for American promises regarding the freedom of shipping to Eilat.

Although Nasser's military defeat at the hands of the IDF was transformed into an Egyptian political victory, this victory, the result of cooperation between the two nuclear superpowers, resulted in three additional developments. First, France finally decided to go militarily nuclear and collaborate with Israel in this regard. Second, France waved her objections to the creation of a European Common Market and agreed, ahead of this reform, to the launching of EURATOM, the first multinational project aimed at the common use of nuclear energy for peaceful purposes as an alternative to the superpowers' monopoly in this field, excluding Great Britain.

France's nuclear cooperation with Israel has been understood in terms of French, not only Israeli, advantage, but the costs related to it, in addition to the enormous costs of the 1956 campaign itself, did concern Finance Minister Eshkol. It is not clear whether Eshkol objected to the nuclear endeavour per se, but its financing was arranged outside of the regular budget[15] and, therefore, beyond the control of the Knesset Finance Committee; the Finance Minister and his right-hand man, Industry and Trade Minister Sapir; and their spheres of influence as Mapai potentates. The project was entrusted to Shimon Peres, Ben-Gurion's Deputy Minister of Defence since the 1959 elections, who, together with Moshe Dayan, now a junior minister in Ben-Gurion's cabinet, seemed to be aspiring to succeed Ben-Gurion in both his offices and thus skip over the whole secondary leadership and its top man, Eshkol.

Additional key details in regard to the acquisition of the French reactor remained obscure and became part of the official policy of nuclear opaqueness that Israel has maintained to this day. I shall return to the origins of this policy later on, noting only that the details at issue pertain to the acquisition by Israel of a plutonium separation plant and nuclear-capable missiles, and the dates thereof.

The reactor itself was acquired in October 1957 in the aftermath of the abortive Suez-Sinai campaign. According to the account by the French author Pierre Pean,[16] the French Socialist-Radical coalition under Guy Mollet and Morris Bourgès-Maunoury was motivated by a 'Munich reflex'. That is, they likened Egypt's President Gamal Abd el Nasser to the Axis leaders in the 1930s and perceived in him a Fascist threat similar to that posed by General Francisco Franco, whom the Third Republic had given free rein to win the Spanish Civil War. The same syndrome was subsequently attributed to the Munich accord, in which Britain and France sacrificed Czechoslovakia for an elusive peace with Hitler. This description is of course a simplistic rendering based on the thinking of one author, since the issue at hand was France's interest in retaining Algeria. Even so, the Suez campaign marked a general crossroads in French foreign policy: its failure, under the shadow of Soviet nuclear threats and American opposition, generated a whole series of major French decisions: most notably, France would finally become a full-fledged nuclear power. The many steps leading to this decision – a crucial one made by radical Prime Minister Pierre Mendès-France upon his decision to pull out of Vietnam – are described by Pean from a Gaullist perspective, as if the Fourth Republic had been dragged by its permanent bureaucracy into going nuclear without clear-cut political willingness to take this step at first and without a clear strategic concept that would explain why the country should adopt a military nuclear posture of its own.

The decision to give Israel the ultimate gift – an entire nuclear weapons production facility, i.e., a reactor for plutonium production and a plutonium separation plant – is described by Pean as a complex political-technological deal that involved much more than sentiment. French domestic complexities required Israel's help in overcoming Leftist Socialist opposition to the decision of Mollet's mainstream Socialist party to go nuclear. Cooperation with Israel, a beleaguered socialist sister-state, could lend the French decision at least a degree of domestic legitimacy if not a measure of international understanding among nuclear scientists, many of whom were Jewish. At this time, the moral-political campaign in the West against the bomb reached one of its spikes and the Americans' anti-proliferation stance prohibited the supply of sensitive tools such as advanced computers to potential nuclear powers such as France. Thus, after Jerusalem and Paris signed a formal agreement on nuclear cooperation in October 1957, Israel allowed the latter to calculate the parameters of the French bomb by using American computation equipment available at the Weizmann Institute of Science in Rehovoth.[17] Soon afterwards, French technicians began to construct the Dimona reactor, which was supposed to be ready, plutonium separation plant included, by the end of 1963.[18] The intended purpose of the bomb was to strengthen isolated Israel vis-à-vis Egypt's Nasser, the political winner of the 1956 Suez-Sinai fiasco and France's main enemy in its struggle over Algeria. At the same time, Israel envisioned growing nuclear cooperation with West Germany and, possibly, Italy, and managed to gain secret military aid from Bonn.[19]

FRANCE RETHINKS, AMERICA OBJECTS

De Gaulle's return to power in 1958 did not seem to interfere with the ongoing nuclear cooperation between the two nations, at least until 1960, when three issues merged to threaten the completion of the Israeli project. First, in 1960 France tested its own bomb successfully and officially joined the nuclear club. It no longer needed Israeli help in this regard; in fact, the Gaullist concept of the French national bomb was exclusive. Having produced its all-French A-bomb, France now demanded that the great powers, that is, the nuclear powers, admit it to their exclusive club, which prohibited the rendering of nuclear aid to a small country outside of it.

Second, de Gaulle manoeuvred the West Germans into accepting his political-strategic leadership, rather than cooperation, in nuclear matters, while the problem of German access to NATO's nuclear arsenal remained a major issue within the Treaty Organization.[20] Hence the Israeli understanding of these changes may have been rather blurry when de Gaulle informed Jerusalem in mid-1960 that the secret of Dimona – the reactor's site in the Negev desert – had been blown and that France would terminate its role in the project.[21] For the time being, construction was indeed suspended, at least officially.

Third, we do not know whether de Gaulle had already decided at this stage to withdraw from Algeria partly or completely. The Algerian Sahara was France's nuclear test field and its ballistic-missile experimentation areas were visited by Israeli military leaders such as the former COGS, Moshe Dayan, and Deputy Minister of Defence Shimon Peres before Paris' sudden decision to terminate its vital involvement in the Dimona project. Dayan and Peres were Ben-Gurion's closest military aides and the architects of the French-Israeli military cooperation that had led to the Suez-Sinai campaign of 1956. Since then, the armed forces of both nations developed intimate relations to such an extent that de Gaulle feared it might jeopardize his Algerian plans. The reason for his decision in 1960 to at least suspend the Dimona project, which was scheduled for completion in 1963, may have been related to the Algerian complex.

The crisis over Dimona was not limited to France and Israel. The Americans got wind of the secret. Serious behind-the-scenes deliberations on how to stop the Israeli venture ensued and would surely leak soon.[22]

The frantic Israeli effort to save the project led to Ben-Gurion's first official visit to France and to negotiations that, on the face of it, had two rather misleading outcomes. First, in December 1960 Ben-Gurion announced in the Knesset that Israel was building a nuclear reactor 'for the development of the Negev' (that is, for peaceful use). Thus, under foreign pressure, Israel's bid for a nuclear deterrent was delegitimized by Israel itself. Second, under these circumstances, de Gaulle allowed the construction of the reactor to resume – holding Israel as a hostage in this regard, in my view, if Jerusalem or any Israel military or foreign-intelligence officials were to support the French Army in any way once he decided to withdraw from Algeria. The official description of the continued French involvement, given years later, was that France had pulled out of the project but Israel continued it 'on its own'.[23] Since the construction of the reactor did continue and, according to Ben-Gurion's biographer, was completed successfully in 1963, the crucial question now was whether Israel had acquired a plutonium separation plant as well and, if it had, whether it was able to operate both facilities properly.[24]

By that time (mid-1962), Ben-Gurion had convened a high-level discussion about Israel's future nuclear strategy.[25] Since it adjourned without the adoption of any overt deterrence posture, some scholars discern in it a decision by Ben-Gurion himself not to embrace nuclear deterrence as the decisive guarantee of Israel's existence.[26] I would seek to prove that such scholars are wrong and that Ben-Gurion did view the bomb as the definitive 'grand equalizer' that would allow the Arabs to descend from the ladder of their undertaking – politically required and strategically attainable in the long run – to destroy a conventionally armed Israel.

Later on, the Americans intervened directly in Israel's domestic politics and contributed their share to Ben-Gurion's final resignation from his two portfolios in the summer of 1963.[27] According to oral testimonies and published Israeli sources that may be compared against primary American records, Ben-Gurion was manoeuvred out of his offices by the combination of the domestic government crisis related to the 'Lavon Affair', his policy of military cooperation with West Germany, the perception that he must be close to retirement due to his advanced age, and American efforts to freeze the Dimona project in exchange for Egyptian concessions on their own – rather useless – missile programme. The

Soviet role in this regard remains obscure as far as primary sources are concerned. According to Mr Peres, however, the Kremlin undertook a major act of intervention with Washington while Ben-Gurion was still in office – a gambit that was averted because no evidence about the existence of a plutonium separation plant available to Israel could be found.[28]

POLITICAL AND ETHNIC RECALIBRATION

The November 1959 elections handed Mapai and its leader a great victory. Mapai won more mandates than ever before at the expense of its rival to the Left, Tabenkin-Galili's and Allon's Ahdut ha-'Avoda, and of the moderate right-wing parties. One of the campaign slogans concerned Ben-Gurion's 'British' reform, which Mapai had officially adopted. The core of Ben-Gurion's reform plan was the introduction of a constituency-majority ballot law after the British electoral system which, while producing a two- or three-party regime, allowed the membership to participate – in contrast with the system practiced by Mapai, and the other parties, of appointing representatives to the Knesset and other institutions from above, by closed select committees controlled by party machines. The British party system was more complicated than that; under extraordinary circumstances in the early twentieth century, it had endured serious schisms and entailed coalition-building between liberals and conservatives in the House of Commons, relied on independent Irish delegates, and even faced repeated general elections as coalitions collapsed before completing their full legislative terms. Press lords had also played an important role in British politics at the time. However, the system had successfully navigated the process of crowning Labour as the successor of the Liberal Party, won the First World War, found a reasonable solution to the Irish question, won the Second World War, and adopted a far-reaching welfare-state programme by means of parliamentary legislation. Thus, it fulfilled Ben-Gurion's main requirements.

For Mapai bosses such as Eshkol, Ben-Gurion's reform meant surrendering power or replacing a governing system that worked – even if it was based on decisions made in smoke-filled rooms and horse-trading with the electorate thanks to Mapai's control of jobs and social services – with an alternative untried in the Israeli milieu. For Ben-Gurion, the reform was absolutely necessary, since to his mind the rank-and-file, especially Israelis from Muslim countries, must be given the option of real participation and the emergence of their own representatives within the Mapai framework, instead of the passivity imposed on most of them as clients of the select committees.

The November 1959 elections, however – conducted under the old electoral system – denied Mapai an absolute majority and thereby foiled the launching of Ben-Gurion's reform, because it entailed the support of other large parties, which refused to join him, or smaller ones, which the reform would have destroyed. These and other factors planted seeds of mayhem that would sprout upon the eruption of 'the Affair' irrespective of the debate that broke out during it. Inside Mapai, a group of 'young Turks' entered politics under the leadership of retired COGS Moshe Dayan. Introduced to the 'system', which traded jobs, healthcare and social services, controlled by Mapai's bosses in the Histadrut, as well as higher wages authorized by Eshkol and Sapir, for political support from the powerful unions organized under the Histadrut umbrella, Dayan was genuinely shocked.[29] Obviously such things were unheard of in the IDF. In response, Dayan launched a much publicized attack against the Histadrut – indirectly an assault on Pinchas Lavon, its powerful Secretary General, and on Eshkol and the elderly Mapai bosses – that sounded like a call to replace a corrupt oligarchy with a new, young leadership devoted to the interests of the state and free of the existing political machinations. The 'bosses' – Eshkol, his right-hand aide Pinchas Sapir, a devoted dove, and Lavon – construed the new démarche as a quest for power and, possibly, a bid for the succession of Ben-Gurion himself, all by a retired general who had retained his military habits. Hence, they banded together urgently to thwart it and keep the succession in their own hands. Dayan's démarche was also immediately rejected by the parties on the Left as a call for 'statism', that is, the imposition of state control over voluntary organizations (such as the highly bureaucratized Histadrut). Behind this call, old wounds pertaining to the dissolution of the Palmach staff by Ben-Gurion and the subsequent emergence of Dayan as chieftain of the IDF, as Ben-Gurion's protégé, created a link between the two and an unmitigated desire on the part of old Palmach leaders such as Allon and Galili to get rid of both men.

But there was more. The Dayan-led gambit marked the emergence of an Israeli-born generation (colloquially termed *sabras*, denoting the prickly-pear fruit – bristling on the outside, soft and sweet on the inside). The individuals involved introduced a new version of spoken Hebrew, Ivrit, as well as a native sense of humour and a new style of writing that by definition was fresh and different from that of the founding fathers. Politically, they were close to the Left in its various parties. One of them, the renowned poet Nathan Zach, quipped when Eshkol took over that, 'There's no one to rebel against now', meaning that Ben-Gurion's authoritarian style, which had invited rebelliousness among members of Zach's generation, had given way to Eshkol's cotton-soft manner of governance, which initially aroused sympathy but later turned to mockery and ultimately to popular uprising.

Within the constellation of parties, Ahdut ha-'Avoda despaired of becoming an alternative to Mapai and began to search for allies within the latter, a large pluralistic party, in order to influence it from within without losing its own identity. Dialectically, Mapai's triumphs over its veteran rival since the 1940s created an opening – which Ben-Gurion felt very acutely – for an attempt by Ahdut Ha-'Avoda to penetrate his party and forge new relations with potential allies within Mapai, precisely because Ahdut ha-'Avoda had performed so poorly at the polls. In the Histadrut domain, at least, Ahdut ha-'Avoda and Mapam, the left-wing Marxist-oriented party, could look forward to a dialogue with Sapir and Eshkol because the left-wing parties' militant stance on wages was hindering economic growth. An alliance between Mapai and these parties would facilitate growth and silence or isolate the militant voices on the Left. A formal parliamentary alliance with Ahdut ha-'Avoda, however, might encumber Ben-Gurion's foreign and defence policies, especially in regard to relations with the Federal Republic of Germany and the development of the nuclear option – an issue on which Yigal Allon had voiced public criticism ahead of the 1959 elections.

Hence my assertion about the seeds of mayhem that were sown in the coalition that Ben-Gurion had to establish with Ahdut ha-'Avoda specifically after the 1959 polls. For this reason Ben-Gurion preferred to coalesce with the moderate-right General Zionist party and also because the General Zionists' electoral fortunes had been declining, and if they were left out of the coalition, he feared they would leap into the arms of Menachem Begin's nationalist Right, thereby creating a right-wing combination or 'alignment' that would counterweigh Mapai's rapprochement with the left-wing nationalist party, Ahdut ha-'Avoda.

Another seed of mayhem was the threat that Ben-Gurion's proposed 'British' reform posed to the Mapai apparatus and the traditional control of voters that it had amassed due to the immigrant-absorption services, jobs and identity that were provided by the Histadrut. The same was true with regard to the government ministries controlled by the party and its associates, and separate Mapai machines in various parts of the country, such as Tel Aviv and Haifa. While they were run by local bosses they were largely under Eshkol's and Sapir's control. If the country were partitioned into direct-majority electoral precincts as Ben-Gurion proposed – following the British and American practice – a new situation, unfathomable to the veteran Mapai bosses, would come about: voters could directly affect the election of candidates in their precincts. The party strongmen did not see how a Knesset elected under the existing method could marshal a majority in favour of this idea. Ben-Gurion's attempt to circumvent the *ancien régime* by appealing directly to public opinion in the 1959 elections did not deliver the definitive electoral results that would make such a comprehensive reform possible. Therefore, Eshkol had to fashion a coalition in the accepted way – with Ahdut ha-'Avoda, of all parties – in order to promote economic growth and silence left-wing militancy in economic and wage affairs, which were Sapir's and Eshkol's principal interest. Sapir, however, was an unmitigated political dove in foreign and defence affairs and had his own doubts about Moshe Dayan, the politically cunning formerly hawkish military man, and Shimon Peres, who had seemingly established a fiefdom of his own at the MOD that controlled lots of money, lots of people and secret affairs such as the construction of the reactor in Dimona, which were beyond Sapir's control. These misgivings planted further seeds of mayhem – one immediate, one for the longer term – that influenced 'the Affair'. Sapir noted that the 1959 elections had prompted Ben-Gurion to promote Dayan to the ranks of the Government, albeit as Minister of Agriculture, a minor portfolio that offered no clout in political and defence affairs.

Eshkol, however, soon found himself in trouble with the new

Minister of Agriculture, when by dint of his obligations as the Government's treasurer (and still as head of the Jewish Agency Rural Settlement Department) he failed to complete the National Water Carrier, the key for the development of the northern Negev. The financing of the Dimona project, very close to Dayan's heart following Ben-Gurion's efforts on its behalf, seemed to be far from Eshkol's priorities. Thus, the money for Dimona had to be raised privately, outside the budget, from individual donors at home and abroad. Dayan raised hell about the Carrier and forced a positive decision about its funding.[30] This, however, hardly earned him Eshkol's affection, and vice versa.

As a newly arrived politician, Dayan was surprised to encounter among urban youth a lack of sense of duty and an overdose, to his mind, of freewheeling individualism,[31] which Ben-Gurion had been trying to counter without much success. Dayan mobilized young people from established moshavim – he was the first-born of kibbutz Degania but his family moved to Nahalal, the first moshav – to help newly created cooperatives, whose population came from Muslim countries, with a degree of success. Eshkol and Sapir, however, held the purse strings for this endeavour and released the funds according to their own priorities and conflicting demands. They focused their attention increasingly on the development towns in the periphery, doing their best to attract investments at least for the establishment of light industries there with the help of direct and indirect government subsidies and continued economic control. Some locations on the periphery seemed to be doing well, foremost the moshavim and several development towns such as Ashqelon, Ashdod, Yavne and Eilat. Others, however, did not flourish, and the so-called mixed Arab-Jewish towns such as Acre were even worse off. The most problematic of all were the enclaves of poverty and accumulated sense of discrimination on the fringes of major cities such as Haifa and Jerusalem, inhabited by immigrants from Muslim countries, especially Morocco, known today as Mizrahim ('easterners'). At this time, Mizrahim counted for little as active participants in the political process; they figured largely as instruments of Mapai's power and policy agents. Most Mizrahim who lived in the periphery were as dependent as ever on Histadrut healthcare services and jobs or on government investments in old and new economic enterprises.

In due course, the Mizrahi enclaves of poverty and growing criticism of this 'system' produced violent protests. The best known of them were the so-called Wadi Salib riots, which started in the Haifa neighbourhood of that name in July 1959 and spread to other towns where Mizrahim felt discriminated against, such as Tiberias, Beersheva and Migdal ha-'Emeq. The trigger was a false story about police brutality against an alleged Mizrahi victim in Haifa. Taken as solemn truth, the incident ballooned into violent demonstrations against Ashkenazi (European-Jewish) neighbourhoods and offices and clubs of Mapai and the Histadrut, resulting in injuries to both demonstrators and police and arrests among the former. The government, shocked, called an emergency meeting in which it appointed a commission of inquiry chaired by a judge. One of those who testified before the commission, the demonstrator David Ben-Harush, called the panel's attention to a list of issues requiring immediate action that he had drawn up while under arrest: an end to discrimination and the regime of *protektsia* (political nepotism and pull), free high-school education, state-run healthcare services, immediate housing solutions for everyone instead of the still-functioning transit camps, and larger social-security benefits for the elderly and the like. For Mapai, this meant in part the surrender of power, for which the party was not yet ready.

Thus, the Wadi Salib riots failed to produce political results at that stage. Ben-Harush did create a Moroccan-ethnic political party ahead of the November 1959 elections but garnered very few votes. The reasons for his failure were several: Mapai was still the party of David Ben-Gurion, the hero of the immigrants from east and west and the embodiment of the Jews' newly achieved national sovereignty and dignity. The melting-pot sociocultural policy, championed by Ben-Gurion and others, remained intact and actually proved rather successful thanks to compulsory and reserve army service. Eshkol and Sapir released some money to alleviate the most immediate housing and schooling problems in the neglected areas. Accordingly, Mapai and the Histadrut maintained their power as before. The introduction of ethnic and ethnic-religious parties would have to wait for decades, first requiring Ben-Gurion's demise and Mapai's related political suicide.

The writing seemed to start appearing on the wall after the 1959 general elections when Pinchas Sapir, reappointed Minister of Commerce and Industry next to Levi Eshkol, the Minister of Finance, noticed that Ben-Gurion had elevated Moshe Dayan to the cabinet and that Ben-Gurion had hoisted Shimon Peres from the bureaucracy to the posts of Deputy Minister of Defence and Member of Knesset. Sapir may have realized that the two newcomers were counterbalanced by pronouncedly dovish ministers – Abba Eban, who had joined the Government after concluding his tenure as Ambassador to Washington, and Giora Josephtal. However, Sapir may not have known that Ben-Gurion wished to bring the retired COGS, Yigael Yadin – now an archeologist – back to political life as a counterweight to Dayan.[32] Although Yadin spurned the offer, these and other démarches show us that the prime minister did not name successors but in fact supported Eshkol if he – or anybody else – could make it on his or her own. It seems, however, that Sapir could not restrain himself, and in 1960, when the opportunity came about, he pitted Histadrut Secretary General Lavon against the defence establishment, from which Dayan and Peres derived their prestige and their public and real power, probably hoping that the information in Lavon's possession would harm the past and present paragons and leaders of this establishment.

THE LAVON–DIMONA NEXUS

I do not wish here to plunge into the ins and outs of the '1960 Affair', the outgrowth of the '1954 Affair' that erupted almost immediately after Sapir gave Lavon new information about what had happened in 1954. In a nutshell, it amounts to this: Avri Elad, chief of Israel Military Intelligence (MI) in Egypt at the time of the '1954 Affair', was prosecuted in Israel in a secret trial in 1960 and found guilty of conspiracy with the enemy after the capture of the cell that he had commanded in Egypt in 1954. (By implication, he had escaped from the Egyptians – with their assistance – in the course of the events.) When he testified, Elad incriminated his superiors at MI and accused them of forging documents and, thereby, prejudicing the quest for truth about the operation in Egypt. His allegations seemed to imply that the IDF – MI – was corrupt and mendacious and that its personnel or their subordinates had operated in Egypt without Defence Minister Lavon's permission. Armed with this information, Lavon, now Secretary General of the Histadrut, approached Prime Minister and Defence Minister Ben-Gurion and demanded that the latter rehabilitate him, that is, absolve him of responsibility for the '1954 Affair'.

Ben-Gurion's response, given in 1960, was that the exoneration of Lavon was a topic for a judicial inquiry and not a political question that a minister or a government should answer. Lavon, then, threatened to seek justice elsewhere – with the Knesset Foreign Affairs and Defence Committee (FADC) – and promptly turned to the media and also to a group of intellectuals composed mainly of professors at the Hebrew University of Jerusalem. This marked the beginning of a campaign on Lavon's part to destroy the political system of Israel by blackmailing Mapai's ministers in order to facilitate his exoneration by pinning responsibility for the Egyptian disaster on Dayan and Peres, his subordinates in 1954. I express the matter in these dire terms because the '1960 Affair' broke out at a historical crossroads: the construction of this system had not been properly completed; the government was still a mishmash that increasingly defied control for historical, political and personal reasons. Ben-Gurion's role in the system was to hold the disparate pieces together. No one knew better than he did that such a mechanism could not last forever and that action must be taken – by him – to replace it by means of appropriate institutionalization. Ben-Gurion's struggle in the '1960 Affair', then, was one facet of a broader attempt to institutionalize political life in Israel as a civilized country deserved.

Just as Lavon revived the '1954 Affair' in May 1960, another grave crisis broke out that eclipsed the foreign and defence policies – which were doing well until then – of Ben-Gurion and his aide, Peres: French President Charles de Gaulle secretly advised Israel that he had decided to abrogate the 1957 accord relating to the construction of the reactor in Dimona. Thus, as the clouds of the '1960 Affair' threatened them domestically, Ben-Gurion and Peres, the latter being Lavon's main target, were preoccupied with the other crisis.

The new Dimona affair was concealed from the public eye and became widely known only years later.[33] The only public expression of internal controversy about it was sounded by the so-called Public Committee for Nuclear Disarmament in the Middle East, headed by Professor Yeshayahu Leibowitz and Eliezer Livne. The latter had been an important activist in Mapai in the 1930s and 1940s but had been ousted from the party before the crisis due to allegations of lifestyle improprieties. The real problem, however, seemed to be his close relations with the American Embassy in Tel Aviv; since then, he had been busying himself with apocalyptic public lamentation of the demise of Israel's pioneering and egalitarian spirit due to the German reparations. Another source of incessant personal incitement against Ben-Gurion was Uri Avnery's *Haolam Hazeh*. This weekly magazine, considered a reliable source of information among members of the erstwhile left-wing youth movements, had been hounding Ben-Gurion from the War of Independence onward. *Haolam Hazeh* disclosed the gist of the '1954 Affair' obliquely and linked it to its previous campaigns against the Mapai regime generally and Ben-Gurion specifically. Now Livne and Leibowitz termed the nuclear option 'an act of lunacy' on the regime's part: 'To stay in power forever', they alleged, 'they're engaging in nuclear deterrence'.[34]

At that time, the international constellation had become much more sensitive to nuclear affairs due to the escalation of the Cold War, the launching of the USSR's Sputnik 1 and the advent of Soviet intercontinental missiles – all of which plunged the United States into spasmodic dread even though it continued to outperform the USSR in all nuclear respects. By campaigning as they did, Leibowitz and Livne sent Israelis a signal: Ben-Gurion and his associates were dooming Israel to immense trouble vis-à-vis the United States, its main patron; we do not know whether they mentioned a possible entanglement in Israel–Soviet relations. In fact, this is what happened in 1967 during the crisis that culminated in the Six Day War, but the nuclear project – Ben-Gurion's main target as far as Israel's long-term survival was concerned – survived and later became a major source of its security and peace negotiations that go beyond the scope of this book. Few Israelis, however, gave much thought to such a secret and serpentine issue.[35] In fact, as we shall see, American intervention and Soviet inputs regarding Dimona would play a role in Israel's road to the Six Day War of 1967, with some ironic if not tragic results.

In political high places, however, the construction and operation of the reactor in Dimona did generate controversy from the very beginning all the way to the early 1960s. After all, the British

Labour Party – several of whose leaders consorted intimately with left-leaning personalities in Israel, especially Yigal Allon – had its own doubts about an independent British nuclear deterrent. It was in view of this stance that they judged Israel's nuclear option and fiercely condemned Shimon Peres behind the scenes.[36] Simcha Flapan of Mapam, editor of the journal *New Outlook,* went so far as to accuse Peres of having strayed after the French chimera of independent deterrence, which had no future in a superpower-dominated world.

If it was Lavon's intention to suggest to prospective supporters of his remarks that Peres had always been a dubious quantity and that he, Lavon, had attempted unsuccessfully to restrain him back in 1954 while serving as Minister of Defence, alluding to the nuclear project as a risky, impractical endeavour initiated by Ben-Gurion and now run by Peres, the resurfacing of 'the Affair' in 1960 served his cause. Ben-Gurion did not stop Lavon from pursuing this course. However, he conducted his own internal investigation of the '1954 Affair' by means of his military secretary and, later, by means of the former Attorney General, Supreme Court Justice Chaim Cohn – an act that Lavon found unacceptable since both investigators were free to judge for themselves. In neither case was it possible to determine once and for all who had given the order to instigate the '1954 Affair', although the inquests made it clear that middle-grade officers had forged documents. Then came another unanswered question: had these officers covered up on their own initiative, or had their superiors put them up to it? After all, Lavon was presumably busy at the Histadrut and Ben-Gurion himself was occupied with the Dimona crisis. Thus, in June 1960, the latter prepared to set out for France in order to discuss the matter with General de Gaulle tête-à-tête.

The aberrant and intrinsically unpredictable behaviour was neither Ben-Gurion's nor Peres', but Lavon's. After all, Lavon broke the 'rules of the game' that had been accepted in Mapai at least since the key elections in 1944, which had created a solid base for future decisions by cleansing Mapai of its leftist nationalist minority, which created its own political party, Ahdut ha-'Avoda-Po'alei Tsiyyon, under Yitzhak Tabenkin, Yisrael Galili, and Yigal Allon. Their role as the originators and leaders of the Palmach, whose separate command they tried to preserve after the War of Independence while preaching for a pro-Soviet orientation and rejecting the partitioning of the country, had been neutralized by Ben-Gurion with Eshkol's help. Now, however, they were Ben-Gurion's coalition partners thanks to Eshkol and his economic priorities. They perceived in Ben-Gurion an old enemy and in Dayan and Peres, his successors in various respects including the Dimona project and sociocultural matters, bureaucrats striving for nothing but power, whose ascendancy should be prevented.

Allon, an outstanding officer during Israel's War of Independence and now a politician representing the Left-nationalist Ahdut ha-'Avoda party, had been exposed to nuclear strategic theories; he and others so equipped might have used this terminology for their own purposes. They did it in a conventional sense, which transformed conventional compellence – an obsolete war aim in the nuclear age – into a valid objective for Israel even during the nuclear era. This would mark a departure from Ben-Gurion's own security thinking, which aimed in the long term at an unconventional solution to Israel's defence problems, in which nuclear deterrence rather than conventional compellence would assume a primary role. For Allon and Galili, deterrence should be conventional, that is, the maintenance of conventional superiority over the Arab states' combined military power plus several 'red lines', such as the presence of Arab armies in the Jordanian West Bank, enemy concentrations and preparations for war along Israel's Armistice Demarcation Lines, the re-imposition of the Egyptian blockade over Eilat, the promise of intolerable arms supplies to the Arabs without adequate supplies secured by Israel. Any of these might justify Israeli pre-emption. Thus, the loss of Israeli conventional deterrence (as formulated) by enemy breaching of the aforementioned 'red lines' would force an Israeli conventional first strike, a concept that the IDF Command would be ready to adopt in due course. Eshkol's understanding of this mindset, as Ben-Gurion's successor at the MOD and as Prime Minister, would be tested during the May 1967 crisis.

Ben-Gurion's security dilemma following the War of Independence was based on his understanding of the Arab-Israeli conflict in terms of 'no final win for Israel but an assured and decisive win for the Arabs'. Ben-Gurion assumed that any new round of conventional hostilities initiated by Israel, however victorious, would not be final from the Arab point of view. The Arabs would recover and try again, since even repeated Israeli victories would not put their existence at stake. Israel, on the other hand, could not afford one decisive defeat, and should avoid the price of accumulated victories. This did not mean that the conventional IDF would be allowed to disappear. On the contrary: the Israeli bomb would rule out a general Arab offensive aimed at Israel's annihilation even if the Arabs acquired the bomb as well, which they might in due course because they would never yield – and would never have a reason to, due to their oil, their strategic significance, and their enormous conventional disparity given their population, hundreds of millions strong, against tiny Israel. The Israeli bomb was a psychological and real threat to their own survival that could, contrarily, help them to accept Israel de facto and maybe even de jure.[37] It would not, however, exclude limited conventional wars. In fact, the IDF should be strengthened to deal with such wars, provided that the political echelon would be clever enough to avoid them when possible.[38]

The conventional strategy touted by Allon and his political colleague, Galili, rested on three assumptions: that the partition of the country was a grave security mistake; that Israeli rule of the unpartitioned country was an ideological obligation; and that Israel's conventional advantages in terms of the IDF's use of modern conventional technology and the superior qualities of its leaders and fighters would not only remain decisive but would grow rather than diminish. Nuclear deterrence was, accordingly, not credible because the Arabs were not 'rational', as abstract Game Theory requires.[39] Worse still, once Israel went nuclear, the Arabs would do the same and, as a result, the existing, pre-1967 lines would be frozen because any kind of conventional hostilities in such an environment would become impossible and Israel's freedom of conventional action would be reduced to nothing, on top of infuriating the superpowers due to this violation of their anti-nuclear proliferation policy.

Lavon's game was heaven-sent. It was aimed at Ben-Gurion's former aide, General (Res.) Dayan, and Peres, and, indirectly, at Ben-Gurion himself, their supposed mentor, as far as they (and the opposition led by Menachem Begin) were concerned.

For Ben-Gurion, Lavon's demands transcended the necessity of bringing the historical truth to light; Lavon was demanding political rehabilitation from the executive branch as though he held a monopoly on this truth, while Ben-Gurion believed that he had given the matter the investigation that it deserved,[40] beyond which it belonged to a judicial inquiry. Lavon's demand that the cabinet – that is, the executive branch – exonerate him of responsibility for the '1954 Affair' was simply unconstitutional in the deepest sense of the term. Slowly the public debate over 'the Affair' ballooned – under the inspiration of Lavon and his supporters – into the grand old menace that Ben-Gurion had always feared: the Jewish predisposition to power struggles on ostensibly moral grounds. Although he sometimes blamed this tendency on life in exile, he noticed it – and discerned the absence of the state-level thinking that is required to surmount it – in the independence era, too, with the nation implanted in the soil of its homeland. The issue, he believed, was the mobilization of justice for the perpetration of an injustice, that is, the rehabilitation of a man who demanded rehabilitation by means of political arm-twisting and availed himself of a politically sensationalist media for this purpose. Lavon was now proven to have been driven by urges and possessed by lust for power, very possibly hoping to taint Dayan and Peres, Ben-Gurion's aides, with responsibility for the '1954 Affair' and, thus, blocking their path to his succession. He may have even hoped to taint Ben-Gurion himself as having ordered them in retirement to carry out the Egyptian operation; thus he, Lavon, might become the successor. Either way, he was willing to trample on accepted procedures at the top of his party – which, having concluded its internal debates, accepted the authority of its elected chief and refrained from arming its political rivals in the FADC. Indeed, the delegates whom Mapai's rivals had posted to the parliamentary committee thirsted for any incriminating information that originated in members of the Mapai leadership – be it wholly true, partly true, or untrue.

What we have, then, is the advancement of personal power interests, driven by lust, in the service of ostensibly exalted beliefs and views, foremost the pursuit of justice. Now, all of these are 'politics' in the accepted sense of the word. Ben-Gurion, however, had never been fond of such 'politics', even though he used it himself on occasion. The question was whether it would become a definitive and accepted public norm. Admittedly, corruption exists in every administration and society. Who realized more than Ben-Gurion, who knew his people too well, that many functionaries in the Mapai apparatus were not angels? The problem, however, involved not a quixotic attempt to banish corruption from the world – the forging of documents by MI wheelers and dealers had been known to occur before – but corruption at the highest levels of the state, that is, in Lavon's struggle to restore his reputation by means of pressure, blackmail and extortion, which would translate into overt corruption on the grounds of the need to eradicate covert corruption. All of which operated under the patronage of mass media and with the support of powerful politicians whose sole interest had nothing to do with the injustice that had ostensibly been inflicted on Lavon. It was this constellation of factors that steadily dawned on him during the public debate over the '1960 Affair', making him a participant in it and prompting Eshkol to intervene in his conciliatory fashion, which however gave Lavon his exoneration. For Ben-Gurion, the issue was more complicated. At that time he was involved in giving Israel a spiritual-ideological new direction, which he termed as the necessary 'vision', or aspiration,[41] based on the old Jewish messianic dream, but converted to moral-political guide to become 'a light unto the nations' morally and practically by settling the Negev and the Galilee, return to nature and develop science and secular learning. This, and the ongoing security challenges required not only support from abroad, West Germany included, but also, for him, the Zionist Revolution entailed the ability, and the obligation, to differentiate between the Bonn Republic and Hitler's Third Reich. But Jewish emotionalism coupled with political gains for those who criticized Ben-Gurion's policy of cooperation with West Germany at the time overshadowed his 'vision' as a matter of principle and practical threats to his defence and foreign policy. The main argument against Ben-Gurion levelled by Right and Left was that Bonn was a direct heir of Hitler's Munich. Since the West German cooperation became a matter of public criticism during the Lavon Affair of 1960 onward, the only way to extricate oneself from this tangle, to Ben-Gurion's way of thinking, was to separate the various sides of the issue and adhere to the historical truth. True, Jews are powered by messianic faith, but this faith is a historical truth. Furthermore, Jewish moral content is associated with the exercise of justice; apart from being a fundamental of Judaism, this is an inseparable part of the 'human conscience'.[42]

By implication, if Lavon were to be granted justice in the form of injustice – after having ignited a public scandal and mobilized growing support for his cause in the media and among sundry 'intellectuals', headed by Professor Nathan Rotenstreich, Lavon's personal and political comrade from time immemorial, a support fanned by others – then Israel was facing more than a scandal. It was actually facing the corruption of public virtues on behalf of these virtues since Lavon was using blackmail methods, threatening to have his personal and political ambitions pursued by opening Mapai's Pandora's Box (possibly relating to the dubious methods of its election funding, not relevant to the mishap in Egypt). Worse still, he and his aides manipulated the press by leaking lies, speculation and half-truths in an irresponsible fashion. This reminded Ben-Gurion of the ailments of mass democracy, the sort that had fettered democracy in the bleak days of the ascent of Fascism and had rendered it helpless for a lengthy period of time. This kind of democracy had been hurtled hither and yon in Third Republic France and Weimar. In such a predicament, it is the statesman's obligation to act against a public opinion that has fallen prey to manipulation – unknown to most of the public – and against the manipulators.

By then, however, the '1960 Affair' was snowballing. The mass media – headed by the newspaper *Ma'ariv* and its editors, most of whom were former Jabotinsky supporters who, in their new role as journalists, were eager to cause the leaders of Mapai to butt heads and by so doing boost their newspaper's circulation – gorged itself on leaks from Lavon, his backers, and opposition and coalition members of the FADC. The 'rules of the game' in security affairs began to crumble, even though the military censor obscured the names of the principals in the '1954 Affair' and the details of the related document forgeries that had come to light in 1960. Indeed, in his appearances before the FADC, Lavon lodged sweeping accusations against the entire army and defence system, as he had attempted to do in the investigation of 'the Affair' in 1954, at which time Peres and Dayan had been his main targets. Now Lavon insinuated that the IDF, the apple of Ben-Gurion's eye, was a corrupt organization and that Shimon Peres – now Ben-Gurion's deputy at the MOD – was capable of any action, no matter how dastardly, that might promote himself and his interests. This gambit placed at risk the enterprises for which Peres was responsible and had laboured tirelessly, such as the reactor in Dimona. Once again, historical truth took a beating for the sake of a unilateral 'truth', to the real detriment of personalities unrelated to the '1954 Affair'. Behind the scenes, the different sides, Peres and Dayan included, calculated each other's ability to deal the Histadrut – which they considered an obsolete and less-controlled bureaucracy under Lavon – a more-or-less severe blow and even made preparations for a struggle over Ben-Gurion's succession.

ESHKOL'S PROTÉGÉS AND THE ANTI-DIMONANS

Given the coincidence of the 'Lavon affair' and the crisis with France over the reactor in Dimona, the stalwarts of the Public Committee for Nuclear Disarmament in the Middle East celebrated the failure of the 'white elephant' under construction in the Negev and even tried – unsuccessfully – to bring it to the public's knowledge.[43] Several of them, however – such as Yeshayahu Leibowitz and the great Talmudic scholar Professor Ephraim Elimelech Urbach – actually became involved in 'the affair' as 'intellectuals' who subjected the treatment of the '1960 Affair' to a crescendo of protest. They and Lavon's comrade, Nathan Rotenstreich, set the bandwagon in motion and quickly were joined by the historian Professor Jacob L. Talmon, the economist Professor Don Patinkin, and many other high-profile personalities at the Hebrew University of Jerusalem. The grounds for their vocal mobilization was the ousting of Lavon as Secretary General of the Histadrut by Levi Eshkol, the Mapai boss, which Ben-Gurion had ostensibly forced by saying, 'either me or him'. This, they said, was an act of tyranny if not a Robespierrean beheading.[44]

Talmon's enlistment in this chorus and his criticism of Ben-Gurion, backed by his expertise in the history of the French Revolution and its degeneration into the Robespierrean one-man dictatorship, is unsurprising in itself. Talmon was no less a political creature than a historian; he even tried, to no avail, to mentor a liberal-conservative centre party that had been established at the time. In his best-known book, *The Origins of Totalitarian Democracy*,[45] published and translated into Hebrew several years before the events described here, Talmon developed and perfected a critique that was well known at the time, dating from the French Revolution itself, against what he called 'political messianism' –

the subordination of society to an abstract vision, an essentially religious aspiration for the redemption of man. As Talmon saw it, this aspiration clashed irresolvably with the individual's aspiration to freedom. As Ben-Gurion's successor in the premiership and later as his rival, Eshkol would try to exploit this yearning for individual freedom at the expense of what seemed to have been Ben-Gurion's 'political messianism', with interesting results. For the time being, however, Eshkol instigated Lavon's rehabilitation by a cabinet committee behind the prime minister's back, thus yielding to Lavon's campaign and threats to open Mapai's 'Pandora's Box'. However, when faced with Ben-Gurion's outrage about this move – made without any authorization – Eshkol engineered Lavon's deposal as Secretary General of the Histadrut. In both cases, Eshkol seemed to have established himself as the real power in Ben-Gurion's cabinet and Mapai, but with some limitations that would subsequently haunt him and ultimately abet his own departure from the MOD under the pressure of public opinion and the collapse of his own standing among members of his coalition in May 1967 – a kind of Greek tragedy that befell Eshkol in the third act of this history, following his triumph in the present act.

Concurrent with Lavon's dismissal as Secretary General of the Histadrut, one of the most militant of Mapai's bosses, the party's Secretary General Yosef Almogi, launched a 'wake-up campaign' to drum up public support for Ben-Gurion. Both démarches – the ousting of Lavon by Eshkol from a post unrelated to the '1960 Affair' on the grounds that he had caused grave damage to Mapai and the accepted 'rules of the game', and Almogi's 'wake-up campaign' – enraged the 'intellectuals' and forced the Prime Minister himself to intervene publicly in the '1960 Affair'. He explained his stance on 'the Affair' by corresponding directly with these personalities and by placing articles in the Histadrut newspaper *Davar.* Topical arguments, however, were of no use. Lavon's dismissal gravely damaged Ben-Gurion's status among the Israeli elites, and one must ask why. One possible reason was that a public much broader than 'the intellectuals' was pleased to behold the demise of Ben-Gurion's 'bill of moral obligations' and to discover that Ben-Gurion himself was seemingly remiss in discharging the obligations of a prime minister and a party leader, that is, the obligation of treating properly Lavon and the majority in his

Government, which had exonerated Lavon of responsibility for what had happened in Egypt. Concurrently, Peres and Dayan – Lavon's targets – operated in the media without consulting with Ben-Gurion, thereby strengthening the impression that Ben-Gurion's actions had been meant to defend their good name and the gift that they expected to receive from him, his legacy.[46]

In the mean time, the Dimona crisis had not blown over; it clouded Ben-Gurion's foreign and defence policies in a field that was literally and figuratively critical.

NOTES

1. In this regard, see Shlomo Aronson, 'David Ben-Gurion and the British Constitutional Model', *Israel Studies*, 3, 2 (Autumn 1998), pp.193–214.
2. See Anita Shapira, *Berl*, Vol. II (Tel Aviv: Sifriyat Ofakim/Am Oved, 1980), p. 470.
3. See Aronson, *Hitler, the Allies, and the Jews* (New York: Cambridge University Press, 2006).
4. The French-Israeli connection was much more complicated than the depiction here; see further in the text.
5. 'Hanukkah Reflections', in David Ben-Gurion, *War Diary, The War of Independence 1948–1949*, in Hebrew (Tel Aviv: Ministry of Defence, 1982), pp.902–3. On the meetings with Bergmann and Rackah, see ibid., p.827.
6. Remarks by Professor Yisrael Dostrovsky at a conference on 'Ben-Gurion and Science', sponsored by the Israel Academy of the Sciences and Arts on 23 April 1987, marking the centennial of Ben-Gurion's birth. Dostrovsky titled his lecture 'David Ben-Gurion and the Development of Science in Israel'.
7. On the Commission's resignation, see the Commission members' letter to this effect, 17 February 1958, given to me courtesy of Professor Shmuel Samburski, a member of the Commission and first director of the Science Council at PMO. According to the members who resigned, the Commission had not been called into session since 1956, i.e., since the opportunity had arisen to import a nuclear reactor from France, obviating the need for home-manufacture.
8. See *Sharett's Diaries*, Vol. E, in Hebrew (Tel Aviv: Sifriyat Ma'ariv, 1978). Sharett reported in this diary not only his meetings with Bergmann but also those with other scientists and the Director General of PMO, Teddy Kollek, ahead of the meetings with Eric Johnston, US special representative for water issues, pp.400, 483, 533–4, 565.
9. See Gabriel Sheffer, *Moshe Sharett, Biography of a Political Moderate* (Oxford: Clarendon Press, 1996), pp.694–6.
10. See Shlomo Aronson, 'Israel's Security and the Holocaust: Lessons Learned, but Existential Fears Continue', *Israel Studies*, 14, 1 (Spring 2009), pp.65–93.
11. See Moshe Dayan, *Story of My Life*, in Hebrew (Jerusalem: Idanim, 1976), p.213.
12. Ibid., p.231.
13. The authoritative scholarly work on the French-Israeli alliance is Benjamin Pinkus, *From Ambivalence to an Unofficial Alliance, Israel, France, and the French Jews 1947–1957*, in Hebrew (Beersheva: Ben-Gurion University Press, 2005). Several versions of the French-Israeli connection, including the acquisition of the French nuclear reactor by Israel and its construction near Dimona, were published or ghost-written by Shimon Peres but cannot be cited in a scholarly work except with the

greatest caution because Peres' current office may give this source unwarranted significance and thus requires caution and verification since he was a party to the events described.
14. Yossi Goldstein, *Eshkol – A Biography*, in Hebrew (Jerusalem: Keter, 2003), pp.400–1.
15. In this regard, see Shimon Peres' interview with the newspaper *Yedioth Ahronoth*, 20 November 2009.
16. See Pierre Pean, *Les Deux Bombes*, in French (Paris: Fayard, 1982, and new edition, 2002).
17. Ibid.
18. Ibid.
19. Michael Bar-Zohar, *Ben-Gurion, A Political Biography*, Part II, in Hebrew (Tel Aviv: Am Oved, 1977), pp.1522–6.
20. See Susanna Scharfstetter, *Die Dritte Atommacht, Britische Nichtverbreitungspolitik im Dienst von Statussicherung und Deutschlandpolitik 1952–1968*. [The Third Atom Power, British Proliferation Policy in service of maintaining its status and its German Policy (1952–1968)] (Munich:DVA, 1999).
21. On the 1960 crisis with France, see Pean, *Les Deux Bombes*, pp.102, 123–40.
22. See Mordechai Gazit, *President Kennedy's Policy toward the Arab States and Israel, Analysis and Documents* (Tel Aviv: Shiloah Center for Middle Eastern and African Studies, Tel Aviv University, 1983), p.40.
23. Bar-Zohar, *Ben-Gurion, A Political Biography*, p.1373.
24. In an interview with the author on 20 February 2006, the late Professor Yuval Ne'eman, a major nuclear scientist and former military official, explained that the actual completion of the reactor under Mr Peres' leadership proved impossible. Only after Peres left the MOD early in 1965 to the opposition party Rafi did the reactor become operational, under Professor Yisrael Dostrovsky of the Weizmann Institute. In the meantime, Israel could have obtained a quantity of fissile material from other sources. A subcommittee of the US Senate secretly investigated the matter at the time. A more plausible explanation of the outcome may come to light due to the recent opening of the Nixon-Kissinger records at the US National Archives. Cf. 'Israel's Nuclear Arsenal Vexed Nixon', *New York Times*, 29 November 2007.
25. See Yair Evron, *Israel's Nuclear Dilemma*, in Hebrew (Tel Aviv: Hakibbutz Hameuchad, 1987), p.17.
26. Ibid.
27. See Aronson, 'Israel Security and the Holocaust', p.86.
28. See Shimon Peres, *Battling for Peace, A Memoir*, ed. David Landau (New York: Random House, 1995), pp.138–9.
29. See Naora Barnach-Matalon, *A Good Place on the Side*, in Hebrew (no publishing location cited, KIP Publishers, 2009), pp.138–9. Ms Matalon was Dayan's aide and a close observer of his military and civilian activities from his appointment as COGS to his death in 1981. She gathered important records and, with others' support and Dayan's approval, actually wrote many parts of his publications.
30. Ibid., pp.146–7.
31. Ibid., p.194.
32. Bar-Zohar, *Ben-Gurion, A Political Biography*, describes Ben-Gurion's attempts to place Yadin at the forefront of the 'Young Turks' circle ahead of the 1959 elections.
33. For details, see Shlomo Aronson, *The Politics and Strategy of Nuclear Weapons in the Middle East,* revised version, Vol. A, in Hebrew (Jerusalem: Academon, 1994), pp.61–82. This is a much more detailed version of the original English publication: *The Politics and Strategy of Nuclear Weapons in the Middle East, Opacity, Theory and Strategy, An Israeli Perspective* (Albany and London: SUNY Press, 1992), both published with the assistance of Oded Brosh.
34. See testimony Yehuda Ben-Moshe, a member the committee, to the weekly journal *Koteret Rashit* [Main Headline], 26 November 1986: 'Twenty-Five Years before [Mordechai] Vanunu'.
35. Ben-Moshe, ibid.; this indifference persisted even though Leibowitz and Livne insinuated this issue and others into articles that they published in the *Hebrew*

Encyclopedia (Jerusalem: Encyclopedia Publishing House, 1967), which Leibowitz edited. For an example, s.v. 'Ben-Gurion, David', supplement volume, pp.666–77, written by Leibowitz.

36. Denis Healey, the British Labour Secretary of State for Defence, took the rhetoric to a higher level by terming Peres a 'fascist'. Testimony by Israel's Ambassador to London, Ephraim Evron, to the author.
37. In his war memoirs, Churchill described the bomb as an 'excuse' for Imperial Japan to surrender, since it was a 'supra natural' cause that absolved the conventional military of its obligation to die to the last man following a conventional invasion (or even to win it in view of Allied losses). Churchill claimed to have advanced this idea himself ahead of Hiroshima, but according to Lord Moran, his physician, he picked it up from Lord Mountbatten years afterward.
38. Following a meeting called by Ben-Gurion in 1962, at which Allon and Galili demanded larger investments in conventional forces while Dayan and Peres advocated the nuclear option, Ben-Gurion was quoted by Yair Evron (see above) as having come down in favour of the conventional choice. This interpretation is misleading because the nuclear option was not ready as yet. At any rate, it was not supposed to replace the conventional IDF, which, in Allon's and Galili's thinking, should have been expanded at the time to deal with under-the-threshold threats such as limited wars and terrorism.
39. Thomas C. Schelling's *The Strategy of Conflict* (Cambridge, MA: Harvard University Press, 1960) was put to extensive use here.
40. In his book *Things as They Were*, in Hebrew (Tel Aviv: Am Hasefer, 1965), Ben-Gurion provides a detailed explanation that he wrote to Martin Buber about his investigations of 'the Affair', to no avail.
41. This endeavour, to propose a 'messianic vision' for the changing Israeli reality, is too complicated to tackle in a footnote. Eshkol was not a part of it. I shall deal with it in the text and return to the support rendered by the 'intellectuals' to Eshkol in his own struggle with Ben-Gurion, based among other things on their rejection of Ben-Gurion's 'messianic vision'. See forthcoming English translation of Shlomo Aronson, *David Ben-Gurion, the Renaissance Leader and the Waning of an Age*, in Hebrew (Sede Boqer: Ben-Gurion Heritage Center and Ben-Gurion University Press, 1999), pp.336*ff*.
42. Ben-Gurion to Yariv Ben-Aharon. See Michael Keren, *Ben-Gurion and the Intellectuals*, in Hebrew (Sede Boqer: Ben-Gurion University of the Negev, 1988), pp.87–8.
43. The journalist Dan Margalit, who launched his career at this time as a junior correspondent for Uri Avnery's *Haolam Hazeh*, was summoned to a meeting with Leibowitz and Livne, who told him about the crisis with de Gaulle and described what they knew about the 'failure' of the reactor construction project. The meeting took Margalit much by surprise; he kept its contents to himself, as he told this author years later.
44. Even a contemporaneous historian such as Professor Yechiam Weitz regards the unseating of Lavon as an uninhibitedly dictatorial act and claims that in the early 1960s, and *a fortiori* later in that decade, Ben-Gurion deteriorated into a vengeful, tragic and marginal personality after having exhausted his 'charisma', the secret of his lengthy rule. Weitz's sources for this matter are Jacob Talmon, Ben-Gurion's rival; Yitzhak Ben-Aharon, a leftist politician, the author Amos Oz, a confidant of Lavon's; and the journalist Amos Elon, on whose criticism of Ben-Gurion Weitz bases himself; for example, in Elon's *The Israelis: Founders and Sons* (New York: Holt, Rinehart and Winston, 1971). See Y. Weitz, 'End of the Beginning – Elucidating the Concept of "Genesis of the State"', in Y. Weitz (ed.), *Between Vision and Revision: a Century of Zionist Historiography*, in Hebrew (Jerusalem: Yad Izhak Ben-Zvi, 1997), pp.244–7. Weitz's lack of historical perspective finds expression in a remark about 'Ben-Gurion's inexplicable rage over the conclusions of the "internal committee of seven"'.
45. London: Secker and Warburg, 1952.
46. Almogi published his version of 'the affair' and Ben-Gurion's downfall years later in

his book, *The Struggle for Ben-Gurion: in the Wake of the Affair*, in Hebrew (Jerusalem: Yedioth Ahronoth, 1988), arguing that the 'Dayan-Peres group' had made unauthorized use of that public scandal to piggyback on Ben-Gurion's reputation and actions and pose publicly as his successors. Actually, Lavon himself had contributed to this because as the public debate over 'the affair' escalated, he insinuated that Ben-Gurion himself had given the order for the abortive operation in Egypt, routing the instruction to people whom he had left behind in the defence system, that is, Lt Gen. Dayan and Shimon Peres. Thus, as it were, he had manipulated them from his place of retirement in Sede Boqer.

Chapter Six

Eshkol's New Era

INTELLECTUALS AND DOERS VS. THE 'OLD MAN'

By late 1960, the Dimona crisis had taken a turn for the worse and spilled into areas that transcended Israel–French relations. Now it seemed as though the United States would intervene in the matter with such force as to threaten to precipitate an incomparably grave crisis between Jerusalem and Washington, to the delight of Leibowitz and Livne. However, things developed differently. The eruption with Washington coincided with the 'seam' between the Eisenhower and Kennedy presidencies. This seems to have happened for good reason: the outgoing president, Eisenhower, chose during the transition to put as much pressure as he could on Israel regarding Dimona and managed to obtain from Ben-Gurion the aforementioned statement in the Knesset that transformed the project into one of peaceful intent. After the American elections, Ben-Gurion tested the incoming chief executive as to how he would behave on the Dimona issue. He quickly discovered that President Kennedy, although a Democrat whose election had been strongly supported by Jews, appeared determined to halt the construction of the reactor, no matter what. His statement in the Knesset, acknowledging the construction of a nuclear reactor in the Negev but defining it as being for 'peaceful purposes', gave the French an out to continue building the reactor and finally leaving Israel to complete it 'on her own'.[1]

Although by making this announcement about the construction of the reactor Ben-Gurion bought Israel time that allowed the work to resume, the disclosure created an obstacle of sorts in both the short and the long term because it allowed the Americans to revise the purpose of the reactor, at least publicly.

From then on, Washington would try to make sure that the facility was not in fact being used for military purposes, basing itself on Israel's public word. Over time, this obfuscation of Dimona's objectives would inflict real damage on the veracity of Israel's defence doctrine, at least in domestic public opinion. After all, the defence doctrine had intended the reactor in Dimona to be decisive as far as Israel's future survival was concerned, making Israel's destruction impossible in terms of its cost to the Arabs. As such, this doctrine was linked to Ben-Gurion's refusal to perceive in the West Bank Israel's 'territorial depth' as formulated by General Allon, or as an ideological-political target for Israel's expansion as it was believed to be by Mr Begin and by Allon's spiritual leader Yitzhak Tabenkin.

At this time, Ben-Gurion broached the idea of visiting the US personally in order to meet with Kennedy and alert him to the dire state of Israel's security needs, and he did so in June 1961. The encounter, which Ben-Gurion had forced on Kennedy and that took place in New York because the president did not wish to host an Israeli premier on an official visit in Washington, shows us how badly off Israel was in those days – and not specifically in regard to the Dimona project. Today we are accustomed to viewing the US as an almost official ally of Israel; the matrix of relations that has developed between the countries over the years lends substance to this perception. Back then, however, Ben-Gurion did what he did in full awareness that Washington was reluctant to get too close to Israel and that the Kennedy Administration would continue to strive to ingratiate itself with the Arabs, foremost Nasser, in view of Kennedy's ongoing and escalating rivalry with the Soviet Union. Research on Ben-Gurion's manoeuvres in domestic, foreign and defence affairs in the early 1960s, including those related to 'the Affair', should be pursued within this inclusive context, with separation maintained between 'the Affair' and foreign and defence concerns, including Israel–German relations. This kind of research is necessary above all for study of Eshkol's own behaviour when he succeeded Ben-Gurion in 1963 and had to address the same or similar challenges.

In the meantime, the military collaboration with West Germany – a controversial arms deal from the Leftist parties' standpoint, concluded between Jerusalem and Bonn and including German aid for the nuclear project – had become far more problematic than it had been before due to the sudden discovery of Egypt's missile and unconventional-weapons programme, which had been pursued surreptitiously by Austrian and German scientists in Nasser's service. What the programme meant, seemingly, was that Germans were involved once again in a looming Holocaust against Israel with the blessing, if not the encouragement, of the Bonn Government, which Ben-Gurion had publicly christened a 'different Germany' some years back when lobbying public opinion for acceptance of his bid to secure West German economic and military aid to Israel.

The 'German scientists affair' did more than overshadow the rest of Ben-Gurion's tenure until his resignation in the summer of 1963; it also tied into the reverberations of the Eichmann trial and the lessons of the Holocaust as construed and used by his critics to attack him, a fact of political life that did not escape the attention of Levi Eshkol and Foreign Minister Golda Meir.

Meanwhile, Eshkol, as the main player in a ministerial committee of seven, engineered the exoneration of Lavon as the latter had demanded, overstepping the panel's mandate. Ben-Gurion refused to accept the verdict, dissolved his coalition, and remained in power as head of an interim Government until a new round of general elections could be held. This gave him time to allow negotiations with the French to reinstate the work at Dimona and to deal as best he could with the Kennedy Administration on the nuclear project and several alarming American initiatives regarding the Palestinian refugee issue.[2] After he went to the polls on 15 August 1961, Mapai emerged with five fewer mandates than it had had before. The lesson – at least in the estimation of the party's main bosses, Eshkol and Sapir – was that the public had not fully embraced Ben-Gurion's stance on 'the Affair' and the Germany issue, causing the party genuine harm at the ballot box. This conclusion only strengthened the bosses' tendency to continue cooperating with the nationalist-Left Ahdut ha-'Avoda in the Histadrut, lest control of the Histadrut be lost and, with it, the necessary control over wages and economic growth which were their main concern. Consequently, they engineered the formation of a governing coalition with Ahdut ha-'Avoda, overruling Ben-Gurion's preference for the moderate right-wing General Zionist party. His desideratum in this regard traced to his fear that the moderate Right would be pushed into Menachem Begin's far-Right Herut (Freedom) Party and that Ahdut ha-'Avoda might upset his German and nuclear policies.

However, opposition to Ben-Gurion's style and his German policy combined to unite all constituents of Left and Right for the first time. It was a development – a wall-to-wall coalition of all parties other than Mapai in areas where Mapai had been the definitive player to date – that Ben-Gurion had foreseen. Such an occurrence, he knew, could not be staved off for long unless the whole political system was reformed and a British-style two- or three-party regime installed. It did seem, however, that Ben-Gurion was rapidly losing control of his own party. His lengthy political career would have to conclude shortly; what mattered now was a struggle for the succession in a new reality. For the time being, it was Finance Minister and party boss Levi Eshkol who hammered out the Mapai–Ahdut ha-'Avoda coalition for Ben-Gurion, who had no choice but to accept it in order to remain in power long enough to see the construction of the reactor finished and to gain as much military support from West Germany as possible. Ben-Gurion still spoke uninterruptedly of the vision of settling the Negev, the importance of vision or a moral-messianic sense of duty and hands-on involvement, and the necessity of relations with democratic West Germany in view of European and global realities. He still immersed himself in the Bible and its interpretation and still engaged the 'intellectuals' in dispute. His image, then, was one of a person who entertained pretensions of omniscience and quasi-Stalinist omnipotence in making rules and ramming them down everyone's throat.

Ben-Gurion, however, was not the sort of person who capitulated to such images or others. Convinced that he was neither a Stalin nor a Robespierre, he believed that the core of the struggle against him in 'the Affair', in regard to Germany and on other issues, concerned a problem that the Jews had in terms of the Zionist revolution. Had the Jews learned, or would they learn, to debate matters on their merits and inhabit a realistic world, or would they tenant a false world, an invented world, or a world that served their lusts? In the midst of 'the Affair', as he stood on principle and insisted that the investigation and resolution of the issue be treated as a judicial matter and not as a political one (indeed, years after his resignation, the State Commissions of

Investigation Act was passed into law due to this stance), the Prime Minister invited eleven senior academicians to a debate over the tenets that preoccupied him at the time: 'Is it at all conceivable that we [Jews] will be a special people and a light unto the nations? Can the redemption of the world and of the Jews really take place'?[3] It was an attempt to grab the bull by the horns, that is, to hear out the 'intellectuals' and the political and natural scientists on these matters, with the clear intention of showing them that no nation, let alone the Jewish people, could manage without a vision, and that in this regard – the idealistic inspiration that Israeli society needed at this phase of its coalescence, an inspiration that should be provided by the statesperson, with the worthy assistance and initiative of 'intellectuals' – the 'intellectuals' offered no real alternative to the vision of this particular statesperson. Levi Eshkol, the *makher* (cunning man of action), had no part in this debate save as an astute observer who would try in due course to mobilize 'the intellectuals' in support of his own role in the '1960 Affair' and, subsequently, of his standing as Prime Minister and the boss of Mapai.

The vision at issue was a matter of principle – 'messianic faith' as Ben-Gurion put it – or a creativity and passion that should be cultivated and not allowed to deteriorate into routine, as I would define it, that would later become Eshkol's manner of doing things his own way. The cause seems to have been, at least for some time, a series of acts toward the democratization of the Israeli polity and liberation from Ben-Gurion's pretentious idealism. This 'idealism' also accommodated quite a few prosaic affairs such as security, settling the Negev, and using the Negev as a gateway to key countries in Asia and the Far East. In response, the 'intellectuals' whom Ben-Gurion invited, challenged, each in his own way, what Michael Keren called the use of 'vision' as the sole guide for action. After the fact, the encounter was more like an acrid collision between the typical views of each of these personalities and the eclectic, 'renaissance-like' jumble of Ben-Gurion's 'vision'. The encounter, however, is of importance in a book about Levi Eshkol because the 'intellectuals' would become Eshkol's ardent supporters later on. He relished this support and even strove to rehabilitate the ousted Lavon and unite him with a group of intellectuals in a bid to challenge Ben-Gurion ideologically. This did more than destroy his relations with Ben-Gurion; it also had grave ramifications for Mapai, Eshkol, Ben-Gurion and the future of Israel's polity.

For this reason, let us dwell on the encounter. Professor E.E. Urbach, an acclaimed Talmudic scholar who had been campaigning against the construction of the nuclear reactor and was one of the main spokespersons on 'the Affair', chose to attack Ben-Gurion's use of the messianic-humanistic vision of the Jewish prophets for his purposes. The prophet Isaiah, Urbach claimed, had addressed only a few verses in his entire prophecy to messianism, devoting most of his message to criticism of the social and political realities in Judea of his time. By implication, the prophets' disciples had learned from their mentors that they should do more than offer a positive vision of redemption that could provide creative inspiration for the construction of a new Jewish commonwealth; they should also critique reality. Martin Buber also emphasized this view of the role of the Jewish intellectual as a critic.[4] Ben-Gurion confronted this challenge as best he could. 'Criticism', he said, does not build a society; instead, perhaps, it shapes and is influenced by public opinion. Indeed, on behalf of principled 'criticism' one could defend Lavon, condemn the construction of the nuclear reactor, and do as one pleases without knowing what is at stake.

This brings us back to the problem of historical truth and the historical and philosophical sources of the arguments relating to it, given the contrasting argument that truths may not exist at all or may be relative, or that there may be moral truths that are left to professional ethicists such as Buber and Leibowitz to determine.

Ben-Gurion found more in the Bible than social or political 'criticism'. In his quest to invest the Book of Books with special importance in the public mind, he deviated from Joshua's conquest of the Land of Israel and the prophets' universal vision by attempting to make conscious use of this trove to lend content to the life of a society that was rapidly divesting itself of at least some of the contents that had motivated its founders. As Allan Bloom put it many years later, the Bible has contents of substance, moral weight and profundity that lead us closer to the truth.[5] What Bloom meant, however, was not the shop-worn argument that people lead fuller lives when they base them on myths, but that a Bible-based life is closer to the truth than its alternative and that the Bible supplies 'material' for deeper investigation of, and more effective access to, the true nature of things. Several of Israel's founders occupied themselves with this Jewish epos, regarding it as a positive, profound and moral instrument for the construction of the most just society possible in Israel. Levi Eshkol excused himself from this group; he was the doer among them, a party man who always cherished compromise among the Labour factions, rather than a thinker or an intellectually endowed statesman.

Ben-Gurion, in the meantime, augmented the intellectuals' interpretations with others of his own invention concerning the abiding relationship between the land and the people of Israel. To his way of thinking, however, this 'invention' was linked with facts, that is, with historical reality as he viewed it as opposed to a reality derived from his conscious imagination. The declared purpose of this interpretation, strongly influenced by Professor Ezekiel Kaufman's original biblical research,[6] should instil consciousness of belonging to the Land of Israel in the mind of the public and of youth, whom, he felt, did not 'belong' to it adequately. He went about this as the 'intellectuals' of the 1960s occupied themselves with modern bureaucracy – deriving from Max Weber and others a principled criticism of bureaucracy, including the Israeli military complex, and its ailments as seemingly expressed in 'the Affair', via which they indirectly tackled the Holocaust as carried out by Adolf Eichmann and other bureaucrats.

To this, the politicization of the Holocaust on the right side of the Israeli political spectrum should be added. Since his abortive 'rebellion' against the British during the Holocaust, Menachem Begin argued directly and indirectly that the Yishuv leadership 'collaborated' with the hostile British authorities in order to maintain its power and control over the Jewish community in Palestine. This very serious blood libel, divorced as it was from the realities of the Holocaust, implied that rescue of Jews from Nazi dominated Europe was possible, but the main stream Zionist leadership failed to pursue it, being ideologically and politically preoccupied with its own power games, and hence the same leadership – Ben-Gurion, Sharett, Chaim Weizmann – was guilty of almost criminal negligence, with ongoing political ideological ramifications.

To Ben-Gurion, however, the Holocaust meant something else. It was so ghastly a disaster, and its interpretation such an inescapable historical-political minefield for its victims and their compatriots outside the killing zone, especially regarding rescue options which hardly existed and yet were undertaken without success, that Ben-Gurion and those of a similar mind spent many years avoiding public debate over the matter and refrained from peering into its depths until, in their estimation, the public became able to contemplate the contemporaneous state of the nation with its eyes wide open. Israel's Declaration of Independence of May 1948 cited the Holocaust, among other things, as proof of the need for Jewish independence, but Ben-Gurion, who had authored the Declaration, avoided *a priori* a deliberate policy of using the Holocaust as the foundation of the reconstituted social democratic society of the Jewish nation in the Land of Israel, for the secular religion of this nation was one of life and not of death. However, as Bloom remarks – seeking the roots of the matter in the penetration of German philosophy in the universities of the West – people (such as, I would say, some successors of the Israeli 'intellectuals' of that time, led by several of today's 'post-Zionists') cannot fathom the essence of evil and doubt that evil exists at all. For them, Bloom says, Hitler is an abstraction of sorts, a place-filler in a null category stolen from Kant but conceived and born in the writings of Hannah Arendt, the successful user of the cliché 'the banality of evil'.[7]

In contrast to Urbach, the economist Professor Don Patinkin spoke about the gap between vision and efficiency.[8] By adhering to a vision, he said, people allow themselves to disregard considerations of the cost and the practical outcomes, to various terms, of their 'visionary' investments. I do not know whether he was referring to the Dimona reactor and its price, the environmental effects of its construction, or similar issues. However, he was quoted as asking whether anyone had calculated how many schools would not be built due to the construction of the National Water Carrier, how many people should be settled in the Negev, how this would affect the economy and the quality of life in the other parts of the country, and so on. This area of inquiry is exactly what an economist would concern himself with, as opposed to the domain of vision, which seemed to have been phrased generally and, therefore, sweepingly and indefinitely.

Indeed, many of Patinkin's graduate students would join Eshkol's Finance Ministry and a few would follow him to the PMO and MOD, thereby contributing their share to the changing Israeli reality under Eshkol. A major contribution to the modernization of the Israeli economy at the time was the creation by Eshkol of the Bank of Israel and the appointment of David Horowitz, the sober professional, as its governor.

Patinkin was undoubtedly right in most of his arguments, from his professional points of view. His remarks, however, mirrored the tendency – long evident among notably Zionistic intellectuals – to separate the ethos of nation-building, one of the major axes in Ben-Gurion's thinking and actions, from the prosaic doings of state and government. Ben-Gurion valued such things per se and regarded them and their improvement as the other side of the nation-building coin. He deemed it unacceptable to separate the two, least of all in regard to Patinkin's remarks about settling the Negev. Patinkin, he ruled, lacked the kind of broad 'political vision' that would see how settling the Negev Desert tied in with Israel's foreign and defence affairs. The value of populating the Negev, Ben-Gurion charged, eluded Patinkin's line of vision in a definitive respect, since a populated Negev would be Israel's strategic depth – rather than the politically hazardous West Bank – and its gateway to the awakening Third World. From this standpoint, the 'vision' embodied the viewing of possibilities that, while not available in the present, might exist in the future. It did not seem totally senseless; Israel did manage to establish close relations with Burma even though its attempts to form ties with the People's Republic of China and neutral India were spurned angrily or coolly. In my opinion, however, the definitive point in this matter lay elsewhere and Patinkin did not give sufficient thought to it: by settling the Negev, Israel would shift its centre of gravity from the coastal strip – vulnerable, narrow and seemingly begging to expand into the Palestinian-inhabited and incomparably politically sensitive West Bank – to the vast, unpopulated and politically un-sensitive Negev. The failure to attain this goal would have an immediate implication – pursuant to the crumbling of Ben-Gurion's status and actions – on the prelude to and the aftermath of the Six Day War.

Eshkol did not seem much preoccupied by intellectual exercises of these kinds. What concerned him instead was how to live with, and maintain a balance between, the leftist flank of the coalition, which was very much anti-West German, and his own pragmatic approach toward the complex of West German–Israeli relations in due course, which is discussed below. As for Patinkin's legacy, many of his graduate students at the Hebrew University, known collectively as 'Patinkin's kids', joined Eshkol's Finance Ministry and later became known as 'Eshkol's kids'. This influx of modern economists into the country's decision-making centre in financial and growth issues contributed to the perception of Eshkol himself as a reformer, an updated *makher*, while he himself – along with Pinchas Sapir – retained ultimate control over the economy, at least for a while.

In the meantime, Ben-Gurion struggled to salvage his country's relations with West Germany, which yielded a large contribution of military equipment to the IDF and some aid for the Israeli nuclear effort, tendered in complete secrecy following a meeting between Ben-Gurion and Chancellor Konrad Adenauer in New York in 1960. As this went on, the relationship came under growing domestic criticism due to Bonn's failure to recall its citizens from Nasser's missile factories, which isolated Ben-Gurion in his own parliamentary faction.[9] Concurrently, Ben-Gurion was fighting to hold the French to their treaty with Israel in regard to the construction of the Dimona reactor. Then a new storm threatened Ben-Gurion's weakened position: in early 1963, President Kennedy issued NSAM (National Security Action Memorandum) 231, instructing the Department of State to devise a plan that would halt the development of advanced weaponry in the Middle East.[10] Kennedy's action prompted Moshe Dayan, now Minister of Agriculture, to come out against the memorandum in an article that he published in the newspaper *Ma'ariv* in April 1963, by which time Peres had already hinted to a foreign newspaper that Israel intended to develop only a very limited nuclear deterrent.[11] Since such a deterrent would naturally be aimed solely at targets in Egypt (such as the Aswan High Dam), claims relating to a 'second-strike capability', the sort that the two superpowers needed, were groundless and a nuclear deterrent against the USSR was not on the agenda.

At the time, however, Dayan and Peres were poorly regarded in the West; both were considered crude and uninhibited elbow-wielders. Reports from Western embassies in Israel depicted Peres as having a corruptive influence on Ben-Gurion himself. By implication, if the Americans wished to stop the reactor project in Dimona, they had to try to approach Foreign Minister Golda Meir and Levi Eshkol, considered Ben-Gurion's successor-designate. To accomplish this successfully, they would have to show Meir some form of commitment to Israel's security and demonstrate achievements of some kind in Egypt. This they tried to do. Kennedy provided the Foreign Minister with a repetition of American promises – non-binding promises long since issued – to defend Israel. Contrarily, however, the State Department focused its main efforts at this stage on seeking Egypt's favour.[12] The President dispatched John J. McCloy, an important Democrat from the Roosevelt era who now specialized in nuclear disarmament (and Arab oil affairs), to the Middle East. McCloy offered a linkage – a deal – which Minister Mordechai Gazit, Ambassador Avraham Harman's subordinate at the Israeli Embassy in Washington,[13] defined in the following way: 'The US will try to talk the Israelis into agreeing to international inspection of the Dimona reactor in return for Egyptian flexibility on [Nasser's] missile programme'.[14] Thus, the Egyptian missiles, which Israel's MI had in the meantime found to be lacking in guidance systems and feasible chemical or radiological warheads, were still an advantage to Nasser. A toothless Egyptian 'white elephant' became an American bargaining chip that could be played to sabotage the Dimona project, which was supposed to sprout its teeth right then. (According to a French source, the construction of the entire complex was to be completed by the end of 1963. In fact the project as reported encountered many difficulties and was finally completed several years later.[15])

Thus, according to one of his biographers, Ben-Gurion postponed his resignation – an inevitable denouement given the state of his party, the coalition, the Knesset and most of public opinion – until the project was completed.[16] Foreign primary sources, however, paint a vastly different tableau that corroborates our conjecture that Ben-Gurion's resignation was related not only to the completion of the Dimona project but also to the expected clash with McCloy and his superordinates. The latter had more in mind than killing off the Dimona project. The Kennedy Administration had from its first days been exploring various ways of solving the 1948 refugee problem and had been discussing with the British – following a tradition dating to the Eisenhower Administration – the revival of the idea of demanding Israeli territorial concessions in the Negev that the Administration thought necessary. After all, one of Nasser's charges against Israel – apart from its very 'illegality', to his mind – was that the country was a regional bone in the throat, a wedge between Egypt and its Arab sisters in northern Africa and the Arab Middle East to its north and east. By inference, if the West wished to find a common language with the most important Arab country and its charismatic leader – against the background of competition and escalating risk of confrontation with the Soviet Union – Israel must at least make concessions to Egypt in the southern Negev in order to establish an overland bridge between Egypt and Jordan, Iraq, Syria and Saudi Arabia.

BEN-GURION, ESHKOL, DIMONA AND THE SPECIAL RELATIONSHIP

Ben-Gurion attempted to repel the Kennedy Administration's overall Middle East policy at several levels. First, he corresponded personally with Kennedy, de Gaulle and other Western leaders in order to show them that unless Israel received a NATO-style guarantee or similar assurances from the two superpowers, it would have no refuge from the inter-Arab dynamic of the 1960s.[17] This dynamic had led to the establishment of a new Arab union – an Egyptian–Syrian–Iraqi federation – sometime after the militant pan-Arab Ba'ath party had seized the reins in Syria. Ben-Gurion heatedly warned his correspondents about this federation's public commitment to the annihilation of Israel. The Administration tended to pooh-pooh the gravity of this attempt at Arab unity; after all, a full Syrian–Egyptian union had just fallen through. Worse still, Kennedy considered the Israeli premier's warnings and entreaties a smokescreen that was meant to conceal the Dimona project and vehemently demanded the right to inspect what was going on there.

As it turned out, no sooner had McCloy set out on his fateful mission to the Middle East than Ben-Gurion resigned. The final pretext for this act was a severe clash between Ben-Gurion and the Foreign Minister, Golda Meir, over an Israeli military training programme in West Germany. Israeli soldiers, uniforms and all, had been sent there to master and operate the L-70 radar-guided anti-aircraft cannon that were needed, among other things, to defend Dimona against low-flying aircraft. Meir, construing the disclosure of the mission as yet another provocation against her and public opinion in respect of the charged German issue, demanded that all information about the mission be censored, and threatened to implement her own resignation. Ben-Gurion refused to order the military censor to blue-pencil the matter, deeming it totally legitimate, but could assume that the resignation of his foreign minister would bring his Government down. Without the support of this member of the Government, who had been loyal to him in the past, Ben-Gurion evidently reached the overall conclusion that he could no longer function. Furthermore, even if he dissuaded Meir from resigning, he could not predict how she would receive the McCloy mission; she might show an untoward willingness to accommodate McCloy if he were to present her with an ostensible Egyptian concession on the missiles. Meir's American orientation, which Eshkol would endorse and further enhance – unlike Peres' emphasis on Paris and Bonn – was not new and eventually proved itself along a serpentine course that originated at this time and continued until after the Six Day War. Israel's special relationship with the United States, nurtured by Golda Meir with all her strength and subsequently approved and pursued by Eshkol, coupled with Washington's willingness to be forthcoming with the Foreign Minister and the Finance Minister specifically among Israeli officials, might be put to a critical test if McCloy landed in Israel bearing offers 'that could not be refused' in regard to Dimona, once Eshkol and Meir would heed Allon's and Galili's counsel about the dubious strategic value of the nuclear project and its price in terms of superpower opposition to it. Therefore, one may say that Ben-Gurion was forced to step down and, no less, that he was ousted from his posts in the summer of 1963 by the combination of the revolt in his faction regarding the West German issue, his succession problem, unrest among his senior officials from within, and American pressure from without.

Ultimately, however, McCloy never made it to Israel. He first stopped in Egypt, knowing as stated that without an Egyptian concession of some kind on the missiles he would not be able to pressure Israel on Dimona. Nasser refused to give him an explicit undertaking for various reasons including his concern that a concession on this sensitive issue would cost him in inter-Arab currency. Therefore, McCloy headed for Athens to wait for Nasser's final response before proceeding to Jerusalem. As he waited, President Kennedy was assassinated and the entire American foreign and defence policy was put on hold for some time as Lyndon B. Johnson, Kennedy's successor, had other priorities.[18] Upon assuming office, Johnson wrote to Eshkol[19] in a relatively forthcoming tenor when it came to Kennedy's secret offer to come to Israel's aid in case of trouble. The new president supported Israel's right to use the water resources in its north – something that the Arabs rejected on principle – as a source for its settlement efforts in the Negev, an old dream of Ben-Gurion's and Eshkol's that was now reaching maturity. However, he repeated Kennedy's (and the State Department's) stance that the Palestinian refugee problem should be settled as a prerequisite for peace. The president also alluded to Dimona and the Israeli missile purchase in France as a problem if the 'situation in the area was to be stabilized rather than be upset'. Eshkol's challenge would be to untie this package, so as firstly, to avoid any concessions on the refugee issue, which must be settled outside Israel; secondly, to obtain American military aid at the least possible cost in order to avoid being completely dependent on France's de Gaulle; and thirdly, to avoid concessions on Dimona and the missiles insofar as this could be done without getting into hot water with Washington. Eshkol would represent himself not just as the prime minister of a tiny and dependent entity but also as a sort of representative of the Jewish people and a pioneer in something like the Texas tradition, ready to make the utmost sacrifice if asked or pressured to surrender vital Israeli interests. The longer-range goal would be a strategic alliance between the United States and Israel, both recognizing the hostile Arab stances toward Israel and the Soviets' political and military support of Egypt, Iraq and Syria. Those circumstances might trigger a new war in due course, necessitating enough deterrent power to head off such a war and, ultimately, the means to win it.

Eshkol would need all his bargaining skills, including Jewish influence in the White House, to accomplish this. As he worked at it, Ben-Gurion looked over his shoulder, remembering well that under past circumstances Eshkol had succumbed to pressure such as Lavon's and his own. Moreover, Eshkol, the quondam treasurer of the Jewish Agency and the outgoing Minister of Finance who had foisted a major economic reform on his reluctant colleagues in 1962,[20] was torn as always between his goals – settling the country and developing the economy – and the realities of resource shortfall, the threat of inflation and the deteriorating balance of payments. Sometimes the treasurer in him won over. Now as prime minister, however, he had the power to strike a new balance by trying to mobilize American aid. Buying weapons in France had become rather expensive and politically insecure since de Gaulle had begun to toy with Dimona in 1960. At least, a decision to scrap the costly Israeli missile project and buy French IRBMs instead had to be justified in view of the Americans' suspicions about the missiles' aims. Since missile development was no simple matter, the purchase of French missiles had given Eshkol some room to play vis-à-vis the Kennedy team, as we shall see.

Now this team, inherited by Johnson, argued that the late president had managed to avoid an unnecessary – in fact, unacceptable to the Arabs – close proximity to Israel that would have pushed them even more firmly into the Soviet embrace. Later on, Nasser's activities against the pro-Western Saudis and Jordan, especially in Yemen, on top of his repeated statements calling for the destruction of Israel, complicated Washington–Cairo relations, led to the suspension of vital American food aid to Egypt, and convinced the Americans that some arms deliveries to Israel had to be considered after all due to Soviet supplies to the Arabs. Such deliveries would have to be limited because the United States wished, as before, to avoid becoming a major weapons supplier to Israel. Israel needed a modern fighter-bomber, for example, but aircraft deliveries to Israel had to be balanced by deliveries of aircraft to Jordan.[21]

Meanwhile, Israel's relations with West Germany based as they were on secret arms supplies from the latter to the former – mostly decommissioned American-made M48 tanks – were exposed to serious threats. At home, Eshkol's partners on the Left, represented by the leaders of Ahdut ha-'Avoda, were implacably hostile to Bonn and even ready to forgo its secret weapon deliveries, still blaming West Germany for the German scientists' involvement in Nasser's missile project. The German side – now led by Chancellor

Ludwig Erhard and his Foreign Minister, Gerhard Schroeder – angrily denied all responsibility for Egypt's unconventional venture and even disclosed that Bonn had officially rendered some aid to the Israeli nuclear project.[22] A short time later, early in 1964, the Germans leaked details to the press about their secret arms supplies to Israel (which had been partly exposed beforehand) and 'responded' to the leak by cancelling the deal altogether due to concern about Arab wrath and recognition of East Germany. At the same time, Bonn avoided the establishment of diplomatic relations with Israel for the same considerations.

When Nasser responded by inviting Walter Ulbricht, the East German strongman, to visit Egypt, Bonn reacted in 1965 by exchanging the cancelled arms deal for the establishment of diplomatic relations with Israel and the provision of some economic aid.[23] The cancelled tank deal, which seemed to have been in danger anyway due to the accession of the new Gerhard-Schroeder Government and the fall of Franz-Josef Strauss, Bonn's Minister of Defence whose role in the arms deal had been decisive, forced Israel to seek new sources – possibly direct American tank deliveries. Thus Eshkol was able to bring the German complex to a reasonable conclusion and avoid trouble with his coalition partners on the Left, who at the time (according to the historian of Ahdut ha-'Avoda) cherished their power as members of his Government more than their socio-economic principles as long as they could keep Ben-Gurion, Dayan and Peres away from the PMO, restrict their influence over the MOD and at least downscale the nuclear and missile projects, discussed further below.

Eshkol tried his luck first by writing to President Johnson in late November 1963,[24] asking him for three types of aid. The first was surface-to-surface missiles. Second, he asked for American tanks, stressing the growing disparity between modern Soviet armor flowing to Egypt and the antiquated Israeli tank force; this argument was based upon Kennedy's – and Johnson's – vague promises to maintain Israel's conventional balance of power. Third, he sought from Washington some means of countering Egypt's growing naval strength.

The result was a rather frank meeting between Johnson's National Security Advisor, McGeorge Bundy, and Israel's Ambassador Avraham Harman, on 10 January 1964. Bundy agreed that the growing imbalance between Israeli and Arab armor 'posed a real problem' but wondered why Israel needed missiles, viewing large expenditures on (conventional) missiles wasteful and unnecessary. Harman countered by saying that ordinary Israelis expected their Government to obtain the necessary means to counterbalance the Egyptian missile threat and that the IDF's legendary superiority over the Arabs was very much a myth in view of the non-European immigration and the problems that had arisen in absorbing it. Bundy then drove straight to the core of the matter: the Egyptian missiles, he said, were meaningless without nuclear warheads, and such were indeed lacking. 'However, if Israel went in for a substantial missile force along with its existing nuclear potential, it would create the real possibility of a whole new dimension of the Middle East arms race.' Hence, 'We would be forced to re-evaluate the whole basis of our Middle East policy'.

Ambassador Harman, who seemed somewhat harassed at this point, switched the subject by asking, 'How about tanks?' What he had in mind were 200 M48A3s and 100 M60s to replace the IDF's old Shermans in view of the modern armor that the Soviets were supplying to Egypt. What is more, he wanted them free of charge. Israel's defence, he reported, echoing Eshkol, 'now [takes up] 40 percent of the Israeli regular budget and 11 percent of GNP'. The arguments – and the linkage between the tank request and the missiles – went to and fro, Harman insisting on Israel's right to obtain the necessary gear for its survival, Bundy expressing denial of the missiles as a precondition, and Secretary of State Dean Rusk reminding the president from behind the scenes that Eshkol's obvious goal – making the United States Israel's strategic ally – might jeopardize American interests in the region, which under Kennedy had been based on a policy of balance between Arabs and Jews.

The next series of *FRUS* documents relates to an American inspection visit to Dimona after the facility was said to have been activated, scheduled for December 26, 1963, and proving that the site was 'clean' of weapons production, and Eshkol's reluctance to 'agree to our passing information on the reactor to Nasser'.[25] The records quoted below attest repeatedly to American efforts to block Israel's missile acquisition and nuclear efforts for fear of an Egyptian pre-emptive strike, supported by

Nasser's repeated threats to do exactly that, or 'at the least, push the UAR (Egypt and other Arabs) closer to Moscow',[26] prompting a letter in this spirit by President Johnson to Eshkol. Soon afterwards, an American military delegation visited Israel and met with Eshkol, repeating these arguments. Eshkol responded regarding the missile issue, as quoted, by telling a half-truth: 'Missiles are dangerous, expensive and not sure decision possible in one year; probably two years more accurate'. Thus, Eshkol did not apprise the Americans of his decision – discussed below – to scrap the Israeli missile programme and order the missiles from France instead – which would take time anyway. He then continued:

> On security basis, price is no object. Israel is home of the Jewish nation, last and only foothold requiring last-ditch stand even if must lower standard of living to lowest African level ... Eshkol suggested US instead of approaching Israelis go to Nasser with arguments to stop production missiles or Israelis would get good missiles from US; this would immediately stop race.

When a member of the American delegation remarked that 'that type of missile Israelis investigating only useful with nuclear warheads, Eshkol looked aghast, appeared to be new thought to him, and finally stated, "Don't try to persuade us to put nuclear warheads on them"'.

This was indeed a new style of negotiation compared with Ben-Gurion's. What is more, it would yield some results since Johnson had other priorities and Eshkol was operating under rapidly changing regional and global conditions. Still, the Americans would learn from their own sources about the Israeli–French missile deal and do their best to scuttle it or, at least, to prevent the deployment in Israel of the French-made medium-range ballistic missile – all of which, on top of their continued efforts to curb Dimona.

Ben-Gurion's retirement began in standard fashion: on 16 June 1963 he transferred his offices to Levi Eshkol by handing his successor both portfolios with neither interference nor rancour, after which he seemed to have settled in Sede Boqer for good. Soon, however, two external and internal circumstances that had led to his resignation changed. One was the assassination of

Kennedy and the succession of Johnson; the other was a series of démarches that Eshkol slowly began to carry out on his own counsel, such as an initial decision to scrap the Israeli-made medium-range missile and opt for a French one only. 'Eshkol has decided to stop the [missile] development programme [and continue the French project] against [Deputy Minister of Defence Shimon] Peres' stance and displeased Ben-Gurion so badly that he would eventually blame Eshkol for major security blunders without specifying details.'[27]

THE NEW PM: NO RESPITE

In Professor Yechiam Weitz's opinion – which, in this matter as in others, follows the lead of the journalist Amos Elon – Eshkol's succession marked the onset of a new era in Israel, one of domestic conciliation as the high-and-mighty recognized the citizenry's maturity and democratic rights. This conciliation was reflected in several gestures. One was the fulfilment by Government resolution of Jabotinsky's request, as expressed in his will, to have his remains exhumed from their place of burial in the US and reinterred in Israel. Another was the readmission to Mapai by Eshkol of Lavon's secessionist group, which had assembled in the Min Hayesod association after his dismissal by Eshkol from his post as Secretary General of the Histadrut – a step that must have outraged Ben-Gurion and ultimately sank into failure. A third measure illuminated the nature of the Eshkol Administration: the transformation of the Voice of Israel, the public radio service, from a department of the PMO into a public state authority. This action converted direct political supervision of public radio, as had been practiced until then (and that was largely ostensible except where Arabic programming was concerned), into the control of an executive committee and a cumbersome plenum in which the governing coalition commanded a majority. The Government appointed the chair and the director general of the authority and subordinated them directly and indirectly to its will. After the fact, Eshkol and his associates hoped to keep the authority very much under their thumb, albeit in a roundabout way. Soon enough, however, they lost control over the journalists, paving the way to the introduction of television in a most haphazard and somewhat corrupt fashion under minister Yisrael Galili.

Finally, Eshkol did away with the military rule that had been imposed on the Arabs of Israel during the Ben-Gurion era and replaced it with indirect supervision by Mapai's party machine and the security services. Military government had been forced on the heterogeneous Arab population of the Galilee and the 'Little Triangle' – an Arab-inhabited region close to Tel Aviv that controlled strategic routes to Israel's settlements all the way to the north, most of which had been reluctantly handed over by Jordan to Israel after the War of Independence. The population at issue was a national minority that belonged, in principle, to the enormous Arab majority in the region – a mass of humanity that, for the time being, rejected Israel and threatened to regroup and destroy it. Given the resulting protracted state of emergency, Israel's Arab minority was immeasurably better off than the American reservation Indians (until recently) and the Nisei in the Second World War. For one thing, Israeli Arabs enjoyed the franchise from the outset. The Nisei, in contrast, were doomed to their quarantined status until Japan surrendered unconditionally and accepted provisional American occupation. Ben-Gurion, however, had been concerned that the Jewish majority's internal fragmentation into camps and sects would invest the Arab minority with scale-tipping power vis-à-vis the majority. The maintenance of military rule was meant to allay these concerns somewhat without denying the Israeli Arabs political representation. Thus, the entire Israeli–Arab sector was totally dependent on the military government for basic needs such as freedom of movement, economic and financial matters and even education. Teaching was done in Arabic, but the teachers were Jews, most of them Iraqi immigrants. The Arab political parties became subsidiaries of Mapai in the Knesset.

Despite his chronic suspicions about Arab political behaviour, Eshkol developed a more benign view of this population group over the years, partly due to pressure from the left-wing parties. He had been surprised to observe those among the Arabs who welcomed the Israelis during the War of Independence by waving Israeli flags and collaborated with the military governors later on.[28] By abolishing military rule without continuing Ben-Gurion's campaign for a 'British' two-party regime, Eshkol gave Ben-Gurion an additional reason to be displeased with his successor.

Eshkol may have hoped that the pattern of Arab dependence

would be replaced by indirect control thanks to the continued collaboration of the Arab political parties and the economic opportunities that the reform would open up for this population. The Jewish teachers, for example, were soon replaced by Arabs, some of whom had graduated from Jewish schools. However, the policy of expropriating Arab land in strategic areas of the country was maintained and caused much resentment among the former inhabitants. Furthermore, the newly hired Arab teachers introduced nationalistic and, later, Islamic teachings in the curricula. When combined with the occupation of the West Bank and Gaza in 1967, Israeli Arabs, and especially their political parties, would move incrementally toward identification with the occupied Palestinian and the Islamic cause in the name of Israeli democracy.

All told, however, Eshkol's Israel put on a more democratic face than it had worn before and the new premier and his associates conducted its affairs in a more graceful and kindly way. In one matter, however, Elon and Weitz were right: under Eshkol, Ben-Gurion's doctrine of national duty, captured in the term 'bill of obligations' that he contrasted with the liberal American Bill of Rights approach – as this was understood by Elon and Weitz – expired. Although it did not happen in one stroke, Israelis of European decent, especially those who were young at this time, began to adopt the bill of rights approach as they construed it. The other Jewish Israelis, those of Mizrahi ('eastern') descent, still counted for little as active participants in the political process. They remained dependent on Mapai's machine control of the Histadrut and its services such as healthcare, jobs and government investments in new and old economic enterprises, which were not free of red tape and corruption. After Eshkol's death, the quest to fight Mapai's machine politics and corrupt legacy would find political expression within the framework of a new liberal party called Shinui ('Change') that would ironically catapult Menachem Begin to the Prime Minister's Office, its criticism playing into the hands of the Right.

The path to that destination was circuitous and owes its immediate origins to the Six Day War and its ramifications, mainly the Yom Kippur War of 1973. In the crisis that preceded the former, Eshkol lost control of the whole system and forfeited his standing even among loyal supporters in his inevitable struggle with Ben-Gurion. In other words, the 'system', whose endless difficulties Ben-Gurion had recognized and within which Eshkol thought he could operate, improve and invoke in order to undertake internal and external moves with considerable latitude, ultimately tripped him up with help from Ben-Gurion himself – a helping hand that deserves a closer look. Furthermore, the thing that Weitz, parroting Elon, described as a surfeit of democracy in Israel created an opening for a new foreign and defence policy that minority factions were allowed to influence perceptibly. By then, in fact, Mapai – and Eshkol at its helm – had lost its definitive status in these fields as the central pillar of the political edifice.

It is but natural that Ben-Gurion would not contemplate from the sidelines the potential of the change that Eshkol had begun to introduce in Israel's domestic affairs and would do his best to keep abreast of Eshkol's moves in foreign and defence affairs. For the time being, Shimon Peres and Moshe Dayan remained in their posts as Deputy Minister of Defence and Minister of Agriculture, respectively. Therefore, one could assume a strong measure of continuity in Eshkol's policies, at least in regard to Dimona if not on the issues of Germany and missiles. We will return to these matters presently. However, Ben-Gurion was now free to investigate the 1954 'Lavon Affair' once and for all and hired the journalist Haggai Eshed as a muckraker. The conclusions of Eshed's inquiry led inexorably to a confrontation between Eshkol and Ben-Gurion, in which the former prevailed and, in effect, manoeuvred the latter out of Mapai.

The dynamics in the Middle East arena, Europe and the global theatre, however, did not give the winner much of a respite. Furthermore, the appointment to the post of COGS of Yitzhak Rabin, an experienced professional military man but nevertheless a protégé of Galili and Allon – Eshkol's senior partners in the coalition that he had reassembled after Ben-Gurion's resignation – had the effect of granting practical and political power to a man who would represent the army vis-à-vis a civilian minister whose experience in this field was marginal compared with the geo-political knowledge and the related in-depth analysis of the domestic, regional and global processes that were unfolding rapidly since Eshkol's accession to the premiership and MOD. Indeed, Rabin would soon respond in his own way to the regional changes that accelerated until their peak in May 1967, doing so largely with reluctant and *ex post* backing from his civilian superordinate, Eshkol. By the time Eshkol bestirred himself to stop the army and preclude the 'preventive war' that all IDF leaders found inevitable, he had lost control of the entire political system, including the IDF.

The regional and global changes that ultimately triggered the war were a mixture of the old and the new – a concurrence of long-standing problems and interests and dramatic changes in regional and global leaderships:

a) Kennedy's assassination in November 1963 and the accession of Lyndon Johnson to the American presidency turned the focus of interest at the White House toward sweeping domestic reforms. The foreign-policy establishments, however, continued striving to stanch the Soviet Union and its allies everywhere. The change was particularly evident in Vietnam, in regard to which the president also had the domestic consideration of avoiding attacks on his home turf for being 'soft' on the Communist enemy. Concurrently, these establishments sought to work out an agreement with the Soviet Union on nuclear anti-proliferation – a goal that took them until 1968 to attain. They also sought compromises in the Middle East that would tilt in the West's favour and looked for ways to stop Israel's nuclear programme in return for some form of Egyptian consideration. When they failed at this, they acted to head off a war over this programme, which developed steadily in the 1960s and became an official Egyptian *casus belli* by early 1965. At that stage, however, the Arabs were taking no direct action as yet in this regard.

b) The downfall of Nikita Khrushchev in 1965 and the accession of Leonid Brezhnev and Alexei Kosygin ostensibly created a new situation in superpower relations that initially centred on vagueness about the Soviets' intentions. However, two pending problems stood out in this 'new' situation: Vietnam and the lesson of the Cuban missile crisis, which seemed to have ended with a victory for Kennedy and may even have contributed to the ousting of Nikita Khrushchev. But why had Khrushchev been deposed? Was it because he had 'capitulated' to Kennedy and removed his missiles from Cuba, or because he had taken the grave risk of sparking a nuclear world war there? This must have been related to the abiding concern of Kennedy himself, as well as his successors in Johnson's foreign and defence establishments, of an even greater entanglement than the one that they had barely escaped in respect of isolated Cuba. Cuba, where Khrushchev had been snared in a web of lies, was their back yard. In its surroundings, the Americans enjoyed total naval and air supremacy. But what would happen if the Soviets were tempted to respond, or felt that they must respond, to challenges in areas of vital concern to them – such as the Middle East – and would station missiles in Egypt or Syria? The development of Israeli nuclear missiles, especially to ranges that would cover not only obvious targets in the Arab world such as the Aswan High Dam but also targets in the Soviet Union itself, could cope with such a challenge. The Soviets, however, might neutralize the Israeli threat by equipping the Arabs with a response of their own or by furnishing them with a nuclear guarantee. In all, this was a threat that could thoroughly destabilize superpower relations and subordinate them to démarches among clients whose conflict had escalated and acquired an internal logic of its own.

An aggressive school of thought seemed to exist, at least in the Soviet defence establishment – surrounding the Deputy Defence Minister, Andrei Grechko – which sought to aggrandize the Soviet Union's status and naval might in Middle Eastern countries such as Egypt, Ba'athist Syria, civil-warring Yemen and Aden, which the British were about to evacuate. These countries' receptiveness to Soviet military influence and presence was rising steadily. The USSR also wished to amass strength in the Third World in response to the downfall of the pro-Soviet regimes of Muhammad Ben Bella in Algeria and Ahmed Sukarno in Indonesia. Indeed, winding up a visit to Egypt in late 1965, Grechko seemed to have given Egypt a prospective nuclear guarantee 'if Israel attains nuclear weapons'.[29]

Concurrently, the Soviets directly approached Israeli delegates during talks in Geneva over the foreseen nuclear anti-proliferation treaty and warned them not to develop the bomb. 'The moment you have the bomb, so will the Arabs', they argued, among other things. This reasoning might terrify various personalities on the Israeli Left who continued to view the USSR with a mixture of affection and immense awe. Such a person was Transport Minister Yitzhak Ben-Aharon.[30] From then on, Ben-Aharon's cohorts in the Ahdut ha-'Avoda faction – ministers Galili and Allon – could argue that such a guarantee severely weakened Israel's nuclear deterrent or, in any event, enjoined Israel against deploying medium-range missiles that might threaten the Soviet Union itself and sabotage superpower relations. As it seemed, Eshkol's newly formed Government would have to make decisions about missile development, it having become clear that a makeshift missile called Shavit II, launched by Peres on the eve of the 1961 elections, had been nothing but a public-relations gimmick and that Israel had no practical missile programme of its own, unless Eshkol were ready to use the existing infrastructure and skilled manpower and spend the related enormous resources. Eshkol decided to abandon the Israeli missile project and opted for France alone, whereas Ben-Gurion would have retained both options. The decision, as Professor Yuval Ne'eman wrote,[31] was to assign the development of two prototypes – a short-range missile called the MD 620 and a medium-range model termed the MD 660 (the initials relate to Generale Aeronautique Marcel Dassault, the vendor) – to France. The medium-range missile was due for delivery in 1967.[32] By implication, this issue – and this year – would present Arabs, the Soviets, and the Americans with a challenge of the highest order if they wished to eradicate Israel's nuclear option before it could pass the point of no return.

c) Events in the Arab world at this time assured inter-Arab rivalry but also guaranteed a measure of unity in regard to Israel and related specific issues – starting with the problem of the Jordan River waters after Israel completed its National Water Carrier and began to pump water from the Sea of Galilee to the Negev, ending with the Dimona problem, and in between an issue as unresolved as ever, the 1948 Palestinian refugees. The last-mentioned problem had itself taken on the typical complexion of inter-Arab rivalry. Since 1964, Syria's militant Ba'ath regime had been aiding Fatah in its guerrilla operations against Israel under the inspiration of the FLN's war against the French in Algeria and North Vietnam's war against the Americans. In 1964, President Nasser had established a Palestinian organization of his own called the Palestine Liberation Organization and stationed Ahmed Shuqairy at its head. This entity was additionally tasked with undermining King Hussein of Jordan and inciting his numerous Palestinian subjects against him. For the time being, however, Nasser did not allow the PLO to operate directly against Israel from the Gaza Strip, which had been surrounded by UN peacekeeping forces since Israel evacuated it in 1957. His restraint in this matter, however, exposed him to accusations from his conservative and radical Arab enemies and rivals to the effect that instead of practicing what he preached – working toward the goal of annihilating Israel – he was hiding behind the skirts of the UN forces.

d) Nasser himself was embroiled in a great many struggles in various arenas during these years. In 1961, he had been forced to withdraw from his union with Syria. In 1963, he countered a militant and provocative pan-Arab Ba'ath regime in Damascus that had clouded his moral and political leadership throughout the Arab world. Concurrently, Egypt had intervened in the civil war in Yemen on the side of the anti-Imam forces and, as a result, found itself in an indirect struggle with Saudi Arabia, which favoured the Imam, and with Jordan. These two countries diligently protected their monarchy regimes and their separate interests, and Saudi Arabia made sure to reserve its oil treasures for itself. Their opponent, the impoverished socialistic Egypt, depended on American aid (cheap grain shipments) to feed its citizens, who were multiplying at an unprecedented pace.

e) Just then, another acute change took place in Syria. In February 1966, an even more radical sect of the Ba'ath Party seized the helm. The new regime seemed willing to take escalating risks vis-à-vis Israel, either on its own or by means of Fatah, and to operate in domains that had been agreed upon at Arab summit conferences from 1964 onward. There were two such domains: an operation in conjunction with Jordan and Lebanon to divert water sources from the Sea of Galilee in response to Israel's use of them to irrigate the Negev, and operations in matters pertaining specifically to Israel–Syria–Palestinian relations, including the shelling of Galilee localities in response to the agricultural use that Eshkol's Israel was making of the demilitarized zones in the north of the country. Yasser Arafat's Fatah organization was even allowed to operate from Syrian bases, provided that this was done under appropriate Syrian supervision, in most cases not directly but via Jordan. Damascus seemed keen on precipitating a general war with Israel and mobilizing Egypt for this cause. At least it was 'doing something' and creating the challenge of a real struggle against the Zionist state, as opposed to Nasser's hot air, which, for the time being, was not being backed by action.

THE LAVON–DIMONA NEXUS II

One issue, however, stood all by itself: how the Arabs should respond to the Dimona project. This matter, which had been the theme of at least one summit meeting in 1965, had given birth thus far to a public pronouncement by Nasser that if Israel crossed the nuclear threshold, the result would be war. The Ba'athists in Damascus and Arafat and his associates could argue that, from their standpoint, the Israeli nuclear option did not present a genuine challenge in this, the era of guerrilla warfare. Egypt, in contrast, could view Dimona as a challenge to itself, a very grave threat that must not be taken lightly by any means while assuring Israel's existence no matter what. Ahmed Shuqairy turned this delicate issue into the topic of shrill public alarm, suspecting that the Arab states would not fight for the Palestinians if they were to face the menace of an Israeli nuclear challenge. If so, the time to fight and destroy Israel was now – before Israel went fully nuclear.

There lay the origins of Israel's future security dilemmas and even the Americans' vigorous endeavours to 'prevent war' from 1965 on. All these factors quickly jelled to bring on the preventive war of 1967. Although Eshkol had neither planned nor wanted that war, it was occasioned anyway by prior plans that became real under the pressure of events. From the standpoint of our discussion, however, the main issue concerns Eshkol's role on the road to that war and what he did in an effort to head it off.

Ben-Gurion's 'contribution' to that road was manifested in several domains up to the 1965 elections. The first was the resurrection of 'the Affair' and the heated struggle pertaining to it, which ultimately brought on his resignation and ousting from Mapai as a traitor. Second, after (or perhaps before) his resignation, Ben-Gurion decided to set up a party of his own for the 1965 elections. Admittedly, the new entity did not do well enough at the ballot box to acquire enough blocking power to influence the structure of the coalition that Eshkol reassembled after the elections. However, its stances during and after the election campaign marred Eshkol's credibility in foreign and defence affairs; these issues entail elucidation in view of the actions of Eshkol's coalition per se. The third question has not been clarified adequately to this day: where the security issue figured in

Ben-Gurion's considerations in running for office in 1965 at the head of his own list, since conventional wisdom usually links his decision to domestic affairs, foremost the resurrection of 'the Affair'.

Indeed, after receiving the findings of Haggai Eshed's investigation of the '1954 Affair' in Egypt, which held Lavon responsible for having given the order to carry out a dastardly and risky action in said Arab state, Ben-Gurion acted at several levels. Most importantly, he tried to have the decision of the ministerial committee that had exonerated Lavon annulled. In this matter, he was supported by Dov Joseph, Eshkol's Minister of Justice. The nullification of the decision – which Eshkol had sponsored at the time it had been adopted – could have several clashing outcomes. One of them, to which Ben-Gurion aspired, would not only establish that he had been right in his lengthy struggle on this issue but would also place him and his principles in new public light after the calumny that he had absorbed from every direction since the beginning of the public debate of 'the Affair'. Debunking the ministerial committee that had exonerated Lavon would set the tenets of 'rule of law' and 'public rules of the game' – cardinal principles in Ben-Gurion's reform policies – on firm ground. Lavon's exoneration after the Government's improper investigation of his case had been a manifestation of trampling of the 'rules of the game'. After such a proceeding, Ben-Gurion's thinking presumably went, people viewing the matter after the fact would think that if Ben-Gurion had personally lost such a game against Lavon and the media, why should they bother to fight a battle of principles that even Ben-Gurion himself had not been able to win? Therefore, it was of supreme importance to restore the deserving 'rules' to their place or to fight for their adoption.

Another possible outcome – that Eshkol had calculated and found useful to him and, from his standpoint, to Mapai – was the prevention of the very démarche described above, for several reasons. One of them, certainly, was Eshkol's sense that he himself would be wounded by the repeal of the Government resolution that he had sponsored back then. Furthermore, his leadership and that of his party colleagues – Foreign Minister Golda Meir, who in the meantime had become Mapai Party's Secretary General, Finance Minister Pinchas Sapir, and Education Minister Zalman Aranne – would be blemished, to the benefit of Ben-Gurion and his young ostensible successors, Dayan and Peres.

After all, the nullification of Lavon's exoneration would automatically clear them of the suspicions and vicious charges that Lavon had levelled against them in the course of the '1960 Affair'. These suspicions and charges had clouded their reputations even though they had never been proven, and in their presence Eshkol could more easily manoeuvre between them (Dayan and Peres) and their traditional foes (Allon and Galili), whose partnership he needed in order, at the very least, to establish internal harmony at the Histadrut.

Another motive was Eshkol's slightly cynical attitude toward the British-style 'rules of the game' and 'state of law'. Eshkol was a man of compromise and a master of give-and-take who, at this stage of his public career, had become a professional politician who was eager to continue holding both of his portfolios and record achievements of his own in them. Ben-Gurion's shadow weighed on him – whether Ben-Gurion was right or not – and at this stage he definitely did not want his predecessor to return to the arena as a moral victor, let alone a political one. He also understood rather well that most of Ben-Gurion's enemies in the '1960 Affair' took no interest in the matter per se; instead, they regarded it as an opportunity to get back at Ben-Gurion in various ideological, personal and political disputes. Therefore, it puzzled them greatly to see Eshkol suddenly inspired to conduct a topical investigation of a matter of which the public had had its fill. Finally, he refused to reopen the case over 'the Affair', knowing that these personalities probably wanted no part of an investigation that had no axe to grind. Lying, legal-political injustice, blackmail and mendacious manipulation of the sort that Ben-Gurion attributed to Lavon were despicable per se and their entrenchment as accepted norms posed an immense danger for the future. Eshkol, however, trusted the Israeli elite to have tired of 'the Affair'. Furthermore, he was convinced that his own style and tactics, aimed at compromises, were very much more appreciated as 'more democratic' than Ben-Gurionic governance and, as such, would be honoured by the 'intellectuals' and many others whom he organized under the banner 'Citizens in Support for Eshkol' ahead of the 1965 elections.

We do not have any information about Eshkol's intellectual-cultural interests at that time. He was too busy to give himself any respite from his official jobs, ruining his health thereby. A 200 per cent political operator, he did not pay attention to the changing spirit of the 1960s abroad and at home and thus seemed, in spite of his more liberal, open style, to be divorced from the younger generation of the elite, as well as from the Mizrahim. Yet the pro-Lavon 'intellectuals' continued to support him against Ben-Gurion, Dayan and Peres, and he courted them as well. Eshkol's Zionism remained an East European, grassroots, popular and natural way of life, divorced from the masses of immigrants from the Muslim countries, Ben-Gurion's darlings, who hardly understood his Yiddish jokes but remained – so it seemed – under the thumb of Mapai's machine even though their standard of living was much lower than that of the union bosses and their members, who 'counted' for more. Eshkol and Sapir were convinced that they were running a state-controlled economy that at least tried to create a more modern version based on the principle of equality, even though within its framework their oligarchy remained 'more equal' until Menachem Begin would teach Eshkol's Labour Party otherwise and harvest enormous profits from the corruption among Mapai's bosses. Although Eshkol had only a limited understanding of the arrival in Israel of the age of Western permissiveness, he seemed to enjoy some aspects of it, especially in his relations with women. His lifestyle symbolized the end of the Puritan age in Israeli history but made no real contribution to the new age; he was too busy for that.

Thus, after appearing to be willing to discuss the ministerial committee's decision to exonerate Lavon per recommendation of the Minister of Justice, Eshkol recanted, resigned, dissolved the Government and put it back together again without subjecting the matter to any debate at all. When the Mapai Central Committee took a vote on the issue, Eshkol came away with a 60 per cent victory, thanks to the mobilization by Eshkol and Sapir of the party machine, whose key bosses figured that the rank-and-file had tired of Ben-Gurion and his arguments, and with support from most of the media. Moshe Sharett, dying of cancer, used the Mapai Central Committee to deliver a prosecutorial and vengeful speech against Ben-Gurion, who had dismissed him from the Foreign Ministry way back then, and in defence of Lavon, whom he himself had once ousted from the MOD in the sincere belief that Lavon had been responsible for the botched operation in Egypt. Ben-Gurion came away with 40 per cent of the tally.

It was a resounding victory indeed. However, it throttled all further pertinent public discussion of the issue and cleared the way, in Ben-Gurion's opinion, for the continued deterioration of public life in Israel into a regime of deceit and mendacity that rewarded its practitioners.

The reader may of course ask: Hadn't this regime originated in Ben-Gurion's defence system, a closed, self-contained system that was exempt from real public supervision? The method, by this reasoning, had sprouted over time and Lavon had merely revealed its true face, irrespective of whether he had been responsible for 'the Affair' in Egypt or had resorted to the forging of documents that had indeed been committed in order to clear his name and expose the system's drawbacks publicly. Furthermore, whether or not Ben-Gurion had designated Dayan and Peres as his successors, after their manoeuvrings following 'the Affair' they were perceived publicly as contenders for the throne; therefore, they posed a threat to Eshkol and his associates. The prime minister and defence minister was not fond of the ambitious Moshe Dayan, the wily, rough-and-tumble minister of agriculture, who seemed to have plenty of media entrée and potential public support. Eshkol, along with his cohorts Allon and Galili, seemed so willing to dump Dayan or, at the least, to crimp his steps that he would eventually claim – nothing less – that he felt as though he had stumbled into a concentration camp where the guards shoved him through the fence just so they could gun him down. After the Central Committee vote Dayan promptly resigned from the Eshkol Government, seemingly bringing his public career to an end.[33] Shimon Peres, in contrast, attempted to survive in the Government and in Mapai due to his conviction that he needed this large and powerful party as a platform for advancement. Therefore, when he ultimately seceded from Mapai and joined the party that Ben-Gurion had established in 1965, we do not know whether it was of his own volition and for reasons of loyalty to its quondam leader, that is, for pertinent reasons relating to disagreements with Eshkol on security matters, or whether he did it through lack of choice.

In 1965 and immediately afterwards, significant disagreements about security affairs might have concerned two issues: a new American move on the Dimona question, which Washington linked for the first time to direct supply of offensive weapons, and a grave crisis in Israel–French relations that germinated in 1964 and ripened in 1965. The latter calamity concerned one Mehdi Ben Barka, a Moroccan opposition leader who had found refuge in France but was extradited to his prosecutors at home thanks to some kind of cooperation between the Moroccan and Israeli foreign intelligence services operating on French soil. The Ben Barka affair prompted General de Gaulle to launch a comprehensive review of France's bilateral relations with Israel and seemed to threaten the delivery of the medium-range missile that Paris had promised Jerusalem.

As for Dimona, the Americans had pinned hopes on Eshkol from the moment he took over the premiership and the defence portfolio and were willing to be more forthcoming with him than they had ever been with Ben-Gurion.[34] The first scholar to publicize the American 'guarantee' of the 1949 Armistice Demarcation Lines, which Eshkol received as soon as he took office, was Professor Michael Brecher. In his public writings, Brecher never clarified the reason for Washington's decision. In an oral communication with this author, however, he explained that it was in fact an American attempt to find a surrogate for Dimona.[35] To my mind, however, the guarantee was problematic in many respects. First, it was secret, and therefore valueless from the standpoint of Israeli public opinion. In fact, if it ever became clear that Washington would not come to Israel's aid as expected, as seemingly happened in May–June 1967, those in the know would ask what Eshkol had obtained from the Americans in return for what he had given – as we discuss below – and the answer would be basically nothing. Second, the right to conclude a secret guarantee such as this was one of the powers that the Administration had arrogated to itself in foreign and defence affairs at this time; its value in American constitutional terms was dubious because the Senate had not approved it, meaning that it could not be deemed equal to an overt NATO-style military alliance. At the critical moment, the president himself might repudiate the guarantee, arguing – justifiably in itself and, therefore, many times worse – that the deal lacked sufficient support in the Senate and in public opinion. This indeed seems to be what happened in the crisis that precipitated the Six Day War.

For the time being, however, Eshkol seemed, contrarily enough, to follow Ben-Gurion's lead on the Dimona issue. Ahead of Eshkol's first visit to the United States on 1–12 June 1964 – where he expected to face direct questioning about Israel's nuclear programme – John Badeau, the American Ambassador in Cairo, sent Washington the following evaluation: the only circumstances that would prompt the Egyptians to even consider a surprise attack on Israel would be their realization that the Israelis had obtained or would soon obtain nuclear weapons. In such a case, Badeau continued, the Egyptians' goal would be to destroy the Israeli facilities with the greatest celerity and efficiency and then pull back behind its frontier, counting on international opinion and its pressure to prevent Israel from hitting back. In this case, the calculus behind the Egyptians' actions would be defensive, not offensive.[36]

By phrasing his last sentence as he did, Badeau indirectly justified an Egyptian démarche of this kind, that is, an overland march on Dimona. Even if the chiefs of the IDF were unaware of the cable, they certainly knew that the Egyptian Army could burst into the Negev and advance on Dimona and Beersheba if this overland front were unprotected. For this to happen, the Egyptians would have to man the trench lines that they had established in the northern Sinai after Israel's retreat from this area in 1957 and to amass serious armoured forces along them. To forestall this possibility, Israel would at the very least have to seal the border by calling up large-scale reserve units. This is how I will explain Israel's initial decision to mobilize reserves in the May 1967 crisis, since Egypt had just then marched into the Sinai and carried out flights over the reactor.

WASHINGTON RESPONDS, ISRAEL MANOEUVRES

As for the Egyptians' motives on the Dimona issue, we may glean some understanding from a document produced by the National Security Council (at the White House) or the Central Intelligence Agency in December 1964, that is, after Eshkol's visit to the US. According to this paper, Israel's nuclear programme seemed to have been pledged to research since January 1964 but might also be suitable for the manufacture of weapons. Prime Minister Eshkol, the paper continued, had told Johnson that Israel's nuclear activity was meant for peaceful purposes. However, neither Eshkol nor his predecessor, Ben-Gurion, had ever ruled out the development of nuclear weapons by Israel if the Middle East situation were to justify this.[37]

As for the question itself, the authors of the document, which was released for publication after censorship and re-editing, determined that Israel had the technological ability to develop a bomb. The US, the authors continued, believed that Israel, without outside assistance, could detonate its first nuclear device two or three years after it decided to develop nuclear capability. The production of more advanced weapons would take Jerusalem another year or two. In the meantime, the US had compelling evidence that a French company was developing for Israel a two-stage solid-fuel missile with a 450-kilometer range, and that a warhead with a 1,500–2,000 pound carrying capacity, usable for both high explosives and a nuclear payload, was being planned. Israel considered the existence of its own military deterrent crucial to its survival. Given this approach, the authors adduced, the Middle East arms race had advanced to a dangerous level. As the United Arab Republic (that is, Egypt) progressed and Egypt's missile technology improved, Israel was acting to develop a counter-deterrent that would be as unique as it was frugal. It would probably lead to the development of nuclear warheads for the missiles that Israel had ordered from France. Indeed, the document added, lower-level Israeli officials spoke openly about Israel's strategy vis-à-vis Egypt: (a) surface-to-surface missiles aimed at the Nile Delta and (b) the ability to bomb the Aswan High Dam and release its waters, which would require a nuclear warhead.

As for Egypt itself, the report had the following to say: among all the countries in the Middle East, Egypt is the most vulnerable to a nuclear attack. A single nuclear device, properly aimed, would send a flood of water 400 feet high down the narrow Nile valley, where the entire Egyptian population was concentrated. Israel was also vulnerable, but due to the nature of its frontiers a nuclear attack against it would harm the neighbouring Arab countries almost as much as it would harm Israel. Therefore, to assure its own survival, Egypt evidently believed it advantageous to obviate the possibility of Israel's using nuclear weapons and, to accomplish this, to ban the introduction of such weapons in the Middle East.

Thus, an official American document dating to this time established explicitly that if Egypt wished to head off the advent of 'the bomb' in its region, it felt this way in order to 'assure its own survival'. And why was its survival at stake? Because Cairo wanted and/or had promised to annihilate Israel *ab initio*, refusing time and again, openly and in talks with the Americans, to accept the regional status quo as we shall see below. Therefore, the introduction of an Israeli bomb would give Israel the only instrument that could assure its own existence by threatening Egypt's. By seeing things this way, however, the Israelis clashed not only with Egyptian ideology, Cairo's public undertaking to destroy the country, and pan-Arab interests, but also with US priorities and global policy at the time.

Indeed, the White House national security team – left over from the Kennedy Administration – not only considered the Dimona project a challenge per se but seemed to expect the Soviets to respond by giving the Arabs at least the belief that they would come to their aid in this respect. Or they might do something much worse, such as station nuclear missiles of their own in Egypt or Syria, avenging Washington many times over for the Cuba incident. America had had its way in Cuba because the latter was isolated in America's backyard and surrounded by American forces that held a decisive edge. Such might not be the case in the Middle East. These concerns must have, or should have, surfaced during Eshkol's visit to the United States in June 1964. After the visit, the State Department circulated a cable that it had sent to the International Atomic Energy Agency in Vienna (posting it to its ambassadors in all Arab capitals and in Paris and Rome). In the cable, the US said that it had restated its undertaking to assure the territorial integrity and the political independence of Israel and the other Middle Eastern states against aggression and the threat or use of force. Washington, the cable continued, had reported to the Israeli side its belief that its commitment to resist aggression would go far to alleviate Israel's security concerns. The US expressed hope that its renewed assurances to Israel would allow progress to be made in the common cause of restraining the arms race.

Further on in the missive, the following was stated:

> the Administration believes that Egypt's missile capability will remain essentially a psychological threat and that Cairo will not develop nuclear capability. The US is concerned

> about an escalation of the Middle East arms race and opposes the proliferation of missiles and nuclear weapons.

Then, quoting Prime Minister and Defence Minister Eshkol, the author of the document said,

> Israel appreciates the United States' support but is convinced that it must maintain its own deterrent in view of the possibility of an Arab offensive. The rank-and-file Israeli regards the Egyptian missile threat as a real one. Just the same, Israel will postpone the public display of missile capability for a year or two.[38]

Given the current state of the documentation, one cannot know whether Eshkol had conceded only 'the public display of missile capability' for a year or two, during which time the French missiles would be developed – therefore amounting to no real concession at all – or whether his American interlocutors noticed this and would eventually apply more adamant pressure in regard to the missiles. At least in regard to the necessity of an independent Israeli deterrent, Ben-Gurion's successor seems to have remained true to his precursor's policy, except with regard to the French missiles, to which we shall return. However, Eshkol may have believed that his charm and manners had found a friend on Johnson's Texas ranch and that, for this reason, he had succeeded in creating a growing partnership with the United States. Such a partnership, he may have reasoned, would eventually allow Jerusalem to acquire conventional offensive weapons from the Johnson Administration without giving up the nuclear option but possibly by merely 'slowing it down', as a contemporary Ahdut ha-'Avoda historian expressed it.[39] For the time being, Eshkol was able to conclude a deal with the Johnson Administration regarding tank and jet supplies in exchange for regular American inspection visits at Dimona. The road leading to this agreement should be understood in the context that follows.

Still in 1965 – in several ways a key year en route to the Six Day War – Nasser decided to cancel his ambitious missile project, finally acknowledging the costly failure that it had become. Under these conditions, he went ahead and promised Johnson that Egypt would not develop weapons of mass destruction.[40] This had been the goal of the mediator McCloy, and for its sake Washington had pressed Israel to scrap its nuclear programme. Now, Egypt had made a commitment in this respect for no prior consideration. Nasser, however, could entertain the expectation that, having taken Egypt out of the race for the manufacture or acquisition of WMD, Israel would come under mounting superpower pressure to quit the race as well. Late that year, the USSR gave Nasser something resembling a nuclear guarantee, which was widely publicized after Deputy Defence Minister Marshall Grechko's visit to Egypt.[41]

Indeed, even before Grechko's visit to Egypt, an American mission headed by the roving ambassador W. Averill Harriman visited Israel on his way to India, where he would attempt to pressure that country, too, to refrain from developing an independent response to the just-tested Chinese bomb. With him was Robert W. Komer, a National Security Council official from the Kennedy days. Komer, who had already invested much effort in trying to head off Israel's nuclear programme, visited the country now as representative of McGeorge Bundy, chair of the council, and had some grave things to say not only about Dimona but also about the missiles.[42] We have quite a few sources about the Harriman-Komer visit, foremost Yitzhak Rabin's Hebrew-language memoir *Service Notes*.[43] According to Rabin, the Israeli COGS at the time, the two American officials wished to predicate the Israeli–American 'strategic understanding' on three agreed principles: (1) Israel would not initiate a preventive war against the Arabs; (2) it would not take comprehensive military action against the Jordan River diversion programmes that the Arabs had begun; and (3) it would undertake not to become a nuclear power in possession of nuclear weapons (indeed, such a distinction was made). If Israel agreed to these provisos, it could send a military mission to Washington to discuss the procurement of aircraft, tanks and artillery.

Thus Washington dangled an enticing carrot along with the stick: an opportunity for Jerusalem to escape its absolute dependency on France and Germany in the procurement of conventional weapons. The offer was made just as West Germany's secret arms deliveries to Israel became public knowledge and the Bonn Government had been forced to terminate them and replace them with the establishment of diplomatic relations and economic aid.[44] Furthermore, the expression 'strategic understanding' with the US carried the important potential of a quasi-alliance with the Western superpower, something that Eshkol had coveted dearly since Ben-Gurion's tenure at the helm. Even though the price seemed unbearably high, Eshkol thought it unwise to flatly reject the outstretched hand. The proper thing, in his judgment, was to try to grasp it as firmly as possible without paying the full price that it entailed. According to Rabin's account, Rabin himself rejected the first two points and Komer – and, to a slightly lesser extent, Harriman – took a very tough line on the nuclear-arms issue. The visitors persisted, refuting Rabin's claim that Prime Minister and Defence Minister Eshkol had announced in his recent visit to the US that Israel would not be the first to introduce nuclear weapons to the region. The Minister of Defence seems to have found this phrasing, which Shimon Peres attributed to himself, satisfactory even after the construction of the reactor was completed and the Arabs had information to the effect that it had already produced 'eight kilograms of plutonium' in 1966.[45] Therefore, Komer requested a personal meeting with COGS Rabin and, after getting his wish, used 'rough language' that contained a threat: If Israel follows this path it is liable to bring on the gravest crisis that it has experienced thus far in its relations with the United States. We do not know what the (Jewish) official was referring to, but he may have apprised Rabin of the danger posed by a Soviet Union that would respond to the arrival of medium-range missiles in Israel and the existence of armed nuclear warheads there – which Moscow might construe as a direct threat against it by an impudent American client. Therefore, the Soviets might hold Washington responsible for this and for the possible outgrowth of an entanglement between its Arab clients and a nuclear Israel, and might respond accordingly.

By implication, Israel's conduct posed a potential threat to the United States itself or, rather, endangered a forthcoming American–Soviet agreement on a non-proliferation treaty. In response, Rabin told Komer that American emissaries had visited Dimona and knew 'exactly' what was going on there. Rabin was referring to a very recent American inspection visit to Dimona that had been kept under wraps. Shortly afterwards, another inspection visit took place and was leaked to the American press. On the basis of the available records, we may assume that these successive inspections (which continued until the Americans terminated them unilaterally in 1968) were the outcome of a deal that Harriman and Komer had concluded with Eshkol during their visit.

We do not know, however, whether the deal was related only to the inspection visits or also to the non-deployment of the MD 660 missiles that had been ordered in France. According to primary sources at the Johnson Library, a deal for the supply of Skyhawk aircraft and Pershing tanks to Israel was signed in March 1966, some time after the placement of Israel's order to France for the missiles had been leaked to the *New York Times*. The question is the price that Eshkol paid for the transaction: was it only the acceptance of the inspection visits or also his consent not to deploy the missiles? Were the medium-range missiles ready, given that we are told that they were due for delivery in 1967? Either way, when Eshkol asked Harriman who would defend Israel from the threats of the Arabs' patron power – the very Moscow that had brandished the bomb as a threat to Israel's existence at the time of the Suez-Sinai War – the American replied that in one matter at least – in an allusion to Cuba – the late President Kennedy had cured Soviet leader Nikita Khrushchev and his associates of the penchant of threatening nuclear war. Harriman's purpose in saying this was to assuage the Israelis' concerns about a 1956-style Soviet nuclear threat and, as it were, to obviate the need for an Israeli medium-range missile. Komer augmented Harriman's diplomacy with a casuistic touch of his own: since Khrushchev had in the meantime been deposed; who knew how his successors would behave? Moreover, as stated, he explicitly threatened a grave crisis with the United States if the missile were set up.[46]

Ultimately, Washington and Jerusalem did conclude the transaction and agreed on the purchase of Skyhawk aircraft (to be delivered several years on) and Patton tanks. The deal, however, was not perfect from the American point of view and, in their opinion, could not placate the Egyptians. After all, American inspection at Dimona was not necessarily an efficient way to deactivate the facility. Egypt could use it in order to accept Washington's reports that the reactor was not serving military purposes. This, however, was only if Cairo wished to accept this and avoid war. If Cairo wanted war, the very fact of the inspection and its concomitant, the continuing delegitimization of the Israeli nuclear programme by both superpowers, would provide Cairo with a *casus belli* at the time and place of its choosing. Indeed, Nasser could argue that the Americans' inspection amounted to a cover-up of Israel's nuclear programme, which Washington itself viewed as illegitimate *ab initio*. However, the timing of the delivery of medium-range missiles created a red line from Egypt's standpoint, since as long as Israel lacked these missiles it furnished Cairo with a good *casus belli* without a nuclear deterrent to speak of. All these points are speculations that must have tormented Eshkol's Government during the May–June 1967 crisis, but they have a factual basis in a cable from the State Department to the US Ambassador in Cairo immediately after Harriman and Komer concluded their visit to Israel. According to the cable, the Harriman-Komer talks had eased the situation '**but the main problems remained unsolved and constituted a potential *casus belli*. The U.S. Government**', the cable added, '**would continue to press Israel not to implement its nuclear program. Nasser must have been aware of the American inspection visit, it having been reported in the press**' (boldface in the original cable).[47]

This inspection visit (and the successive visits in 1966) plunged Eshkol into domestic hot water and failed to placate Nasser. Thus, the Administration was trapped between Cairo and Jerusalem: its power of influence was limited to one side only if the other side were to opt for war in the belief that the US lacked the ability to restrain Israel in this respect. Such is implied by an exchange between the State Department and the US Embassy in Cairo to Washington in mid-April 1965 about a meeting conducted by the Ambassador, Lucius Battle, and the Assistant Secretary of State for Near Eastern Affairs, Philips Talbot, with President Nasser.[48] Talbot explained to the Egyptian president why the problem of American inspection at Dimona had come up – that is, why the US had become involved – and said that the Israeli side had refused to accept appropriate inspection by the International Atomic Energy Agency. The US, Talbot added, would 'also' be concerned if the Israeli reactor were to be put to use for military purposes; this, he said, would create an issue between the US and Israel and not only between Egypt and Israel.

Talbot may tell Nasser, the cable continued, that the State Department has satisfied its curiosity in this matter. Nasser replied that while understanding Washington's concern he must note that Egypt, unlike Israel, had no influence in the United States. In response, Talbot termed nuclear proliferation a global problem and urged Nasser to believe that Washington was dealing with it from the perspective of the service of global interests (that is, not merely those of American domestic politics, possibly alluding to Jewish influence in the latter domain).

The whole thing did nothing to placate the pan-Arab leader and equally enraged Israel. Things reached such a point that in July 1965 the editor of the newspaper *Ma'ariv*, Aryeh Dissenchik, met with the director of the US Arms Control and Disarmament Agency, William Foster, and allowed himself to comment explicitly about Dimona.[49]

Dissenchik was as intimate with Moshe Dayan and Shimon Peres as he was with Levi Eshkol and Menachem Begin. There is no telling whether he was acting with authorization and, if so, with whose. Either way, he told his stunned interlocutor – who hurriedly reported the Israeli newspaperman's remarks up the ladder – that given Nasser's incessant threats to destroy Israel he 'regretted' having leaked to American television what, he said, the US knew about goings-on in Dimona. This leak, he continued ruefully, must have damaged the credibility of the Israeli deterrent and, at the very least, delegitimized it in American eyes. In the same breath, Dissenchik went on to say that Israel did not want war with the Arabs – even a victorious war – due to its cost in human life and property. What seemed important to him was that the other side should realize that Israel had a four- to five-year head start in the nuclear domain and could quickly put the finishing touches on a bomb. Under these conditions, he continued, the Arabs should think twice; therefore, Israel possesses a crucial deterrent. Foster sharply expressed his hope that Israel would go no farther in the military direction than it already had gone and explained Washington's concern about the threat that would ripple through the entire Middle East if Jerusalem were to persist. Dissenchik continued in his own vein. The main threat, he said, was the expected nuclear non-proliferation treaty, since presumably it would omit India – Egypt's close friend, which by then was considerably advanced in developing a bomb of its own.

It is hard to believe that the editor of *Ma'ariv* was pursuing a private initiative in this matter, but he fanned the flames. Shortly after his visit, the Soviet Deputy Defence Minister came to Egypt and gave Cairo at least the appearance of a Soviet nuclear guarantee if and when Israel were to obtain the bomb. It was then, too, that the Administration leaked to the *New York Times* the fact of Israel's order of medium-range missiles from France.

NOTES

1. See Michael Bar-Zohar, *Ben-Gurion, A Political Biography*, Part II, in Hebrew (Tel Aviv: Am Oved, 1977), p.1388.
2. The refugee issue, that is, allowing them to choose between compensation for their property or the right of return to their homes in Israel, Israel's withdrawal from the southern Negev in order to give Egypt overland access to the east, and a return to the 1947 UN partition plan were raised by Nasser back in December 1955 – see Bar-Zohar, *Ben-Gurion, A Political Biography*, p.1162 – and repeated again and again with a degree of support by Washington and London at the time and later. Although the proposals pertaining to the Negev and the 1947 partition lines were dropped after the Suez-Sinai War, the refugee issue remained on the American agenda during the tenures of Presidents Kennedy and Johnson; see below in the text.
3. For a detailed account and discussion, see Michael Keren, *Ben-Gurion and the Intellectuals*, in Hebrew (Sede Boqer: Ben-Gurion University of the Negev, 1988), pp.90–2.
4. Ibid.
5. Allan Bloom, *The Closing of the American Mind*, Hebrew translation (Tel Aviv: Am Oved, 2002), p.294.
6. Yehezkel Koifman (his Hebrew name spellings), *History of the Israeli Faith*, Vol.1, in Hebrew (Tel Aviv: Dvir Publishing House, 1954).
7. Ibid., p.64. For a moral-philosophical critique of Arendt's argument see Elhanan Yakira, *Post-Zionism, Post Holocaust, Three Essays on Denial, Forgetting, and Delegitimation of Israel* (New York: Cambridge University Press, 2009).
8. In Keren, *Ben-Gurion and the Intellectuals.*
9. The parliamentary faction had no formal power; the governing institutions of Mapai since 1956 were the National Convention, a smaller Party Center elected by the membership, and several executive bodies (the Secretariat, a larger Council and a Political Committee). The members of the Government convened informally when necessary. See Moshe Lissak, chief editor, *The History of the Jewish Community in Eretz Israel since 1882, Israel, the First Decade*, in Hebrew (Jerusalem: The Israel Academy of Sciences and Humanities, 2009), pp.488–97. Next to them was a powerful informal political machine that controlled the membership by trading jobs and other benefits for votes for the party's elected institutions, maintaining party control of the Histadrut, and nominating Mapai candidates in general elections. Ibid., pp.497–500. Eshkol's and Sapir's roles as economic and agricultural leaders gave them a major advantage in controlling the machine whenever necessary.
10. See Shlomo Aronson, *The Politics and Strategy of Nuclear Weapons in the Middle East, Opacity, Theory and Strategy, An Israeli Perspective* (Albany and London: SUNY Press, 1992), chapter 4.
11. See 'Independent Deterrent Force for Israel', editorial, *Jewish Observer and Middle East Review*, 28 December 1962. This journal, which often solicited Peres' views, stated in this editorial that the Cuban missile crisis had demonstrated overtly how hesitant the United States would be to embroil itself in a nuclear war on behalf of interests that it considered marginal, and that Israel understood this. Pursuant to this lesson and its precursor, the Holocaust, however, the Israelis realized that a much smaller and more

sophisticated deterrent, one that was deliberately kept limited from the potential aggressor's standpoint, was crucial for their security and existence.

12. On the State Department's actions, the President's directives, and Ben-Gurion's responses to them, and on my sources, obtained thanks to the assistance of Dr Oded Brosh, mostly from the Kennedy Archives in Boston and in smaller part of Israeli origin, see Aronson, *The Politics and Strategy of Nuclear Weapons*, pp.296ff.
13. Source of Gazit's title: http://www.gwu.edu/~nsarchiv/israel/documents/first/index.html.
14. On McCloy's mission, see Aronson, *The Politics and Strategy of Nuclear Weapons*, pp.79–92, n.317–20.
15. Statement by nuclear scientist Professor Yuval Ne'eman to the author.
16. Bar-Zohar, *Ben-Gurion, A Political Biography*, Vol.III, pp.1522–6; cf. ibid., pp.1554–9.
17. On Ben-Gurion's correspondence with Kennedy and his concurrent appeals to the leaders of other Western powers, see Bar-Zohar, *Ben-Gurion, A Political Biography*. Ambassador Gideon Rafael, a high official in Israel's Foreign Ministry, in an oral communication with this author, added that it was he who had phrased Ben-Gurion's messages. Their purpose, he said, was to justify the Dimona project, which was Ben-Gurion's principal concern at the time.
18. Notably, quite a few Arab newspapers alleged at the time that Israel had been behind the President's assassination.
19. See *Foreign Relations of the United States* (hereafter referred to as *FRUS*), Vol. XVIII, *Arab-Israeli Dispute 1964–1967* (Washington, DC: US Government Printing Office, 2000), pp.1–2.
20. On Eshkol's New Economic Programme, see Yossi Goldstein, *Eshkol – A Biography* (Jerusalem: Keter, 2003), pp.372–7.
21. *FRUS*, Vol. XVIII, pp.502ff.
22. This author, at the time the Israeli Broadcasting Authority's correspondent in Germany, was warned not to continue his negative coverage of the German scientists' story due to the damage that it might inflict on secret German–Israeli cooperation in 'scientific matters'. Since the official Israeli criticism in this regard continued as before, State Secretary Karl-Günter von Hase, the Chief Government Spokesman, referred to it in a press conference. The newspaper *Frankfurter Rundschau* interpreted his remarks as relating to nuclear research.
23. Israel State Archives, *Levi Eshkol, the Third Prime Minister of Israel, Selected Documents on Chapters in His Life,* in Hebrew (Jerusalem: Israel State Archives, 2002), pp.464–5.
24. Memorandum for Record dated 10 January 1964, Meeting between National Security Advisor McGeorge Bundy et al. and Israeli Ambassador Avraham Harman et al. regarding Israeli Arms Needs, *FRUS,* pp.11–13.
25. *FRUS*, Vol. XVIII, pp.329–31.
26. Ibid., pp.33–4.
27. See Yitzhak Greenberg, 'Creation of the Foundations for R&D and Defence Production: Policy and Budgeting Aspects', *'Iyyunim bi-tequmat Yisrael, Studies in Zionism, the Yishuv and the State of Israel, A Research Annual*, Vol.9, in Hebrew (Sede Boqer: Ben-Gurion Research Center, Ben-Gurion University of the Negev Press, 1999), pp.167–87.
28. Interviews with Dr Zvi Elpeleg, Dayan Center, Tel Aviv University. Lt Col Elpeleg is a veteran military governor and a scholar of the post-1967 occupation regime in the West Bank and Gaza.
29. Grechko visited Cairo in December 1965; a report that the USSR would guarantee Egypt's security if Israel were to develop or obtain nuclear arms appeared in *The New York Times* in early 1966.
30. Former transport minister Yitzhak Ben-Aharon, in interview with this author.
31. Yuval Ne'eman, 'Why I Resigned from MOD', *Ha'aretz*, 6 February 1966.
32. Interview by the author with Ze'ev Sheck, Israel's envoy in Paris at the time. Sheck spoke explicitly about the 'medium-range missile' and regarded its continued current

development by France as a principal test of the soundness of relations between de Gaulle and Israel.

33. On Dayan and his published writings at the time, see Aronson, *The Politics and Strategy of Nuclear Weapons in the Middle East*, revised and updated Hebrew version, Vol. B (Jerusalem: Academon, 2006), p.17.
34. In this matter, see Michael Brecher, *Decisions in Israel's Foreign Policy* (New Haven, CT: Yale University Press, 1975), p.332, and cf. Gazit's detailed and even-handed study, partly based on primary sources from the John F. Kennedy Presidential Library and Museum in Boston: Mordechai Gazit, *President Kennedy's Policy toward the Arab States and Israel* (Tel Aviv: Shiloah Center for Middle Eastern and African Studies, Tel Aviv University, 1983).
35. Exchange with Professor Brecher in 1976 (no exact date).
36. Department of State, Cable 737A, 11 April 1964, on US–Egypt relations (Secret). Source: Lyndon Baines Johnson Presidential Library and Museum, Austin, TX, NSF (National Security Files) UAR – Container 158, Item 39. Badeau was a typical 'Arabist' who had served as president of the American University in Cairo before entering the US Foreign Service.
37. Limited circulation. Source: ibid, NSF, Committee on Nuclear Proliferation, Container 1–2, Problem 2, Item 1.
38. Diplomatic Cable 2447, sent to Vienna on 26 June 1964, to International Atomic Energy Agency in a circular to all Arab capitals (classified Confidential). Source: UPA microfilms, Israel: National Security Files 1963–1969, K4-128b [Kathy], Library of Congress Microfilm Reading Room, 86-89264 (85-4561 MICRR).
39. Uri Yizhar, *Between Vision and Power, The History of the Ahdut-ha-'Avoda Po'alei Tsiyyon Party*, in Hebrew (Efal: Yad Tabenkin, 2005), p.313.
40. Secretary of State Dean Rusk to President Johnson. Source: Johnson Library, Austin, TX, UAR (Egypt), Containers 159–161, Cables, Vol. 2, Item 99a.J.
41. The visit took place in late 1965, even though the wording of the nuclear 'guarantee' that Moscow would give Egypt, if Israel were to 'develop' or 'obtain' nuclear arms, did not appear in the *New York Times* until early 1966.
42. Previously Komer had been involved in simulation games that were set up by Thomas Schelling of the Rand Corporation, a renowned social scientist and activist against nuclear proliferation. In this matter and on the firm stance against nuclear proliferation of McGeorge Bundy, national security advisor to Presidents Kennedy and Johnson, see Aronson, *The Politics and Strategy of Nuclear Weapons in the Middle East*, Vol. A (Jerusalem: Academon, 1994), p.155 and sources *ad loc*.
43. Yitzhak Rabin, *Service Notes*, in Hebrew (Tel Aviv: Sifriyat Ma'ariv, 1979), pp.129–30.
44. On Israel–German relations at the time, see Aronson, *The Politics and Strategy of Nuclear Weapons in the Middle East*, Vol. B, pp.45–51.
45. See cable US Embassy in Egypt (signed by the Ambassador, Lucius Battle), no. 2379, sterilized wording (without names), Johnson Library, NSF, UAR File, Containers 159–161, Item 20.
46. Efraim Evron, subsequently Israel Ambassador to the United Kingdom, to the author.
47. Johnson Library, NSF, UAR File, Containers 159–161, Item 6.
48. Ibid., Item 21a.
49. US Arms Control and Disarmament Agency, memorandum about a talk on the prospects of a non-proliferation accord and related matters, 13 July 1965, for restricted circulation, UPA – Library of Congress, copies to White House and US embassies in Moscow, Cairo, Paris, UN mission, and Special Ambassador Harriman.

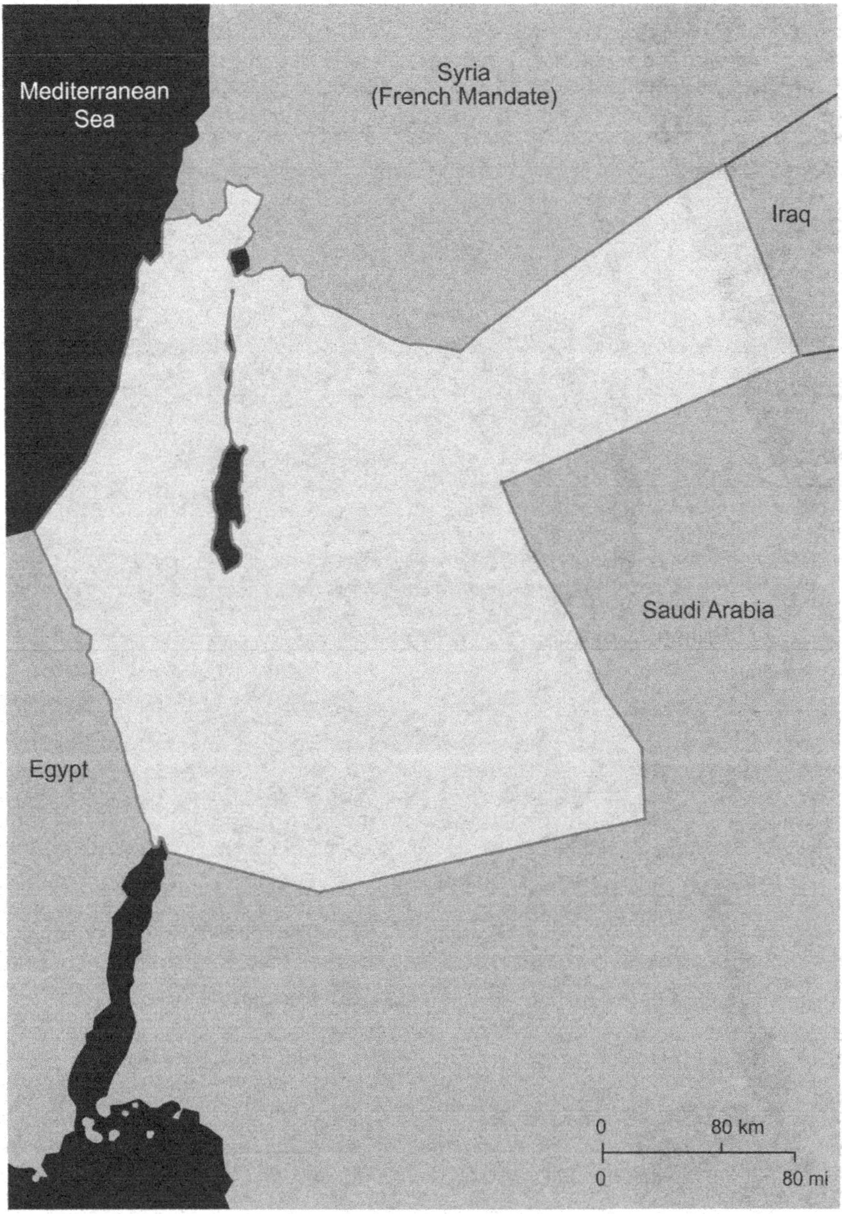

1. British Mandate. Copyright 2003 Koret Communications Ltd.

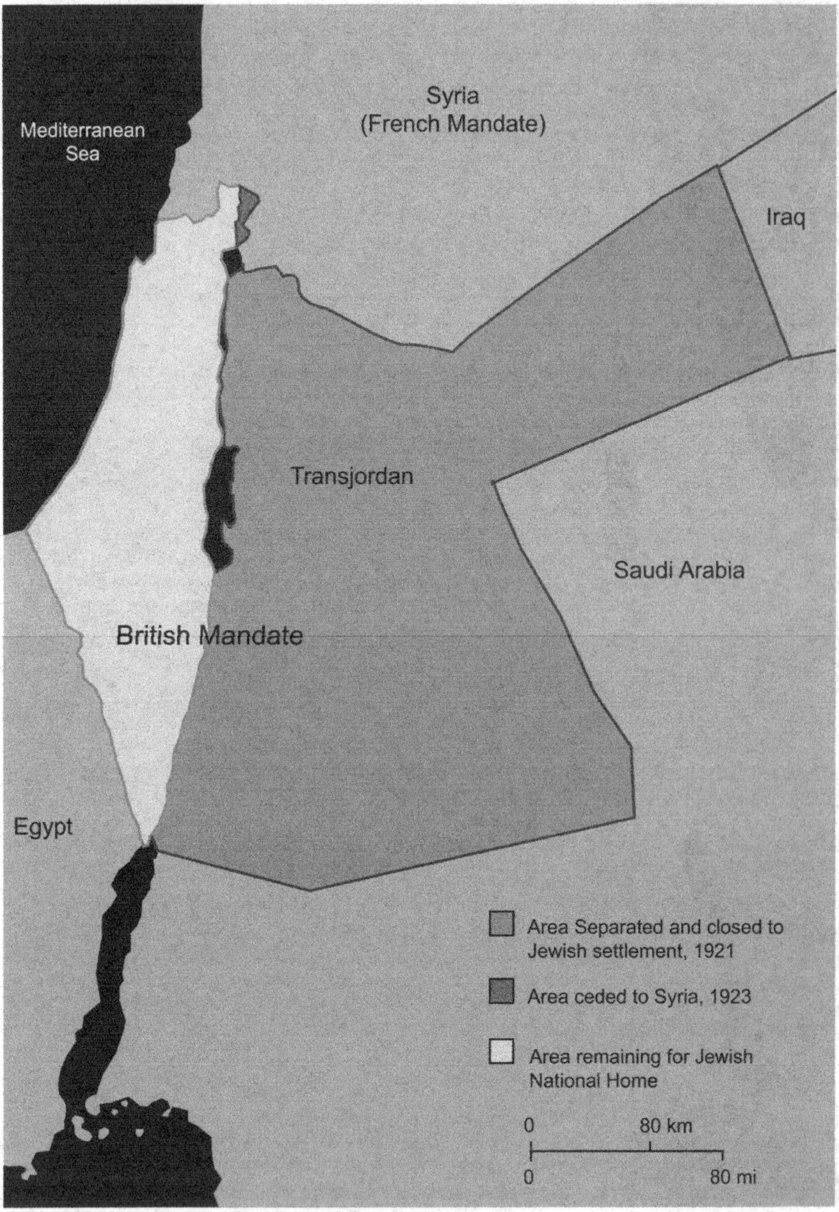

2. 1922: Separation of Transjordan. Copyright 2003 Koret Communications Ltd.

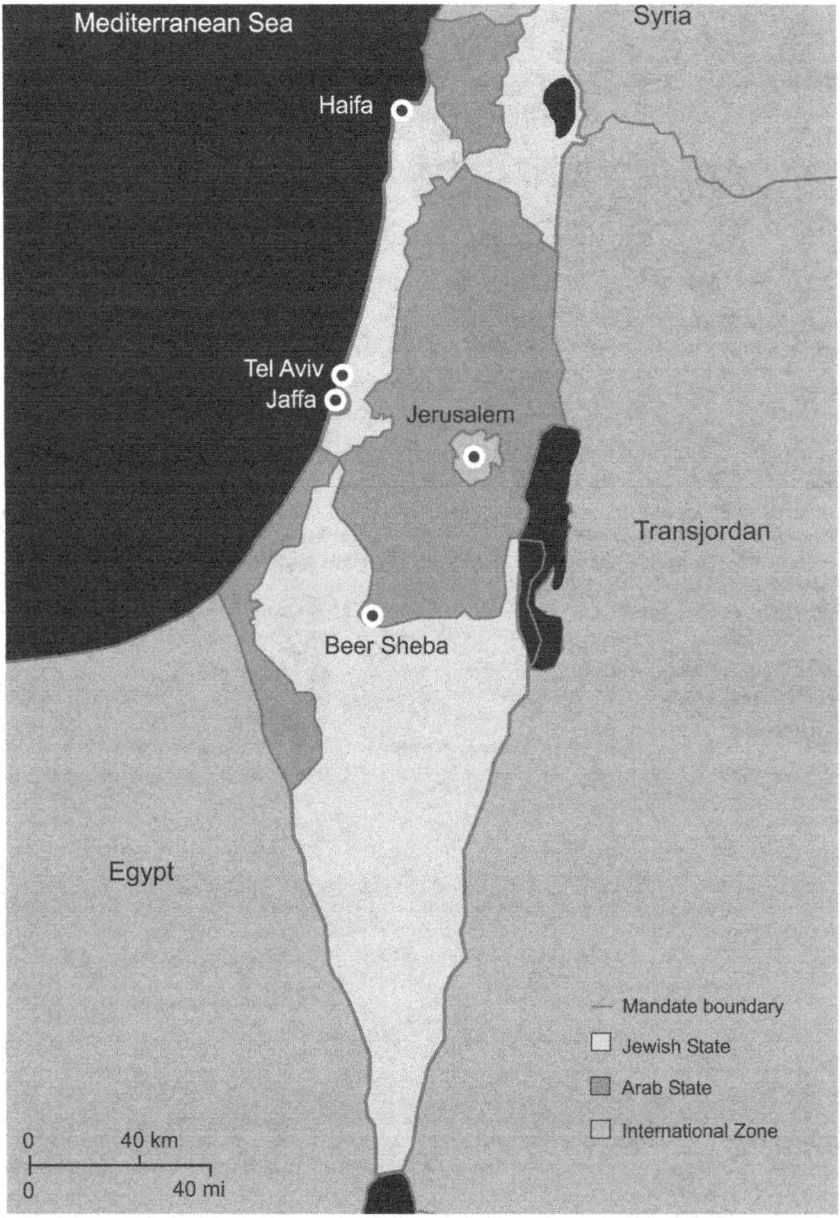

3. 1947 UN Partition plan. Copyright 2003 Koret Communications Ltd.

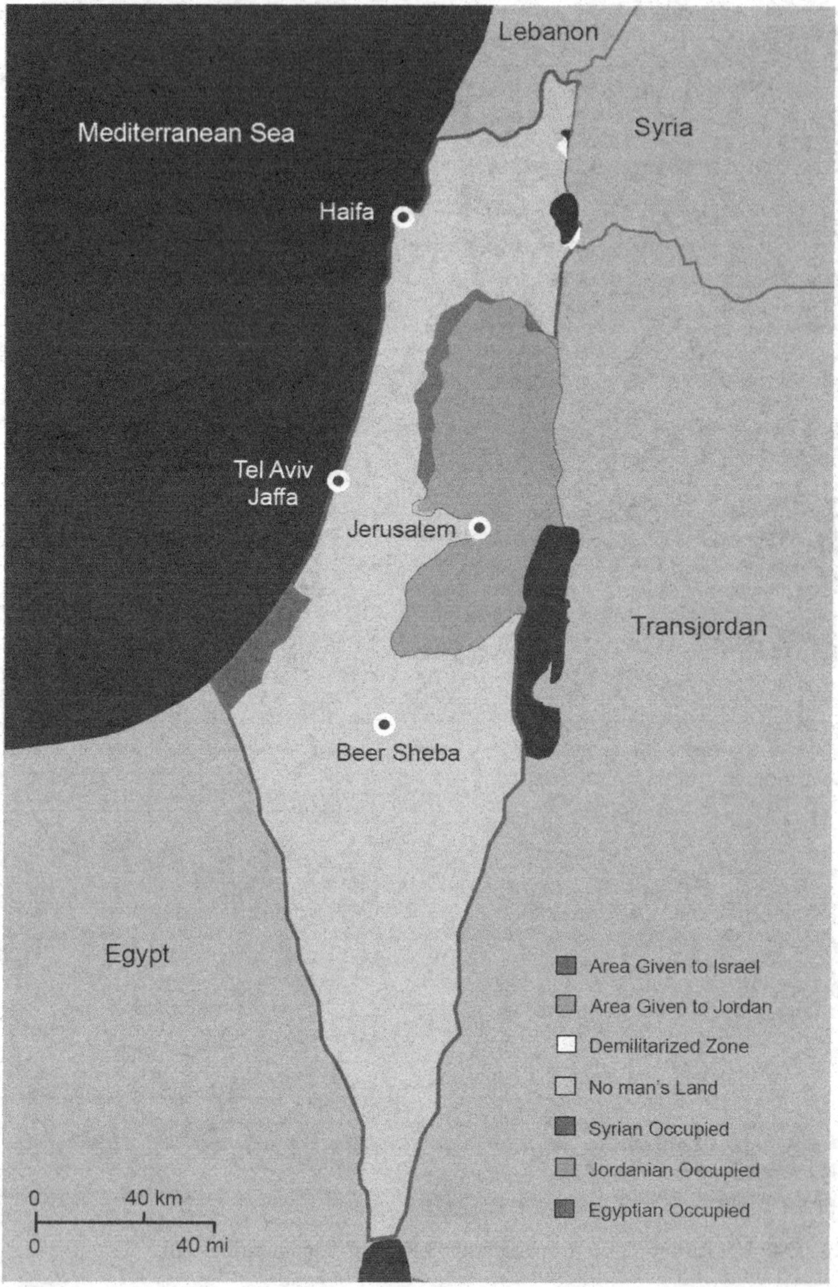

4. 1949 Armistice Lines. Jordan annexed the West Bank, ceding some territory to Israel. Egypt occupied the Gaza Strip. Syria occupied the Hema area. Some territory along the Syrian and the Egyptian lines declared as demilitarized. Copyright 2003 Koret Communications Ltd.

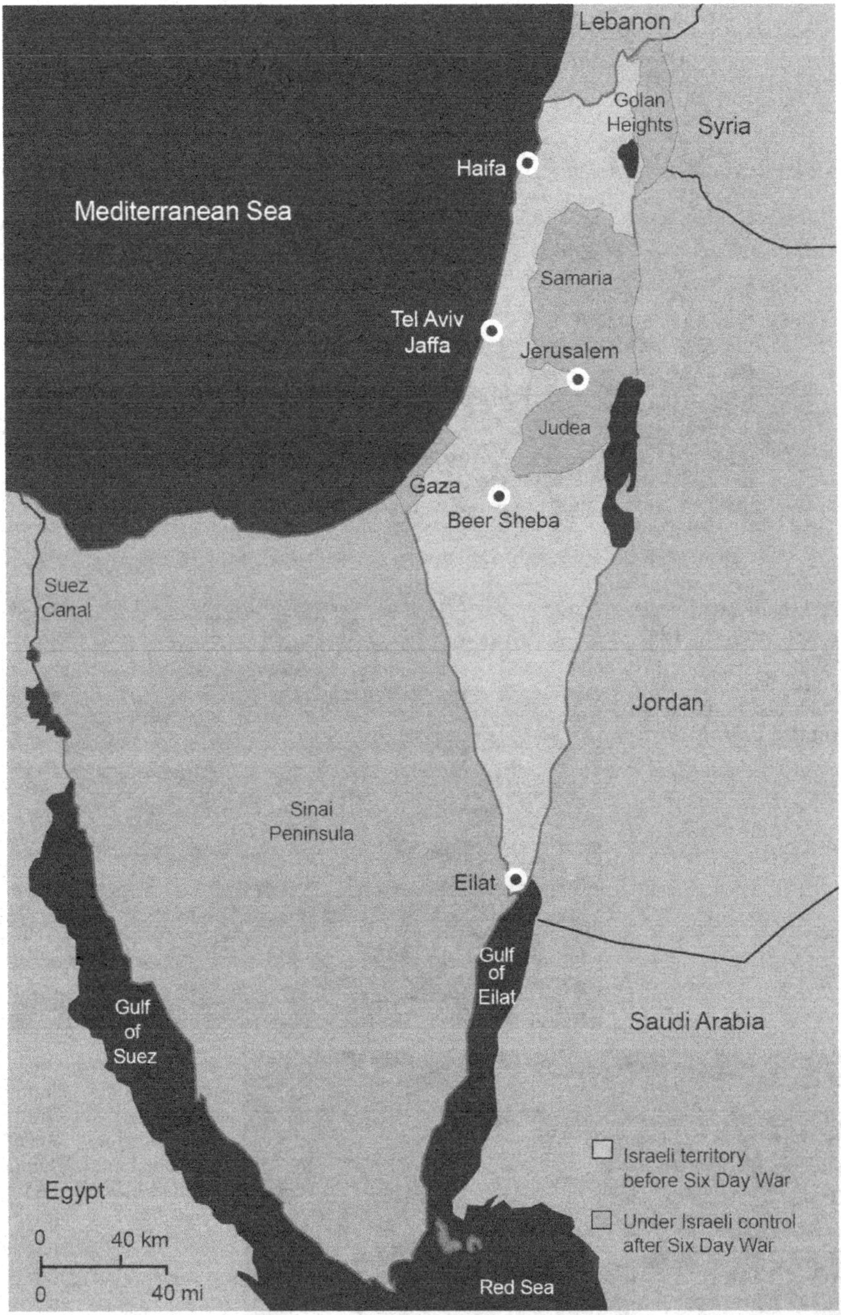

5. Israel's armistice lines before and after June 1967. Copyright 2003 Koret Communications Ltd.

6. Eshkol as a student in Vilnius High School, 1913. Photo courtesy of Am Oved Press, Tel Aviv, published in its Album entitled *Eshkol*, 1965.

7. Eshkol at a Negev water project, 1947. Photo courtesy of Am Oved Press, Tel Aviv, published in its Album entitled *Eshkol*, 1965.

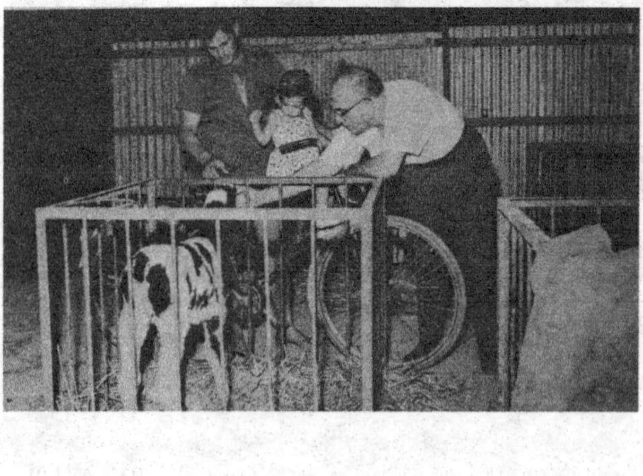

8. Eshkol in a new moshav, 1955. Photo courtesy of Am Oved Press, Tel Aviv, published in its Album entitled *Eshkol*, 1965.

9. Eshkol with Yemenite settlers, mid-1950s. Photo courtesy of Am Oved Press, Tel Aviv, published in its Album entitled *Eshkol*, 1965.

10. Eshkol breaks the ground for a new moshav, late 1950s. Photo courtesy of the Israel National Fund, Jerusalem.

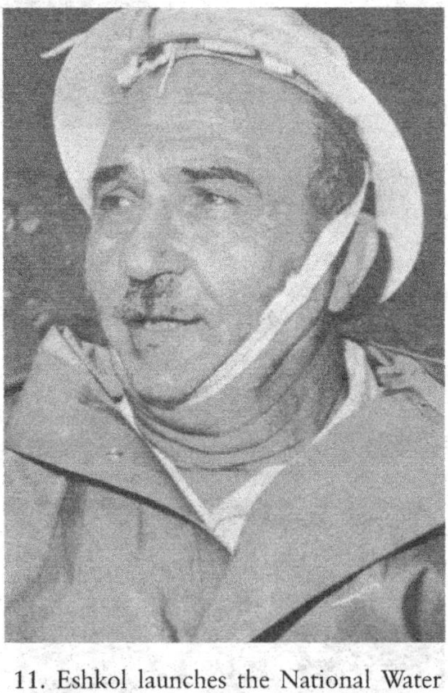

11. Eshkol launches the National Water Carrier, 1962. Photo courtesy of Am Oved Press, Tel Aviv, published in its Album entitled *Eshkol*, 1965.

12. Defence Minister Eshkol surveys a bombed kibbutz from the Syrian Golan Heights on the eve of the Six Day War, 1966. Photo courtesy of the Israel National Fund, Jerusalem.

13. Prime Minister Eshkol with his 'friend' President Johnson, Miriam Eshkol and Lady Bird Johnson, mid-1960s. Photo courtesy of the Israel National Fund, Jerusalem.

14. The Prime Minister is invited to visit the Wailing Wall, June 1967. Photo courtesy of the Israel National Fund, Jerusalem.

Chapter Seven

Eshkol Response to a Stormy Period

THE GENERATION-GAP COALITION

There is no final, documented way of knowing how the powers' manoeuvres affected Eshkol's Government. One may conjecture that the Ahdut ha-'Avoda ministers, Galili and Allon – long apprehensive about a Soviet response to the French missiles and disparaging of the nuclear deterrent at the end of the Ben-Gurion era – had reached the general conclusion that Israel would do best not to deploy the missiles and, perhaps, should content itself with aircraft. One option in that regard would be the French craft already in Israel's possession that could deliver nuclear payloads to short ranges. Another might be the American Skyhawk, which Washington had offered. Its use for such purposes would be forbidden. Alternately, to the minds of Galili and Allon, Israel should at least 'slow Dimona and the missile projects down'[1] in favour of conventional deterrence and compellence. Building on the assumption that modern conventional warfare would always leave the Arabs behind the IDF, both ministers would opt for better boundaries as security zones; ideologically, this had been their party's most important obligation since the pre-state days. Eshkol himself accepted the American inspection visits to Dimona at roughly this time and even decided to 'civilianize' the Atomic Energy Commission and forgo the services of Professor Ernest David Bergmann, the commission's veteran chairman since Ben-Gurion's days and, in Washington's eyes, a longstanding symbol of Israel's quest for the bomb. This clutch of measures did create the impression that Israel had downscaled, if not scrapped, its nuclear programme.

One cannot know whether, at least in regard to the missiles, Israel's actions did much to free the Egyptians of their apprehensions about the bomb. They did believe that Israel possessed nothing but a few antiquated French subsonic bombers and, in all probability, had no aircraft advanced enough to threaten the Aswan High Dam and the delta – and, by extension, Soviet targets – as seriously as a medium range ballistic missile could. One doubts, however, that the Egyptians believed that Israel had truly written off the missiles; therefore, the delivery date in 1967 became critical from their standpoint and possibly from a Soviet one as well. Since the Egyptian archives are not accessible to scholars, we cannot ascertain the Egyptians' considerations. The Soviet aspect of this complex will be discussed shortly. The Government of Israel, however, could not afford a hiatus such as this, since in 1965 its crossing of the nuclear threshold became an official Egyptian *casus belli*, as Nasser said again in 1966 despite the American inspection visits to Dimona. At this time, the Eshkol Government hid this *casus belli* from the Israeli public by making extensive use of the military censor and the media. However, when the Egyptian army made its sudden thrust into the Sinai in May 1967, and when Egyptian photo reconnaissance flights over Dimona immediately followed, the Government – unaware that the Egyptian MiG 25 jets were manned by Soviet pilots, whose role will be discussed below – had to determine the reasons for these actions and to weigh counter-measures, all of which without the public correctly understanding – to this day – the true reasons for the Government's concern and its protracted hesitancy.

Before we bid farewell to 1965, however, we should remember that this was the year when el Fatah embarked on its Vietnam- and Algeria-style guerrilla operations from Syria via Jordan, which severely troubled the IDF high command. Under Lt Gen. Rabin, the IDF was preparing to meet conventional challenges and was much more concerned about a Vietnam-inspired guerrilla onslaught by Yasser Arafat and other Palestinian organizations, based on and supported by the radical Syrian regime, than a half-baked nuclear deterrent.

It was also in 1965 that Ben-Gurion returned to political life, established the Rafi (Israel Workers List) Party, brought Dayan back from the wilderness, forced Shimon Peres to join him, and tackled Eshkol head on at the ballot box. Rafi engraved a large collection of slogans on its standard: restoring public life to health in view of the handling of 'the Affair', instilling proper *mamlakhtiyut* ('state-worthy' behaviour) in the spirit of Ben-Gurion's government reform, and so on. Cognoscenti, however, called Rafi 'the nuclear party'. Eshkol met the Rafi challenge by, among other things, mobilizing a group called 'Citizens for Eshkol', to which Ben-Gurion's 'intellectual' enemies since the days of the battle over Lavon and many others belonged. These 'citizens' viewed Eshkol's persona and style as a sort of guarantee against what they considered Ben-Gurion's authoritarian method of rule and as a promise for a more democratic form of government.

In the 1965 elections, Rafi came away with ten Knesset seats – quite a failure relative to the pretensions of a party headed by David Ben-Gurion. Levi Eshkol reassembled a centre-left coalition with Ahdut ha-'Avoda and Mapam, the leftist dovish party, after the former faction had joined a parliamentary 'Alignment' with Mapai without risking its status at the ballot box and continually retaining the option of seceding from the Alignment – to the immense rage of Ben-Gurion, who loathed such manipulations in the party constellation. Indeed, the Alignment had reserved the small faction's seats in the Knesset without elections and allowed it to secede from Mapai, the larger party at any time, or to threaten to do so in order to promote its own goals when such were incompatible with the views of the larger faction. On top of this, the Alignment's power has been based upon the Histadrut, which had become very much the guardian of the power and privileges of organized labour and the unions that controlled most of the nation's key services and many industries. Dayan and Peres had criticized this state of affairs in public back in 1959, without Ben-Gurion's explicit support, but the limits of social democracy based on a number of old-fashioned yet powerful bureaucracies supported by partially corrupt multiparty political alignments had become a fixture in Israeli politics, and so it would remain at least until the political system was reformed.

Having won the 1965 elections, Eshkol found himself in the middle of a problematic coalition. Most of his ministers, especially those from the National Religious Party (NRP), made many demands on domestic religious matters, but were relatively moderate – much more than Eshkol himself – on foreign affairs and security. Only Galili and Allon of Ahdut ha-'Avoda, true to Allon's 'deterrence-conventional compellence' doctrine, were more ready to take action under the circumstances than Eshkol was. This coalition structure, however, to which Eshkol added two more 'dovish' parties, would impair his own freedom of action as Rafi, and foremost Mr Peres, flayed his foreign and security policies mercilessly.[2]

Concurrently, the establishment of the centre-left Alignment brought an old fear of Ben-Gurion's to fruition: the relatively moderate Right, embodied in the Liberal Party as it was known back then, now established an alignment of its own with Menachem Begin's Herut movement (named Gahal, signifying 'Herut–Liberals'); by implication, the spineless Liberals fell into the snare of the populist-nationalist Right. Indeed, the Liberals' action rescued Begin from the political wilderness into which Ben-Gurion had manoeuvred him and created a parliamentary infrastructure for the changes that the Six Day War would bring on. The political instrument of Ben-Gurion's own creation, Rafi, would also slip from his control and become a factor of the highest order on the eve and in the aftermath of the war.

At home, after Eshkol's electoral victory, 1965 saw the beginning of a move to restrain and stabilize the economy after the election year. The intolerable length of an Israeli election campaign, among other factors, had forced the incumbent Government to avoid the necessary economic corrections required due to the high rate of inflation and the deteriorating balance of payments that its own policy of economic expansion at all costs until after the elections had caused. When Eshkol now sought to restore control over the economy, however, a severe recession ensued – the first of its kind in a society whose upper crust had become accustomed to a perpetually rising standard of living. Although one cannot say that this slice of society had attained genuine affluence, the unexpected recession took a toll on its morale. An additional outcome of the recession, growing unemployment that badly hit the underprivileged newcomers from the Muslim countries, hardly commanded the attention of Eshkol and his Finance Minister, Sapir, at first.[3]

Eshkol's decision-making strategy was based upon endless consultations with his aides, his coalition partners, and many figures relevant to his final decision, including those who did not accept his own views or compromises. When done, he presented his decision by announcing that this or that would be done according to 'my humble, decisive, opinion'. Once he finally made up his mind, however – as Yosef (Yossi) Sarid, his spokesperson during his days as Mapai's boss, described it – Eshkol could be extremely tough and uncompromising, transforming his decision to a matter of personal prestige. He made extensive use of the press, leaking information to eager reporters while complaining about leaks from his own Government meetings. Generally, his style was more modern and democratic than, say, Ben-Gurion's, based on political horse-trading; at the same time it was quite patriarchal, as Eshkol was prone to keeping sensitive issues largely to himself. His responsibilities spread so far and wide that one would only expect him to make bad compromises or exercise lax control over issues that escaped his attention, such as the Ben Barka affair in France, to which we shall return, and the need to keep Chief of General Staff Rabin under control. On top of this, from 1965 on Eshkol managed his court in a strictly personal fashion as a perpetual battlefield against Ben-Gurion and the latter's political partners, Dayan and Peres. This acted in favour of Ben-Gurion's old rivals, Allon and Galili of Ahdut ha-'Avoda, who were not only Rabin's mentors but also Eshkol's official partners in his two-party bloc in the Knesset.

In due course, this modus operandi invited criticism from a biting, competitive press, which Eshkol courted, and also responses by his ruthless young spokesman, Yossi Sarid, who labelled Ben-Gurion 'an old tyrant' and attempted to tar him as semi-racist in his attitudes toward Israelis who had emigrated from Arab countries. Although Sarid lost that case,[4] it was only the first round in a remarkable career. Sarid, Mapai's spokesman in 1964–66, was a protégé of Finance Minister Sapir who had been exposed to Sapir's intrigues and behind-the-scenes machinations. He performed his duties in fresh *sabra* Hebrew, tossed inhibitions to the wind, and cantilevered these qualities, which earned him the nickname of the 'national snake' from his political adversaries and victims, into a political career of his own. His method was based on media smearing and behind-the-scenes manipulation of politicians against each other, as Sapir himself had tried to do when he restarted the Lavon affair in 1960.

Even Sarid, however, could hardly plug Eshkol and Sapir into a new generation of Israelis. For one thing, the Ashkenazi youth considered Eshkol's partisan wheeling and dealing irrelevant to the new progressive era of the 1960s. For another, Eshkol was wearing out. His electoral victory in 1965 was followed by the serious aggravation of a heart condition, entailing lengthy periods of hospitalization. He carried an almost inhuman workload as economic czar, a defence minister who spent much time resolving issues of procurement and its financing, not to mention many visits to IDF bases, a prime minister in charge of Israel's security services at home and abroad, the civilian boss of the Israel Atomic Energy Commission, the chairman of Mapai, and the chief negotiator in assembling the post-election coalition – a very time-consuming task also thanks to his style of decision-making.

THE DOER ENGINEERS A RECESSION

Once his coalition was in place, Eshkol decided, in consultation with David Horowitz the veteran Governor of the Bank of Israel, and his own 'Patinkin kids', to put the economy through a controlled slowdown. The overheating that he had engineered in order to win the election had created growing wage demands due to high inflation, continued expectations of only upward movement in the standard of living – at least among members of organized labour and other veteran population groups – and a threatening gap in the balance of payments. The necessary antidote had been worked out before the elections, and Eshkol and Sapir now administered it: less construction, smaller capital imports, exposure to competing imports, and a major cutback in government spending – except for Eshkol's dream of desalinating water by using nuclear energy in cooperation with the United States, which, however, was on hold until Israel would join the Non-Proliferation Treaty (NPT), which it has not done to this day.

Did Eshkol hope that his endorsement of the American inspection visits at Dimona would suffice to allow such cooperation, and did it contribute to his decision to 'slow down' the Dimona project in this connection? The answer is not clear and little came of it anyway. A decision to slow the work at Dimona had been made, but its machers were Galili and Allon, according to the historian of their political party. The two Ahdut ha-'Avoda ministers – like Eshkol himself – focused on Israel's conventional preparedness and, as Eshkol would soon learn, on a conventional war of pre-emption. Finding himself harshly criticized by Ben-Gurion's Rafi Party regarding the American inspection visits at Dimona, Eshkol did his best to make the visits ineffective while securing conventional American military aid. In so doing, he piqued American suspicions and threats from Washington to leave Israel to its own devices should the Arabs decide to fight it on account of Dimona – a point that we return to below.

In the meantime, Eshkol's attention was riveted on the recession that followed his austerity programme. The relevant numbers were indeed alarming: in 1965, the deficit on balance-of-payments account ballooned by about 80 per cent; a series of strikes, typical of an election year, prompted huge wage increases in the bloated public sector; immigration plummeted; and many immigrants left the country. The defence budget and, especially, procurement outlays grew enormously and to pay for them the government borrowed growing sums from abroad. Major programmes such as the National Water Carrier, a new port in Ashdod, and the modernization of the Dead Sea Works, not to mention Dimona, had been completed, and nothing new was offered to restrain rampant unemployment, especially with government spending having been slashed. The high rate of inflation pushed direct and indirect taxes upward, the development budget went almost entirely on payback of foreign loans, and food subsidies were slashed. All this brought the Government under growing criticism in the Knesset and even in Mapai's own governing institutions. Various intellectuals still backed Eshkol in his battle with Ben-Gurion; some of them, such as the economist Don Patinkin, the historian Yehoshua Arieli, and the sociologist S.N. Eisenstadt, even founded a group that called for voluntary reduction of salaries in the public sector provided that the Government would curb the high rate of inflation. The Government responded by reducing its spending and taxation a bit. Taking to the airwaves, Eshkol justified his economic measures by stressing that the Israeli standard of living had skyrocketed in the past five years or, to be more precise, since he had assumed the premiership. The irresponsible quest for the individual good life, he continued, threatened the nation so badly as to justify unpopular measures that aimed to boost exports and curb imports.

Eshkol's strictures dealt the weak strata a particularly dire blow.

The immigrants from Muslim countries who had congregated in development towns in the south and in the north had an unemployment rate in excess of 20 per cent. As if their sense of discrimination at the hands of the veteran European elite were not enough, Israel had no unemployment insurance at the time, meaning that the recession plunged this group into real misery that almost totally escaped Eshkol's attention. His Mapai had indeed become the party of the established upper classes and had begun to shed its original social-democratic character, portending the decline of the Labour Party later on. In the meantime, the unemployed demonstrated in Dimona, Ashdod and Jerusalem in what spiralled into violent confrontations with the police. The intellectuals' movement in favour of voluntary salary reductions disappeared. As emigration outpaced immigration, a bitter quip circulated: 'Will the last one out of the country turn off the lights at the airport?' Eshkol's popularity sank dramatically, manifested in the publication of a booklet sarcastically titled *All Eshkol's Jokes*. The butt of these jokes saw no choice but to keep up the austerity programme and toss the unemployed a few ineffective measures of relief. In fact, the Government had lost control of the recession, which would end only after the Six Day War of June 1967 and largely as a result of it. Abroad, the economic decline invited some, foremost the Arabs and the Soviets, to view the country as a failed experiment. This would contribute its share to the outbreak of the 1967 war, as we discuss below.

In the meantime, Eshkol did what unpopular leaders regularly do: set his sights abroad. He embarked on a round of state visits in Africa, reaping the rewards of the efforts of Golda Meir, his erstwhile foreign minister, to forge good relations with, and offer development aid to, the newly independent countries in that continent. Eshkol also turned his attention to the European Common Market, whose evolution into a growing economic bloc he followed with much interest. He and Finance Minister Sapir envisioned full membership in the Common Market or, barring that, preferential agreements with the new association and, possibly, with the United States. The problems here were twofold: political issues related to allowing a non-European nation to join the Common Market, and the dilemma of how to accommodate Israel's government-controlled, highly bureaucratized economy with the relative free-market principles of the European community. It would be quite a domestic challenge to renounce Mapai's instruments of power and those of the Histadrut, even if the conclusion of limited preferential agreements made these measures only partly necessary, in view of the growing trouble created by the deepening recession. Indeed, by early 1967 unemployment had reached such a peak as to lend credibility to the criticism that Ben-Gurion, Dayan and Peres were levelling against Eshkol's foreign and security policies. Eshkol's strength in the increasingly gloomy domain of defence had become susceptible to challenge due to repeated guerrilla operations by Syrian-based Palestinians and Syrian shelling of Israeli settlements when inhabitants of these settlements cultivated disputed frontier areas – areas that Eshkol, the settler, had opened to cultivation. At first, Eshkol responded to the guerrilla acts by saying that 'the book is open, and the hand is taking notes'. In other words, he preferred not to respond to the challenge at all, at least for the time being, thus generating much public resentment.

STAYING THE COURSE

As for the style of his leadership, Eshkol remained clever and humorous, self-confident and seemingly untouched by the gathering clouds. As far as the contents of his leadership was concerned, ideologically and culturally it was hollow compared with Ben-Gurion. He had no real message to communicate in terms of Ben-Gurion's old vision. The only alternative vision he offered was the maintenance of a previously successful, unchanged political and spiritual reality since he took over – a reality that slowly came under attack as the new breezes from America and Britain of the 1960s encountered a population cringing under domestic troubles and security challenges. It was precisely this that had prompted many Israelis who had tired of Ben-Gurion's constant admonishments about diminishing spiritual commitments and moral demands, plus his warnings that the existing multiparty system might make Israel ungovernable, to take pleasure in Eshkol for a while. Eshkol, too, had started out as a practical pioneering founding father but had evolved into an establishmentarian in his partisan interests who nevertheless fulfilled a quest for change that many Israelis appreciated. Now Israeli society, a 'mobilized society' until then, was left to pursue new interests and absorb the spirit of the 1960s, flowing in from abroad, as best it could, under the baton of a benevolent but uninspiring old-style leader who mixed partisan loyalties with modern economic measures that quickly backfired.

The eclipsing of Eshkol coincided with the decline of Mapai's intellectual leadership, which had been ruptured since 'the Affair', and the growing transformation of the party into a vehicle of the upper classes, costing Mapai its traditional support among the Mizrahi masses and their progeny. It is true that Eshkol and Sapir were mindful of this population group's needs and proposed to meet them by directing new investments to the places where they lived. At the same time, however, these Mapai bosses paid much attention to the established unions and their wage demands. While the Histadrut seemingly guaranteed political control and stability through its control of the healthcare system, vast numbers of jobs, and social and cultural services, it was heedless of the intellectual-psychological vacuum that had come about and the profound change in the behaviour of the young. The offspring of the elite had been raised to join pioneering kibbutzim but were repelled by the communes' rigid doctrinaire priorities, which inhibited their quest for personal progress by attending institutions of higher learning and pursuing individual aspirations. Most of those who had done the leaders' bidding left the collectives in short order, joining academia, the career army, the state service and even the Histadrut's own apparatuses. For them, however, Mapai had ceased to be a source of inspiration; it was but a tool of power.

For some time, the contextual void had been filled by the immense personal grace, cleverness and the twinkling eyes of Levi Eshkol. Now his economic and defence leadership would be put to steadily escalating tests, of which his Government told the population nothing due to the secrecy involved, the ongoing negotiations over sensitive security matters, and the policy of undeclared threats vis-à-vis the Arabs, in response to Arab threats and actual acts of aggression.

BEHIND ESHKOL'S BACK

We noted a visit to Dimona by American inspectors in 1965 that was leaked to the American press, justifying Israel's fears of an

Arab attack against Dimona rather then calming the Arab side down. Another American visit ensued in March 1966; this one seemed conclusive as no plutonium separation plant was found. Still, the Americans were not wholly satisfied; they feared some dark side to the Dimona story.

On 7 January 1966, the *New York Times* published an article by John W. Finney, which stated, among other things, 'The United States believes Israel ordered 30 intermediate-range ballistic missiles from France, a move seen as indicating an intention to develop atomic weapons.'

In April 1966, the legendary chairman of the Israeli Atomic Energy Commission, Professor Ernst D. Bergmann, resigned from his post. Bergmann was known to have been the 'father of the Israeli bomb', at least in the spiritual sense, and had chaired the commission, which had been subordinate to the MOD, since the early 1950s. Now Eshkol reconstituted the commission under the PMO as if it were something in opposition to the MOD, seemingly making it not only a new commission but also a civilian one.

We now consult the Public Records Office (PRO) documentation on these moves and secret talks about them among British, Israeli and American officials. The records paint an apparently confused picture of the Israeli intentions, American activities and Arab reactions to the public and behind-the-scenes American manoeuvres.

We have at our disposal the British documentation pertaining to the Dimona complex in consultation with the Americans, now, following Eshkol's elections victory of 1965, having appointed Mr Abba Eban, a well known dove, to serve as his Foreign Minister. According to the British records, Mr Eban was quoted as if, as foreign minister, he seemed to have given – may already have given – 'watertight private safeguards to the Americans about Dimona,[5] i.e., safeguards which will permit the Americans to do proper inspections, and *possibly use them to give private assurances to the Egyptians*' (italics added). By implication, the Americans were trying to avoid war over the Dimona issue. Mr Morris of the Foreign Office in the same document went on to say,

> Mr Bergmann of the Israel Atomic Energy Authority told Mr Beith [another British official] last year that he believed that

> Eban had sold the pass to the Americans and said so as one who quite openly held the view that Israel should keep the nuclear option. Mr Eban said when he was here in February that Israel could not give IAEA safeguards because of 'parliamentary' objections, but he made satisfactory arrangements for American inspections.
>
> We know that the 'parliamentary' objections are real – it is a euphemism for the government's reluctance to face violent attacks from Ben-Gurion, Peres, Rafi [their political party] generally who lose no opportunity of accusing Mr Eshkol and Mr Eban of spinelessness.

Indeed, following the 1965 elections and mainly during 1966, Ben-Gurion openly accused Eshkol of various 'security blunders' of the utmost significance, without going into details, declaring him unworthy to continue serving the country as Minister of Defence. One of these blunders may have been the so-called Ben Barka affair, an intelligence failure in France that occurred due to Eshkol's vague, typically unclear instructions given to the Israeli Foreign Intelligence Service in this regard, which had prompted President de Gaulle to order a general inquiry on the depth and ramifications of French–Israeli military cooperation and that may have endangered the delivery of the missiles, if they were ready.[6] Another possible blunder was the 1965 American inspection deal, followed by the second inspection visit in March 1966 and Bergmann's resignation in April 1966 which, to Ben-Gurion's mind, as I interpret it, had damaged Dimona's deterrent value. After all, he may have reasoned, nuclear weapons were a psychological-political weapon. If their own owners deny their legitimate existence when ready to the minimum degree, their deterrent use is diminished accordingly. A third possibility was Eshkol's assurance that the medium range missiles would not be deployed during the next two to three years. If the missiles were ready for delivery in 1967, their non-deployment would render Israel's deterrent almost dead while Dimona would remain a justified target for Egyptian attack; after all, since neither the Americans nor the British fully believed the 'private' American assurances, Egypt surely would not believe them either. Thus, the American inspections aggravated key Israeli politicians, failed to satisfy the Arabs – especially Ahmed Shuqairy's Egyptian-supported

PLO, which hysterically called for war before Israel went nuclear[7] – and left 1967 as a crossroads for the delivery of the missiles. According to Morris of the Foreign Office,

> Another point is that Mr Komer of the White House told Sir Roger Allen [a British high official] in February that he thought one way of stopping the Israelis making a bomb was to be generous with conventional arms – hence their attempts to sell British bombers last year, and their decision to sell [American] bombers now.
>
> All this evidence, however, can be interpreted the other way round. *As one of those wanting to keep the nuclear option, Mr Bergmann's best tactics would be to persuade us that the pass had been sold and that we had nothing more to worry about*. [Italics added.]

Hence, one may add, even the removal of Professor Bergmann would not bluff the Western Allies, let alone the Arabs and the Soviets. Morris continued:

> The plain meaning of Eban's statement here was that the inspections made by the Americans hitherto are all that is required, and *we know them to be unsatisfactory* ... Mr Komer's statement to Sir Roger Allen certainly implied that the Americans were not at that date persuaded that the Israelis had given up the option. [Italics added.]

A handwritten remark, circled by Morris or by one of his Foreign Office readers, added: '*Mr Komer thought they never would*' (italics added).

Hence, in my view, the major issue remaining among Israel, the United States, Egypt and the Soviets was the medium-range missiles. This is because, as I see it, a nuclear Israeli Intermediate Range Ballistic Missile (IRBM) system would have the range to threaten not only the Aswan High Dam – its obvious, main target, as the aforementioned 'Israeli officials' made clear – but also Soviet targets. This, in my view, made Israel into a cause for Soviet threats or at least into a superpower problem.

To test this hypothesis, we should further consult the new records – all British – dealing with the missile issue, and juxtapose their information with oral evidence given to me by Mr Efraim Evron, Israeli Minister in Washington at the time.[8] According to

Evron, Robert Komer threatened Jerusalem with the 'most serious break conceivable' between the United States and Israel 'should the missiles be deployed'. Hence, in my view, the bomber offer was made. After all, the 'bombers' in question were short-range A-4 Skyhawks, which could not threaten anything beyond their limited radius of flight and could easily be taken care of by Soviet anti-aircraft guns and missiles in the event that Israel would ignore the expected American precondition that these aircraft must not be used as nuclear platforms. Since the United States was hoping to negotiate an NPT with the Soviets (and did so successfully in 1968), the emergence of a new, however small, nuclear power armed with missiles capable of threatening a superpower was not in the interest of either Washington or Moscow. But obtaining the nuclear option *before* the ratification of the NPT would have been the most urgent Israeli goal since Ben-Gurion's days.

Following the *New York Times'* reportage in January 1966 about the Israeli IRBMs purchased in France, Mr Morris asked the British Embassy in Tel Aviv for its opinion: 'What will happen when the Israelis deploy an effective medium range ballistic missile system (assuming they have no nuclear warheads)?'[9] The ambassador, Michael Hadow, attached an assessment drawn up by his defence and air attachés, according to which they did not expect the Israelis 'to get anything effective from the French in the near future', adding that, 'Apart from the psychological effect, missiles with conventional warheads would not really be a very useful addition to the Israel armory'.

The second part of the letter, however, made it 'all the more difficult to explain away [the] general line taken with you' by Brig. General Aharon Yariv, director of Israel Military Intelligence:

> [Yariv] clearly seems to have suggested that the Israelis expect to be in possession of effective French missiles by the end of the year. I do not know how we resolve this contradiction. It may well be that the whole question is largely a matter of psychological warfare and that the Israelis, as part of their campaign, think there is no harm done if they leave us with the impression that they are going to have a missile system, and fairly soon. In their minds there would be no disadvantage in

> the Arabs learning from British sources that we thought this was the case. This would all be in line with the Israel 'deterrent' philosophy.

The same file contains American speculations that the *Times* story had been leaked to its rapporteur, Mr Finney, either by Abba Eban himself or by Shimon Peres, one of the architects of Dimona, who happened to have been in the United States at that time. In the past, Peres had used John Kimche, editor of the London-based *Jewish Observer and Middle East Review,* to express his view in favour of an Israeli 'economic' nuclear deterrent.[10] In this connection, Ambassador Hadow reported that he had met Kimche recently and

> added my voice to the general chorus abjuring him from writing 'nuclear' pieces about Israel ... The only interesting thing he had to say was that he had seen [General] Yariv and that *Yariv was very worried about the possibility of the Egyptians, at some stage, mounting and carrying out a sort of cutting-out expedition against Dimona* ... Perhaps the theme was started at a time when it looked as if Nasser might pull out of Yemen – and the Israelis were laying advance plans for a situation when the returning heroes of the Yemen were all stationed in Sinai. But all this is very speculative.[11] [Italics added.]

By going on to reject Yariv's worries as unfounded, the British ambassador managed to blind himself to the origins of the Six Day War.

Now when we go back to the Israeli report, mentioned above, to the effect that the French missile had already been tested in 1965, we have at our disposal a British inquiry in Washington, dated 11 April 1966, quoting Lebanese press reports in mid-1965 stating that Israel had indeed purchased such French missiles. What is more, Mr Morris of the Foreign Office considered these reports accurate.[12] Mr Everett, the British diplomat in charge, asked Harrison Symmes, director of the State Department Office of the Near East, about the missiles and was told that on top of previous information given to the British in this regard, 'The missile tests appeared to have run into some sort of a problem and it seemed likely that *delivery would not begin to take place until some time in 1967*' (italics added).

This and other British reports on their talks in Washington hardly reflected the rather strong pressure that the Americans were bringing against Israel in regard to Dimona and the missile issue, with which we shall deal on the basis of the relevant volume of *Foreign Relations of the United States* (*FRUS*).

NOTES

1. See Uri Yizhar, *Between Vision and Power, The History of the Ahdut-ha-'Avoda Po'alei Tsiyyon Party*, in Hebrew (Efal: Yad Tabenkin, 2005).
2. Israel State Archives, *Levi Eshkol, the Third Prime Minister of Israel, Selected Documents on Chapters in His Life*, in Hebrew (Jerusalem: Israel State Archives, 2002), p.491.
3. This section is based on ibid., pp.498–504, 510–19.
4. Interview with former Mapai member of Knesset Yehuda Hashai, March 1989.
5. Commentary by W. Morris, Eastern Department, for internal use of British Foreign Office, dated 5 April 1966, on reports from Washington and Tel Aviv as quoted below, PRO, FO 371/186864.
6. On the Ben Barka affair, see Shlomo Aronson, *David Ben-Gurion, Renaissance Leader and the Waning of an Age*, in Hebrew (Sede Boqer and Beersheva: Ben-Gurion Research Institute, 1999), pp.41–2.
7. As reported by the well-informed Lebanese press of the period. See, for example, *Filastin,* Beirut, 17 November 1966: 'Preparations must be made to destroy the nuclear reactors in Israel', and cf. *Al-Muharar,* Beirut, 11 November 1966, 'A preventive war against Israel must be undertaken by launching missiles and [mounting] an aerial surprise attack against the reactor in Dimona'.
8. Interviews conducted in 1991–92.
9. Ambassador Michael Hadow to Mr W. Morris, Foreign Office, received 30 March 1966, PRO, FO 371/86851, original No.1199/66.
10. 'An Independent Israeli Deterrent', *Jewish Observer and Middle East Review*, 28 December 1962.
11. See note 9, above.
12 .C.H.D. Everett, British Embassy, Washington, to W. Morris, Foreign Office, secret, PRO, FO 371/86851, original No.11946G.

Chapter Eight

Mr Eshkol's Tea and Coffee

THE COMPROMISER WINS

According to an apocryphal anecdote that remains current among Israelis, Levi Eshkol, asked if he wanted a cup of coffee or a cup of tea, replied, 'Half and half'. The quip reflects the reputation that Eshkol had acquired even before assuming the highest office in the country: the master of compromise. Mockery aside, he was in fact witty, clever and self-confident. Ben-Gurion commanded people, argued with them, and fought with them to create a solid political base for future decisions that he would make. Eshkol imposed his views by charming people, being ready to hear them out, acknowledging their political power, and steering them toward compromise with a smile and a chat. Under certain circumstances, he was willing to bluff people, yield to those who possessed power, or beat political partners and even enemies into submission by the sheer length of the negotiations that he imposed on them toward the solution or compromise that he favoured. When his ego was at stake, he fought his adversaries even when the cause seemed hopeless. When no reasonable compromise was possible, he cheated or fought his adversaries ferociously. He always remained loyal to old partisan affiliations and did his best to maintain them by spending time with them and by applying his own position of power, which he had carved out by dint of arduous toil. He was also loyal to his party's machine, which he cherished as a matter of pride and as evidence of his unmitigated personal success. As a result, Eshkol was a slow and cumbersome decision maker, much in contrast to Ben-Gurion, who was quick to identify 'windows of opportunity' and leap through them as swiftly as possible, repeatedly threatening to resign in order not miss an important historical chance justified by Israel's special needs, or deciding in favour of inaction, especially in regard to Israel-initiated wars.[1] Eshkol invested much time in his daily schedule[2] in speaking with the press, to which he was rather sensitive – in contrast to Ben-Gurion, who only occasionally apprised the press of his doings. Yet Eshkol kept the public uninformed about major issues, such as his negotiations with the Americans on sensitive matters, and issued only vague warnings against enemies such as Fatah and Syria, admonitions that appeared weak and hence counterproductive.

On the face of it, then, Eshkol's 'compromise' with the Americans, as Robert Komer explained to President Johnson, was the following:

> In short, we'll sell Israel 48 A4Es (about $50 million), and they will undertake in return to: (1) quietly support our sale of 36 second hand F-104s to Jordan; (2) reaffirm their promise not to go nuclear unless others do; (3) keep the whole matter quiet until we decide to publicize it; and (4) not bother us any further on planes for the next several years.[3]

Komer seemed quite sure that Foreign Minister Eban 'essentially settled for our terms', as one would expect him to do after Secretary of Defence Robert McNamara had 'dusted him off in twenty no-nonsense minutes'. However, Komer was cautious enough to note that the Israelis 'added enough oral caveats ... that we think we'll insist on the terms in writing'. As we have seen above, Komer told the British that he knew that the Israelis would never give up the bomb. Hence, his construction of the expression 'going nuclear' may have referred either to an open nuclear stance or the acquisition of nuclear missiles.

The next day, President Johnson himself reassured Anwar es-Sadat, president of the Egyptian National Assembly, that the US was not as 'alarmist' as the Egyptians about the possible acquisition of nuclear weapons by Israel. Washington was watching the situation closely. 'The US would be against such a development because of our firm policy against the proliferation of nuclear weapons.'[4]

From this we learn at least that the Egyptians were 'alarmists' about Dimona. This made the Israelis even more alarmed, especially when they read an Egyptian-inspired report about the same meeting in the Lebanese newspaper *Al-Yaum* after President Nasser had again threatened overtly to launch a preventive war if Israel were to acquire nuclear weapons. Sadat was quoted in the report as having told Johnson that Israel was still working toward the development of nuclear weapons, according 'to the reports Egypt receives', and that General de Gaulle

> admitted in a [recent talk] with [Egyptian minister of war, Field Marshal Abd el Hakim] Amer [during a visit to Paris] that Israel is capable of producing nuclear weapons ... Following this, and Israel's refusal to allow American observers to control the Dimona situation, [a fact] which confirmed the information at Cairo's hands, President Johnson was perplexed and asked ... Sadat to convey in his name his promise, which was an official undertaking, that the US would not allow Israel to produce a bomb at any price, and would even use force if necessary ... but Egypt, who knows the value of American promises, and especially when they deal with Israel, cannot trust them. Therefore the *President [Nasser] made an open and clear warning, when he spoke of a preventive war.* [Italics added.][5]

In fact, this warning was a repeat of one issued by Sadat in a meeting with Secretary of State Dean Rusk on 25 February 1966, also claiming that the only obstacle to the improvement of American–Egyptian relations was Israel.[6] Sadat was quoted further as having said that

> small size Israel plus policy encouraging Jewish immigration made expansion inevitable. UAR hated spend scarce foreign exchange on arms, but did not want become nation (of) refugees like Palestine.
>
> c. *Secretary asked whether fear Israeli expansion or existence Israel governed UAR attitude. Sadat said both. Secretary observed if former something might be done, if latter not so sure.*
>
> d. Secretary stressed unalterable US commitment oppose proliferation nuclear weapons. Applied worldwide to all countries. Injection nuclear weapons into Near East arms race would cause US react very harshly. [Italics added.]

Thus, the Lebanese press report quoted Johnson as having promised to 'use force' against Israel if it went nuclear. This, however, was merely the newspaper's inflated interpretation of Dean Rusk's formulation about 'reacting very harshly', to which Sadat responded by saying that Egypt '*felt equal concern* and would be forced to launch preventive war if Israel acquired bomb. Secretary hoped for effective preventive measures short of war.' (Italics added.)

Hence the United States became responsible in Egyptian eyes and in its own for the preclusion of an Egyptian preventive war if Israel went nuclear. We have no room here to discuss the rest of this memo, in which Sadat again singled out Israel as the only problem in US–Egyptian relations. 'Might not be solved this generation, but time had also solved problem 80-year Crusader occupation Egypt.'

At this time, however, Washington had problems with Egypt that were unrelated to Israel. Very much troubled by Nasser's role in Yemen due to his threats against Saudi Arabia and Jordan, it was unwilling to renew vital grain shipments to Egypt – precipitating accusations of an American 'starvation' policy by the Egyptian ambassador and, subsequently, an angry outburst by Nasser himself against the departing American ambassador, Lucius D. Battle.[7]

During the period between 31 March and 4 April 1966 a three-man team of US nuclear experts visited Israeli atomic energy sites and reached the conclusion that 'the reactor has been operated at significantly reduced power' and that '[there is] no chemical reprocessing facility at Dimona'.[8] The team admitted that it 'may have been deliberately deceived by the Israelis' but judged this to be 'unlikely'. Today, after the Israeli nuclear technician Mordechai Vanunu published photographs of the reprocessing facility, we know that it had been installed underneath the reactor.[9]

The next document is a report on a meeting between the American Ambassador in Israel, Walworth Barbour, and Prime Minister Eshkol on 24 May 1966, following American instructions circulated on 10 May to renew the April 1964 missile discussions with Eshkol, and, 'in particular, to try to halt any delivery to Israel of missiles falling under the initial French-Israeli contract for 25 missiles'.

> 2. After I made pitch pursuant [the aforementioned circular] PM assured me
> a) there are no strategic missiles now. b) *there will be no such missiles in Israel at least for two more years from now, perhaps three.* [Italics added.][10]

This statement clashes frontally with General Yariv's statement to the British, quoted above, concerning Israel's intention of deploying the French IRBM as soon as possible. In the following elocutions, Eshkol indeed mixed his tea with his coffee:

> c. [Eshkol] sincerely hopes that within this period of time UAR will abandon its missile programme, in which event Israel will do likewise. In any event Eshkol indicated that GOI [Government of Israel] not contemplating purchase of more than 'two dozen, maybe one dozen more or less'. He implied they were having developing problems, and finding costs nearly prohibitive.

Barbour was impressed by Eshkol's arguments, which in fact were contradictory. The Prime Minister, the ambassador said, was 'fervently desirous avoiding further qualitative escalation in area arms'. However, the question of why he had given up on the missiles for the time being, given that they were not even ready yet – was it due to real development problems or due to complications with France following the Ben Barka affair? – remains moot. No Israeli sources are yet available to answer this question, except for the aforementioned 'Dimona downscale' decision, made under the influence of Allon and Galili.

If Israel was worried about Soviet guarantees to the Arabs if it went nuclear and deployed the IRBM, the next Memorandum of Conversation on Nuclear Weapons in the Middle East between Secretary of State Dean Rusk and Soviet Ambassador Anatoly Dobrynin, on 26 May 1966, probably failed to alleviate their fears. In the conversation, Rusk suggested to the Soviets that both superpowers obtain private assurances from their clients that the clients would not produce nuclear weapons and would inform them accordingly. Rusk then added his conviction that Israel would not produce such weapons because she had promised not to, an assessment that Dobrynin answered with scepticism. While promising that the USSR would furnish no country in the region with nuclear weapons, Dobrynin stressed that until the Big Powers took some steps toward disarmament and set an example, it would be 'difficult' to convince the nations of the Middle East not to acquire missiles.[11] Thus, the issue of the Israeli IRBM may have been seen in Western eyes as a possible reason for the Soviets to supply missiles to Arabs and for Arabs to acquire them.

Such a perspective may have driven Eshkol to strike one of his compromises: Dimona, yes, but as opaquely as possible; IRBMs, no. Thus, Israel would rely instead on aircraft, even though they were much less credible, hardly had the radius for the delivery of a nuclear strike against main targets such as the Aswan High Dam, and obviously excluded Soviet targets.

Concurrently, Arthur Goldberg, the American Ambassador to the UN and previous to that a prominent Jewish Associate Supreme Court Justice, tried his luck in trying to solve the Palestinian refugee problem and seemed to have found a positive response among members of the task force that Mr Eban had set up for this purpose, with Eshkol, Goldberg said, fully aboard. 'They are looking for ways to break down the "fortress Israel" idea and to build bridges to the Arabs', the former Associate Justice of the US Supreme Court judged.[12] Indeed, the Israelis had been concerned about the revival of the Palestine issue since 1964, and the emergence of Fatah and the PLO as rivalling outfits, the former carrying out commando actions against Israel from its bases in Syria via Lebanon and Jordan. The PLO, under Ahmed Shuqairy and sponsored by Egypt, was not allowed to operate from the UN-guarded Gaza Strip but remained very militant and extremely loud – in fact, the most vocal Arab outfit calling for preventive war before Israel could go nuclear.

The State Department quickly returned to the nuclear issue. Building on the latest inspection visit, Secretary Rusk repeated,

> We consider it most important there be no misunderstanding on part of GOI of utter seriousness which USG, at highest level, attaches to prevention nuclear proliferation in Near East. As Secretary told Eban this is matter of fundamental significance to US-Israeli relations.[13]

Thereupon, Rusk demanded for technical reasons that

> Periodicity needs be semi-annual. Scientific reason given to

> Embassy in Deptel 938, June 15, 1963[14] (but apparently not then relayed to GOI because of Ben-Gurion's resignation) which you may give Eban is as follows: ... a reactor size of Dimona could be operated so as to discharge single fuel load approximately every six months if intended for ultimate production of weapon grade plutonium ... As previously stated on several occasions, what *we want is full access to Dimona's facilities and records every six months.* [Italics added.]

This was the half-cup of coffee that Eshkol would not serve Washington and, hence, not Cairo either.

FROM THE WEST BANK TO MOSCOW

A major problem for the Israelis was the attitude of the Soviet Union, not only as a patron power of Egypt and Syria but also as the supplier of conventional weapons to both Syria and to Iraq, which greatly enhanced these countries' firepower and possibly, in turn, their growing willingness to use it.

Would Israel be willing to trade the nuclear option for Soviet restraint in conventional weapons supply to the Arabs? It was a remote possibility that came up in a rather unpleasant exchange between Ambassador Gideon Rafael of the Israel Foreign Ministry and Secretary of State Dean Rusk, as reported to the American Embassy in Tel Aviv on 28 July 1966. Accordingly,

> After discussion Israeli proposal on refugee problem ...[15] Secretary tried question of Israeli nuclear intentions. He noted Soviet interest in denuclearization [not exactly a credible description of Rusk's previous meeting with Dobrynin, possibly using a Soviet threat to make the Israelis give ground – SA] and said that if Israel would agree to IAEA safeguards, he believed its Arab neighbours would also agree and USSR would go along. Would Israel agree to IAEA safeguards he asked.
>
> Israel Ambassador Rafael said Israel was not giving any thought to it at present because GOI's concern for broader problem of conventional weapons. Rafael said *Soviets did not indicate to Israelis* in Geneva *they would be willing to limit conventional arms in the area in exchange for nuclear*

> *ban*. He added Israel made clear its position it would not be first to introduce nuclear weapons in Near East.
>
> *Secretary noted our assumption GOI does not wish to go nuclear and added: If you do, you will lose US support* . If on the other hand, you accept nuclear ban ... your neighbors would follow you and that would be first step toward reduction of tensions. Secretary said we cannot guarantee USSR interested in conventional arms limitations, but nuclear question can be separated out and that consideration is fundamental to US position.
>
> Secretary then told Israelis that nothing would be more disastrous to GOI than enter nuclear weapon field, and urged them to agree to international safeguards. When Rafael protested nuclear ban does not take care of GOI's problem with conventional weapons, Secretary said: *This means then you want to hang on to the threat of nuclear weapons*. Rafael said no, GOI has made position clear in Knesset, but there are some people in Israel – not in govt [Ben-Gurion and his Rafi colleagues – SA] – who say Israel should go nuclear.
>
> Secretary said either this card is in your deck, or it is not. If it's not, then get it out of the way by accepting safeguards. He again noted that if Israel is holding open the nuclear option, it should forget US support. We would not be with you, he said. [Italics added.][16]

In other words, if Israel were to find itself at war because of Dimona, it would stand alone – as Jerusalem increasingly felt during the May 1967 crisis despite Eshkol's gestures in making the nuclear option opaque by allowing at least annual visits at the site and, possibly, by not deploying the French IRBM if they were ready and available. At that time – the spring of 1966 – President Nasser publicly renounced the American grain aid and his spokesman, Mohammed Heikal, promised a 'hot summer' in the Middle East.

A short time before, early in 1966, a militant Ba'athist group took over in Damascus and its Foreign Minister, Ibrahim Mah'us, propagated an 'Algerian' or a North Vietnamese model of liberation struggle against Israel that would be sure to stay under the nuclear threshold, a strategy that made the Israelis seriously concerned.[17]

The Vietnam War was also escalating at this time. Criticism of the war, also ascending, included fierce domestic campaigns in which American Jews figured conspicuously. This troubled President Johnson so badly that he spent his time with the Israeli President Zalman Shazar at the White House, on 2 July 1966, discussing the significance of 'the US stand against aggression in Vietnam and its implications for US assurances [that] it will seek to deter and prevent aggression against other smaller states', such as Israel. Specifically, Johnson wanted Israel's help in tempering American-Jewish criticism of the Vietnam War. Shazar, however, explained that he was 'president only of Israel, not of World Jewry'.[18]

Since Johnson had not brought up Israel's nuclear option at all, one may jump to the conclusion that he was much less interested in it than his Secretary of State and the NSC officials. However, in a meeting with the tireless Egyptian Ambassador Mustafa Kamel on 12 August, Johnson interposed that 'the US remain[s] adamantly opposed to the proliferation of nuclear weapons in the Near East', when Kamel pronounced Egypt ready to accept IAEA safeguards, thereby indirectly making the Israeli nuclear option a major threat to Middle East stability in the context of an American–Egyptian relationship that was otherwise rather promising.[19]

Ambassador Barbour again tried his luck with Foreign Minister Abba Eban on 14 September 1966, before Eban left to attend the annual UN General Assembly where he was scheduled to meet Secretary of State Rusk.[20] Barbour added a fillip of his own to the Administration's previous arguments, stressing Rusk's personal interest in and concern about Israel's nuclear programme. After all,

> since it is obvious, as a result various leaks [about the inspection visits], that Israel in fact not embarking on weapons production, GOI had nothing to lose and everything to gain in making gesture suggested [e.g. adopt IAEA safeguards at Dimona].

Eban responded by expressing his opinion that 'nuclear arms race somewhat more remote contingency in area than it had been, less pressing immediate possibility for example than clash with Syria'. Then, asking Barbour whether Rusk was threatening to impose sanctions on Israel if it retained its nuclear option, Eban was told, 'It not matter of sanctions, on contrary it matter of losing US support'. Barbour entertained some hope that Eban would be authorized to proceed in 'the direction we desire'. Meeting with Eban again on 3 November 1966, however, he was given a package of contradictory arguments that also related to the forthcoming NPT that Ambassador Rafael had endorsed in the meantime in the hope of gaining enough time to make the NPT a reality. Eban said,

> From all evidence available to GOI, Egypt now fairly relaxed as to Israeli intentions re nuclear weapons. In fact, PM has been convinced by President Johnson that effort keep Nasser uncertain as to Israeli intentions is no longer worth risk of Egyptian weapon escalation.
>
> However, due Egyptian predilection for sabotage and plotting, GOI must find middle ground between letting Egyptians be assured GOI not manufacturing bombs and giving them full info as to Israel's scientific nuclear facilities ... Therefore, GOI cannot accept IAEA system of controls to which Egyptians have access at all levels and ... it wishes be sure we [and presumably others] do not pass on to Egyptians specifics as to location or functions of Israeli installations ... Israelis too have hopes of being included in general non-proliferation treaty before long which they would prefer to being singled out in some special arrangement [e.g. the American inspection at Dimona] in way contrary Israel's sovereign status.[21]

In response, Ambassador Barbour clarified that the NPT was 'not yet a reality and, much as we all support it, we do not know when it will be'.

Thus we may add that if Israel secretly went nuclear around that time, it became a de facto member of the 'nuclear club' long before the NPT was signed and ratified in 1968–70. The Americans saw such a development as an immediate danger, pertaining to Arab threats: 'This being an imperfect world, *Israeli gesture to assure its suspicious neighbors that it not moving toward nuclear weapons would promote peace in the area*' (italics added).

In other words, the United States took seriously the Arab and, especially, the Egyptian threats to launch a preventive war because of Dimona. Worse still from Jersusalem's standpoint, Washington might be perceived as even justifying the threats, thereby making Israel the source of instability in the Middle East – which in fact it was, due to its mere presence there. Barbour went further, proposing IAEA safeguards, a 'verification scheme including Israel and Egypt with third country', or unilateral invitation by Israel, as a sovereign state, of foreign scientists or other countries to participate in research projects at Dimona.

The American ambassador then returned to the missile issue, reminding his interlocutor that Prime Minister Eshkol

> stated missiles were at least two years away ... and suggested that since UAR running into difficulties in missile development, this type of sophisticated weaponry (Israel's primary hope to deter its enemies) too should be subject to control arrangement.

After protesting his ignorance of the history of Israel's missile discussions, Eban promised to raise the matter with PM Eshkol, leaving the Americans with the impression that 'we are making progress' and that President Johnson had convinced the Prime Minister 'that tactic of keeping Nasser in state of uncertainty as to GOI intentions [re Dimona] was dangerous'.

On 13 November 1966, Lt Gen. Yitzhak Rabin, the Israeli Chief of Staff, sent an armoured brigade into then-Jordanian territory, in broad daylight, in order to retaliate against the Palestinian-inhabited village of Samu' in the southern tip of the West Bank. Samu' was suspected of having supported or sheltered Fatah guerrillas on their way from Syria to Israel territory, where they planted mines that killed several officers and men. The Israelis expected Jordanian intervention and they got it; the Israelis ambushed the forces sent to Samu', causing heavy losses among them, and the operation developed to an air battle. No action of this type had ever been authorized back in Ben-Gurion's time. Israel was perennially reluctant to challenge an Arab regime in such a far-reaching way, and King Hussein in particular was doing his best to curb guerrilla operations from his territory into Israel. Hussein was relatively weak and Western-oriented compared with the militant, Soviet supported Ba'ath regime in Damascus, and had a Palestinian population that was imbibing continual propaganda from Ahmed Shuqairy's Egypt-based PLO.

Once exposed to the harsh Israeli action, the West Bank exploded, threatening the stability of the Hashemite state, which introduced armour to subdue the Palestinians. Everyone wondered why the seemingly moderate Eshkol had punished a semi-ally in this manner; his move appeared to signal fear of the stronger and Soviet-backed Syrians, who had unleashed Fatah against Israel and now engaged in direct cross-border challenges.[22] The Samu' incident also precipitated an extremely angry American reaction, followed by efforts to save Hussein's regime, which, in turn, would have to adopt a more hostile attitude toward Israel. This stew of circumstances occupies most of the last part of the *FRUS* volume under consideration here.

CONTAINING THE ARMS RACE – NOT AT ISRAEL'S EXPENSE

In Israel, the recession following Eshkol's election victory in 1965 prompted the prime minister to seek an increase in American economic aid. The dependence on such aid seems, in turn, to have imposed defensive measures on his Government on the Jordanian front. In the meantime, Rabin turned full attention to Syria. At home, the combination of the recession and guerrilla attacks from both Syria and Jordan, coupled with the clashes along the Israeli-Syrian border, seriously eroded Eshkol's public standing. Opaque accusations from Ben Gurion's party in regard to Dimona and the Ben Barka affair only greased the skids.

At the same time, Egypt's ambassador to Washington kept pressing the US – almost hysterically – for food aid. 'Maintaining that key to peace and stability in Near East is the continuation' of this aid; he assured his interlocutor that Nasser was not trying to topple King Hussein.[23] The Americans, in turn, wondered whether 'it was not in UAR's [Egypt's] own interest to allow Shuqairy to "lead Egyptians around by the nose"'.[24]

Much occupied by the challenge of controlling the rapidly growing and contradictory forces in the Middle East, the Americans returned with a sense of urgency to Dimona. Building on what may have been his belief that Eshkol had realized the danger of keeping Nasser in doubt about Dimona's true nature, Ambassador Barbour asked Foreign Minister Eban on 29 November 1966, for an appointment with the Prime Minister to pursue the matter,[25] adding, 'In line our understanding we would like to have another visit to Dimona and that AEC [the U.S. Atomic Energy Commission] team is prepared to do so any time during next three weeks. I commented that it *almost eight months since last visit*' (italics added). Eban promised to take up the matter with Eshkol. Two weeks later, however, Eban met with Nicholas Katzenbach, the Acting American Secretary of State, and expressed concern about Israel's new strategic situation, no doubt reflecting a prevailing opinion among Rabin's General Staff:

> Israel's deterrent capacity had achieved a viable balance in that no neighbouring state wished military confrontation. He [Eban] praised various warnings made by Nasser and his spokesman Heikal that Egypt would not be led by Syria to premature hostilities, [but added that] Israel's enemies now employing new method of expressing active hostility, guerrilla warfare as practiced in Algeria, Viet-Nam, etc ... This technique plus the ideology of adding the 'sixth entity', the Palestinian nation, to five opposing Arab states created a major problem.[26]

Thus Eban explained the Samu' raid and accused Nasser of trying to undermine King Hussein's regime. Dimona was not mentioned. Yet on 11 January 1967, Ambassador Barbour raised the demand for IAEA safeguards with Mr Eban again, and this time the Foreign Minister gave him a rather detailed response,

> centred about three points: (A) 'national dignity' (B) national security (C) domestic political considerations. Re (A) Eban objected to Israel asked to give up something while the same demands were not being levied on UAR. He rejected idea that somehow Israel 'owed UAR something' in this matter.[27]

Eban repeated 'Israel's own disposition on area nuclear matters' as he had made them publicly known several times. Barbour said in reference to Eban,

> His researchers showed him that a basic premise of arms control agreements was mutual recognition of sovereignty, right to existence of partners to agreements. There seemed to be no disposition on part of UAR make such elemental concession in case of Israel. Instead one only heard talk of war of liberation. He [Eban] wondered whether USG was

> not seeking do too much to increase range of assurances to UAR and not taking sufficient account Israel's concerns. He said Israel's hopes for progress in this problem rested largely on the achievement of general non-proliferation treaty.

Barbour responded that Israel would serve its own interest and 'broader interest world peace' if it accepted IAEA safeguards, since 'Nuclear variable lent whole new dimension to Middle East arms race and was regarded by us with utmost seriousness', while Egypt's nuclear effort was practically nil. Barbour refused to wait for the birth of an NPT and went on to say that the domestic political consideration might be accommodated by a unilateral Israeli concession following assurances that Israel had already given. However, following remarks by Moshe Bitan, an assistant director general of Eban's ministry, that 'he [Barbour] thought progress along lines we were pressing was unlikely', commented to his superiors that 'the going is heavy'. At the same time, the border clashes with Syria intensified so badly that Eshkol warned the Americans 'carefully' that while the Israelis' 'patience with Syria has about run out',[28] he was refraining from action due to the Americans' 'reaction to [the Israeli] raid on Jordan, [which] shook them badly'. Secretary Rusk now moved toward authorizing food aid to Nasser's Egypt. This, he thought, would maintain at least some degree of control over the Egyptian President's behaviour in the rapidly destabilizing Middle East, after Nasser had publicly accused the United States of fighting a 'starvation war' against Egypt;[29] it would also match the Soviets' offer of similar assistance. The main outstanding issue, however, remained Nasser's involvement in Yemen and Egypt's military operations there, which involved Saudi Arabia directly or indirectly.[30]

As the Americans debated about what to do with Nasser, who in the eyes of Walt Rostow, the National Security Adviser, was still 'the most powerful figure in the Middle East', Secretary Rusk responded to a cable from the American Embassy in Tel Aviv on 23 February 1967,[31] as follows: 'Your A-478[32] describing conversations with two Israeli contacts suggests *Israel could be much closer to nuclear weapons capability than we had supposed*' (italics added).

This opening sentence requires our commentary since the Israeli 'nuclear lobby', headed by Mr Peres, was not silent about

Dimona, and Peres himself was known to have used such tactics in order to make 'his' deterrent much more visible than Prime Minister and Minister of Defence Eshkol wished. Eshkol hoped for a degree of ambiguity that would not ruin US–Israeli relations. He may also have hoped to secure desalination facilities in return for the (so-far ineffective) American inspections and the undeployed missiles and to keep the Arabs wondering about Israel's actual nuclear preparedness. This complicated mixture of tea and coffee, however, exposed as it may have been by Peres as a sheer bluff, merely inspired Secretary Rusk to tell his ambassador that:

> We are requesting urgent assessment these and other recent reports by Washington intelligence community ... potential implication these reports makes it even more pressing to obtain response from Eshkol on our request for visit to Dimona.

Reminding him that on 16 January Eshkol had promised a visit 'within a few weeks', Rusk instructed the Barbour to inform Eshkol that 'highest levels of USG are aware you requested GOI agreement to visit as long ago as November and are frankly disturbed at lack of GOI response'.

On 22 February 1967, President Nasser of Egypt unleashed a far-reaching verbal attack on the United States 'for creating, supporting, arming, and protecting Israel, supporting Arab reactionaries such as Jordan's King Hussein, King Faisal of Saudi Arabia, applying economic and psychological pressure against Egypt', and even refusing to provide military aid to Egypt in the 1950s.[33]

In a farewell meeting with Nasser shortly afterwards, American Ambassador Lucius D. Battle was exposed to a highly emotional speech by the Egyptian President. Nasser frankly defined the Yemen problem as a prestige issue for him, one that would dictate his subsequent behaviour during the crisis leading to the 1967 war. He also, however, addressed himself to the future of Aden, which the British were about to evacuate. He then angrily refused the American offer to resume wheat deliveries, complained about the behaviour of the International Monetary Fund toward his country, and threatened instead to cooperate with the Soviet economic bloc or, possibly, with China.

'Re Israel', Battle's report to Washington continued,

'[Nasser's] views are well known. He hoped Arabs would return.'[34] This may have meant that the exiled Palestinians should do their own fighting, with possible support from the Arab states. Nasser's dilemmas, however, were rather complicated here: Egypt was involved directly in the Palestinian problem by virtue of her control of the Gaza Strip. Since Israel's withdrawal from Sinai and the Strip in 1957, however, UN troops had been deployed along the Strip and at Sharm el-Sheikh, at the southern tip of the Sinai Peninsula.[35] No military action was possible in these areas as long as the UN troops remained there. Nasser's Arab rivals had begun at this time to accuse him of 'hiding behind the UN' instead of acting on his own inflammatory rhetoric about Israel and the Palestinians' rights. Syria, in contrast, was allowing Fatah to do some real fighting and was escalating its direct confrontation with Israel.[36] Samu' had exposed Nasser as ostensibly having allowed Israel to hit the West Bank Palestinians badly while sitting on his hands.

Deliberating among themselves about whether and how to meet Nasser's food requests (even though the Egyptian President had rejected them) and deal with his grievances against the IMF, the Americans received Israeli requests for military and economic aid following the recent developments described above, which had the further aim of balancing a possible American shift toward the Arabs as a result of them. Here, however, the outstanding Dimona safeguards and 'Israeli officials [who were] not forthcoming about their missile development' were stumbling blocks.[37] Thus, in a conversation with Abe Feinberg, an American-Jewish go-between,[38] President Johnson 'indicated, 1. That before we moved on the Israel package, we would like a date set for a visit to Dimona'. Johnson did not make the one 'explicitly contingent' on the other but 'referred to the failure of Eshkol to respond to the President's letter of March [May] 1965 recommending accepting IAEA safeguards'. Just the same, he instructed Walt Rostow, his National Security Adviser, to assure that State, Defence (which was strongly against military aid), and AID (the US Agency for International Development) come closer together on an agreed-upon package.

The nuclear issue remained a major concern of the Interdepartmental Regional Group for Near East and South Asia, as stated in its report of 28 March 1967.[39] The Group agreed that,

'It remains particularly important to avoid the introduction into the area of sophisticated new types of weapon systems, including nuclear weapons'. It also agreed that Soviet cooperation was essential for effective arms control in the Near East and that

> We should continue to explore on all appropriate occasions the possibilities of an understanding with the Soviet Union on this subject; and that an effective understanding would also require the cooperation of various other European countries (e.g. the United Kingdom, France, the Federal Republic of Germany, and Italy, as well as Czechoslovakia).

How exactly could this be done? Possibly within the framework of a forthcoming NPT. Since the Israelis had been concerned about this likelihood for several years, Jerusalem, in my view, would have moved faster rather than slower in order to beat the treaty, but it would do so in the most ambiguous fashion possible.

Concurrently, the Group recommended that 'Despite Soviet shipments to the Arabs we should avoid becoming involved as the major supplier of arms to Israel and should encourage the Government of Israel to look generally to Western European suppliers'.

Shortly after these recommendations were made, Israel submitted requests for armoured personnel carriers. At this occasion, Walt Rostow, Johnson's special assistant, wrote to the President:

> We ought to keep the brakes on the Middle East arms race. When we completed the Israel aircraft deal in March 1965, we told Nasser that sale completed a round of escalation. We said we didn't foresee further sales soon unless the Soviets made more. As far as we know, they haven't, and our December sale [of F-104s] to Jordan was too small to affect the balance.[40]

Hence the new source of imbalance was perceived to be Israel's nuclear and missile programme, on top of net American interests in the Arab world that required some distance from Israel. Thus, Rostow recommended further – now in connection with an NPT as a 'long shot' – that

> We should be tough as long as they play coy on their nuclear

> position. Eshkol has invited our technicians to visit Dimona on 22 April.[41] It will be more than a year since our last visit. Only when they report will we know whether we should use all our leverage to make them agree to visits every six months.

Referring to the Israeli arms requests, Rostow returned to the Middle East arms race:

> The only approach that could work is an understanding with the USSR to stop big shipments. We've probed before, and the Soviets have shown little interest. But in the context of persuading the Israelis to sign the Non-Proliferation Treaty, they might show more.

Rostow then acknowledged the anticipated role of domestic Jewish pressure on Johnson to supply more arms to Israel. 'If he [can] stand the heat, a pause in sales might be worth a try.'

On 7 April 1967, Israel escalated the Syrian border clashes into a major air battle in which the IAF downed seven MiG 21s, including several that it chased into the suburbs of Damascus. The incident began when the Syrians opened fire on an Israeli tractor ploughing in the Demilitarized Zone along the Israel-Syrian frontier, which Damascus regarded as forbidden for cultivation by Israel. The resulting battle lasted most of the day and involved mortar, artillery and tank fire. Opposition leaders David Ben-Gurion and Lt Gen. (Res.) Moshe Dayan regarded the whole clash as an unwarranted and badly handled step toward war,[42] whereas COGS Rabin, while probably having persuaded Eshkol that such an operation might deter the Syrians, had overstepped Eshkol's authorization and would later usurp his powers by threatening a war to precipitate a regime change in Damascus. Under the circumstances, Eshkol himself was willing to consider inflicting a major blow on the Ba'athist Syrians due to the escalation of Syrian-supported Palestinian guerrilla operations inside Israel and the shelling of Israeli settlements from the Golan Heights. A regime change in Damascus, however, went far beyond his intentions and might trigger unwanted Soviet and Egyptian responses. Eshkol considered firing Rabin as a result, but his alliance with Allon and Galili of Ahdut ha-'Avoda – Rabin's mentors – tied his hands.[43]

Still, Nasser's dilemmas, and possibly his opportunities, seem to have started narrowing down toward a controlled confrontation with Israel, with enough Soviet backing – now that their Syrian client needed protection – to allow him, possibly, to manoeuvre much more effectively vis-à-vis the Americans, who were 'starving' him and supporting his 'reactionary' rivals (Hussein of Jordan and Faisal of Saudi Arabia), and vis-à-vis his radical Arab competitors. As these options became available to the Egyptian leader, the American National Intelligence Estimate of 13 April 1967, acknowledged that 'Rivalries and disputes among the Arabs ... create some danger of precipitating crises from which large-scale Arab-Israeli hostilities could develop'.[44]

In the Americans' estimation, however, the main factor that might prompt the Arabs to initiate a war remained the Israeli nuclear programme and its missiles:

> If and when the Arabs come to believe that the Israelis are at the point of deploying strategic missiles,[45] a phase of sharply increased Arab–Israeli tensions will probably arise. This is likely to occur within the next two or three years. In this event, the Egyptians would probably press the Soviets for help.

The missing link in this otherwise rather balanced estimate was the assumption, or rather a suspicion that the Israelis had been entertaining for several years, that the Arabs would strike *before* the missiles were deployed. This seemed not to be an immediate threat since Egypt was still mired in Yemen, but about a month later Nasser marched his troops into Sinai. The Intelligence Estimate quoted above rejected the possibility that the Soviets would give Egypt nuclear missiles in response to the Israel challenge but admitted that 'missile systems' could be delivered. Reassuringly, however, the Estimate noted that

> Both sides appear to appreciate that large-scale military action involves considerable risk and no assurance of leading to solution. In any event, the chances are good that the threat of great power intervention will prevent an attempt by either side to resolve the matter by military force.

Nasser, however, might construe these givens as allowing him room for a limited action that, if it provoked a larger Israeli response, could justify his own reaction – an attack on Dimona, for example – while the ensuing Israeli counter-response would be staunched by the superpowers and his allies around the globe. At least Eshkol had to calculate it that way, and he did. He still, however, continued to hope for American support, which seemed to have been menaced not just by US interests in the Arab world but also by Dimona – the very project that Israel had launched to free itself from dependence on American help and resolve the Arab–Israeli conflict once for all – which he had tried to minimize as best as he could by allowing American inspections and deferring the deployment of the French missiles, if they were available at all.

On 18 April 1967, Rostow repeated 'concern over too close a relationship [with Israel] while Israel's nuclear intentions are in doubt'.[46] Rostow informed the President that 'Our inspection team will visit Dimona this weekend for the first time over a year. With NPT ahead of, we may need a clear expression of Israel's position.' Eshkol, Rostow added, believed that 'we promised something in return for their keeping quiet on our Jordan package last November' but suggested various fallback positions in regard to the armoured personnel carriers and food aid to Israel. However, in a memo to the President dated 20 April 1967, ahead of Johnson's meeting with Abe Feinberg, Rostow even suggested to the President that

> The main reason for holding off [on the Israel aid package] is to demonstrate that you're serious about nuclear non-proliferation. Even this year's whole aid package wouldn't be enough to bargain with on this life-or-death issue (as Israel sees it). However, as we approach the time when we may need to press Israel to sign the NPT, we must consider how much leverage we need to hold in reserve. So far the Israelis have succeeded in keeping this apart from the rest of our relationship.[47]

This statement was not accurate in the sense that Eshkol had agreed to the inspection visits, which had made the deterrent value of the Israeli nuclear programme questionable. However, Israel was pursuing the programme itself and, therefore, may have given the Arabs a *casus belli* that was legitimate in American anti-proliferation terms. What is more, Eshkol may have delayed the actual completion of the deterrent programme by yielding to American pressure not to deploy the French-built missiles.

However, once the Egyptians would march into Sinai in May 1967, expel the UN buffer force from Gaza and Sharm el-Sheikh and finally close the Straits of Tiran (which led to Eilat), no American countermeasures would be forthcoming. Thus, knowledgeable Israelis would view Eshkol's concessions to Washington in the nuclear-missile complex as bad bargains. More than that, they would inspire Ben-Gurion to try to remove him from his offices altogether and Peres to suggest an interesting way out of the May–June 1967 crisis: testing a nuclear device in the Negev Desert, thus making Israel an official member of the club and eliminating the American–Egyptian common cause, based on the illegality of Dimona.[48]

In the memo quoted above, Rostow expressed the issue in the following terms:

> The only counter big enough to sway Eshkol, I suspect, will be the US–Israeli relationship itself ... I realize this creates a domestic dilemma, but I should think the Jewish community itself with its liberal tendencies would be strongly attracted to the NPT.

Rostow repeated his 'serious concern' about the French missiles, adding an attachment to his memo, dated 20 April 1967, in which he defined the nuclear question in the following terms:

> This is critical for large US interests. We have been able to live with this ambiguous Israeli defense policy in terms of conventional weapons. Should they wish to have both a national nuclear capability and US guarantees, we would be in almost impossible position. Moreover, if they insisted on it, it might well destroy the possibilities of a non-proliferation treaty throughout the world.[49]

Having thus formulated the American dilemma, Rostow might have defined Eshkol's tea-plus-coffee tactics as follows: the Israeli Prime Minister seems to have authorized an effort to make Dimona bomb-ready due to the eventuality of the NPT, the deteriorating situation in the Middle East, and the pressure emanating from Ben-Gurion's camp. Concurrently, he hoped to have given the Americans enough, by way of the inspection visits and the missile issue, to obtain an informal guarantee of some kind. Nasser's moves in May–June 1967, however, placed both Eshkol and the Americans in a serious quandary because Egypt did not attack Israel directly. As long as Cairo did not start a shooting war, Nasser might respond to Israeli pre-emption by attacking Israel's most vital target, Dimona. This explains better than any previous explanation Eshkol's lengthy cabinet deliberations after the May 1967 crisis began, which ultimately destroyed his public standing, brought Dayan back to a national emergency coalition, and precipitated the cabinet's final decision – under Dayan's influence – to terminate the escalation by striking at Egypt.[50]

READYING THE DEFENCES

The relevant volume of *FRUS* does not bring us this far. The last document that we quote from that volume, however, concurs with the British documents quoted above in the sense that Under Secretary of State Katzenbach wrote to President Johnson on 1 May 1967, just a fortnight before Nasser moved to create the drama leading to the Six Day War:[51]

> Nuclear Weapons. Concerned that over the long run the Arabs will achieve superiority in conventional forces, Israel is carefully preserving its option to acquire sophisticated weapons, including, we believe, nuclear weapons. We have no evidence that Israel is actually making a bomb, but we believe Israel intends to keep itself in a position to do so at reasonably short notice should the need arise ... Our suspicions that we do not know the full story have been heightened by the Israeli unwillingness to tell us what happened to 80–100 tons of unsafeguarded uranium concentrate that they bought from Argentina 4 years ago.[52] Israelis have stressed to us their concern that information obtained by IAEA inspectors, which might be available to UAR, could aid the latter in planning a military or sabotage operation against Dimona.

Indeed, these – a military operation against Dimona and the closure of the Straits of Tiran – were the most troubling consequences for Eshkol once he judged Nasser's aims following the eruption of the May 1967 crisis. An Egyptian reconnaissance flight over Dimona on 17 May, after the march of Nasser's troops into Sinai had set the crisis in motion, was the deciding factor in

Eshkol's decision to follow Lt Gen. Rabin's recommendation to mobilize reserves and seal the Israeli–Egyptian border. The Israeli mobilization, however, added a domestic Israeli dimension to the crisis and posed a prestige dilemma for Nasser, escalating the crisis further until all parties involved lost control of it.

In the aforementioned document, Under Secretary Katzenbach went on to describe Israel's longer-range plans pertaining to its missile programme, hoping to achieve a reasonable understanding between Eshkol and Nasser in this regard, related to the Soviet interest in NPT. *FRUS* 2000 does not divulge President Johnson's response to his officials' urgent advice. Former Israeli diplomats such as Efraim Evron, however, told this author that Johnson was less inclined than his bureaucrats to bring pressure on Israel due to the president's growing domestic troubles, an assertion to be discussed. In the meantime, the initiative passed into Nasser's hands. And one of Nasser's main reasons for doing what he did must have been his troubles with the United States, that is, the food issue, Yemen and the ensuing crisis with Hussein and Faisal. These factors, plus his dilemmas in view of his radical verbal position on Israel's right to exist and his exposure since Samu' as having done nothing to counter Rabin's strategy of conventional deterrence, combined with Israel's nuclear challenge and may have pushed him to his calculated march into Sinai in mid-May 1967 with Soviet support.

In my view, Nasser's gambit rested on the assumption that he could march into the Sinai amid a torrent of publicity because this would give him the appearance of alleviating the Israeli pressure on Syria, with a degree of Soviet blessing that he may have had or hoped to be able to mobilize following the events of 7 April and Rabin's overt threats against the Syrian regime.[53] Thus, the Egyptian Army manned its usually unoccupied positions in northern Sinai. Believing that an Israeli attack against them would run aground against the Egyptian defences, allowing various responses once Israel justified them by firing the first shot, the bulk of its offensive force – its armour – remained in the Suez Canal area in a defensive posture. Later on, one special tank unit was deployed in Sinai against Eilat. Thus far, Nasser operated in Egypt sovereign territory. But he still had to deal with his most vulnerable spot in terms of inter-Arab relations, the accusation levelled against him by King Hussein and his other enemies of hiding behind the UN troops along the Gaza Strip (and in Sharm el-Sheikh or the Straits of Tiran). His way of dealing with it was to ask the UN commander to withdraw his forces from their line of deployment to their permanent camps. This, coupled with the integration of a Palestinian unit into his forces in Gaza, would transform the Strip to a base of guerrilla operations, protected by the weight of the Egyptian army in neighbouring Sinai. UN Secretary General U. Thant gave Nasser a choice: allow the UN force to remain along the line or have it withdrawn altogether. By doing so, he pushed Nasser to ask for their complete removal, allowing Palestinian action to be undertaken from the Strip as a matter of course.

At this stage, accompanied by the Dimona fly overs and the ensuing Israeli mobilization, Nasser escalated the crisis further by closing the Straits of Tiran. The Israeli dilemma, as I see it now, was this: If Nasser wanted to provoke Israel to start a shooting war that might in turn justify an attack against Dimona, why give it to him? The proper Israeli decision would be to ask the United States to lift the obviously illegal Egyptian blockade of the Straits. For the time being, Eshkol ordered upon Rabin's recommendation a general mobilization of the whole Israeli reserve army. If the Americans and their allies proved successful in defusing the Egyptian *casus belli*, Israel would be relieved of the necessity of doing this by itself, that is, starting a shooting war on its own, placing Nasser in confrontation with the United States and its allies, if any. President Johnson, however, did not see himself, as yet, as having allies in such a move against the Egyptian blockade and was loath to do it on his own, on top of his growing troubles in Vietnam. Paradoxically enough, then, Israel found itself alone, as it always feared, in a situation in which her long-range remedy was something that, as a matter of Egyptian–American understanding, she had no right to possess. Israel did possess the remedy, but not in a form that could deter Nasser. That would have entailed the French missiles. Were Egypt left unharmed in spite of her aggressive moves without being punished, the Americans would be more, rather than less, willing to recognize Nasser as 'the key figure in the Middle East', as Rostow put it.

Mulling what to do, Eshkol still hoped for succour from Washington. His inaction, however, damaged his public standing among the mobilized and therefore idled nation beyond repair. In fact, Eshkol found himself facing the very phenomenon that he had yielded to and had been encouraging since the Lavon affair: media pressure to resign as Minister of Defence, mobilization of public protests against him in an ironic transformation of 'Citizens for Eshkol' into 'Citizens against Eshkol', a growing revolt against him among members of the imbalanced coalition that he had cobbled together in 1965 – based on the realities of the partisan system that he had failed to reform – and, finally, an open revolt against him in the decision-making institutions of Mapai. When this had happened to Ben-Gurion, Eshkol had stepped in to repair the situation. It now happened to Eshkol.

NOTES

1. Ben-Gurion's stance against the Six Day War is discussed below.
2. See Eshkol's files at Israel State Archives, catalogue Eshkol 153.8, files meetings with journalists, no. 7935/9-k.
3. Memorandum Robert Komer, President's Deputy Special Assistant for National Security Affairs, to President Johnson, 22 February 1966, *Foreign Relations of the United States* (*FRUS*), 2000, Doc. 273, pp.556–7.
4. Ibid., p.559, Memorandum of Conversation, Subject US–UAR Relations; Yemen.
5. Israeli Army translation, 1 May 1966.
6. Telegram State Department to Embassy in UAR, 28 February 1966, signed by Rusk, *FRUS,* 2000, pp.562–3.
7. The grain-supply problem was a subject for many conversations with the Egyptians and internal American deliberations, as reflected in the quoted volume of *FRUS*. On Nasser's final angry rejection of the American linkage between the grain supplies and his behaviour in Yemen and elsewhere in the Middle East as a destabilizing factor, see telegram embassy in UAR to State Department, 4 March 1967, signed by Battle, *FRUS*, 2000, Doc. 393, pp.768–70.
8. Memorandum from Director of the Defense Intelligence Agency [Carroll] to Secretary of Defense McNamara, 4 May 1966, signed by Joseph F. Carroll, Lieutenant General, USAF, ibid., Doc. 289, pp.582–3.
9. See *The Sunday Times,* 5 October 1986.
10. Telegram Embassy in Israel to State Department, signed by Barbour, *FRUS,* 2000, Doc. 293, p.588.
11. Memorandum of Conversation on Nuclear Weapons in the Middle East between Secretary of State Dean Rusk and Soviet Ambassador Anatoly Dobrynin, 26 May 1966, ibid., Doc. 294, pp.589–90.
12. Special Assistant Walt W. Rostow to President Johnson on 31 May 1966, ibid., Doc. 297, pp.594–5. 'State' was sceptical about the whole initiative, which came from Johnson himself. Cf. ibid., p.594, n.2.
13. Rusk to Embassy in Tel Aviv, 11 June 1966, ibid., Doc. 298, pp.596–7.
14. Editor's note 3 re: previous publication in *FRUS,* 1961–1963, vol. XVIII, Doc.274.
15. See Doc. 310, p.619, in which Ambassador Rafael rejected any repatriation of Arab refugees to Israel 'at this stage' because 'repatriation is symbol of Arab hostility to Israel'. The main hope was attributed to King Hussein's policy of absorbing Palestinians.
16. Ambassador Gideon Rafael of the Israel Foreign Ministry and Secretary of State Dean Rusk, as reported to the American Embassy in Tel Aviv on 28 July 1966, *FRUS*, 2000, Doc. 312, pp.622–3.

17. See Uzi Narkiss, *A Soldier of Jerusalem*, in Hebrew (Tel Aviv: Ministry of Defense, 1991), pp.130–246.
18. *FRUS*, 2000, Doc. 314, pp.625-7.
19. The meeting took place on 22 August 1966. Ibid., Doc. 315, pp.628–9.
20. Ibid., Doc. 322, pp.637–9.
21. Ibid., Doc. 331, pp. 654–6.
22. See details below and in Shlomo Aronson, *David Ben-Gurion, Renaissance Leader and the Waning of an Age*, in Hebrew (Sede Boqer and Beersheva: Ben-Gurion Research Institute, 1999).
23. *FRUS*, 2000, Doc. 350, pp.688–9.
24. Ibid., Doc. 348, p.687.
25. Ambassador Barbour to Foreign Minister Eban on 29 November 1966, ibid., Doc. 351, p.690.
26. Meeting between Foreign Minister Eban and Nicholas Katzenbach, the Acting American Secretary of State, ibid., Doc. 366, pp.715–18.
27. Meeting between Ambassador Barbour and Foreign Minister Eban, 11 January 1967, bid., Doc. 377, pp.735–7.
28. Special Assistant W.W. Rostow to President Johnson, 16 January 1967, ibid., Doc. 380, pp.742–3.
29. Draft memo Rusk to President, ibid., Doc. 384, pp.750–3.
30. Telegram Lucius D. Battle, American Ambassador in Egypt, to State Department, about meeting with Deputy Vice President Zakaria Muhieddin, sent on 1 February 1967, ibid., Doc. 386, pp.754–6.
31. Ibid., Doc. 391, p.766.
32. See ibid., pertaining to airgram A-478 from Tel Aviv, 7 February, filed as an attachment to a 22 February memo to Rusk, which summarized reports suggesting that Israel's nuclear programme might be moving at a faster pace than previously indicated. The same note quotes a memo to Ambassador Ellsworth Bunker, in charge of desalination equipment that had been promised to Israel – and Egypt – if IAEA safeguards were accepted. The memo, dated 17 February, outlines the views of State's Near East Office about the Israeli desalination project and then states, 'Israel may be constructing a chemical separation facility and proceeding so far in the production of bomb components that assembly of a nuclear weapon could be completed in 6–8 weeks'. NEA, however, was cautious about this; Ambassador Barbour welcomed its caution, adding that 'My own impressions from such information available to us is that Dimona is not running at full blast'.
33. Ibid., Doc. 392, p.767, n.2.
34. Ibid., Doc. 393, pp.768–71.
35. For a brief summary of the 1957 arrangements pertaining to the UN troops, see Aronson, *David Ben-Gurion*.
36. Ibid.
37. Rostow memo to Johnson, 15 March 1967, *FRUS*, 2000, Doc. 395, pp.774–5.
38. Ibid., Doc. 397, p.778.
39. Ibid., Doc. 400, pp.782–5.
40. Rostow memo to Johnson, 7 April 1967, ibid., Doc. 401, pp.786–9.
41. See cable 3020 from Tel Aviv, 23 March, quoted in ibid, p.788.
42. See Ezer Weizman, *On Eagles' Wings, The Personal Story of the Leading Commander of the Israeli Air Force* (Jerusalem and Tel-Aviv: Steimatzky's Agency, 1976), p.207.
43. Miriam Eshkol to this author.
44. *FRUS*, 2000, Doc. 404, pp.791–2.
45. A footnote in the source text defined 'strategic' missiles as those capable of striking major population centres or military installations of the enemy – in this case, missiles with a range of roughly 100–500 miles.
46. Special Assistant to President Johnson, subject: Israel Aid Package, *FRUS*, 2000, Doc. 406, pp.794–6.
47. Ibid., Doc. 407, pp.796–7.
48. See Dan Margalit, *I Have Seen Them All*, in Hebrew (Tel Aviv: Zmora-Bitan, 1997), p.60.

49. *FRUS*, 2000, Doc. 408, p.799.
50. See Arie Baron, *Moshe Dayan and the Six-Day War*, in Hebrew (Tel Aviv: Ministry of Defence, 1997). General Baron was Dayan's aide after the Six Day War and had access to IDF studies on the war and its origins.
51. *FRUS*, 2000, Doc. 415, pp.814–17.
52. Missing in this document is the allegation that Israel 'diverted' a quantity of enriched uranium from a nuclear plant in Pennsylvania, which became a subject for a – still secret – congressional investigation.
53. See in this regard Yitzhak Rabin, *Service Notes*, in Hebrew (Tel Aviv: Sifriyat Ma'ariv, 1979), p.150. Accordingly, Ben-Gurion criticized Rabin's moves from Samu' all the way to the May 1967 mobilization; cf. Michael Bar-Zohar, *Ben-Gurion, A Political Biography,* Part II, in Hebrew (Tel Aviv: Am Oved, 1977), pp.1588–9. Dayan also criticized these actions in the Knesset Foreign Affairs and Defence Committee: 'You [Eshkol's Government] made several undue decisions: you flew over Damascus. You attacked Samu' in daylight'. Rabin remarked, 'It is as though [Dayan] were saying, "You yourself brought this trouble on us"' (Rabin, *Service Notes*, p.137). As the escalation process continued, however, Dayan played a decisive role in bringing about the pre-emptive strike against Egypt. This isolated Ben-Gurion, who wanted to limit the operation to the opening of the Straits by joining a National Emergency Coalition.

Chapter Nine

Eshkol's Supreme Test

THE APPROACHING ECLIPSE

Eshkol's keen political instincts failed him after the general mobilization, which badly limited his domestic freedom. Concurrently, he focused his attention on his 'friend' in the White House, who warned him not to act against Egypt after the closure of the Straits of Tiran. Eshkol still hoped that the United States and several maritime nations would force the Straits open, but they failed to do so, a matter on which we elaborate in due course. Israel felt it necessary to refrain from starting a shooting war in the absence of due process, as it believed that it must demonstrate patience and exhaust diplomatic options. Only thus could it justify unilateral pre-emption and its ensuing requests for United States political-strategic support as a counterweight to Soviet support for the Arabs, not to mention American resupply of weapons. At first Eshkol went so far as to contemplate a request for American financial aid in order to maintain the reserve troops on the Egyptian front, since their mobilization had paralyzed the domestic economy.[1] Under no circumstances, however, could he muster the necessary majority in his own coalition – most of whose members were 'doves' who feared Soviet backing of Nasser's gambit – for immediate pre-emption. Yisrael Galili, who had been removed by Ben-Gurion during the 1948 war from his position as civilian COS of the embryonic IDF because of his partisan loyalties and pro-Soviet views, was now Eshkol's political right-hand man and most important aide, in charge of writing the Prime Minister's speeches and formulating government statements. Galili and his colleague Yigal Allon, soon to return from a visit to Moscow, did opt for immediate military action after Nasser closed the Straits of Tiran, perceiving this a breach of Israel's conventional red lines and an unacceptable challenge to Israel's conventional deterrence posture.

We do not know whether Eshkol was acquainted with Allon's doctrine of 'pre-emptive counterstrike', published in his 1959 volume, *Curtain of Sand.* Challenging Ben-Gurion's embryonic nuclear-deterrence posture, Allon used the contemporary terminology of nuclear deterrence by invoking Thomas C. Schelling's 'red lines' in a conventional context. Such lines, Allon postulated, must be upheld vis-à-vis the enemy, or – if breached or threatened to be breached by him – checked by a 'pre-emptive counterstrike'. Departing from the very different context of 'strategy of conflict' in the nuclear age, as formulated by Schelling, but invoking Schelling's 'rationality' theorem that requires two 'rational' rivals in order to achieve and maintain a stable nuclear balance, Allon proclaimed the Arabs to be 'irrational' and, therefore, capable of escalating acts of war unless stopped from the outset after they challenge the status quo by plans or actual acts. This frame of mind was very much known and accepted among the generals of the IDF, who watched Nasser's escalations with dismay since the political level had chosen thus far not to respond to him, but may have been unknown to Eshkol. If so, Israel's civilian minister of defence was inadequately acquainted with his own army general headquarters and his field commanders – an initial prerequisite pursued by Ben-Gurion during the 1948 war – and had failed to create a political base that would allow him to follow the necessary decision-making procedure during the war.

Eshkol's coalition was imbalanced and the Prime Minister himself was being severely criticized by a raucous opposition, led by Ben-Gurion, Dayan and Peres, for being too tough on Jordan and Syria and too weak on his American 'friends'. Also, Eshkol's way of doing things was to listen, talk, tell stories and jokes, and wear out his adversaries while countenancing other people's views until rendering his decision according to his 'humble, decisive opinion'. This method backfired now.

Lt Gen. Rabin, the COGS, was caught in an increasingly stressful situation. On the one hand, Eshkol authorized his requests for the partial and, later, total mobilization of the reserves. The prevailing opinion among the IDF's generals, however, was that time would play into the enemy's hands if the political echelon disallowed immediate action. The argument was that the Egyptian troops, newcomers in the previously empty bases in the northern Sinai, were acclimatizing quickly, laying vast minefields and placing other obstacles around and among their fortifications, thereby making an Israeli offensive costlier by the day. On top of these worries, the IDF command expected its top-secret aerial attack on the enemy's air bases – the key to the success of the whole campaign – to be leaked in one way or another to too many reservists, who might talk about it sooner rather than later. The generals may have interpreted Eshkol's indecision as evidence that the prime minister and his coalition were not sure whether the army could be trusted at all. The resulting tension between the generals and Eshkol climaxed on 24 May when Rabin seemed to have collapsed under the strain of the events.

Before his ostensible breakdown, Rabin had met with David Ben-Gurion and Moshe Shapira, the dovish leader of the National Religious Party, and complained to them that the political echelon expected him to tell it what to do instead of the other way around. In fact, Rabin's real grievance may have been that Eshkol was frantically trying to persuade President Johnson to reopen the Straits. The premier's ostensibly strong relations with the White House, however, proved disappointing despite Eshkol's boasting of intimate ties with Lyndon Johnson since his visit to the president's ranch in 1964. In the meantime, Israel's economy was grinding to a complete halt and the reserve army awaited a decision in vain.

Although we do not have a transcript of Rabin's meeting with Ben-Gurion, Ben-Gurion's biographer and other secondary sources[2] tell that us Ben-Gurion blamed Rabin and Eshkol for the crisis that had evolved since the Samu' operation. It was odd, Ben-Gurion supposedly said, that Rabin was suddenly asking others to tell him what to do after he had been telling them what to do, without success. The main responsibility for the crisis, however, in Ben-Gurion's judgment, resided with Eshkol: 'He attacked a civilian village' – referring to Samu' and alluding to his own retaliation policy, which forbade such actions ever since the Qibbia affair in the early 1950s[3] – 'flew over Damascus, turned a reprisal operation into a quasi-war, [and] ordered premature mobilization. As a Prime Minister, he is a liar and a coward', hinting at Eshkol's handling of the Ben Barka affair and the downscaling of Dimona. Due to the latter decision, Ben-Gurion alleged – by implication, of course, since no one spoke of this openly – Eshkol was now left with two or three makeshift nuclear devices and no French missiles, all of which on top of a crisis that Eshkol had abetted by his unwarranted decisions, made under public pressure, vis-à-vis Jordan and Syria.

Just the same, Ben-Gurion argued against an Israel-initiated conventional pre-emptive war, as he had in 1956, as a matter of principle. After all, the enemy would merely recover and prepare for a new and costlier round in due course. Ben-Gurion favoured pre-emption only if it were supported by a foreign power, as it had been in 1956, and under circumstances that would guarantee real strategic gains, weapons supplies and minimal Israeli losses. What he had in mind was skilled management of the crisis, something that required several things: a statesman who had firm powers of judgment and knew how to distinguish among priorities, in contrast to the habitual wheeler-dealing of a machine politician; rehabilitation of relations with de Gaulle, which Eshkol seemed to have ruined due to the Ben Barka affair; the completion of the endangered nuclear project in the sense of amassing a real arsenal including missiles; and the exclusion of Allon's and Galili's dangerous influence, which would extend Israel's conventional deterrent posture into the West Bank, with its teeming Palestinian population.

In fact, it was Rabin who had stood behind the aforementioned operations against Samu' and Syria; Eshkol had merely authorized them, although not on the scale in which they had been carried out. Rabin did blame himself for the ensuing escalation and suffered what seemed to be a nervous breakdown. After a day of rest, however, his malaise proved to have been a mild case of fatigue compounded by an overdose of nicotine. On 27 May Rabin resumed his interface with Eshkol and his ministers and again recommended action at the soonest possible opportunity. The Government, however, had just heard a message from President Johnson that conformed to the previous impression, newly conveyed by Foreign Minister Eban (who had recently returned from a meeting with the president), that the United States was committed to helping remove Egypt's blockade of the Straits. Eban misled the Government by reinforcing this impression, since the new message explicitly asked Eshkol not to mention any such a commitment in his public speeches in the Knesset.[4] Eshkol suggested to the cabinet that Israel do one of two things: either go to war immediately or wait some more – perhaps two or thee weeks – and leave the mobilized army massed on the borders, especially since the United

States was not willing to intervene as yet. Eshkol chose war or, at least, voted in favour of it. The cabinet, however, was divided fifty-fifty and Eshkol refrained from exercising his prerogative as Prime Minister to cast a double, decisive vote in the case of a draw of this kind. He must have counted the votes ahead of time and realized that he lacked a clear-cut majority in his coalition for such a vital decision. Thus, although voting in favour of war would have satisfied his 'hawkish' friends such as Galili and Allon, the actual result of the cabinet meeting was no war now, and maybe none ever in the event of the hoped-for American or even international intervention to open the Straits.

THE TIPPING POINT

Thus having stirred his coffee with a healthy dose of tea, or of boiling water, Eshkol proceeded to the radio station to inform the nation that the waiting period would continue instead of the immediate action which was expected. Eshkol read out a written statement in which an aide had inserted corrections in illegible handwriting. When the Prime Minister reached the amended part of the note, he asked the aide to explain the corrections in the middle of the live broadcast, making his typical bass voice appear to stutter. It was the definitive moment in Eshkol's perceived legacy. The 'stutter speech' compounded the disappointment of the mobilized nation and, especially, the troops, who were waiting in vain in their improvised camps for the thing they expected: immediate war. Many believed – wrongly, as we have seen – that Ben-Gurion had launched a preventive war against Egypt in 1956 under much less threatening circumstances but that Eshkol was dragging his feet now. As a witness to this scene,[5] my impression was that Eshkol was unaware of the deterioration of his personal standing brought about by his ostensibly unclear course, which he failed to explain in that broadcast.

Eshkol then proceeded to a meeting with the members of IDF GHQ and senior field commanders. The proceedings of this encounter should be quoted at some length[6] because at this occasion he sounded 'Ben-Gurionic' all the way through. However, failing to exercise the authority of a Ben-Gurion, he soon came under growing public pressure to resign his defence portfolio in favour of Ben-Gurion. Had he acceded to this demand, he would have changed the course of events profoundly even though, while the generals appreciated Ben-Gurion's analytical power, they considered him hopelessly detached from realities on the ground.

Eshkol opened his meeting with the generals – which was not recorded but was later reconstructed by his *aide-de-camp,* who had taken notes – by stating that Israel still faced serious danger and that the state of preparedness must be maintained. The closure of the Straits, he added, was 'like an act of aggression', but noted that there was an international 'willingness' to solve the problem.

> At this very moment, we are using power plus brains. This may not be a pleasant situation for the generals of the IDF ... but in the meantime things have happened in the political level that require restraint and the husbanding of our [military] power. The political problems dictate a delay.

Eshkol went on to describe the Soviet and the American positions in a rather alarmist but nevertheless promising action, full of inaccuracies that would make his situation vis-à-vis the generals even worse. The maritime powers, he said, were preparing an expeditionary force that would sail through the Straits. Eshkol knew very well that President Johnson forbade him from quoting such an American commitment in public and that this was the reason for the Government's refusal to go to war with a reasonable degree of American support against the Soviets either way, that is, via American action to force the Straits open or in an Israel-initiated war. Continuing, Eshkol said that in view of recent political developments and under these 'political, maybe moral' circumstances, we 'must restrain ourselves and husband our power for two or three weeks and maybe altogether'. Two major-generals, Yeshayahu Gavish (GOC Southern Command) and Rehavam Ze'evi (Assistant Chief of Operations), disputed this, arguing that nothing would alleviate the current danger and that the time lost would strengthen the enemy. Eshkol replied, 'Should the great powers deceive us, the Government will decide to act. In the meantime, *based on my personal acquaintance with [President] Johnson*, I do hope that he will keep his promise.' (Italics added.)

What ensued was a hiatus typified by a blend of action and inaction in Washington. Since his 1965 agreement with the United States on conventional arms deliveries and the American inspection visits at Dimona, Eshkol felt bound to a clause requiring consultation with Washington before going to war, if he thought that such action was required. This did not mean that Israel had totally relinquished its freedom of military action, but it seemed to Eshkol that such a commitment on his side would commit the Americans to an effort to maintain the balance of conventional power among the parties in the volatile Middle East and, under certain circumstances, to come to Israel's aid in some manner once consulted, that is, justifying American intervention or an Israeli unilateral act of war when necessary. Although Israel's part in the 1965 deal, regarding more frequent American visits to Dimona, remained unfulfilled, Eshkol had been trying since the beginning of the crisis in May 1967, and especially since the resumption of the Egyptian blockade on Eilat, to transform the crisis into an Egyptian–American problem related to freedom of shipping. Thus, instead of taking summary military action, he had dispatched Mr Eban to Washington (and Paris) first, in order to discuss the crisis with President Johnson. Many of Eshkol's ministers feared that the Soviet Union was behind Nasser's gambit, a possibility that Eshkol himself did not rule out. Consequently, Eban's mission seemed to be the right move for the time being.

For this reason, we quote here the American deliberations with Eban before we return to Eshkol's meeting with his generals, which developed into something like a shouting match.[7] By now, Johnson was under pressure from three sides: the Israelis and their American-Jewish supporters, who otherwise objected to his war in Vietnam; the Arabs, including 'moderates' such as the oil-producing Gulf states like Saudi Arabia, which furnished jet fuel for his operations in Vietnam and linked the current crisis to the Palestinian refugee question and, hence, to Israel's very survival; and Soviet support for the Arabs, who were destined to gain from any American support given to Israel.

Johnson had a meeting with his key secretaries and under-secretaries, agency directors and his Jewish friend Abe Fortas on 26 May 1967. There he was told by Gen. Earl Wheeler, Chair of the Joint Chiefs of Staff, that the Egyptian deployment in Sinai was defensive and that Israel could maintain its present level of mobilization for two months without suffering serious economic troubles. The president also believed that if Egypt attacked Israel, it would lose its defensive positions in the Sinai for little advantage. This point was also clear to Eshkol and David Ben-Gurion, both of whom believed that no action was necessary at that stage. By failing to mobilize Ben-Gurion to his assistance, however, Eshkol would soon have to surrender his defence portfolio to the much more hawkish Moshe Dayan. Dayan had blamed Eshkol for the current crisis, but its causes became irrelevant now, in his view, when Nasser took the initiative and threatened to ride the storm to his advantage. Be this as it may, we can assume that Nasser – and the Soviets – preferred an Israeli first shot that would justify a counterstrike.

The first target of such a counterstrike would be the Dimona reactor, that must have been shut down by then so that it would emit no radioactivity if attacked, justifying an Israeli nuclear response. Secretary of State Dean Rusk summarized the situation by saying that Foreign Minister Eban has been told that Eshkol's message about an imminent Egyptian attack was not supported by American intelligence estimates. He cautioned against a preventative Israeli attack, adding that 'we could not be responsible if Israel goes off on its own'. Secretary of Defense Robert McNamara repeated Rusk's warning and interpreted the Eban–Dulles accord pursuant to Israel's withdrawal from the Straits in 1957 as if Washington had made no real commitment to Israel to use American power in the event of a renewed Egyptian blockade, at least without congressional approval. (The question of American commitments of this kind would drive future Israeli Governments to seek rock-solid obligations, as far as possible, before surrounding occupied territories.) Lucius D. Battle, the former Ambassador to Egypt, now in charge of the State Department Near East Division, identified 'a vigorous Soviet effort to turn this crisis into a US–Arab confrontation' and argued that 'Whatever we do we are in trouble. If we fail to stand by Israel, the radical Arabs will paint us as a paper tiger. If we stand by Israel, we will damage ourselves seriously with all the Arabs.' Battle offered one line of consolation: 'We must know that the Arabs never stick together for long. We know that eventually strains will reappear.' Johnson's way out of this was to adopt the Rusk–McNamara view plus an effort to resolve the crisis in the UN Security Council (which basically had been paralyzed by the Soviets' veto power) while seeking ways to organize a force of several maritime nations to sail through the Straits, but no military action without congressional approval. Urging Eshkol to stay patient, Johnson was far from the picture painted by Eshkol at his meeting with the generals. The *FRUS* volume quoted above contains several additional remarks about Nasser's economic plight and the effect of the American grain embargo as possibly a mistake,[8] but nothing about Dimona – perhaps due to censorship by the editors.

With this background in mind, we return to the 'night of the generals'.[9] Maj. Gen. Ariel Sharon (Head of Training, GHQ, and division commander on the Egyptian front) argued that Israel had

> destroyed its deterrent power by its own hand. We have broken our main weapon – the enemy's fear. If we give up on the issue of the Straits, we open the road to the demise of Israel altogether. We also must take into consideration the demise of the people's morale ... The people understand and feel that they must pay a price. The problem is not the Straits. The problem is maintaining Israel's very existence.

The Prime Minister countered Sharon's arguments by positing that they contained a contradiction in terms with regard to forfeiting the Straits and Israeli rights. Sharon stuck to his guns, retorting that the Israeli inaction exposed Israel as a powerless, humiliated nation. 'I do not share this consideration', Eshkol responded:

> We have dealt with it and taken it into account. We believe that the foreign powers are indeed interested in Israel's safety. We must remember that destroying the Egyptian army now will not bring it to an end. It will recover. Israel won't without foreign aid. If we can avoid war, we must spare no effort to do so. There is a good hope that Britain and the United States, for their own considerations as well, will do it instead of us. Israeli generals must understand the considerations of the statesmen and not allow their unhappiness to be decisive ... The Government has to view the matter as a whole, the question of blood, the problem of property, and damage to the military machine.

Here, whether he knew it or not, Eshkol repeated almost verbatim Ben-Gurion's arguments against a preventive war in his debate with General Dayan in 1956. The generals, however, continued in succession to raise issues that the Minister of Defence should have clarified with them earlier, not in the middle of such a crisis. Maj. Gen. Avraham Yoffe, a division commander in the south, warned him that, 'Our feeling must work itself out to the troops. We won't leave here all smiles. And even if we pretended to, we'd be exposed as liars.' His colleagues, Armoured Corps Commander Maj. Gen. Israel Tal and Quartermaster General Matitiahu Peled, lectured their civilian boss on two counts: there were no assurances that the Americans could force the Straits open and, more important, Mr Eshkol did not realize that the IDF was not designed to remain mobilized for many weeks. The reserves had been called up and must act quickly. Others repeated these arguments, adding that not only could the Arab armies be destroyed easily but Nasser's unpunished challenge necessitated this outcome.

Eshkol's response again ignored a fundamental of Israel's conventional security doctrine – propagated years ago by his political ally Yigal Allon, who had joined Eshkol during the meeting but had said nothing in his presence – that his audience had evidently internalized:

> We need to take a long breath. Nobody said that we are an army of pre-emption ... I do not accept that an Egyptian army deployed in the Sinai dictates war ... We are not alone in the world. The very term 'power of deterrence' requires long breath ... It certainly enrages those who all their lives have been educated to attack, to wage war. But we were talking about deterrence. Deterrence [as opposed to pre-emption – SA] does not mean action ... I argue that the power of deterrence can wait and allow all other possibilities to be exhausted ... Must we live by our sword all our lives? If we have a reason, we would do it. Did you need more hardware? Fine. You wanted 100 warplanes? You received them. You received tanks as well. You received everything necessary to win if necessary. We have been educated not to fight a pre-emptive war.

That was exactly Eshkol's problem: most if not all members of this group of military men had been educated to fight a conventional war of pre-emption according to the Allon doctrine that their civilian boss had suddenly discovered. It was too late, especially since the same mechanism that had contributed decisively to Eshkol's public success since 'the Affair' had now begun to erode his public standing. The combination of media pressure to take immediate action, obvious displeasure with his inaction on the part of the public and the mobilized nation, and, finally, the loss of confidence of his coalition partners and his own party's central committee in Eshkol's leadership escalated into growing demands that he relinquish at least his defence portfolio. It is not clear whether Eshkol's 'deterrence' posture, as quoted above, was also based on the nuclear option as a last resort if conventional deterrence were to fail and a military catastrophe occur. In fact, Col. Shlomo Gazit, the IDF spokesman who briefed the Israeli war correspondents at that stage of the crisis, myself included, did allude to a 'Samson Option' if other measures to save the nation failed.[10]

We do not know how such an option would work without the French missiles. It is possible that the IDF had converted some old French-made subsonic Voutour medium-range bombers to carry the few bombs that were available. Censorship, however, would have eliminated any trace of nuclear deterrence from the text quoted above. By itself, the IDF under Rabin had never adopted the nuclear option as an operative part of its strategic doctrine; instead, it adhered to Allon's conventional-pre-emption doctrine.[11] And, of course, the question of the missing French missiles, coupled with Eshkol's concessions to the Americans in this regard and on the American inspection visits at Dimona, should at least have brought about some serious American action regarding the blockade of Eilat. However, no such thing seemed to be forthcoming, despite increased Jewish lobbying of President Johnson. Levi Eshkol may have expected this sort of action to work in the longer run, but his young Israeli generals and the general public, who had been raised since Ben-Gurion's times to believe in self-reliance, but were less attentive to his warnings about an Israeli-initiated war alone, were less convinced. Soon, however, they would be surprised to discover that the 'old man' was much more cautious than his reputation.

A DISSONANT SONATINA FOR TWO DOERS

At this stage, let us move back to Washington, DC. According to Robert Dallek, Johnson's biographer,[12] the American President 'had struggled' during the first three years of his tenure 'to contain an Israeli nuclear programme which Israel perceived to be essential to its survival'. As we noted above, the struggle for containment was the source of ensuing arms deals and conditional American assurances to come to Israel's aid in case of emergency. Concurrently, Johnson's State Department was trying to cultivate its relations with 'moderate' Muslim states such as Jordan, Iran and Saudi Arabia, while reducing its economic aid to radical Egypt and trying to isolate Ba'athist Syria. Since the beginning of the May 1967 crisis, however, given Johnson's warnings to Eshkol not to act alone on pain of being left alone, 'The President came now "under tremendous pressure" from American Jewish groups'. Dallek recounts Foreign Minister Eban's visit to Washington in mid-May – 'a little miniature Winston Churchill', in Johnson's acerbic language, sent by Eshkol's Government to explore the Administration's response to what Israel considered the illegal Egyptian blockade of Eilat. The issue, including American obligations to lift the blockade, possibly with British naval support, proved legally and practically complicated in view of Johnson's conflicting priorities. Since the *FRUS* records dealing with this complex issue may have been censored to exclude the nuclear issue and possible Soviet support of the Arabs in that context, Dallek says that, in any case, the President's dilemma was how to prevent a war or, failing this, how to head off a US confrontation with the Soviet Union. This seems to have been de Gaulle's main concern as well. It explains his warning to Israel not to fire the first shot and his enforcement of this injunction by imposing a weapons embargo on Israel, including shipments already paid for, and his wish, expressed in a conversation with Abba Eban, to join a four-power Middle East crisis forum in which France would be an equal member at last.

Johnson's worries focused on the growing domestic opposition to Vietnam, which he considered now a distraction from the 'more important' Middle East conflict. Also, the Administration still hoped for an NPT agreement with Moscow. For the time being, the US Sixth Fleet was ordered to stay away from the potential belligerents' shores and Eshkol was warned again not to start a war. Even when King Hussein of Jordan flew to Egypt on 30 May and placed his army under Egyptian command, breaching yet another Israeli red line, the President counselled Eshkol to maintain patience while having no other idea how to come to his 'friend's' help.

On the afternoon of 5 June 1967, a State Department spokesman declared the United States 'neutral in thought, word and deed'. One can imagine what this statement meant for Eshkol's standing at home; after maintaining for years that he had forged an alliance of sorts with Johnson, he was now shown to have entertained an illusion. Now, according to Dallek, American Jews stepped in unleashing 'a fire storm of criticism' that would crimp Johnson's freedom to apply effective pressure on Israel should she decide to pre-empt. After such pre-emption, too, in my judgment, the Johnson Administration would adopt a new policy on Arab territories occupied by Israel. There would be no repetition of Eisenhower's strict demands for Israeli withdrawal from such territories in exchange for UN peacekeeping forces – now gone, at Nasser's behest – and vague promises about freedom of shipping to Eilat, now proven to be a matter of interpretation by the UN and, possibly, the International Court at the Hague, as repeated by Walt Rostow, Johnson's aide.[13] Furthermore, as it turned out, the combination of these circumstances, Eshkol's lengthy patience, and Israel's stunning victory secured American resupplies for Israel. Given the fact of Soviet resupplies for Egypt and Syria, however, this would take some time to become the official American position.

After the fact, Egypt complained that the United States (and the British) had been directly involved in the IAF's destruction of its airfields. The US's declaration of 'neutrality' was aimed to head off Arab sentiments of this kind, especially after several Arab states broke relations with Washington. The immediate outcome of the neutrality statement, however, was that Johnson found himself attacked by Arabs and Jews alike. Hence, he instructed Secretary of State Dean Rusk to reiterate a statement that he had made on 25 May about supporting the territorial integrity and independence of all countries in the region and eagerness for a cease-fire and a long-term settlement. Also, according to Dallek, Johnson asked prominent Jewish friends to get the word out that he was working to assure Israel's security and that attacks against his Administration were uncalled for and unproductive. Some in the Jewish community were not so sure about this; they suggested that the President issue a statement to a rally that was scheduled to take place at Washington's Lafayette Park. The idea was endorsed by two Jewish aides at the White House, Larry Levinson and Ben Wattenberg, who argued that such a statement might even help Johnson win support not only from Jews but also among his anti-Vietnam foes. In response, the President, catching sight of Levinson down the hall, shouted at him, waving a clenched fist:

> You Zionist dupe! You and Wattenberg are Zionist dupes in the White House! Why can't you see I'm doing all I can for Israel? That's what you should be telling people when they ask for a message from the President for their rally.[14]

By referring to 'all' that he was doing, Johnson may have had in mind the Sixth Fleet, which, although ordered to maintain its distance from the belligerents' shores, effectively neutralized the Soviet Mediterranean flotilla and gave Israel freedom of action if attacked, in the expectation that she would win anyway.

When hostilities did erupt, Walt Rostow busied himself trying to determine who had fired the first shot. The White House and State may have dropped the matter once Israel made public an intercepted phone conversation between Nasser and Hussein of Jordan, which exposed them as having conspired to hold the United States responsible for the Israeli air offensive against Egypt. Soon afterwards, attention focused on an Israeli attack on the American surveillance ship USS *Liberty,* a tragic mistake that we discuss further on.[15]

THE OTHER SUPERPOWER

But let us discuss the Soviet role in this crisis as well: Isabella Ginor and Gideon Remez's *Foxbats over Dimona: The Soviet Nuclear Gamble in the Six-Day War*[16] adds yet another dimension to the story. The authors argue that the USSR instigated the 1967 crisis deliberately in the context of blocking Israel's nuclear programme, committing Soviet personnel and weapons to direct military intervention on the Arabs' behalf. This important study substantiates Israel's fear in the spring of 1967 that the Soviet Union was indeed the main actor behind Nasser's manoeuvres that culminated in the Six Day War.

While the authors' argument for direct Soviet military intervention is weak and contradictory, the argument that the USSR instigated the crisis deliberately is spot on. According to Ginor and Remez, it was the Israeli Prime Minister and Minister of Defence, Levi Eshkol, who had initially set the May 1967 crisis in motion against his better judgment. Beginning with assurances from Isser Harel, Eshkol's intelligence advisor, to the Soviets that Israel's nuclear programme was not yet ready, the authors assert that this unconventional endeavour, including the ordering of intermediate range ballistic missiles from France, had kindled Moscow's wrath. Therefore, it was Eshkol and his allies at home, mainly the Ahdut ha-'Avoda politicians Yigal Allon and Yisrael Galili, who seemed to have feared a Soviet nuclear guarantee to Egypt without Israel possessing missiles capable of threatening the USSR, thereby providing Egypt with an umbrella in case Israel's atomic bombs were ready. This, in turn, eventually prompted Nasser to move forward to eliminate the Dimona nuclear reactor if not Israel itself.

The real power behind Nasser's gambit of May 1967, according to Ginor and Remez, was Moscow, that is, the Soviet military under Marshal Andrei Grechko and Admiral Sergei Gorshkov, in cooperation with their Egyptian counterpart, Marshal Abd el Hakim Amer. The highest political level in both countries – Secretary General Leonid Brezhnev (and Alexei Kosygin, his more cautious premier) and President Nasser – endorsed military preparations in view of Israel's imminent nuclearization. Yitzhak Rabin's part in this drama, which would lead to the tragedy of his assassination years later, was purely conventional, aimed at maintaining conventional deterrence vis-à-vis hostile Arab states and preventing Palestinian guerrillas from operating inside Israel from bases in Syria or havens in Jordan. Thus, in November 1966, Rabin embarked upon the large-scale reprisal operation against the then-Jordanian-Palestinian West Bank village of Samu', prompting not only American wrath but the Palestinian turmoil noted above. As a result, Rabin moved on to Soviet-backed Syria, whose radical and aggressive Ba'ath regime was not only behind the Palestinian incursions into Israel but was also fighting Jewish farmers working along the contested frontier by shelling large parts of the Galilee from the Golan Heights. A series of air battles initiated by Rabin, one which ended with the downing of Syrian MiGs over Damascus, was followed by open threats by Rabin to induce regime change in Syria. To place this chain of events in its context, we must understand that the Soviets operated on two levels. Trying to protect their allies in Damascus gave them the pretext to prod Nasser into moving his army into fortified yet empty positions along the open, hardly protected Israeli southern border. Essentially, Rabin's conventional deterrent postures backfired.

Foxbats over Dimona makes an important contribution to the study of Soviet behaviour by analysing Israel's rights and problems, which changed abruptly when Brezhnev adopted a belligerent posture towards America's standing in the region. Using sources based on the memoirs of former Soviet officials and interviews with Soviet military personnel, Ginor and Remez describe Brezhnev's policy actions in detail. First, they explore his demands to withdraw the US Sixth Fleet from the Mediterranean and his adoption of an extremely hostile attitude toward Israel, including the territories that it had won after the Arab aggression of the 1948–49 war – all of which thanks to Soviet-authorized supplies via Czechoslovakia, which the Kremlin now regarded as 'occupied'. Second, the authors analyse the implications of Soviet military strategies for the newly born cause of the Palestinian refugees. All of which combined with Eshkol's internally weak and externally isolated Government. Indeed, Israel's woes under Eshkol – its first-ever economic recession, its inability to stop Fatah's guerrilla attacks, and a hesitant but later escalatory policy toward Syria – prompted growing domestic criticism among ordinary Israelis and Ben-Gurion's opposition party, Rafi. Finally, Eshkol had also presided over the Ben-Barka affair (the aforementioned rogue Israeli intelligence operation in France), which may have driven a furious General de Gaulle to cancel the delivery, scheduled for 1967 or early 1968, of French-made medium-range nuclear-capable missiles – prompting a torrent of criticism from opposition leader Ben-Gurion without the disclosure of its reasons.

Eshkol, along with Foreign Minister Abba Eban, while trying his best to temper Washington's criticism of the Israeli nuclear programme by allowing ineffective American inspection visits at Dimona, also attempted to placate Moscow. One of these attempts may have been a message conveyed to the Kremlin that the Israeli nuclear programme had not become operational yet. Remez and Ginor use various terms to denote the thing that had not become operational, such as a 'deliverable weapon', which may have included not just an assembled bomb but a credible means of delivery – in my view, the French developed medium-range missiles that indeed could cover Soviet territory and practically every vital Arab target. Eshkol, in my opinion, may have hinted to the Kremlin that it need not concern itself with this threat to Soviet territory as an unacceptable provocation. Indeed, when the first Israeli satellite was launched years later, the Soviet official in charge quoted Eshkol's political ally and conventional-pre-emption strategist, Yigal Allon, as having promised Moscow not to deploy missiles capable of launching satellites (and nuclear warheads as well).

At any rate, Ginor and Remez argue that since it was clear that the Israeli nuclear project had neither materialized yet nor had been adopted by Israel as its strategic deterrent – based on Eshkol's assurances, as I may add – the Soviets and the Egyptians plotted the 1967 May crisis. The Soviets planned to draw Israel into striking Egypt first; this, they figured, would end with the destruction of Israel's most important instrument of survival: its nuclear capability. The plan would have extended a Soviet 'nuclear guarantee' to Egypt while Russian pilots, employing the new MiG 25 (the 'Foxbat'), flew spy sorties back and forth over Dimona. This activity followed Nasser's march into Sinai and his decision to blockade the Straits of Tiran. In the end, however, the Soviets instructed Nasser (or he preferred) to engage in a 'legitimate' game based on international norms, one that prohibited the Egyptian army and air force from starting a shooting war. Indeed, Ben-Gurion and several of Eshkol's ministers were correct in rejecting the 'first shot' approach adopted by Rabin and supported by Galili and, later, by Allon, who actually returned from a visit to Moscow during the peak of the crisis. Eshkol himself also favoured this approach, as noted above, albeit against the votes of half of his own cabinet.

Foxbats over Dimona suggests that the Soviets believed that a ground war would end in a draw and that the United States, whose client would be practically defeated and otherwise stranded in Sinai by a Soviet-allied client, would suffer a major humiliation. The United States, the Soviets assumed, would not risk direct intervention on Israel's behalf because this would provoke a direct confrontation with the powerful Soviet naval squadron that had been amassed in the eastern Mediterranean. I would add to this the traditional American fear of provoking the entire Arab world by coming to Israel's aid. The Kremlin would protect Soviet clients such as Syria from Rabin's open threats against the radical regime in Damascus by prodding Cairo to initiate the May 1967 crisis. This line of reasoning is not mere speculation. Ginor and Remez's argument is well documented and supported by President Johnson's behaviour, which followed the Soviet scenario almost to the letter with the exception that he believed Israel would win a conventional war if the initial crisis evolved into one.

Foxbats over Dimona deepens and enlarges our understanding of these events, providing a more nuanced view not only of conventional accounts of the war, but also of contemporary accounts of Cold War history. Ginor and Remez also help us to understand better the subtleties surrounding Israel's own deliberations at the time, at least as far as the political elite, as opposed to the mobilized masses, was concerned.

Although *Foxbats over Dimona* makes important contributions to the literature on the 1967 war, two issues remain problematic even from the authors' standpoint: Nasser's point of view and the credibility of a 'Soviet nuclear guarantee', and Soviet forecasting of American behaviour, that is, the reaction that could be expected despite the State Department's official policy of 'neutral[ity] in thought, word and deed'. According to Ginor and Remez, the Kremlin deployed nuclear-capable submarines (and other vessels) that, under the circumstances, would have 'nuked' Israel if Jerusalem used nuclear weapons against Egypt and even prepared landings on Israeli shores. The difficulty with this thesis, from Nasser's point of view, was that 'nuking Israel' would have followed a nuked Egypt, a proposition that the Egyptian President would have hardly tolerated regardless of Soviet assurances. Indeed, the landing of Soviet troops on Israeli shores contradicts the authors' own description of the extreme precautions that the Soviets took to disguise, or rather to hide, their presence (mostly as pilots) on Egyptian soil even during the peak of the crisis, a fortiori an overt marine landing.

The Soviet-Egyptian plan developed in a more sophisticated fashion than that. Having marched his troops all the way to the Israeli border, Nasser created a direct threat to Dimona, forcing Israel to shut the reactor down and mobilize reserves to seal the frontier. A 'cold' reactor, one that did not emit radioactivity, was not a live nuclear target and, therefore, would not justify a nuclear counter-response by Israel. The threat to Dimona was now from the air; indeed, the Soviets helped to gather intelligence on the facility's defences, as illustrated by Ginor and Remez. But since neither the Soviets nor Nasser allowed the Egyptian air force a first-strike option, the Egyptian army in the Sinai remained in defensive positions. As the authors of *Foxbats over Dimona* argue convincingly, both Moscow and Cairo did their best to provoke an Israeli first strike that would justify Egyptian countermeasures against Dimona above all. Nevertheless, I would argue that the Soviets never intended to be engaged in the conflict directly because the Americans had ordered the Sixth Fleet away from the countries involved, but not too far away. What is more, as Ginor and Remez also claim, the US fleet was stronger than the Soviet Mediterranean flotilla.

Nasser's own targets may have been limited to the following scenario: first, if Israel fired the first shot, he would retaliate by bombing the 'cold' Dimona reactor, thereby assuring Arab conventional potential to deal with a conventional Israel in due course. Second, at this stage, should Israel try to invade Sinai, the IDF might be trapped between Egyptian fortified positions while trying to relieve a blockaded Eilat. The Egyptian special forces, poised across the border, would isolate Eilat from Israel's mainland and capture it, restoring Egypt's land connection with the other Arab countries to the north and east. Third, Soviet diplomatic support in the Security Council, backed by its satellites and Third World votes, could stop the hostilities whenever Nasser wished, while the United States would hardly intervene in a war whose real *casus belli* was Israel's nuclearization (unacceptable as it was to both Moscow and Washington).

Having studied the Egyptian deployment in Sinai, David Ben-Gurion realized that it was defensive and concluded that Nasser would not move any further regardless of the Soviet 'nuclear guarantee' that Marshal Grechko had given Egypt publicly, if tentatively, in early 1966. Ultimately, Dimona remained intact despite the Soviet intelligence over flights that Ginor and Remez describe in detail. Only if Israel delivered the first strike would it justify Nasser's response. Had it been his decision, Ben-Gurion might have opted for two options other than giving the other side what it wanted, an Israeli first strike. One would have been the removal of Eshkol from both his offices, the premiership and the MOD, thereby repairing the seriously impaired relations with de Gaulle's France, French missiles included. The other option would have been the revival of Israel's own missile programme, which Eshkol had scrapped when he took office in 1963, including the accumulation of a nuclear arsenal on top of the two or three makeshift devices that had been hurriedly readied at the height of the crisis despite the lack of credible means of long-range delivery. All of this required patience, time and a clear-cut order of priorities. Therefore, Ben-Gurion concentrated his focus away from resolving the crisis to de-escalating it and managing it until Eshkol could be removed.

When Nasser's gambit prompted escalation across the Arab world including Jordan, Ben-Gurion might have endorsed limited action centring on opening the Straits of Tiran, for which some measure of international consensus existed. He might also have advocated some limited action in the West Bank once King Hussein joined Nasser, but never occupation as touted by Allon, Galili and Rabin and (later) by Moshe Dayan and Menachem Begin, who joined Eshkol's Government in early June 1967. Since the Israeli Air Force enjoyed complete control over the West Bank (and would in due course destroy an Iraqi expeditionary force on its way to Jerusalem), the occupation of the West Bank was militarily unnecessary.

Although the Soviet behaviour as described by Ginor and Remez was indeed aggressive, when the long hoped-for Israeli first strike threw Moscow (and Cairo) off balance it was the Soviet Union, not Washington, that was humiliated for a while – all of which without the Americans' lifting a finger to help Israel. The nuclear issue seems to have briefly disappeared from the (censored) American records that are available to us; the official American position before the outbreak of the war was expressed in favour of maintaining the territorial integrity of all nations in the region, while Moscow rushed to turn the Straits into Egyptian territorial waters. More interestingly, the new American Ambassador in Egypt, Richard Nolte, suggested on 25 May a possible package deal in which Israel 'would give refugees a choice between peaceful repatriation or full compensation, international status of [West] Jerusalem, and the question of frontiers under the original partition arrangements' that would be subject to negotiation. Israel's existence would 'in effect' be recognized by the Arabs and Israel would gain freedom of passage through the Gulf of Aqaba and an end to the Arab boycott.[17] In a meeting with Robert Anderson, Johnson's personal envoy, however, Nasser asserted that all Palestinian refugees, without exception, would return and transform Israel to a Jewish-Arab state of sorts. Thus, the refugee issue as well as the nuclear question would remain on the American agenda even after the Israeli victory, which President Johnson would hardly celebrate.

NOTES

1. See Eitan Haber, *'Today War Will Break Out', The Reminiscences of Brig. Gen. Israel Lior, Aide-de-Camp to Prime Ministers Levi Eshkol and Golda Meir,* in Hebrew (Tel Aviv: Edanim, 1987), pp.118*ff*.
2. See ibid, p.174; Michael Bar-Zohar, *Ben-Gurion, A Political Biography,* Part II, in Hebrew (Tel Aviv: Am Oved, 1977), pp.1588–9.
3. After a Palestinian terrorist attack in Israel in which a mother and her two children lost their lives, Defence Minister Ben-Gurion authorized a raid against the Palestinian village of Qibbia, then under Jordanian rule, on 14–15 October 1953. Many civilians were killed in the raid. From then on, Ben-Gurion ordered the IDF to target military objectives only, a policy that remained in force later during his tenure as Minister of Defence.
4. Haber, *'Today War Will Break* Out', 192, and cf. American documentation in Notes 7 and 17 below.
5. After the general mobilization, I was called up for reserve duty as war correspondent for the Voice of Israel's combined military-civilian emergency radio network and happened to be in the studio during Eshkol's speech.
6. Haber, *'Today War Will Break Out'*, pp.194*ff*.
7. See *Foreign Relations of the United States* (*FRUS*), Vol. XIX, *Arab–Israeli Crisis and War, 1967,* and cf. Robert Dallek, *A Flawed Giant, Lyndon Johnson and His Times, 1961–1973* (New York: Oxford University Press, 1993), pp.425*ff*.
8. See Rostow to Johnson, ibid., pp.146–7.
9. Haber, *'Today War Will Break Out'*, pp.195–8.
10. I do not remember the date, but the briefing followed a speech by Nasser in which he referred to the outright destruction of Israel, echoed by mass hysteria in the Arab world.
11. See address at meeting of IDF high command, 4 January 1964, in Yemima Rosenthal (ed.), *Yitzhak Rabin, Prime Minister of Israel 1974–1977/1992–1995, Selected Documents, Volume I, Early Years and Military Career 1922–1967*, in Hebrew (Jerusalem: Israel State Archives, 2005), pp.336–7, top secret.
12. Dallek, *A Flawed Giant*, p.423.
13. Rostow to President, 26 May 1967, *FRUS*, Vol. XIX, p.122, partially censored.
14. Dallek, *A Flawed Giant*, pp.428–9.
15. See lengthy exchange about the *Liberty* incident in *FRUS*, Vol. XIX, pp.205–319.
16. New Haven, CT: Yale University Press, 2007.
17. See *FRUS*, Vol. XIX, p.115, note.

Chapter Ten

Levi Eshkol and the Lost Glory

TERRITORIAL GAINS AT WHAT PRICE?

On the eve of Israel's pre-emptive strike in June 1967, it seemed as though the whole Arab world had been mobilized by Nasser to eradicate the Jewish entity in its midst, which stood alone.

At home, the 'waiting period' took an irreparable toll on Eshkol's public standing. While deliberating what to do and still hoping for a remedy from Washington, Eshkol, for decades a 'doer', had become in the eyes of the public a do-nothing prime minister, the embodiment of inaction amid public fears that a new Holocaust was brewing, that 'the world' was as indifferent and estranged as it had been during the Holocaust, and that pre-emption, even alone, should be pursued as it supposedly had been pursued in 1956. The sense of imminent doom created by Nasser's moves and open threats was couched in Holocaust-related terms.

When Eshkol was asked by his own party and coalition partners to give up the defence portfolio in preparation for the unavoidable pre-emption, and when Ben-Gurion's name was mentioned in this regard, he said, 'These two horses won't push the same cart', but added that the Americans, too, would find Ben-Gurion 'undesirable' because they looked upon him as the father of Israel's nuclear programme. Eshkol's view on military action at this stage of the crisis was not far from Ben-Gurion's: both believed in delaying such action, harbouring doubts about its wisdom. Eshkol's ego, however, prevented him from handing the MOD to his personal rival. His vendetta had fateful consequences. Ben-Gurion would never have undone the partitioning of the country between Arabs and Jews, always fearing that Jewish rule over large numbers of Arabs would delegitimize Israel itself. Had he been in power at the MOD, he would have endorsed two limited actions, one to reopen the Straits and the other to restrain King Hussein, Nasser's new ally; but would have refrained from occupying the entire West Bank. In the end, Ben-Gurion was deserted by his own comrades, Moshe Dayan and Shimon Peres, who joined Eshkol's emergency coalition and remained on the sidelines to watch a tremendous victory take place – West Bank, Gaza and all – the results of which Israelis and Arabs live and die by to this day.

Thus, before surrendering his hopes for some form of American intervention to open the Straits and before starting to prepare for war, Eshkol created a National Unity Government under pressure from the media, his coalition partners and his own party. He had been rather responsive to such pressure during his handling of the Lavon affair. This syndrome, although advantageous to him back then, now made him a tragic hero in his own eyes. Eshkol named General (Res.) Moshe Dayan as Minister of Defence in the new national emergency coalition. Apart from Dayan's role as an opposition leader since the 1965 elections, Eshkol roundly disliked the man, nicknaming Dayan 'Abu Jilda' (an Arab robber chieftain) behind his back and fearing his cunning character, his highly developed style of manipulating the media as best he could, and his pronounced disloyalty to anyone if his personal interests were involved. However, given the enormous pressure from his coalition partners, the press and finally his own party colleagues, he preferred Dayan to Ben-Gurion. Vendettas make history.

Eshkol's appointment of Moshe Dayan as his replacement at the MOD electrified the country – an Israel-born war hero, the 1956 COGS, succeeded the dithering Eshkol, an 'exilic' Jew (who had arrived in the country close to Dayan's birth) – and electrified the expanded Government as well. Stepping right into the job, Dayan decisively prevailed on the cabinet in the direction of war. He also tore up Rabin's initial war plans,[1] opting instead for an across-the-board pre-emptive campaign against Egypt and, together with Eshkol, allowing the IDF to occupy the whole West Bank following King Hussein's surrender to Nasser and intervention in the Israel–Egyptian war. Furthermore, he revised the original GHQ operational plan, aiming it at the destruction of the whole Egyptian army in the Sinai and the occupation of most of the peninsula. Only later on were Jordanian, Syrian and Iraqi forces swiftly defeated after they had intervened in Israel's war against Egypt. The occupation of the Golan Heights is discussed farther on.

Israel's tremendous victory over Egypt, Jordan, Syria and the Iraqi expeditionary force imbued the Israeli populace with a sense of salvation, expressed in terms of a Jewish ghetto that had fought and won, this time, on its own and against the Arabs' Soviet support and American neutrality. Dimona survived and was later tacitly recognized by the Nixon-Kissinger Administration, provided that Israel would not go nuclear publicly. What is more, the war gave Israel enough defensive room to allow its bomb to be hidden in the basement. The bomb remained visible enough, however, to impose limitations on the combined Egyptian-Syrian offensive in 1973 and contribute its share to the Israeli-Egyptian peace treaty in 1979; it may also serve to restrain Iran's nuclear ambitions in the future.

All this, however, remained overshadowed by what became the occupation of the West Bank and Gaza, following the initial decisions made about the occupied territories by Eshkol's wall-to-wall coalition and thanks to his own initiatives. The occupation of the West Bank, unintended though it had been, prompted various changes of short and longer ranges that are mentioned here briefly and developed below.

As noted, the birth of Eshkol's National Unity Government introduced Mr Menachem Begin and his right-wing political bloc (then Herut, later known as Likud) into Israel's supreme executive institution, next to the already-represented nationalist Left under Galili and Allon. Both parties were committed to maintaining, in various ways, Israel's control over the West Bank or at least parts of it (Begin wanted the whole place) for ideological reasons as an old Zionist entitlement and due to a political-strategic calculation that viewed these territories as an indispensable security belt. Dayan tried at first to suggest more pragmatic options in regard to the West Bank and Gaza. However, reluctant to sound less patriotic than others and isolated in Eshkol's Government as an unwanted, imposed semi-partner, he needed allies such as Mr Begin, at least on the face of it.

Among many Mapai activists and intellectuals, a Greater Israel movement, favouring the establishment and maintenance of settlements in the unpartitioned Land of Israel, came into being and sank roots. Eshkol himself, at first rather sceptical about whether most of the West Bank could be retained, endorsed his Government's resolution to unify Jerusalem under Israeli rule, expand its municipal boundaries, and, later, establish Jewish neighbourhoods in the annexed areas. Moshe Dayan, as Minister of Defence in charge of occupied territories, intervened immediately after the fall of eastern Jerusalem and ordered the administration of the Temple Mount, including the Al-Aqsa Mosque – the third-holiest place in Islam – and the nearby Dome of the Rock, to be restored to the Waqf, the Islamic charitable trust organization that had been in charge of the Mount before the war. Thus, civilian authority in charge of law and order on the Mount became Israeli and adherents of all three monotheistic religions could now visit this very sensitive place, but the Waqf retained its custodian role, as it has to this day.

Soon enough, too, a national-religious movement actively launched settlement efforts of its own, initially near Hebron, with the support of Yigal Allon, Eshkol's coalition ally, which Dayan tried unavailingly to prevent. Later on, Allon conceived a long-term plan for the West Bank that called for Israeli control only of strategic parts of the territory, including the Jordan Valley, and the creation of a narrow corridor from Jordan to the Arab-populated parts of the West Bank so that this population could establish a state in that area or rejoin Jordan.[2] This 'Allon Plan',[3] albeit never officially endorsed, became the blueprint for Israeli settlements in the West Bank until it was eroded by religious and other forces, including imported religious-nationalistic elements from the United States, as discussed below.

The peculiarities of the Israeli proportional-balloting electoral system, which produced a multiparty constellation and unstable coalitions, should be mentioned here again because they were the source of difficulties in decision-making on the future of the occupied territories. For the time being, as far as Sinai and the Golan Heights were concerned, Eshkol's national coalition offered to negotiate peace with Egypt and Syria in exchange for these territories. Hopes in this direction were publicly dashed by an Arab summit conference in Khartoum in September 1967, also discussed at greater length below. Consequently, Eshkol's grand coalition carried on uneasily, buffeted not by conflicting ideological-political differences among its components but also by personal rivalries among key members such as Eshkol, Allon and Dayan, and their prickly sensitivity to media and public opinion and the public's newly won sense of salvation and glory. Typically, Eshkol tried to merge his Mapai Party, Dayan's Rafi and Allon's Ahdut ha-'Avoda into a new, united Labour Party in 1968, but personal, ideological and political-power differences allowed formal, rather than real unification, until his death in early 1969. David Ben-Gurion, the founding father of Israel and of Rafi, was left alone to preach for withdrawal from occupied territories at almost all costs.

For Eshkol, it was all in vain. Dayan reaped all the glory of a victory that had been made possible by Eshkol's decisive contribution to IDF procurements and preparedness and his patience and ongoing dialogue with President Johnson, which later secured needed military resupplies and seemed to have proved his claims that a sort of a strategic alliance did exist between Washington and Jerusalem. The relatively young, Israel-born and charismatic Dayan, who even looked so unlike Eshkol and whose from-the-hip but high-level Hebrew was far from Eshkol's blend of Hebrew and Yiddish, was the winner of the day, or of the six days. On top of that, the new coalition marked a major step toward the future accession of the nationalist Right under Mr Begin. True to their ideology of a non-partitioned Palestine, the nationalist Left, under Allon and Galili, bid for strategic control of the West Bank (and Gaza) all the way to the Jordan Valley, believing that this would alleviate Israel's dependency on the nuclear-deterrence strategy.

The hardest step for Eshkol had been the relinquishing of his defence portfolio. He clung to it with all his skills, brandishing his old power of negotiating compromise (for example, by naming Yigal Allon as his military aide) and manoeuvring among members of Mapai's Central Committee and his coalition partners, all for naught. Moreover, Eshkol's decision – misinterpreted as indecision – to wait for an American intervention that would resolve the blockade crisis, neutralize the Soviet Union and thereby help cement American–Israeli strategic cooperation, rejected as it was by Washington in order to avoid the impression that such cooperation indeed existed, contributed not only to Eshkol's political demise but also to the inclusion and the legitimization of Mr Begin's far-Right bloc. Had Eshkol pre-empted immediately, in the estimation of Maj. Gen. Ezer Weizman, Chief of IDF Operations at the time and later Begin's Minister of Defence, he would have reaped the glory without including Dayan and without legitimizing Begin.[4] Here as in other tragedies, Eshkol could not and would not pre-empt until he had no other choice, thereby missing out on the glory, to his immense regret. It was strange to watch this man, normally quite cynical and humorous but now diminished by the heart condition that would soon kill him, mourning his lost glory and squabbling with Dayan over who would administer the occupied West Bank and Gaza. That, too, was a lost cause, it being presumed that anything Israel might decide to do in these territories would be undone in the event of a future negotiated peace with 'the Arabs'.

Presiding over a huge, unstable coalition that had been created to win a long, bloody war, and maintaining it after a conflict that had been much shorter and much less costly than feared, Eshkol found his voice blurred among the voices of his partners, especially those of Dayan, Dayan's old rival Allon, and Begin, amid a domestic euphoria that seemed to have transformed the country's psycho-political reality. Previously, Eshkol was careful to define (in Yiddish) Israel's posture as that of a 'poor Samson', emphasizing the hidden nature of its power in order not to provoke unnecessary reaction among her enemies and to secure foreign, especially American, military aid. As we have seen above, this had not prevented him from authorizing, albeit failing to control, the major operation in Samu' and the escalating actions against Syria. Now, by continuing to serve as premier and displaying the relative toughness and impatience that also belonged to his character traits, he seemed to represent a real (and rather arrogant) Samson at least in the eyes of the proud American Jews and in the hearts of the awakening Soviet Jewry, although not in those of Lyndon Johnson and some of his aides, including Rostow.[5] In fact, the Six Day War marked a profound change in the overt and behind-the-scenes behaviour of American Jews, which we describe briefly below. In Israel, however, Eshkol seemed to belong to the past, especially when Dayan and Rabin visited the liberated Western Wall without him for a historical photo opportunity. Thus, the now-ailing Prime Minister was determined not to accept his low standing in the polls and the abuse that continued to pummel since his pre-war 'stutter speech'.

When the National Emergency Government decided on 4 June 1967 to go to war alone, very much under Dayan's influence, Eshkol and the others had in mind a military operation aimed at breaking the Egyptian threat and its blockade of Eilat.[6] They formulated no political goals and no strategic goals of any other kind. Israel warned King Hussein of Jordan, now Nasser's official ally, to stand aside, assuring him that in the event of compliance no action would be taken against the Jordanian presence in eastern Jerusalem and on the West Bank of his kingdom. As for Egypt itself, Dayan ordered the IDF not to advance to the vicinity of the Suez Canal, a vital marine link between European Russia and the far Eastern provinces of the USSR and a supply line to North Vietnam, lest Nasser close the Canal as he did in 1956 and also interrupt the flow of oil to the West. Dayan also ordered the IDF not to confront Gaza at least until the Egyptian army in Sinai, its source of strategic support, could be destroyed. The victorious IDF ignored both orders and Israel's presence along the Canal dictated future policies. Syria, one of the sources of the whole trouble, was left aside for a while.

The scenario that had originally been envisaged began to change when Jordanian troops opened fire on Israeli positions in western Jerusalem and along the entire Armistice Demarcation Line, advanced toward the neutral UN headquarters on a commanding hill in Jerusalem, and bombed and shelled Israeli military airfields and civilian neighbourhoods in central and north-central Israel. Having destroyed the Jordanian Air Force on the ground, Israel made its decision to occupy eastern Jerusalem.[7] Although the entire cabinet endorsed the decision, Allon and Begin set the tone, as expected.

The original decision to occupy the West Bank, made by the cabinet executive committee, was part of a process of extending Israeli incursions into the area in order to stop Jordanian shellings into operations geared to destroy the Jordanian forces in the northern part of the Bank and the Jordanian military presence in the southern part. The Iraqi expeditionary force that had reached Jordan shortly before the war was destroyed on its way to Jerusalem by the IAF. Eshkol and Dayan seemed to have worked together in this regard, with the support of the full Government, without asking themselves – as Chief of General Staff Rabin did – why a thrust into the entire West Bank was necessary when the IAF's complete command of the air sufficed to control and quell any further Jordanian threats from that area.[8] Rabin and many of his army comrades, however, belonged to the generation of 1948 fighters who had been bled white at the hands of the Palestinians and the Jordanian Army in the 1948 War of Independence and now thought it high time to finish the job.[9] Several of them also believed that Israel should integrate the West Bank into the previous 'small' Israel for strategic and ideological reasons and that the Arabs' demographic advantage there could be reversed by an enhanced Jewish immigration effort and Arab migration.[10] Eshkol, while harbouring doubts about this, 'was very much enthused by the occupation of the parts of the Land of Israel that had been lost in 1948', in an allusion to Ben-Gurion's failure to occupy them in the War of Independence.[11]

In the meantime, the Syrian Army had been subjecting Israeli settlements in the north to heavy artillery shelling since the beginning of the hostilities with Egypt and attempted to attack Israeli targets from the air without much success. However, it refrained from a serious ground operation despite the Ba'ath Government's radical behaviour before the war. Eshkol was approached by representatives of the kibbutzim in the area that was under Syrian artillery attacks and, supported by several ministers in his cabinet, contemplated action including the occupation of the Syrian Heights overlooking northern Israel. Moshe Dayan was adamantly opposed to such an operation, fearing intervention by the Soviets on behalf of their clients in Damascus; after all, this had been the official source of the Soviet initiative that officially precipitated the Egyptian march into Sinai in May. But Dayan suddenly changed his mind and, without telling Eshkol about it, ordered the IDF to occupy the Syrian Heights, known since as the Golan Heights, to Eshkol's immense fury.

What followed was an enormous sense of joy and momentous historical change that engulfed most Israelis after eastern Jerusalem fell into Jewish hands, bringing the entire city under Jewish control after two thousand years of exile, coupled with their rage over King Hussein's alliance with Nasser and his military aggression upon the beginning of the operations against Egypt. Eshkol rode this tide of euphoria by initiating several activities relating to the reunification of the city. The Jordanian wall that had divided it and prohibited Jews from visiting the Western Wall and other Jewish holy places was removed – to the benefit of adherents of all religions – and united Jerusalem was declared Israel's capital by various acts of the Knesset. The city limits were greatly enlarged despite Eshkol's persistent doubts about whether this was a temporary measure that ultimately would be replaced by some form of Israeli withdrawal. The Arabs of eastern Jerusalem became residents of Israel but were allowed to keep their Jordanian passports.[12]

Eshkol brought the whole issue of the occupied territories to his expanded cabinet on 18–19 June 1967.[13] According to the official history of Eshkol's premiership quoted here, most of the ministers were ready to offer Egypt peace based on an Israeli withdrawal to the international boundary in Sinai, subject to the demilitarization of the peninsula and guaranteed freedom of shipping in the Straits. Such a guarantee might mean an Israeli presence in Sharm el-Sheikh – at the mouth of the Straits – and overland access to it. The Golan Heights triggered a debate and ended with Eshkol's remark that he was hardly able to decide about returning it to the radical Ba'ath regime. The main topic of debate was the West Bank and the identity of Israel's partners for negotiations on its future. Although Menachem Begin recommended de facto annexation, most ministers adopted the view that the Jordan River should be Israel's security border but were divided about the negotiating partner, some favouring the Palestinian population of the West Bank and others favouring Jordan. Eshkol himself initially remained undecided except for the unification of Jerusalem and de facto annexation of the Gaza Strip despite its teeming Palestinian population. Soon enough, however, he adopted the initiative of various kibbutzim that wished to settle on the Golan Heights, the previous source of their troubles. In these debates he acted as the chairman of a board would but without the decision-making power that he had possessed in the past and without clear-cut targets except for his wish, shared by others, not to repeat the withdrawal trauma of 1956–57 and previous failures to achieve peace. Hence, he adopted an open quest for direct negotiations with the Arabs for the purpose of concluding formal peace treaties. He heeded Allon's counsel on making the Jordan River Israel's security boundary with Jordan and endorsed it; he also accepted – unofficially – Allon's plan for settlement of the uninhabited parts of the West Bank, unaware that Allon would soon ignore it regarding Hebron. He monitored Dayan's growing involvement in West Bank and Gaza affairs with ineffective criticism and, of course, kept abreast of changes in public opinion since May 1967.

ESHKOL VS. DAYAN: SCEPTICAL COMPROMISER VS. COMPROMISING SCEPTIC

Eshkol was certainly aware of Israeli disappointment with the Armistice regime since the signing of the 1949 Armistice Agreements with Arab states other than Iraq, on the grounds that the accords had failed to lead to peace treaties as they were supposed to. Subsequently, the quest for an end to Arab belligerence via formal peace would preoccupy Eshkol no less than it would his Government partners. The issue for Eshkol was whether most if not all of the occupied territories should be used as bargaining chips for peace but, absent peace, would be retained by Israel in some reversible way. Among his colleagues, however, alongside his old partners Allon and Galili, committed as they were to an unpartitioned Palestine, an ad hoc, personal alliance was emerging between Dayan, who had been imposed on Eshkol and now enjoyed enormous prestige at Eshkol's expense, and the radical nationalist Menachem Begin, whom Eshkol himself had legitimized by inviting him to join his emergency coalition, even though Begin's far-reaching wish for territorial control if not outright annexation of the West Bank was not included in the deal.

The political landscape of the country, including that of his own party, Mapai, was changing rapidly and Eshkol knew it. Apart from the aforementioned new groupings, the loud extra-parliamentary association, the aforementioned Greater Israel Movement, favoured the retention and, later, the settlement of the occupied territories, especially the historically cherished West Bank. Others felt that most if not all of the territories should be returned in order to ensure a solid Jewish majority in the Jewish state or to head off corruption and serious political ramifications abroad as a result of occupation rule over alien Arabs. The old anti-nuclear group under Yeshayahu Leibowitz and Eliezer Livne split, Livne joining the Greater Israel Movement and Leibowitz aligning with its antagonists.

Here Dayan revealed his Janusian double or triple face. His first face was quite tough, responsive to the enemy's challenges by using force; his second could be rather cautious, willing to eschew force due to possible risks. He zigzagged between these approaches at high speed while maintaining his public standing and position of power as a contrast to Eshkol's 'exilic' manners.[14] The time had come, it seemed, for resolute Israel-born leaders, native speakers of high Hebrew – as embodied by Dayan's glowing image at the time – to succeed Eshkol's mixture of tea and coffee, just as Dayan had left Ben-Gurion, his previous mentor, in the cold. Now Ben-Gurion was promoting his own public stance that Israel should exchange the occupied territories (except eastern Jerusalem and, possibly, the Golan Heights) for peace agreements, possibly with Jordan in view of the post-war realities – a position that Dayan and practically everyone else considered unacceptable due to the domestic changes under way and King Hussein's conduct during the hostilities.

Dayan's third face was his complex view of Arabs. At one level, he was determined to cure them of their perception of Jews as *walad al-mit* – that is, a nation deserving of death due to their small numbers and the Arabs' supposed moral, historical and conventional superiority. This, for Dayan, entailed the maintenance of Israel's nuclear option, among territorial changes in Israel's favour, especially in Sharm el Sheikh. For Allon and his peers, in contrast, the bomb could rest deep in the basement from now on because Israel had just acquired territorial strategic depth on all fronts. Dayan brushed aside Shimon Peres' suggestion before the outbreak of the hostilities that war be avoided by conducting a nuclear test somewhere in the southern Negev. If preventing Israel from going nuclear had been the Arabs' *casus belli,* they would be shown in this way that they had missed the bus. By conducting a test, Israel would also officially join the nuclear club as formulated in the draft NPT, hereby ending the chapter of Israeli official ambiguity, American inspections at Dimona, and Egypt's use of Washington's anti-proliferation policy for its own purposes. Dayan believed that the test would bring about just the opposite – growing superpower pressure to relinquish the nuclear option when only a few, makeshift bombs were ready but no missiles, quipping that the nuclear option should wait 'until the next war' – which indeed it did,[15] at least by limiting Egypt's and Syria's aims and efforts in the 1973 Yom Kippur War and, later, by doing its share for the 1979 Egypt–Israel peace treaty.

Eshkol agreed with Dayan about the basic Arab posture that the Six Day War and its immediate results ought to change. Absent any positive response from the Arab states, however – except some overtures made by King Hussein while allowing Arafat's Fatah to launch guerrilla raids against Israel from his territory – Dayan also had naive trust in his own ostensible 'knowledge' of Palestinians as an Israel-born 'expert' who had grown up among them. This led him to the concept of an 'enlightened occupation', manifested in the opening of bridges to Jordan to commercial and civilian traffic, granting inhabitants of the West Bank and Gaza access to Israel proper (in order to show them 'our real, positive face'), and applying various other measures that would contribute to the eventual rise of Palestinian nationalism in the

West Bank and Gaza, as discussed below. At first, the Palestinian state of shock following the 1967 war and the seeming success of the 'enlightened occupation' regime in the West Bank and Gaza appeared to offer a practical alternative to Eshkol's fears that Israel might compromise its future by 'enriching ourselves by [adding] a million Arabs to two and a half million Israelis'.[16] In reality, Eshkol feared Dayan's resignation from the grand coalition even more, due to the one-eyed challenger's popularity in Israel and abroad. The gods would wait for Dayan until 1973, when he was blamed for the IDF's initial setbacks at the beginning of the Yom Kippur War. By then, however, Eshkol would be four years in the grave, the only Israeli prime minister to have died in office.

Dayan became the most important figure, if not the only one, in discharging responsibility for the West Bank and Gaza, which indeed was Israel's because international law requires occupied territories to be administered by the occupying military authorities. As for Gaza, the Defence Minister and others, such as Allon, had conflicting views at first. Some suggested the forcible removal of Gaza's refugee population to Egypt, but Dayan initially pondered their removal to the uninhabited parts of the West Bank.[17] Dayan's 'enlightened occupation' soon became the rule: the crossings to Jordan and Israel itself were opened to Palestinian traffic, labour and commercial activities, and direct Israeli rule over the Palestinians was minimized. Although Dayan had little if any fluency in Arabic, he deliberately refused to engage experienced military governors and instead appointed a variety of young Arab scholars, who suddenly became brevet colonels, reserving important engagements and decisions to himself.[18] This led to the collapse of the tight controls that had been exercised by native Palestinian networks and had been used by alien rulers such as the Jordanians, comprised of leading clans that depended in daily praxis on the alien authorities and were powerful enough to carry the message downwards. The result was an inviting vacuum for political activities that Palestinians had avoided until then due to traditional power structures and the alien authorities' iron rule. Freedom of expression, unheard of during the Jordanian occupation of the West Bank and the Egyptian occupation of Gaza, was allowed. Institutions of higher learning, which had never existed before, received operating licenses and inevitably became hubs of anti-Israeli thinking. The rising standard of living allowed Palestinians to invest more time in issues of self-identity, self-image, history and politics.

As time passed, Dayan authorized, with some reluctance at first, Israeli settlement in Hebron – a venture initiated by Allon – and later declared that the whole area should be opened to Jewish settlement. Eshkol, his settler instinct awakened, started to authorize initial settlement activities in Jerusalem, northern Sinai and especially the Golan Heights, whence most of the population had fled to Syria. As for the West Bank, Eshkol was in two minds. At first he considered a Palestinian entity of sorts that might also contribute to the resettlement of Palestinian refugees; then he changed his mind in favour of Jordan, believing that a Palestinian entity in the West Bank would adopt a hostile stance toward Israel due to Yasser Arafat's Fatah and other anti-Israeli inputs from Syria, Iraq and possibly Nasser's Egypt, if no peace treaty were concluded with the latter. In his thinking about Jordan, however, Eshkol was conscious of the problem of eastern Jerusalem – a non-negotiable issue for King Hussein – and the Government's decision made in the meantime to reconstruct the Jewish settlements in the Etzion Bloc, in the West Bank south of Jerusalem, which the Jordanians had occupied and destroyed in the 1948 war.[19]

Concurrently, the domestic intellectual-psychological vacuum of the Eshkol years was filled with the resurrection of old passions about the partitioning of the country reverting to the 1930s, the 1940s, the War of Independence, and its results, including the absent peace treaties with the Arabs, new hopes, challenges and political developments that were taking root, especially among radical contenders for power in the National Religious Party, formerly Eshkol's most moderate partner in issues of foreign and security affairs. On top of these, personal ambitions intruded. Ailing or not, Eshkol felt that he had to maintain his public standing vis-à-vis Dayan, COGS Rabin, and Rabin's mentors Allon and Galili, by adopting his own rather hawkish policies in view of the post-war situation.

NOTES

1. See Naora Barnach-Matalon, *A Good Place on the Side*, in Hebrew (no publishing location cited: KIP Publishers, 2009), p.184, quoting Rabin's memoir, according to

which Rabin had no concrete plan for the Egyptian army in Sinai, preferring instead to wait for the outcome of the IAF's attack on the Egyptian air bases. Only in the event of a successful outcome would he order a limited Israeli advance in the northern sector of Sinai, in order to engage enemy forces there and there alone.

2. See Shlomo Aronson, 'David Ben-Gurion, Levi Eshkol and the Struggle over Dimona: A Prologue to the Six Day War and its (Un) Anticipated Results', in *Israel Affairs,* 15, 2 (April 2009), pp.114–34; cf. further Yeroham Cohen, *The Allon Plan*, in Hebrew (Tel Aviv: Hakibbutz Hameuchad, 1972).
3. Cohen, *The Allon Plan.*
4. See Shlomo Nakdimon interview with Ezer Weizman, 'The Generals' Mutiny', *Yedioth Aharonoth,* 15 September 1985.
5. See *Foreign Relations of the United States* (*FRUS*), Vol. XIX, 2004, pp.398, 436, 445, 457, 468, and below in the text.
6. Israel State Archives, *Levi Eshkol, the Third Prime Minister of Israel, Selected Documents on Chapters in His Life,* in Hebrew (Jerusalem: Israel State Archives, 2002), pp.562–9.
7. Eitan Haber, *'Today War Will Break Out', The Reminiscences of Brig. Gen. Israel Lior, Aide-de-Camp to Prime Ministers Levi Eshkol and Golda Meir*, in Hebrew (Tel Aviv: Edanim, 1987), p.229.
8. Ibid., p.228.
9. One of them was Maj. Gen. Uzi Narkiss, OC Central Command during the Six Day War, who pushed as hard as he could toward the occupation of eastern Jerusalem and its surroundings to the west and north. See his book, *Jerusalem the One and Only*, in Hebrew (Tel Aviv: Am Oved, 1975).
10. In a radio interview with this author years later (no date recorded), Prime Minister and Defence Minister Rabin explained his decision to freeze Jewish settlement in the West Bank by arguing that, 'The Jewish people failed to settle there to begin with'; hence, to his mind, the demographic balance in favour of the Palestinians imposed limitations on Jewish presence in the West Bank. By then – in the early 1990s – the veteran soldier had become a full-fledged politician.
11. Israel State Archives, *Levi Eshkol*, p.574. One politician who warned against the unforeseeable ramifications of the occupation decision was the leader of the National Religious Party, Home Minister Moshe Shapiro. This seemed odd given his party's sentiments and principles, and indeed, Shapiro would soon be succeeded by the NRP's young Turks.
12. On the cabinet deliberations in this regard, see Haber, *'Today War Will Break Out'*, pp.236–7.
13. Israel State Archives, *Levi Eshkol*, p.575.
14. Dayan was born in Kibbutz Degania in 1915, a year after young Levi Eshkol reached the country, but his family moved to Moshav Nahalal shortly afterwards.
15. See Dan Margalit, *I Have Seen Them All*, in Hebrew (Tel Aviv: Zmora-Bitan, 1997), pp.60–1, quoting Avner Cohen, 'Cairo, Dimona and the 1967 War', *Middle East Journal*, 50, 2 (1996).
16. Israel State Archives, *Levi Eshkol*, pp.600–602.
17. At the early stage of the post-war deliberations, Dayan appointed a small group of Hebrew University experts to study this idea, as reported by Dr Nimrod Raphaeli, a member of the group, in a conversation with this author. This option, however, was quickly shelved in favour of the 'enlightened occupation' regime in the West Bank as well as in Gaza.
18. Interview with Dr Zvi Elpeleg, and cf. Shlomo Gazit, *The Stick and the Carrot, Israeli Rule in Judea and Samaria*, in Hebrew (Tel Aviv: Zemora Bitan, 1985).
19. See Eshkol's meeting with the generals, 5 December 1967, in Israel State Archives, *Levi Eshkol*, p.601.

Chapter Eleven

Eshkol's Exploitation of a Problematic Victory

WASHINGTON RETHINKS

We now turn to the American perspective on the foregoing developments. The initial American reaction to Israel's war – except for a lengthy and repeated angry exchange regarding the Israeli attack on the USS *Liberty*, an electronic surveillance ship that Israel strafed during the hostilities – as formulated by Walt Rostow, President Johnson's aide at the National Security Council, on 7 June 1967, was quite interesting.[1]

As a prologue to Rostow's remarks, we quote Secretary of Defense Robert McNamara concerning the last stage of the war, that is, the Syrian chapter and related Soviet threats.

> We had had a carrier group in the Med and fairly close to Israel, and we'd sent it on a training exercise toward Gibraltar. And then we thought the situation was so tense in Israel that perhaps the Syrians, fearing Israel would attack them, or the Russians supporting the Syrians might wish to redress the balance of power and might attack Israel. So we turned the carrier group around and sent it back toward Israel, not with any intention whatsoever of supporting an Israeli attack on Syria, or any Israel offensive moves whatsoever, but rather purely to be able to defend Israel in the event of further attacks on Israel. The Soviets learned of that and they interpreted our action as offensive.[2]

Whether this was done in response to Soviet preparations to attack Israel directly, as Remez and Ginor speculate, we do not know. McNamara was probably not ready to share intelligence about it with his interlocutor even years later. The very movement of the Sixth Fleet itself, however, was enough to prevent such a threat. Dimona, too, is mentioned only once in the published *FRUS* records as a possible Egyptian (Soviet?) target. Indeed, a memorandum signed by Sherman Kent, Chairman of the CIA Board of National Estimates,[3] describes Nasser's motives from the start of the crisis as follows:

> There may have been some element of desperation in Nasser's attitude, arising from the parlous condition of the Egyptian economy, the worsening relations with the US, a belief that some sort of US-Israeli plot against him existed, and perhaps a fatalistic conclusion that a showdown with Israel must come sooner or later, and *might best be provoked before Israel acquired nuclear weapons*.[4] [Italics added.]

Since the conventional literature largely ignores the nuclear dimension of the Six Day War, it overlooks the American threats quoted above, that is, that Israel would find itself alone should it come to war if it maintained Dimona. The Dimona issue resurfaced after the war and stayed on the table as long as Lyndon Johnson remained in office, but the incoming Nixon-Kissinger Administration buried it, seemingly for good.

Kent added, somewhat in the spirit of the Israeli generals' criticism of Eshkol's stance, that Nasser

> may also have concluded ... that he could gamble on US influence [i.e., avoiding war as best he could due to Vietnam and maintaining position in the Arab world – SA] and perhaps some Israeli indecisiveness [Eshkol's image at home and abroad – SA] to prevent an Israeli offensive at the early and most vulnerable stage of his deployments.

The Americans did, however, intervene late in the war in order to restrain the Soviets regarding Syria. The Kremlin swallowed the occupation of the Golan Heights under these circumstances; from then on, the Soviets made themselves spokesmen of 'the Arabs' at large vis-à-vis Washington and rearmed Egypt as their first practical act.

This, of course, was very much on Rostow's mind even before Israel occupied the Golan Heights on 8–9 June. Rostow began his remarks by saying that the Israelis had indeed captured Sinai and the West Bank, including eastern Jerusalem, and 'have in their hands the administrative control of perhaps two-thirds of the Arab refugees'. Rostow wondered whether the Arabs were considering the use of 'the leverage of oil' (in fact, several small oil producers declared an oil boycott against the United States when the hostilities began) and whether

> the settlement of this war shall be on the basis of armistice arrangements, which leave the Arabs in the position of hostilities toward Israel, keeping alive the Israel issue in Arab political life as a unifying force, and affording the Soviet Union a handle on the Arab world; or whether a settlement emerges in which Israel is accepted as a Middle Eastern state with rights of passage through [the still-blockaded] Suez Canal, etc.

President Johnson was very sceptical about the latter possibility and, further, did not hide his objection to the Israeli démarche, as I demonstrate below, being conscious of Soviet behaviour and his domestic situation on the eve of an election year. His standing was deteriorating because of the war in Vietnam and the growing unrest in the Democratic Party, which also had something to do with his civil rights and economic policies.

Rostow elaborated:

> The US objective is evidently to try to move from the present situation to as stable and definitive a peace as possible. This will require Israeli concessions [adding later that the Israelis should move quickly, from their present position of strength and – alleged – political unity] – as well as important moves by the others – on the refugee issue.

Rostow, sounding like today's politicians, speaks about 'Arab moderates' who will replace 'the present radical Arab mood' (with a larger role to be assigned to Iran and Turkey), regional arms-control arrangements, and 'the beginnings, at least, of systematic regional cooperation in economic development', including water resources.

In a meeting of the NSC on 7 June, President Johnson was quoted as having said that he was 'not sure we were out of our troubles'.[5] He could not visualize the USSR admitting to miscalculation and then walking away. Johnson's assessment followed an assertion by Secretary of State Rusk, expressing a degree of sympathy for Eshkol, that the situation on 8 June appeared 'more manageable than five or three days ago', and that 'We do have something to bargain with in that Israel must be grateful to the US [for neutralizing the Soviets and the UN from the outset – SA] and Israel requires continuing US support'. In this sense, Rusk seems to have appreciated Eshkol's long wait before the outbreak of the war (in his angry exchange with the Israeli generals). The Secretary quoted some initial Israeli positions on the occupied territories: the Israelis would insist on final peace treaties with firm, accepted frontiers; would not allow international organizations to supervise; would retain parts of Sinai, including Sharm el-Sheikh, from which they had withdrawn (under American pressure) in 1957; and would expect other adjustments to widen its twelve-mile-wide 'waist' between the West Bank and the Mediterranean.

The president, supposedly Eshkol's personal friend – after all, he had used this title while trying to prevent Eshkol from embracing the war option – went on to state, '*It is important for everybody to know we are not for aggression*' (italics added), perceiving the US as the victim in Vietnam.

> *We are sorry this has taken place ... We thought we had a commitment from those governments* [not to start a war] *but it went up in smoke very quickly ... By the time we get through with all the festering problems we are going to wish the war had not happened.* [Italics added.]

That very day, President Johnson received a plea from a Mrs Krim, one of his most important fundraisers,[6] regarding Israelis who 'felt they had won the war not with the United States but in spite of it'. American Jews, she said, were getting ready to hold a rally at Lafayette Square that would threaten to become an anti-Johnson demonstration. This was accompanied by a message to the president from his Jewish 'dupes', Levinson and Battenberg, stating that while the Jewish leadership understood that State's 'neutrality' statement did not represent Johnson's policy, this was 'certainly not' the opinion among the Jewish rank-and-file. The major concern among Jewish leaders, they added, was that '*Israel, apparently having won the war, may be forced to lose the peace again*' (italics in the original) as in 1956. They expected the UN to sell Israel down the river unless stopped by the US. Finally, David Brody of the Anti-Defamation League apprised Johnson of his conviction that Israel would not withdraw from some parts of the newly occupied territory 'no matter who demands what'.

In a Memorandum for the Record submitted on 17 November 1968, Walt Rostow recalled 5 June 1967, by reiterating that 'President Johnson has never believed that this war was ever anything else than a mistake by the Israelis. A brilliant quick victory he never regarded as an occasion for elation or satisfaction.'[7] In this sense, Johnson's views were not far from those of the isolated Ben-Gurion, except that the latter hailed the end of the partitioning of Jerusalem, and his views were far from Eshkol's quest for his lost 'glory'. Participants in such an epic drama naturally wish to become heroes; the gods, however, refused to make Levi Eshkol a Ulysses in the eyes of his own people.

Ben-Gurion was direly afraid that the war and its ramifications would reopen the whole issue of Israel's legitimacy instead of adding occupied territories to its previous land mass, free of alien Arabs, based on the partitioning of western Palestine. Additionally, he worried about the possibility of the recently concluded round of violence breeding its successor. It is true that, enthralled by the Israeli victory in 1956, Ben-Gurion had proclaimed the birth of the 'third Israelite kingdom' thanks to the occupation of Sinai and Gaza. Soon enough, however, he regained his senses under American pressure, withdrew in favour of UN peacekeepers and American promises about freedom of shipping, and in due course attained his main strategic goal – the acquisition of the Dimona reactor from France.

Significantly, Dean Acheson, former Secretary of State and a grand old statesman among the veteran 'best and brightest' who had served Presidents Franklin Roosevelt and Harry Truman in key foreign-affairs matters, was invited to express his opinion by President Johnson and, according to Rostow's account quoted above, 'looked back on the whole history of Israeli independence and, in effect, said that it was a mistake to ever create the State of Israel'.[8] Such was not the view of McGeorge Bundy, whom the President appointed to chair a special committee to deal with the Middle East crisis. On 9 June 1967, Bundy told the president that his committee would report, 'our own view of what has in fact happened and pin a rose or two on Nasser as a liar and others who have slandered the US' (following a phone conversation between Nasser and King Hussein, taped and made public by Israel's Intelligence according to which Nasser has conspired to make the US and the British responsible to the destruction of his air fields by flying the main sorties against them).

Bundy also recommended that Washington 'make [it] clear that we have now seen a historical event which necessarily changes the landscape'. He further recommended that the president 'project a positive picture of our hope for a strong and secure Israel in a prosperous Middle East'. Emphasizing that this task is in the first instance a task for the nations in the area, he added that this is 'good LBJ doctrine and good Israeli doctrine to get out in public'. Bundy, a quondam National Security Adviser to the president who had been recalled to chair the special committee, was a new voice in the chorus that was being conducted by Johnson himself. He expressed himself freely about 'officers in the State Department who want to underline the territorial integrity clause of the mid-May statement [which had stressed the primacy of this issue before the war – SA]. Old boundaries cannot be restored. Bundy believes we should promptly resume conversations with the Soviets.'[9]

Thus, Bundy introduced a dissonant voice in the president's chorus, one that seemed closer to Eshkol's own even though it had not yet fully crystallized any territorial and political demands except for Eshkol's quest for direct negotiations leading to formal peace. Much depended on the American policymakers' distinction between 'moderate' and 'radical' Arabs and some degree of Soviet cooperation. Such cooperation was necessary at least in regard of the ongoing Soviet rearming of the 'radicals' while no American weapons for Israel were authorized as yet and France had imposed an embargo even on weapons already paid for by Israel. Moscow's role concerned deliberations toward a new Security Council resolution on a possible solution of the crisis, which indeed would follow a Soviet draft calling for Israeli withdrawal from the occupied territories (the definite article included) in exchange for nothing.

On 19 June 1967, President Johnson issued a five-point statement regarding peace in the Middle East. 'The first and greatest principle [is] that every nation in the area has a fundamental right to live, and to have this right respected by its neighbors.' The second was 'another basic requirement for settlement: justice for the refugees'. Third, 'Free navigation rights must be respected'. Fourth, the conflict had demonstrated 'the danger of Middle Eastern arms race of the last 12 years'. As an initial step toward dealing with this problem, Johnson proposed that the United Nations immediately urge all members to report all shipments of military arms into the area. Fifth, the crisis underlines the 'importance of respect for political independence and territorial integrity of all the states in the area'. Having reaffirmed this principle, the President added that it could be effective 'only on the basis of peace between the parties'. He further stated that, 'What the nations of the region [need is] recognized boundaries and other arrangements that will give them security against terror, destruction, and war'. Finally, there must be 'adequate recognition of the special interest of three great religions in the holy places of Jerusalem' (as had not been the case when Jordan had controlled eastern Jerusalem). While offering the assurance that the US Government would 'do its part for peace in every form, at every level, at every hour', Johnson declared that the main responsibility for the peace of the region depended on the peoples and leaders of the region.[10]

The president's statement, plus further clarifications that he made, were interpreted by Eshkol and his colleagues as positive developments in the sense that Johnson had not mentioned unilateral withdrawal and his principles regarding peace and security might involve territorial changes.[11] At this juncture, Eshkol declared himself ready for direct negotiations with the 'moderate' King Hussein of Jordan. The king, however, was not ready for peace, insisting on a state of non-belligerency only,[12] and Eshkol lacked a clear-cut majority in his extended coalition for any far-reaching withdrawals in the West Bank, let alone eastern Jerusalem. Furthermore, much depended on the Arab concert with its internal dynamics, cleavages, economic disparities and old and new rivalries, and on the Soviet Union. Moscow was expected to endorse Nasser's position anyway.

POST SIX-DAY ISRAEL: TEA AND COFFEE

On 18 July Israeli Minister Efraim 'Eppie' Evron returned to Washington from Israel and reported to Walt Rostow 'vividly the impact on him of being in Israel. He said it is impossible to understand at this distance the extent to which Israeli emotions and political life have been changed by the war'. By this, Evron meant not only the enemy equipment that Israel had destroyed or captured (Soviet-made hardware was immediately offered to the Americans for inspection)[13] but also, and above all, the fact of

Israeli access to and control of eastern Jerusalem. He said that he had found himself getting caught up in this fever – which, notably, followed eighteen years of a Jordanian wall dividing the city, barring Jews from visiting their most important holy places, coupled with the destruction of Jewish shrines in the Old City and occasional sniping at Israelis in western Jerusalem. Evron was now 'convinced' that just as it would take the Arabs some time to come to grips with reality, it would also take the Israelis some time to recover from euphoria and tackle the difficult real problems that lay ahead. Evron, however – a former aide to Pinchas Lavon – also offered his opinion that 'Israeli politics is in complete ferment with men taking positions not so much on traditional party alignments as on age basis', since the war was bringing to the fore a new and younger crop of policymakers. The results and new directions in politics could not be predicted.[14] Evron had in mind the obvious decline in Eshkol's public stature and the emergence of Moshe Dayan and, possibly, of Yigal Allon. The latter, claiming personal credit for the conventional pre-emption strategy and its success, as opposed to the nuclear option, rushed to republish his 1959 book *Curtain of Sand* in 1968. Evron's tally of new and young policymakers also included the victorious young generals.

I take the liberty here to quote my own impressions about the changes in Israeli public opinion following the Six Day War – after all, I lived through this period as an active observer – quoted in a book published in 1978, rather close to that war.[15]

> One factor in the formulation of post-war Israeli policy was the change in the political consciousness of a large section of the population, which began long before the war. Of particular importance was the change regarding the parts of Palestine not conquered in the 1948 war. Ben-Gurion had managed to restrain the desire for a revision of the strategic status quo and even for the conquest of all of Palestine ...
>
> To use James Chace's distinction between innocence and experience, as expressed in a *New York Times Magazine* article, Israelis began to lose their innocence with regard to friend and foe alike and tended to lean heavily on their collective experience. Innocence, in Israeli terms, had domestic and foreign policy ramifications. Domestically, Israel's lifestyle, egalitarian simplicity, the concentration on social and moral

achievements that had already proved to be incongruous with the bargaining habits of a population demanding an ever-increasing standard of living, and of a responsive but not always successful government, were slowly giving way. Guilt feelings toward the Arabs refugees – typical of the left, especially Mapam and its followers – were replaced by a new-old set of 'rights'.

First, there was the 'right of the lone defender' who had managed to help himself against open aggression. If he had not managed, he would have been annihilated for nobody would have rescued him. Slowly and logically, the 'right of the lone defender' created 'the right of occupation'. Occupation of sovereign Arab lands and Palestinian-Jordanian territories could always be temporarily justified in terms of bargaining for peace (and self-defence in the absence of peace) but Israel's belief in a 'historical' and strategic right to some of these territories was modified by its most recent experience. The role of the same territories as a bridgehead for a deadly attack against Israel's heartland, and a 'liberal' approach toward Arabs living under Israeli control (especially in comparison to the behaviour that Jews anticipated from the Arabs if they won the war) gained significance.

To this was added the 'right of fear', or the methodical right to the worst possible case analysis. Israel was justified, in its own eyes, in making an almost unconscious decision not to take further risks and not to rely on any American promises, UN forces, or Arab talk when defeated that might allow a new escalatory process when recovered. It may have been the case with Egypt that Nasser had intended a limited confrontation at the outset of the May 1967 events that had led (by Nasser's definition, endorsed by all Arabs) to a war to eliminate Israel altogether when hostilities to deter Arab aggression commenced in June 1967. Thus, a limited Arab aggression acted to trigger an all-out attack that included Jordan, almost an Israeli ally, Iraq, and, to an extent, Syria, the source of the trouble.

I inject a speculation here as to the frame of mind of the Mizrahim, Jewish immigrants from Muslim countries, who along with their offspring accounted for a majority in the Israeli society and electorate. Normally absorbed by Mapai and the NRP and having adopted the elite's foreign policy stance without much questioning during Ben-Gurion's reign, the Mizrahim had begun slowly to develop a more autonomous view of the affairs of state in the early 1960s. Long-established bargaining habits used by the secondary elite to approach them gave the immigrants a growing sense of their right to social progress, one that was not completely being fulfilled. This growing autonomy of thought could hardly coincide with Ben-Gurion's traditional defensive stance in foreign policy when a moment of truth would challenge his bold style and offensive gestures and force a choice between his substance and his style ... at this historical juncture ... Ben-Gurion could mobilize their enthusiasm, using his bold style, his emphasis laid on the Bible as the common denominator between all Jewish-Israeli groupings and old-new sovereignty by engineering a subtle compromise that had skirted war and territorial changes pending international realities and maintaining Jewish majority in partitioned Palestine in 1949–1956 and 1957–1963 ... The demise of Ben-Gurion's popular leadership combined with Mr. Begin's legacy of his 'rebellion' against the British during the Holocaust. Thus the Holocaust has been politicized in the context of the new Holocaust, averted as it was in June 1967, with Mr. Begin – always trying to woo the Mizrahim and exploit their sense of discrimination – at the helm of the victorious government of national unity, which won the war so soon with seemingly decisive results. To this one may add Mapai's political suicide thanks to Mr. Lavon and Eshkol's intervention in this barely comprehensible matter to the rank and file, which ultimately delivered Ben-Gurion's portfolios into Eshkol's hands. As Premier and Defence Minister, Eshkol projected the perception of an Ashkenazi benevolent macher whose style and language were alien to many. Not only could he not be ignored, for he was the economic master of the country, he seemed to have been responsible for the plight of the Mizrahim from the transit camps all the way to conditions in the 'development towns' and economic recession, which had not yet ended ...

The humiliating experience of having lived under Arab rule may have taught Jews that Arabs would never accept any form of Jewish sovereignty in Palestine, which the Arabs considered *dar al-islam*. If this was so, why make any concessions? If Jews

> had a right to Palestine, that right was exclusive, biblical, historical, and political in the sense that no other political choice to supplant Jewish sovereignty could be made. Arab rights could be compensated for in the vast, twenty-one-state Arab world.
>
> Israeli scholars such as former General Yehoshafat Harkaby, who studied official Arab positions toward Zionism, Jewish rights to statehood, Jewish history, and Jewish behaviour as manifested in official Arab publications and teaching materials, religious propaganda, and secular writings, painted a very gloomy picture indeed for a pessimistic Israeli audience ...
>
> The next right, the 'right of the strong', who in the Israeli perception also happened to be the just, was enhanced by enthusiastic comments from abroad about Israel's lightning victory and its new role as a 'regional power'. Many Israelis developed the consciousness of having 'the right of the bastion of the West in the Middle East' after defeating a heavily Soviet-armed Arab world. This perception led to the belief in special ancillary 'rights' in Israeli popular and military thinking, including confidence in Israel's military capabilities, far beyond Ben-Gurion's limited projections, in the event of a renewed Arab challenge.
>
> The fear and the need for self-assertion that dominated Israel's public psychology until June 1967, and that had brought about a subtle compromise under Ben-Gurion, were replaced by a growing sense of confidence. However, fears returned whenever territorial changes (i.e., withdrawals) were mentioned abroad or at home due to the perception of the Arab regular forces' obvious numerical and strategic advantages when deployed along Israel's 1949 Armistice Demarcation Lines ... These national characteristics, in the minds of many Israelis, were embodied in Moshe Dayan's public behaviour. 'Just let me handle these Arabs', Dayan said to the public, though not in so many words.

Efraim Evron's impressions, quoted above, also ignored the 'system', that is, the proportional-balloting method and its outcome, parliamentary fragmentation that resulted in the creation of unstable alignments. The National Emergency Government seemed to have been much more stable, but it was far from it. The grand coalition harboured ongoing infighting between 'young Turks' such as

Dayan and Allon and Levi Eshkol, who while considerably weakened and buffeted from various sides remained alive and kicking and committed to leaving his mark as best he could. Thus, the hardening of the Israeli position in July, agreed upon by Eshkol's cabinet as the Arabs resisted any kind of negotiations, was understandable at least in the eyes of President Johnson's aide, McGeorge Bundy. Bundy, as quoted above, stated at the time that unless the Arabs

> make a drastic change in their bargaining position we have no practical way of opposing this Israeli position. We can insist on the principle of 'withdrawal from danger' [of a new war, of demographic change in favour of Arabs – SA] but as a practical matter the Israelis will continue to confront the Arabs – and us – with small accomplished facts ... and we will find it unwise to take any practical action in reply.[16]

Indeed, by authorizing settlements in the greater Jerusalem area and, later on, by reviving the pre-1948 Etzion Bloc in the West Bank and establishing settlements in northern Sinai and the Golan Heights, Eshkol did 'create facts' on the ground, partly in response to Arab intransigence but also due to his own settler instinct and initiatives by various settler groups. He comforted himself with the belief that at least some of these efforts might be temporary and could be removed in exchange for contractual peace with solid partners (King Hussein was still perceived as a weak traitor in many eyes, especially Dayan's), but Eshkol was a bargainer all his life, and making unilateral concessions to enemies was simply unthinkable to him as a matter of principle, and as the party that held enough cards now for a fair bargain. Eshkol did harbour, as we have seen above and will further see below, grave doubts about demographic change in favour of Arabs if Gaza were annexed on top of the West Bank situation, but he did not countenance any sort of concession without a clear-cut political quid pro quo and territorial changes in Israel's favour.

The early voices heard in this regard in favour of complete withdrawals from the occupied territories, excluding eastern Jerusalem, possibly including the strategic but unpopulated Golan Heights in exchange for 'true peace', were offered by none other than David Ben-Gurion and Pinchas Lavon, joined soon afterwards by Professor Yeshayahu Leibowitz. The latter, in his new role as an anti-occupation Cassandra, would eventually become the hero of the Israeli left despite, or because of, his ultra-Orthodox mannerisms, for which they developed an exotic fondness. Having set his crusade against Dimona aside in favour of the more promising jeremiad stance about the occupation, Leibowitz might have believed that Eshkol had drifted away, albeit slowly, from Ben-Gurion's nuclear strategy.

McGeorge Bundy, however, was still adamant:

> When the Israelis come to us for major military supplies ... I begin to think that our bargaining power even on this issue is not overwhelming. I think we can trade hard on such matters as nuclear policy and perhaps even get them to back off from the French missiles they have had on order, but as long as the Arabs remain adamant, I doubt if we can or should make the Israeli view of Jerusalem or the West Bank a federal case. We can't tell the Israelis to give things away to people who won't even bargain with them.

It was true that neither Eshkol nor Dayan, let alone Begin and Allon, would do this, but due to conflicting motives.

THREE 'NO'S AND HALF A 'MAYBE'

For the time being, the Americans and the Israelis waited for the outcome of an Arab summit conference among both 'radicals' and 'moderates' in Khartoum in late August and early September 1967, including the radical el-Fatah leader Yasser Arafat. The summit produced three 'no's – no negotiations with Israel, no recognition of Israel and no peace with Israel. The interpretations given to this result, however, varied widely. For Eshkol, his colleagues, Israeli public opinion and Israeli historiography of the conflict to date, the 'no's (shorthanded as 'Khartoum') were taken literally. Moreover, Arafat was quoted as having used the summit to threaten Arab leaders' lives if they agreed on any concessions to Israel at this time, believing that the war had given him an immediate base in the West Bank to launch guerrilla operations against Israel from the occupied territories. He proved to be wrong about this; the summit itself was interpreted by Nasser as if paving the way to a diplomatic, rather than a military, solution of the conflict. An incentive to view the matter this way may have been suggested to Nasser by the Soviets, as Foreign Minister Andrei Gromyko did in his ongoing talks with the Americans on a new

Security Council resolution on behalf of 'the Arabs' – describing them as 'wanting peace'.[17]

Gromyko seemed to have forgotten Nasser's promises, issued only a few weeks earlier, to eradicate the 1956 and the 1948 'aggressions'. If he was Nasser's adviser, however, the adoption of a diplomatic solution and peace talks amounted to the brandishing of old weapons in the Soviets' Cold War arsenal, because open belligerence and threats of annihilation of adversaries might justify enhanced resistance on their part and support to them by others while 'the Arabs' remained too weak militarily, or as the Kremlin lost its previous confidence in their military capabilities at least for the foreseeable future. If the Arabs wanted their territories back, peace terminology would transform Israel to an intransigent villain as far as its acquisition and occupation of territory were concerned. Peace itself, however, would remain linked to the refugee problem, which President Johnson, too, linked to a final settlement.

Eshkol, of course, was aware of this complex and retained his traditional scepticism about Arab intentions. For Eshkol, Arab refusal to accept responsibility for their own misbehaviour since 1947, if not earlier, was a major reason not to make concessions to them without a significant quid pro quo. The Khartoum decisions, however, were couched in terms of the recent war: they demanded withdrawal from the territories occupied since 5 June, terminated the partial oil boycott that smaller Arab producers had declared during the hostilities, ended the war in Yemen, and promised economic support to Egypt and Jordan, signifying a new direction toward domestic development.

A flare-up on 20 October 1967, when the Israeli destroyer *Eilat* was attacked and sunk by Soviet-supplied Egyptian missile boats with many Israeli hands lost, requited by the destruction by Israeli artillery of the Egyptian refinery complex in Suez City, led to no escalation.

In the meantime, the Americans had not forgotten Dimona and the French missiles.[18] On the early occasion of 27 June, Ambassador Barbour reported to Washington that the war

> will be seen to have had considerably less effect on ultimate Israeli nuclear and missile intentions than what happens in coming ... months ... Israel has come through a harrowing experience in which its national existence was in jeopardy. It

> did so by dint of its own efforts, a fact of which Israelis are proud and from which they draw lesson that they must continue to rely increasingly on themselves. If peace proves impossible and only another nebulous state of armistice results, making another clash possible, then prudent assumption would seem to be Arabs next time may be better. Israelis, who have technical capability to build bomb, would, it may be argued, be foolish not to produce extra-conventional weapons against enemies whose total conventional military capabilities conceivably could outstrip Israel's within another decade. If powerful nation such as Soviet Union is rearming Arabs this could reinforce Israel conviction it irrational to eschew nuclear weapons ... We have seen in recent weeks increase of popularity of Dayan, who has been associated with those favouring the nuclear weapons development. If his star continues to rise, and that of his associates Peres and Ben-Gurion (who made the decision to build Dimona), then, if outlook for Israeli security appears still uncertain, it would seem fair surmise that Israel might be led closer to nuclear route and development of necessary vehicles for nuclear weapons [plus the embargoed French weapons, missiles included – SA]. Much, perhaps everything in this regard as in so much else, will depend on degree Arab readiness to come to terms'.

Ambassador Barbour was unaware here of the conventional strategy touted by Ministers Galili and Allon, who hardly believed in nuclear deterrence. For them, as we have seen, the occupation of the West Bank carried the additional justification of defensive depth. Nor was he aware of Eshkol's refusal to have anything to do with Ben-Gurion, for reasons including Ben-Gurion's nuclear shadow that the United States might not like, and Dayan's departure from his previous alignment with Ben-Gurion. In this respect, Eshkol remained in the middle. Loath to forgo the nuclear option, he would transfer it to the 'cellar' thanks to the newly acquired defensive space in the West Bank, Sinai and the Golan Heights. As a part of this strategy, Eshkol would seek conventional aid from the Americans in the event that Washington would push him toward the nuclear option without offering it on its own. In the meantime, he watched Nasser's diplomatic manoeuvres with growing doubt.

Here, Nasser's meeting on 3 November 1967, with Robert Anderson, President Johnson's special envoy, should be quoted at some length not only because it reflects Nasser's way of addressing an American friend, but also due to its relevance in understanding various parts of the Middle East conflict to that date. Having survived the war and tendered his resignation but asked by his people to stay in power, Nasser sounded reasonable yet cunning, ready to go as far as he could to retrieve his territories by diplomatic means using President Johnson's own ideas, and seemingly capable of dropping the Palestinian refugees, no less, for his purposes.[19]

Nasser opened the conversation by saying, 'Above all else, try to make clear to your government and your people that we are eager for a political settlement, for a political peace'. He admitted that this had not been true at the very beginning, after the cessation of hostilities on 9 June, because 'We were in a state of confusion, uncertainty, and doubt'.

Now, he said,

> We know that our interest lies not in war, but in peace ... Please try to convince your people and your government that any question of direct negotiation, or even of negotiations with a third party mediator present, would be an act of suicide. It would be so for me, and it would be so for any other Arab leader.

Even if he attempted or agreed to do this, he added, it would be suicide on the part of any other Arab leader not immediately to denounce it and demand the resumption of hostilities against the Israelis. Therefore, Nasser said, 'Under these circumstances, let us try to be practical and, if we all want peace, and we do, then let us find a way to settle our differences and live in peace'. He did not believe that the details of an agreement could be worked out in public or that anything could effectively be begun by negotiations by a committee or any mediator appointed by the UN until some formal action were taken by the UN 'as a first step'. Nasser then suggested that a resolution be proposed to the Security Council on the basis of President Johnson's five points, which he described as follows: (a) the right of Israel and of all other nations in the area to live; (b) free movement of 'innocent' shipping in the waterways of the Gulf of Aqaba and the Suez Canal; (c) full withdrawal by the Israelis from the territories that they had occupied during the hostilities; (d) a declaration of non-belligerence between the Arab states and Israel; and (e) settlement of the refugee problem.

In Anderson's view,

> ... 'It is quite clear that he is willing to undertake contractual obligations, just so long as they are not incorporated into a simple treaty jointly made and signed between the UAR and Israel.' This point he made from time to time, referring always to the fact that even such an agreement would be suicide. Nasir then said that the most difficult problems were going to be the Suez Canal and Jerusalem. I asked if he could agree to let any ship, including the Israelis, transit the Suez Canal if such ships carried not the flag of the country involved, but the UN flag. Nasir said, 'I do not rule this out but there is still the question of logs, manifests and trouble with the people. On the other hand, if you will settle the refugee problem then I can allow Israeli ships to transit', he said. I told him I was skeptical that the Israelis would ever negotiate for a resettlement in Palestine. At this point, Nasir said, *'All right then, let us settle them by agreeing to pay them compensation'. In order to clarify this point, I stated again that I wanted to be quite sure that he would agree to a mutual settlement of the refugee problem without giving the refugees the alternative choice of resettlement [in Palestine] or of taking money instead, and he again said that if resettlement is not possible, we can agree on a mutual compensation. He continually links the free passage of Israeli ships through the Suez Canal with the settlement of the refugee problem.* He then brought up the question of territory. Here, Nasir said that the key point is that Israel cannot be allowed to expand, that for every Muslim nation, regardless of whether or not it borders on Israel, the consuming fear is that Israel plans territorial expansion. He said this is one of the basic problems in trying to unite the New and the Old City of Jerusalem. It is regarded by everyone of the Muslim faith as a violation of their religious rights and as Israeli expansion ... [Italics added.]
>
> Nasir said that except for territory, most of the Arab nations are leaving other details of the Arab settlement to him ... He said, 'Please try to explain to your government

> that however desperately we want peace, we cannot have it at the price of destroying ourselves or any other Arab leader, when you can be absolutely sure that anybody who succeeds me or any of the other Arab leaders will be much more radical against the Israelis than we are'. Nasir said that some of the Arab states, notably Syria and Algeria, had been very vehement with him in stating, 'You cannot agree to a resolution or a declaration which includes the right to live for Israel'. Nasir said, 'I merely pointed out to them that we are no longer talking about Israel's right to live. We are talking about our own right to live ...' Nasir ended the conversation by saying, 'I want nothing but peace. I want to go as far as humanly possible to achieve it. But I must not be asked to do the impossible. I must not be asked to do something that would be condemned by every other leader and by my own people ... I asked Nasir if he would consider permitting both the Old and New City of Jerusalem to come under a single Israeli administration with respect to such things as public utilities, etc., but with each faith to have custody and supervision of its Holy Places. Nasir replied that even if he agreed to this any such solution would leave Israel ultimately confronted with war or resistance so far as anybody could see into the future. He said that nothing he or any other ruler in the world could do would prevent that people will do things in the name of religion that they would not consider doing in the name of politics. On the other hand, he thinks Jerusalem could be zoned so that each faith would have the administration of its own sector. 'My country is Muslim, Christian and Jewish, and I expect it always to be so. Each has his own particular interest in how we settle the issue of Jerusalem ...'.

Later on Anderson met with Zakariyah Muhyi al Din, a top aide of Nasser's who repeated the President's 'peace offer' with its limitations, argued that at Khartoum Nasser was the source of moderation not only toward Israel but he also pursued the end of the Yemen War and reconciliation with Saudi-Arabia. Muhyi al Din further hinted toward the removal of PLO leader Shuqairy, possibly opening the road for a resolution of the Palestinian refugee problem acceptable to the United States, if not to Israel.

Was Nasser ready to forgo the Palestinians' 'right of return' in exchange for compensating them for their lost homes by some 'mutual means'? Was Zakariyah hinting at the replacement of Shuqairy, an Egyptian appointee, with someone who would agree to this as PLO chairman? Would Ba'athist Syria and its protégé, Fatah leader Yasser Arafat, accept this? Was it a sort of punishment to be inflicted on Damascus following the dissolution of the Egyptian–Syrian union in the early 1960s and Syria's meagre contribution to the recent war, which it had in fact triggered by harbouring Arafat? How would revolutionary Iraq respond to the treatment of the Palestinian refugees at the hands of their previous mentor? And as far as Jerusalem was concerned, how could the pan-Arab leader talk about the 'zoning' of the holy city, in which the old part had been barred to Jews by the Jordanians from 1948 until the recent war?

Had Eshkol been privy to this extraordinary report, would he have leaped at the opportunity to solve the refugee problem, the ostensible core of the Arab–Israeli conflict, once and for all in exchange for the occupied territories, including eastern Jerusalem, and less-than-formal peace? Or would he have treated Nasser's diplomatic démarche as a sly, insincere mélange of remarks that the Egyptian president unleashed in order to regain his occupied land without suggesting where the refugees should be finally settled and who should compensate them 'mutually', and who should speak for them? Nasser may also have hoped at this opportunity to mobilize renewed support among the State Department's Arabists and maybe even in Johnson's White House. Now that he had ended the war in Yemen that he had indirectly fought with the Saudis, admitted a few of his mistakes and seemed to offer a new programme for his country: to concentrate on improving Egypt's poor economy, and pursue a new policy toward Israel based on President Johnson's own five points. All this he seemed to have proposed, without renouncing his close relations with Moscow. It is true that Nasser spoke of the rage that would engulf the Arab masses if he negotiated with Israel. More than anyone else, however, it was Nasser who had inflamed the Arab masses, in the past and also recently, to the heights of hysterical agitation against Israel. Now he was hiding behind skirts of his own making, asking for favours resulting from his own miscalculations.

This would have been Eshkol's view of Nasser and also of Syria. It would have been that of his ministerial colleagues as well, amid the steps they had already taken in Jerusalem, the Golan Heights, and, in the sense of establishing a few temporary settlements, in northern Sinai. Thus, on 30 October Eshkol informed the Knesset that Israel would accept no return to the *status quo ante* (that of 5 June 1967) on the Golan Heights, in Sinai, at the Gulf of Eilat and along the Suez Canal.[20]

NOTES

1. *Foreign Relations of the United States* (*FRUS*), Vol. XIX, pp.339–41.
2. Source: Lyndon Baines Johnson Presidential Library and Museum, oral history, special interview with historian Robert Dallek, 26 March 1993.
3. Dr Kent started his distinguished career as member and chair of the Board of Estimates, serving at the headquarters of the Office of Strategic Services, the predecessor of the CIA, during the Second World War.
4. *FRUS*, Vol. XIX, p.148.
5. Ibid., pp.347–8.
6. Ibid., p.349.
7. Ibid., pp.287–92.
8. Ibid., p.291.
9. Ibid., p.436.
10. Ibid., pp.520–1.
11. Israel State Archives, *Levi Eshkol, the Third Prime Minister of Israel, Selected Documents on Chapters in His Life*, in Hebrew (Jerusalem: Israel State Archives, 2002), p.575.
12. Ibid. Dr Ya'akov Herzog, Eshkol's Director General at the PMO, sounded out King Hussein about a peace treaty but the answer was 'non-belligerency' only. Cf. Nasser's position in this regard in the text below, which was binding for Hussein at that stage and much longer.
13. *FRUS*, Vol. XIX, p.634.
14. Ibid., pp.686–7.
15. The quotation that follows is a slightly abridged and revised version of my remarks in Shlomo Aronson, *Conflict and Bargaining in the Middle East, an Israeli Perspective* (Baltimore, MD and London: Johns Hopkins University Press, 1978), pp.82–5.
16. Bundy to Johnson, *FRUS*, Vol. XIX, pp.739–40.
17. On Gromyko's role as advisor to and representative of 'the Arabs', as he defined them all, see ibid., p.676: Accordingly, Arthur Goldberg, American Ambassador to the UN, quoted Gromyko as having said in an exchange with Anatoly Dobrynin, Soviet Ambassador to Washington, reported in a cable to the State Department on 17 July 1967, that the Soviet Union and Japan had on 19 October 1956 concluded an agreement terminating their state of war and reestablishing peace and friendly good-neighborly relations, even though they did not have and had not yet signed a permanent peace treaty. Goldberg agreed that 'this was the basic concept we had in mind'. It would lead to Security Council Resolution 242 and Israel's reservations about it, as described below in the text.
18. *FRUS*, Vol. XIX, pp.569–70.
19. Ibid., pp.973–81.
20. Israel State Archives, *Levi Eshkol*, p.589.

Chapter Twelve

Eshkol's Last Acts

LEGACY: A MAN OF THE SYSTEM

At this point, Eshkol pledged himself to various activities that marked the end of the economic recession, occasioned by the war effort, Jewish financial contributions in the wake of the war, and his own austerity measures. Although ailing, Eshkol was still a dynamo, possessed of enough strength to pursue a large number of causes. Prime among them was an appeal to the Americans for military replenishment, which was ultimately granted during the autumn with various strings attached (discussed below) as a result of ongoing Soviet arms deliveries to Egypt and Syria and political support for Nasser at the UN.

Since Moscow had broken diplomatic relations with Israel during the war, in persistent interaction between the US and Foreign Minister Gromyko, the Soviets searched for a formula that would yield a new Security Council resolution without 'humiliating the Arabs' by even mentioning Israel by name. Secretary Rusk was willing to honour the Soviet desideratum but could not ignore the Israeli quest for 'just and lasting peace' among the states in the area and their 'right to live in peace within secure and recognized boundaries'. Furthermore, the new resolution was supposed to result not only in an end to the state of belligerency but also in a 'just solution to the refugee problem'. Thus, this goal, which the Arabs repeatedly presented as a *casus belli* in their ongoing state of war with Israel, was incorporated into the draft resolution. Finally, the territorial-withdrawal clause was formulated in the English draft as 'withdrawal of Israeli armed forces from territories occupied in the recent conflict', and in the French version as withdrawal from *the* territories.

On 22 November 1967 the Security Council adopted the draft

as Resolution 242, entailing an operative clause regarding the designation by the UN Secretary General of a Special Representative to proceed to the Middle East to establish and maintain contacts with the states concerned, 'in order to promote agreement and assist efforts to achieve a peaceful and accepted settlement in accordance with the provisions of the resolution'.

Nasser accepted the resolution but Israel did not for the time being, hoping that the superpowers would impose its implementation on the other side in a way that Israeli demands would not be ignored. The Johnson Administration, however, was determined not to pursue non-existent Arab concessions toward a nebulous state of peace and secure boundaries, believing instead that these issues entailed negotiations between the parties themselves. The Administration's strategy of staying on the sidelines was furthered by the good services of Dr Gunnar Jarring, the Swedish Ambassador to the UN, whom the Secretary General appointed his Special Representative. Eshkol considered this a blatant departure from his demand for direct negotiations, but Foreign Minister Eban convinced him to accept it reluctantly as the best possible option since it had been endorsed by the United States and introduced by the British, as opposed to Soviet and non-aligned draft resolutions. Dr Jarring was an expert in Turkic languages, especially Uygur; as a young scholar he had visited Xinjiang – known at the time of writing for the anti-Chinese activities of its Muslim population – before holding major diplomatic posts for the Swedish Government. Even these qualifications, however, could not bridge the gaps between the parties. Jarring failed in his attempt to summon the Arab sides to negotiations with Israel in Cyprus, preceded by an Israeli gesture allowing the salvaging of sunken ships in the Suez Canal by the Egyptians in order to facilitate the reopening of the Canal.

The rebuff of Jarring hardened Eshkol's and Dayan's approach, which in turn hardened Nasser's. Military clashes initiated by Nasser along the Canal and by Arafat's Fatah in Israel and the West Bank claimed a steady toll of casualties and required counter-measures that ultimately drove the Fatah guerrilla back across the river to Jordan. In competition with Allon's settlement plan for the West Bank, Dayan proposed now one of his own: the establishment of five military 'fists' at quondam Jordanian Army camps across the West Bank as adjuncts of his 'enlightened' occupation regime, leaving the final status of the area moot for the foreseeable future. Unlike Allon, who believed that foreign pressure could be ignored, Eshkol and Dayan were conscious of the American stance that a final-status agreement must entail Israeli withdrawal to the pre-5 June lines with minor modifications, possibly close to the 'Jerusalem corridor' (the pre-war route of access from the foothills to the capital). Given the Arab refusal to negotiate, however, Israel could come under pressure to affect an immediate withdrawal; for this reason, Eshkol considered negotiations with Palestinian leaders on the ground or with King Hussein. The king now reverted to the relatively moderate policy toward Israel that he had applied before the war – without, however, preventing Fatah operations against Israel from his side of the Jordan River – hoping to recover his territory with American support and Nasser's permission. Concurrently, however, he allowed Fatah to continue its guerrilla activities from Jordan against Israel while maintaining his status as the official sovereign in Jerusalem and in the West Bank in terms of the population's citizenship and the financing of religious and educational institutions.

In the meantime, the Arabs in eastern Jerusalem became 'permanent residents' of the annexed Israeli territory on the basis of a census that immediately followed the annexation. Permanent residents are entitled to live and work in Israel, travel in Israel, carry Israel ID cards, affix Israel license plates to their cars, receive Israel social-security and health benefits, and vote in municipal but not in parliamentary elections. They may apply for full Israel citizenship if they meet preconditions such as pledging allegiance to the Jewish state, demonstrating some knowledge of Hebrew, etc. Most of these Arabs rejected these terms summarily and have done so ever since. Instead, they maintained their Jordanian citizenship and were able to cross the Jordan River into the Hashemite Kingdom at will. Soon enough, construction of new Israeli neighbourhoods in the greater Jerusalem area got under way for the purpose of surrounding the Arab quarters with Jewish dwellings and securing Israel's majority in the city.

Behind the scenes, Dayan's policy of open borders between Israel and the West Bank and the permission granted to West Bankers and Gazans to work in Israel attracted the opposition of the powerful Finance Minister Pinchas Sapir (who was, however, helpless in the case of the occupied territories which remained under military administration according to international law). The flow of cheap labour into Israel, Sapir argued, outside the regulated job market and its control and welfare mechanisms (administered by Sapir himself) might create a new and exploited Arab proletariat, not to mention the conversion of Greater Israel into a binational state due to its swelling Arab population. Eshkol himself was painfully aware of these problems, but his short-term challenge lay elsewhere: to persuade the Johnson Administration to extend more and better military supplies to Israel in view of Soviet rearmament of the Arabs and the limited supplies otherwise available to Israel, mainly of short-range Skyhawk fighter-bombers, authorized two years before but delayed upon the outbreak of the Six Day War. Gone were the French supplies, including fifty Mirage fighters that Israel had already paid for. Eshkol decided to take up the matter directly with President Johnson but expected the latter to make the supplies conditional on Israeli political and territorial concessions; he may also have expected a demand for new discussions about the Israeli nuclear option.

Before setting out, Eshkol met with the General Staff and other generals on 5 December 1967.[1] It was a different Eshkol, almost a humble beggar asking for advice from a forum that seemed to be more serious and capable of giving it than his fractious coalition was. No longer was Eshkol the Minister of Defence who had tried to teach GHQ some basics about the subordination of the military to the political echelon and had referred them to promises allegedly made by his 'friend' in the White House – of which little had been implemented. Even now, Johnson seemed to be rather diffident, if not hostile, toward most of Israel's territorial and political demands. Israel, however, needed the Administration's military and political support more than ever, given France's complete volte-face from its previous military cooperation with Israel, Soviet arms for the Arabs, and non-aligned pressure on Israel at the UN.

This time Eshkol sounded lost in his thoughts, or perhaps he was trying to use President Johnson once again but in a different way. He wanted the assembled generals to help him propose various alternatives for the future of the West Bank, which in the meantime had become Judea and Samaria – the historical/Biblical names for this area – among those who favoured its retention.[2]

In his rather awkward way of speaking, confronting Moshe Dayan and others who were known to favour a permanent Israeli presence in the West Bank, including settlements and hopes for Jewish immigration and Arab emigration, the prime minister raised grave doubts about two options of that kind – Dayan's open-ended presence in the West Bank and Allon's hope of retaining at least the Jordan Valley and the strategic areas in the region, plus Hebron and the Etzion Bloc. Eshkol's point of departure was his expected meeting with President Johnson and the Jarring mission. Eshkol started by saying that Washington was very much behind King Hussein now, trying to mobilize the 'moderates' among the Arabs in order not to lose them to Moscow. Therefore, Israel must formulate a policy vis-à-vis Jordan and explain it to the Americans. He added that the Soviets were making deeper and deeper inroads in the region; he took it for granted that this was another reason to understand American sensitivities. Then he moved on to Judea and Samaria, citing the 600,000 Arabs who lived in the area along with 220,000 in the Gaza Strip, almost a million in all, on top of those who had left during the recent war. He continued:

> We shall be asked about a solution to the [1948] refugee problem and we can respond that they should be resettled all over the world and that we can help to bring this about. But it would be inconceivable for anyone among us to tell Johnson that we're going to blot out the name of Nablus [the Arabic name of the town historically known in Hebrew as Shechem] or that we're proposing the exiling to Brazil of anyone whose name is Ja'abari [a prominent Arab family in Hebron]. Everybody knows that we're not happy about being enriched by a million Arabs, so we'll be asked, 'What do you [really] want?' Now we say, to begin with, we want them to come and discuss peace with us ... [However] if we sat face to face with King Hussein, what could we tell him? He will demand all his territories back, eastern Jerusalem included; he would promise freedom of worship in it for everyone, Jews included. If we sat face-to-face with him and told him to go to hell, it could be done by means of a cable or a letter.

In other words, the quest for direct negotiations would prove pointless unless the Government of Israel made up its own mind about the future of the West Bank. Gaza seemed to be left aside, to be incorporated into Israel as a part of Mandatory Palestine that happened to have been under Egyptian occupation. Eshkol concluded by expressing his misgivings about the incorporation of hundreds of thousands of West Bankers into Israel in whatever way, but asked 'this forum [the GHQ] whether there is no other option that would guarantee us more security and fewer Arabs'. The status quo might somehow be maintained for two or three years, he predicted, but it would perish in due course. While Eshkol displayed at least some degree of farsightedness in this respect, he overlooked the combination of security and ideology that was taking shape, that is, the transformation of the West Bank into security depth for pre-1967 Israel in many eyes, including most if not all of his generals.[3]

In response, COGS Rabin insisted on the Jordan River as Israel's security boundary but rejected three possible corollaries: the return of the West Bank to Jordan, Israel control over a large and disenfranchised alien population, and the idea of a Palestinian state in the West Bank. Instead, he argued in favour of a 'special status' for the area and demanded 'permanent and true peace' as a precondition for talks with the Arab states. Much more radical was the vision of Maj. Gen. Ezer Weizman, the Chief of Operations, who started by saying that he 'trusted the Arabs more than he trusted the Jews' in the sense that the Arabs were incapable of making any reasonable offer and rallying around it. He added, however, that this reality would absolve Israel from the need to 'make important historical decisions'. Since Arab hate prevents any chance of talking with them, Weizman continued, the 'rush to peace' on the Israeli side is unwarranted 'as long as we are well situated [in the occupied territories] and our main target should be the economic and military consolidation of Israel [which may] take 50, 100 years'. Weizman's prestige was extremely high at this time due to his previous role as GOC of the IAF and his decisive contribution to the destruction of the Arab air forces during the June war.

Eshkol listened to Weizman rather carefully and did not argue. Nor did he try to contradict Gen. Rehavam Ze'evi, the Assistant Chief of Operations, who did not expect even a 'true peace' to endure but added that it might allow Israel 'to assimilate into the

Arab environment'. Then he lectured the prime minister about the historical rights of the Jews in the unpartitioned country, criticized him for having failed to encourage Arab emigration, expressed the belief that more effort to this end could still be made, and recommended a Jewish settlement drive in Judea and Samaria, 'the heart of the State of Israel'. Ze'evi had come to this meeting after having chaired a committee that drew Greater Jerusalem boundaries that included parts of the occupied West Bank north and south of Jerusalem. The committee's recommendations, although adopted by the Government, have never been recognized by foreign powers or international organizations to this day.[4]

Yisrael Lior, who as Eshkol's military adjutant recorded the minutes of this meeting, summed up the encounter by saying that the prime minister left the assemblage without offering clear-cut answers, possibly because they were not available and 'none are available to date'. By so doing, he invited initiatives and actions by competing ministers and action groups.[5]

Later in Eshkol's term, the West Bank evolved to a national-religious sacred cow whose horns were grasped by many Israelis, including several members of his own cabinet. To break this nexus, Eshkol would have had to take almost an impossible and daring action. He certainly could have resigned and created a narrow coalition excluding Mr Begin, but he could not trust ministers Galili and Allon, his closest colleagues, let alone Dayan and Peres, and the representatives of the NRP would have betrayed him quickly after a unilateral withdrawal from the West Bank – but not from eastern Jerusalem, for this would have been totally unacceptable to the nation at large.

Mired in these thoughts, Eshkol met with President Johnson on 7 January 1968, at the President's Texas ranch.[6] The president, too, had lost much political altitude, facing not only a growing nationwide campaign against his war in Vietnam, but also serious cleavages that had split the Democratic Party into four parts. Having not yet made up his mind about running for re-election – his decision not to run again would be announced two months later – Johnson displayed a degree of sympathy for Eshkol's military requests but told him bluntly that it would be a pity if Eshkol's mission were limited to a quest for Phantom jets. The F-4 Phantom was indeed the most advanced fighter-bomber of its time; its enormous payload and long range would give the IAF a distinct advantage over the Arab air forces. Johnson added, however, that this was not the solution to Israel's security problems in the Middle East. The real question, he judged, was how two million Jews could live together with a hundred million Arabs. This required a formula that he expected Eshkol, who searched for it himself, to offer. Secretary of State Rusk, attending the meeting, noted that absent Israeli flexibility on territorial issues the situation in the region would deteriorate, Soviet influence would grow, and American influence would decline considerably. 'Which Israel does Israel want?' Rusk asked, as if the American response to Eshkol's requests depended on Eshkol's answer. Then, however, he suggested three areas in which Israel might display flexibility: action on the Palestinian refugees, the return of UN peacekeepers to Sharm el-Sheikh, and the return of two islands in the Straights of Tiran to Saudi Arabia, which claimed to have leased them to Egypt in 1954. Eshkol rejected all three by saying that Israel would not return to the pre-5 June *status quo ante* and was no longer willing to trust UN peacekeepers after Nasser had demonstrated his readiness to remove them whenever it suited him.

At a private meeting between the two, the president told Eshkol that he intended to pursue arms-control agreements with the Soviets; this was no doubt related to the forthcoming agreement between the superpowers on the Non-Proliferation Treaty, which indeed was signed on 1 July 1968. This must have evoked the issue of Dimona, which, while not mentioned in the official Israeli sources, Johnson would soon link to the supply of F-4s which, apart from their nuclear capability, had a sufficiently long range to disturb the Soviets and trigger their response by supplying the Arabs with the most modern hardware, if not more. Eshkol's response on this occasion is not known, but his remarks in the ensuing negotiations with Paul C. Warneke, Assistant Secretary of Defense and the presidential representative in charge of curbing Dimona in exchange for the Phantoms, are quoted below from the official American source.

In regard to Eshkol's visit in early January 1968, we are told that the Administration promised him more short-range Skyhawks and agreed to train Israeli pilots to fly Phantoms pending a decision on supplying the latter later in the year. The

Administration found this necessary in order to withhold the decision until the Dimona issue could be negotiated to the Americans' satisfaction, especially when President Johnson, who in the meantime had announced his decision not to run for a second term and 'work for peace' afterwards, would at least be credited for the NPT. The treaty was waiting to be signed in July, but Eshkol may have tried to drag out the Warneke negotiations until a point in time when the Americans could hardly maintain their own, unilateral inspection at Dimona – ineffective as it was – and concurrently preach for the international control mechanisms specified in the NPT. Probably having satisfied themselves that the missile issue has been resolved for the time being due to the French embargo on military supplies to Israel, Warneke still demanded of Israel[7] that it abandon its quest for the French missiles and refrain from developing strategic missiles of its own without prior information given to and agreed upon by Washington. Israel, he said, should also agree to biennial inspection visits to various Israeli sights, Dimona included, and should supply the necessary information about her nuclear-weapon procurement plans. Finally, Jerusalem should sign and ratify the NPT in due course, which it never did.[8]

Behind the scenes, the American Embassy in Tel Aviv warned the US team that Eshkol was seriously ill and too weak to sustain concessions of this kind, which might jeopardize indirect negotiations with Jordan and Egypt, assuming that such were possible. Thus, Eshkol's weakness became an asset, plus the intervention of Abe Feinberg, President Johnson's Jewish friend and his mediator between the White House and the Jewish lobby (rather self-conscious since May 1967), on top of Johnson's 'Zionist dupes'. Feinberg advised the President to forgo Warneke's demands but to insist in turn on the NPT clause. However, with Johnson progressively weakening and election fever running high, this would have to wait until after the presidential elections in November, when the new Administration – either under Johnson's designate-successor Hubert Humphrey, who enjoyed massive Jewish support, or under Richard Nixon – would make a final decision on what *Ha'aretz* military correspondent, Amir Oren, called 'Phantoms for Atoms'.

However, the Israeli delegation to the Warneke talks, headed by Yitzhak Rabin, had made it clear in advance that Warneke's approach was unacceptable. It was a different Rabin now. He had been named Israeli Ambassador to Washington; his negotiating style was different from that applied vis-à-vis the Harriman–Komer Mission in 1965; and the substance was also different from the Israeli position back then. Rabin now came as the victor in the Six Day War, and he told the American side rather 'brutally' that, 'We did not come here to mortgage Israel's sovereignty'. He then engaged Warneke in a lengthy discussion over the definition of nuclear weapons and strategic missiles. Rabin argued that the 'introduction' of nuclear weapons into the region required overt testing and that strategic missiles were by definition those that could reach Arab capitals. Israel had met neither condition. Just the same, Rabin agreed not to use the US-made F-4s (as agreed beforehand about the Skyhawks) as nuclear platforms. Then, returning to the threat of the Egyptian missiles, he argued that Israel needed missiles to deter Egypt from launching missiles equipped with biological and chemical warheads. In response, the Americans brandished an answer that they had prepared before meeting with Rabin: Israeli nuclear missiles would not deter the Arabs and would have the opposite result, the deployment of Soviet nuclear missiles in Egypt and other Arab countries.

Warneke also responded to Rabin's arguments by warning him (very much along lines similar to those published in Allon's *Curtain of Sand*) that the Arabs in countries including Egypt, Syria and Iraq, were not known for rational, long-range, calculated behaviour, especially under continued pressure. 'We believe', he added, 'that [nuclear deterrence] would work only if the other side is not emotional and properly balanced'. Warneke would prove to be wrong about this. Neither the Soviets nor the Arabs behaved 'irrationally', as Presidents Sadat and Hafez Assad proved in the 1973 Yom Kippur War, a limited conventional offensive launched with limited Soviet conventional aid against a nuclear Israel, while the final decisions about the Phantoms required a new Administration and its different approach to nuclear friends and allies, not to mention a new Israeli prime minister.[9] Eshkol came away with one achievement: the American inspections at Dimona were abruptly and totally halted during his last months.[10]

Back home from his last trip to the United States, a tired Eshkol faced an escalating campaign by Palestinian guerrillas, this time operating from Lebanon. The campaign peaked with the attack on an Israeli airliner in Athens late in December 1968, killing one crew member. This new tactic had to be countered and the decision, authorized by the prime minister and carried out by Defence Minister Dayan, was a raid on Beirut's international airport. The operation 'had to be impressive', as Eshkol's military adjutant, Yisrael Lior, described it,[11] so that the Arab governments and especially the Government of Lebanon would be aware of the implications for themselves if they allowed the Palestinians to continue using their new tactics. The actual outcome, however, went far beyond Eshkol's intentions. According to Lt. Gen. Chaim Bar-Lev, Rabin's successor as COGS, Eshkol believed that only four or six planes were targeted at the airport but the Israeli commandos actually destroyed fourteen. Eshkol was outraged.

So, too, was General de Gaulle. Before the outbreak of the Six Day War, de Gaulle had warned Israel not to fire the first shot and, even before Jerusalem disobeyed, he suspended military deliveries to Israel. Later, he took various positions on the Palestinian refugee issue and the status of the Straights of Tiran that signified a clear-cut change in his foreign policy. The change was based on two premises that de Gaulle had adopted: the great powers must be precluded from dangerous rivalry in the Middle East, a volatile region close to France, and Paris should play an active role in regional politics as an equal of the great powers, if only due to its longstanding traditional ties with Lebanon and Syria. Consequently, he used Israel's Beirut raid to make the suspension of arms deliveries permanent. In all other respects, de Gaulle remained a fringe player in regional developments, and Eshkol's anger at Dayan for having expanded what should have been a relatively modest operation in Beirut only contributed to the prime minister's sense of having been outmanoeuvred once again by his Minister of Defence. When it came to major military operations against the Palestinian guerrillas, however, Eshkol tended to adopt Dayan's hard line against the advice of his civilian experts, possibly due to his own sense of impatience with the Arabs or because he wanted to avoid an open rift with the one-eyed coroneted hero of the Six Day War, who enjoyed immense popularity in Israel and abroad.

In March 1968, Eshkol and Dayan authorized a major Israeli

operation against Yasser Arafat's Fatah following guerrilla acts against Israel from Fatah's bases in Jordan. The ensuing battle of Karameh proved costly: Israel suffered a military blow due to Jordanian Army intervention on behalf of Arafat's guerrillas, failed to eradicate Arafat's presence in Jordan, and left behind what was hailed as a Palestinian-Arab victory. This immediately drew Nasser's attention to Arafat: the Egyptian President invited the Fatah chieftain to Cairo, met with him and his principal aides, and offered them arms and financial support.[12] Nasser also advised them, according to the same source, 'to think of peace with Israel and establishing a Palestinian state in the West Bank and Gaza'. Accordingly, 'Nasser decided to cede his leadership of the conflict with Israel to Arafat'.[13] These seemingly conflicting quotes seem to suggest a double-edged strategy vis-à-vis Israel coined in contemporary terms, during which a two state solution is negotiated between the Palestinian Authority and Israel. Yet it would have been nothing new for Nasser: when it suited his priorities, he expressed support of the Palestinians' own struggle against Israel in terms of their 'right of return', after he had created the PLO, but imposed limits on their operations from Egyptian-controlled Gaza. When he was carried away by his own anti-Israeli rhetoric before and during the May 1967 crisis, he assumed leadership in the conflict with Israel and proposed to retain it until Israel's hoped-for destruction. Now, affairs having reached a new stage, he may have given thought to reverting to support for the promising guerrilla war that Yasser Arafat was spearheading from Jordan. Whether a Palestinian West Bank plus Gaza state was suggested to Arafat at the time by Nasser, we do not know; but such an independent Palestinian state could have deprived King Hussein of his role in the West Bank for good, and serve a base for further claims and action against a 'small' (pre June 1967) Israel. Later, Nasser crowned Arafat as Chairman of the PLO instead of Shuqairy, the Egyptian tool in the now less-relevant competition with Syria. It seems, however, that Nasser advised Arafat to adopt a political plank next to his military activities by talking peace and demanding Palestinian independence in the West Bank and Gaza.

How could Arafat 'think of peace' with Israel, against his own declared aim of destroying her, while Nasser himself was unable to negotiate peace or, rather, 'true peace' as Eshkol expressed it?

And how would this 'think[ing] of peace' solve the question of the Palestinian refugees, whose 'right of return' to pre-June 1967 Israel Nasser seemed to have abandoned in his aforementioned conversation with Robert Anderson? We do not know, but Nasser may have decided to leave the matter to the ruminations of Arafat and other Palestinian leaders in order to free his hands to deal with Egypt's own priorities.

Either way, Arafat's PLO became an umbrella organization for various Palestinian outfits operating in Jordan, an uncontrolled, armed Palestinian presence inside Hussein's state that the king finally destroyed in 'Black September' 1970. At this time, all sides – the PLO, the Arab states and the Israeli leadership – descended into fragmented coalitions, some weaker than others. Syria invaded Jordan, Israel saved Hussein by threatening to move against Damascus, and Nasser intervened in a quest for some way to save everyone's face in Jordan. He died during the crisis, by which time Eshkol was a year in the grave.

In the meantime, Nasser was preparing his own military option along the Suez Canal, which Israel would eventually term the 'War of Attrition', and launched it early in 1969. One would expect Eshkol to meet this challenge with a tough response, as he would toward the growing alliance between Nasser and Arafat, the entrée to Moscow that Nasser had created for Arafat in 1968, and the appointment of Arafat as PLO Chairman. Eshkol did not live to carry out such a crackdown, succumbing to his heart condition on 26 February 1969, and leaving his legacy to be studied by the historians.

THE LAST ACT: MAPAI DEPARTS, THE LABOUR PARTY FORMS, TELEVISION ARRIVES

Since January 1968, Eshkol had been operating within a seemingly new domestic political structure that might have allowed him greater freedom of action than before: the new Labour Party. In fact, however, the new framework was old enough to sustain and even institutionalize the ongoing frictions and rivalries. Preparations for the merger of Mapai with other labour parties on the nationalist and non-nationalist Left began immediately after the Six Day War.[14] While Eshkol devoted most of his attention to the political and the military outcomes of the war, he did travel around the country at this time and gain the impression that the nation was united as never before. Thus, he thought the divisions among the labour parties and factions, which he had always considered an anomaly, could be overcome – at least as far as Mapai and Ahdut ha-'Avoda were concerned, since they had been partners in a parliamentary bloc since 1965. Eshkol's own career, of course, overlapped the entire history of fragmentation in the Zionist Labour Movement. Originally the leader of a small social-democratic party that had joined others to create Mapai early in the 1930s, Eshkol had witnessed the fracture of Mapai in 1944, the creation of the united leftist Mapam in January 1948, Mapam's ferocious pro-Soviet campaign against Mapai in the early 1950s, and the subsequent division of Mapam into Ahdut ha-'Avoda and the Marxist far Left, which retained Mapam's name. Now the time had come, Eshkol argued, to unite them all into one social-democratic party.

The problem was how to accommodate Rafi, the party that Ben-Gurion had established in 1965. Ben-Gurion's main deputies in this venture, Moshe Dayan and Shimon Peres, had left the 'old man' on his own when Dayan joined Eshkol's National Emergency Coalition on the eve of the Six Day War. From the standpoint of Dayan and of Peres, Secretary General of Rafi, the erstwhile sources of Rafi's harsh personal criticism of Eshkol, such as Dimona, the French missiles and the Ben Barka affair, were either under control – and more so thanks to Dayan's new role as Minister of Defence – or belonged to the past. It is true that Rafi had raised other issues in 1965, such as British-style electoral reform, the quest for public virtues and rules of the game instead of the Mapai method of party-boss and party-machine governance, that is, the Levi Eshkol way. These issues, however, as formulated by Shimon Peres in response to Ben-Gurion's expectations in 1965, were mentioned but not pursued.

In a nutshell, the old 'system' was here to stay, except that in the new Knesset faction, within the framework of the new Labour Party, Rafi would receive the same number of seats as the previous elections had given it. This was Eshkol's way of roping Peres and Dayan into the new corral. These two no-longer-so-young Turks were tired of Rafi's role as an opposition party and wished to rejoin Mapai, the large ruling party, without forfeiting their parliamentary base. The outcome that they attained gave them more influence over the Labour Party than they ever could have had over Mapai from the outside. In fact, both Ahdut ha-'Avoda and Rafi were awarded 22.5 per cent of total seats in the new party's governing institution. Although Mapai retained a formal majority, the three-faction regime gave the minorities enough flexibility to manoeuvre within the new party's framework and threaten to leave it, along with their parliamentary faction, at any time of their choosing.[15] Eshkol tried his best to accommodate the leftist Mapam as well, but the latter preferred to retain its independence and agreed only later to form a common parliamentary bloc with the new Labour Party.[16] Ahdut ha-'Avoda was torn now between Yitzhak Tabenkin, its legendary leader who continued to campaign for Greater Israel and its settlement, and Yigal Allon and Yisrael Galili, who pursued their own settlement schemes in strategic areas, in Hebron, and in the southern tip of Gaza Strip by means of creating a new Israeli town separating the Strip from the occupied Sinai, continued to conduct their vendetta against Moshe Dayan and Shimon Peres, did their best to minimize the significance of the nuclear option, and offered Eshkol close support in his personal struggle against his own Minister of Defence. Upon the birth of the new Labour Party, Dayan declared that Rafi had joined Mapai in order to reform it and get rid of Eshkol and Sapir and their machine politics. This rhetoric, however, led only to expressions of discontent in the cabinet, in which Minister Menachem Begin concurred, and to no real action.

And what about Ben-Gurion, number one on the Rafi list? He came aboard only to leave again. He wished his former Rafi colleagues good luck, repeated his acerbic criticism of Eshkol's behaviour since his handling of 'the Affair', and refused to join the new party. His political career was over for good this time. After a while, he abandoned his involvement in current affairs and adopted the posture of a benevolent elder statesman until his death on 1 December 1973, during – as far as he was concerned an anticipated new round – the Yom Kippur War. It was in that conflict that Moshe Dayan, Ben-Gurion's COGS and Eshkol's popular successor as Minister of Defence in 1967, would lose his reputation.[17]

Rafi's continual latent threat to bolt from the new Labour Party deprived Eshkol of nearly all of the freedom of action that a truly united party might have given him. During the time he had left, Eshkol tasked Yisrael Galili, the Minister of Information in his Government, with introducing television in Israel.[18] The story of Israel TV is significant for our account in various ways. During Ben-Gurion's reign, the prime minister opposed the introduction of this medium on the grounds that 'the People of the Book should continue to read books'. Ben-Gurion based his impression of the way television affected its viewers on the replacement of the written word by the picture, which to his mind would have two effects: the encouragement of emotionalism at the expense of rational thinking and the instigation of an unavoidable quest for a lower, if not the lowest, common denominator that the expectations of most viewers would dictate. Ben-Gurion's elitist view of this issue won the day due to the state's control of the airwaves at the time and the support of the religious parties, which feared the influence of television on their own membership.

Soon after Eshkol's accession to the premiership, he established a public radio authority with a chair and director general appointed by the Government, plus a governing body comprised of public figures. Several members of the public body, along with the professionals who worked under their auspices, were able to assume more and more freedom vis-à-vis the Government as a result of the growing role of the media during the Eshkol years. The prime minister himself was approached many times about introducing television. Two things got in the way: the 1965–67 recession which argued against the huge investments that were needed for the establishment of the necessary broadcasting infrastructure and the purchase of imported TV sets, and the religious parties' traditional objections. A compromise had to be struck. Eshkol's Government resolved to study the matter in order to pursue it in the future and contracted with CBS to do the research. CBS was willing to do this at no charge, but the Director General of the Radio Authority, a crusader for the new medium, advised CBS to demand relatively high compensation instead. His Machiavellian idea was to place the Treasury in an investment trap: the American network should be paid so much as to allow only one justifiable outcome – going on to the real thing. In the meantime, the overworked Eshkol named Yisrael Galili minister in charge of public broadcasting and gave him a great deal of latitude.

At that time, I was studying history in West Germany and serving as the correspondent of Israel Radio in Bonn and Berlin, where I was taking a course in TV reporting as well. Amid these activities, I was approached by Klaus von Bismarck, chief of the West German radio and TV system, who offered the non-existent Israeli TV his help in creating the station's technical infrastructure. The scion of the family of the founder of the Second German Reich was – unlike other members of the family – a non-Nazi, and as the 'Intendant' of his broadcasting network he avoided the politicization of the public system while doing much to expose his audience to the crimes of the Third Reich, which had honoured him twice with the Knight's Cross as a distinguished officer of the reserve. I forwarded his offer to his Israeli counterpart who spurned it due to Minister Galili's anticipated reaction to any mention of Germans. So the preparations dragged on, entailing among other things the amendment of the Broadcasting Law. In this respect, Galili solicited the advice of various broadcasters, myself included, but became really interested when one of us dropped the name of Moshe Dayan. Here Galili's ordinarily amiable expression immediately gave way to a look of hate and disgust, which taught us neophytes something about the highly personal character of Israeli politics.

Due to Galili's response to the German offer, among other factors, the technical infrastructure for Israel's First Channel (commercial TV followed years later) had to be purchased under heavy time pressure once the decision to go ahead was made. CBS executives forced the founding team to deal with American equipment manufacturers whose connections with the network were dubious. The resulting transaction landed some of the Americans in prison in due course. Their Israeli counterparts avoided that fate because, in my estimation, kickbacks of this kind were considered legitimate in those days – provided, of course, that they served a 'good cause' such as the interest of the party or some new venture that entailed shortcuts. Such, in part, was the legacy of Eshkol's own permissive approach to this and other manners of conduct, which – years later – not only contributed to Labour's decline in the polls, but brought about the introduction of draconic laws governing the proper use of public finances.

The decision to introduce television in Israel dragged on until May 1967, and then it was made suddenly. The reason: residents of southern Israel were in a state of panic. Able to receive Egyptian TV, they watched the Egyptian army marching into Sinai and if they knew Arabic – as many of them did – they understood Nasser's threats and the related anti-Israel hysteria that had engulfed the whole Arab world.

Once the embryonic TV station was up and running, I ignored the forewarning that I had received in my meeting with Galili and invited Defence Minister Dayan for an interview at the improvised TV studio in Jerusalem. The first major Palestinian terror attack in Jerusalem after the Six Day War had just taken place, and in my capacity as Director of News and Current Affairs it was my professional duty to interview the minister in charge of responding to it. In discharging my duty, I earned truly astonished gazes from Galili's political aides who were in the studio, one of whom turned out to be Galili's expert on nuclear-deterrence theory. To add insult to injury, I and other medium-level executives went on to complain about the enormous waste of public funds expressed in the CBS deals and the chaotic circumstances of the continued development of the station. In these respects, we were told that it was this method, based on improvisation and whatever shortcuts were necessary, that had 'made the desert bloom'.

This was followed by a change in priority: Israel TV was supposed to broadcast foremost in Arabic for West Bankers and Gazans. Few of them had TV sets, however, because electricity lines in the former Jordanian- and Egyptian-controlled territories were scarce; they had to use batteries until their areas were connected to the Israeli grid. The priority had been chosen by an American professor of mass communications who had been appointed director of the newborn medium as a 'bridge to the Arab population'. Then this priority was suddenly dropped in favour of immediate full-scale operation in Hebrew in order to meet the expectations of the Jewish population. These zigzags, combined with my political *naïveté*, soon drove me back to the ivory tower of the Hebrew University at Giv'at Ram.

At day's end, the 'system' worked here as well. Since Eshkol's Israel was highly unionized, the new medium was taken over by the old Broadcasting Authority, which gave its personnel tenure that conferred on them the protection of the Histadrut. Soon enough, television started to change the political climate in a major way. The tenured TV professionals exercised their monopoly power by imposing their judgment and political inclinations on the medium – inclinations that tilted to the Left, sometimes prompting rather caustic criticism of Eshkol's Government and its Labour successors. Consequently, they contributed their share to Labour's decline and loss of power in 1977 and to the rise of the Right. Eshkol's commitment to prior study, however, did not include reflection on the long-range impact of the new medium anyway.

The never-ending story of the West Bank and Gaza belonged now to the reality that followed the Six Day War – a war that Levi Eshkol had tried to prevent but one carrying ramifications that he, among others and in competition with them, helped to shape. In this reality we live, and die, to this day.

I conclude by quoting Winston Churchill's characterization of Eduard Beneš, which, I think, captures the subject of this study with all the obvious differences:

> As this was the last time I ever saw President Beneš I will record my tribute to him ... He was a master of administration and diplomacy. He knew how to endure with patience and fortitude long periods of adverse fortune. Where he failed – and it cost him and his country much – was in not taking violent decisions at the supreme moment. He was too experienced a diplomatist, too astute a year-to-year politician, to realize the moment and to stake all on victory or death.[19]

Eshkol never feared death but refused to be dragged to a risky war; he wanted, however, to be crowned as its winner, but to no avail. He realized that he had won a problematic victory, with which he did not know what he – the old pioneer turned into a year-to-year politician – could or should do.

NOTES

1. Israel State Archives, *Levi Eshkol, the Third Prime Minister of Israel, Selected Documents on Chapters in His Life*, in Hebrew (Jerusalem: Israel State Archives, 2002), pp.600–2.
2. Ibid, pp.603–6.
3. Eitan Haber, *'Today War Will Break Out', The Reminiscences of Brig. Gen. Israel Lior, Aide-de-Camp to Prime Ministers Levi Eshkol and Golda Meir*, in Hebrew (Tel Aviv: Edanim, 1987), pp.297–8.
4. In due course, Ze'evi created his own political party, which stood for the encouragement of Arab emigration, among other things, and served as minister in various Israeli Governments. He was assassinated in 2001 in Jerusalem by Palestinians.

5. Haber, *'Today War Will Break Out'*, p.298.
6. For details, see Israel State Archives, *Levi Eshkol*, pp.608–9, and cf. Haber, *'Today War Will Break Out'*, pp.300–21.
7. See *Foreign Relations of the United States* (*FRUS*), Volume XX, Arab-Israeli Dispute, 1964–1967 (Washington, DC: Government Printing Office, 2001). From here on, notes quoting *FRUS* are culled from this volume or from published summaries of these *FRUS* records.
8. This and the ensuing discussion are based on a summary of the *FRUS* records pertaining to the Warneke–Rabin negotiations, published by Ha'aretz military correspondent Amir Oren on 31 July 2009.
9. See Avner Cohen in Chapter 10, note 15 (above) on the Nixon–Meir agreement in this regard. According to my interview with Professor Yuval Ne'eman above, Edward Teller, the 'father of the hydrogen bomb' and Nixon's close advisor, was involved in the President's decision to allow Israel to retain its nuclear option provided that it would not announce it publicly.
10. Dayan to this author, interview in the Knesset on 17 April 1980.
11. See Haber, *'Today War Will Break Out'*, pp.325–34.
12. Said K. Aburish, *Nasser, the Last Arab* (New York: St Martin's Press, 2004), p.281.
13. Ibid.
14. Israel State Archives, *Levi Eshkol*, pp.610–12.
15. I am indebted to Professor Nathan Yanai of the University of Haifa for this information.
16. Israel State Archives, *Levi Eshkol*, 610–12.
17. Dayan mounted a comeback. After Begin won the 1977 elections, he made Dayan his Foreign Minister. As such, Dayan, who resigned from Labour's parliamentary faction in order to assume the office, became a major player in Begin's effort to negotiate peace with Egypt. This effort and the related Israel–Egypt peace treaty of 1979, which endures to this day, entail separate discussion. See my 'Anwar Sadat and Peace with Israel', *Israel Studies*, forthcoming.
18. I base this section on my reminiscences as Director of News and Current Affairs for the Israel Television Foundation Team.
19. Letter, 6 January 1944, in Winston S. Churchill, *The Second World War,* Vol. V: *Closing the Ring* (London: The Reprint Society, 1954), p.353.

Epilogue

Levi Eshkol emerges from our narrative as a key figure, less known today, operating at various, important junctions of the history of Israel and of the Middle East as a major actor, whose contribution to its further developments to this day was very important indeed. His supreme test, the challenges of the May 1967 crisis and its immediate resolution, require a balanced judgement, from our vantage point of 2010.

Eshkol shaped Israel's society, its economic foundations and development under the most difficult conditions thanks to his own pioneering zeal, supported by the idealistic spirit of the Zionist pioneers who had laid the foundations of Israel. He did what many dreamed of, by invoking a relentless drive and practical measures, which transformed him to a political operator of much influence. As such, Eshkol was the conciliator, a go between for the major leaders of the Zionist enterprise, and finally, their successor. Having assumed the highest offices of the nation in a period of vast domestic and foreign political changes, Eshkol introduced to Israeli politics a more benign, less demanding, seeking for compromise philosophy of government at home and abroad, which had to confront first rate challenges. His reign, at first welcomed by upper-class Israelis as salvation from David Ben-Gurion's authoritarianism, also projected weakness under the pressure of enemies at home and abroad, when in fact Eshkol proved to be a tough defender of his own views and of his search for compromises. Thus, Eshkol found himself in a most important position of power at a crucial period of time. This was the period in which his Zionist national liberation movement was transformed from a voluntary outfit, to a large extent, to a sovereign state. Many such movements were confronted with this challenge, which required new institutions, the reform of existing ones, the adoption of new public rules, and possibly old-new values. Eshkol was not able to meet all these challenges, as did the American Founding Fathers under entirely different circumstances. He became too much of an ordinary politician to pursue a major constitutional reform during his heyday, and in fact used the old political system with its deficiencies as his source of power.

Perceived by the American administrations of John Kennedy and Lyndon Johnson as a compromiser, Eshkol was able to develop closer relations with the United States and yet avoid American demands which he deemed unacceptable. Truth to tell, during the May 1967 Crisis he was left alone by his American 'friend' in the White House, but this very act, combined with the IDF victory in June, helped in opening a new chapter in the US–Israeli relations, thanks to the input of the activated American Jewry, and to Soviet and Arab behaviour. Also, the Six Day War, which Eshkol had tried his best to avoid, contributed much to the revival and activation of Soviet Jewry, which in turn would immensely contribute to doubling the population in Eshkol's 'small Israel' and to changing its social and economic structure.

Eshkol could not foresee the longer range ramifications of the Six Day War, to which he contributed his share, although he did sense some: the revival of religion, in the context of the 'liberation' of the West Bank, and of the unification of Jerusalem; the gradual radicalization of the occupied Palestinians in the West Bank and Gaza, and the ensuing nationalization and islamization of Israeli Arabs; the emergence of Menachem Begin's Likud Bloc as an alternative to Eshkol's Labour Party, which Eshkol legitimized upon creating his National Emergency Coalition in early June 1967. One could certainly ask whether he had any other alternatives, facing the Arab challenge with no help from Washington, in spite of the concessions made to the Johnson Administration on Dimona and related issues. The answers remain open to this day. Eshkol could have, theoretically, refrained from occupying the West Bank and Gaza. But this option would have hardly resolved the Palestinian Refugee Problem, the growing role of the Palestinian military organizations and prevent Nasser and the Syrians, also Iraq, from supporting Arafat's tactics in competition with other Palestinian groups, at that period of time. Indeed, this is what Eshkol had to struggle with in his dying days, during which he accepted the occupation of the West Bank and Gaza, authorizing several settlements therein, as the least threatening evil. Did Eshkol realize that the victory of 1967 entailed Jewish settlements in the West Bank and in Gaza that would complicate any potential negotiations on the future of the occupied territories till this very day? Could Eshkol be strong enough to keep the occupied territories as temporary trump cards for negotiated peace, and was he misleading himself when he hoped that Israeli-created 'facts on the ground' in the occupied territories, even in the Greater Jerusalem area, were reversible? The answer could be found in Eshkol's modus operandi as a practical politician, whose decisions were dictated by domestic, partisan givens, by public opinion and by his own values as an old settler who came to an unpartitioned Palestine in 1914, and soon enough found himself confronted with Arab enmity.

Later on, having played a major role in creating the tools of economic development of the Yishuv and the young state by means of the Histadrut, the Jewish Agency and government inputs, Eshkol presided over huge bureaucracies, controlled by Mapai and its leftist associates. Mapai's voting system, based on machine politicians or 'ballot captains' supplying votes in exchange for benefits, was necessary under the circumstances in order to manage the economy and ensure enough parliamentary support. However, this 'system' would generate not only an ongoing quest for a regime reform, not successful as yet, but above all drive Israelis to seek for individual freedom and economic affluence. This change in the priorities of many Israelis, the introduction of commercial television, the fierce competition among the printed media, and the continued division among secular Israelis, national religious settlers and ultra orthodox groups, combined with anti-corruption, draconic legislation and its implementation by police and the courts. Much of this was the result of Eshkol's times and the developments resulting from them for good or bad.

Eshkol would have been proud of Israel's recent membership in the OECD, and its major scientific-commercial achievements. Much less so would the old socialist like the gap opened since his times between the very rich and the poor, or Israel's isolation among the nations as a result of the post-1967 developments, which, however, was sometimes even worse during his reign. He would have offered something in Yiddish about the poor Samson, who had managed to break the previous siege by opening the doors to America, and that the current siege is serious, but compared to his own experience in the 1930s, 1940s and 1950s, Israel proved to be a success story beyond his own imagination.

Bibliography

ARCHIVES

Ben-Gurion Archive, Ben-Gurion Institute, Ben-Gurion University, Kiryat Sede Boqer
Central Zionist Archive, Jerusalem
CID Archives, British, kept with the Hagana Archive, Tel-Aviv
Franklin Delano Roosevelt Presidential Archive, Hyde Park, New York
German Federal Archive, Berlin Lichterfelde
Hagana Archive, SHAI (Hagana Intelligence), Tel Aviv
Jabotinsky Archive, Tel Aviv
Lyndon B. Johnson Presidential Archive, Austin, TX
John F. Kennedy Presidential Archive, Boston, MA
Israel Defense Forces (IDF) Archive, Tel Aviv
Israel State Archive, Jerusalem and the related publications of the series pertaining to Prime Ministers David Ben-Gurion, Levi Eshkol and Yitzhak Rabin
Mapai Secretariat Archive, Tel Aviv
Public Record Office, Kew, Surrey
US Library of Congress, records pertaining to Israeli nuclear weapons
United States National Archives, College Park, Maryland, and the related volumes of *Foreign Relations of the United States* (*FRUS*), Arab-Israeli Dispute, especially Vols. XIX and XX

INTERVIEWS

Ben-Aharon, Yitzhak
Ben-Gurion, David (TV interview by author)
Brecher, Michael
Burg, Yosef

Dayan, Moshe
Elpeleg, Zvi
Eshkol, Miriam
Eshkol, Levi (media interview as above)
Evron, Efraim
Gazit, Mordechai
Hadari, Ze'ev 'Venia'
Harel, Isser
Hashai, Yehuda
Ne'eman, Yuval
Peres, Shimon (media interview as above)
Rabin, Yitzhak (media interview as above)
Rafael, Gideon
Rotenstreich, Nathan
Samburski, Shmuel
Sheck, Ze'ev
Yanai, Nathan

PUBLISHED SOURCES

English and Other Non-Hebrew Sources

Aburish, Said K., *Nasser, the Last Arab* (New York: St Martin's Press, 2004).

Aronson, Shlomo, *Conflict and Bargaining in the Middle East, an Israeli Perspective* (Baltimore, MD and London: Johns Hopkins University Press, 1978).

Aronson, Shlomo, *The Politics and Strategy of Nuclear Weapons in the Middle East, Opacity, Theory and Strategy, An Israeli Perspective* (Albany, NY and London: SUNY Press, 1992).

Aronson, Shlomo, 'David Ben-Gurion and the British Constitutional Model', *Israel Studies*, 3, 2 (Autumn 1998), pp.193–214.

Aronson, Shlomo, *Hitler, the Allies, and the Jews* (New York: Cambridge University Press, 2006).

Aronson, Shlomo, 'Israel Security and the Holocaust: Lessons Learned, but Existential Fears Continue', *Israel Studies*, 14, 1 (Spring 2009), pp.65–93.

Aronson, Shlomo, 'David Ben-Gurion, Levi Eshkol and the Struggle over Dimona: A Prologue to the Six-Day War and its

(Un) Anticipated Results', *Israel Affairs*, 15, 2 (April 2009), pp.114–34.

Aronson, Shlomo, *David Ben-Gurion and the Jewish Renaissance* (New York: Cambridge University Press, 2010, in press).

Aronson, Shlomo, 'Anwar Sadat and Peace with Israel', *Israel Studies,* forthcoming.

Bauer, Yehuda, *Jews for Sale? Nazi Jewish Negotiations 1933–1945* (New Haven, CT and London: Yale University Press, 1994).

Brecher, Michael, *Decisions in Israel's Foreign Policy* (New Haven, CT: Yale University Press, 1975).

Churchill, Winston, S., *The Second World War,* vol. V: *Closing the Ring* (London: The Reprint Society, 1954).

Cohen, Avner, 'Cairo, Dimona and the 1967 War', *Middle East Journal*, 50, 2 (1996).

Dallek, Robert, *A Flawed Giant, Lyndon Johnson and His Times, 1961–1973* (New York: Oxford University Press, 1993).

Dallek, Robert, *Lyndon B. Johnson, Portrait of a President* (Oxford and New York: Oxford University Press, 2004).

Foreign Relations of the United States (FRUS), various volumes (Washington, DC, Government Printing Office).

Gazit, Mordechai, *President Kennedy's Policy toward the Arab States and Israel, Analysis and Documents* (Tel Aviv: Shiloah Center for Middle Eastern and African Studies, Tel Aviv University, 1983).

Gensicke, Klaus, *The Mufti of Jerusalem and the Nazis. Amin al-Husaini: The Berlin Years 1941–1945* (London and Portland, OR: Vallentine Mitchell, 2010).

Gensicke, Klaus, *Der Mufti von Jerusalem und die Nationalsozialisten. Eine politische Biographie Amin el-Husseinis,* ed. Klaus-Michael Mallmann (Darmstadt: WBG, 2007).

Ginor, Fanny, *Socio-Economic Disparities in Israel* (Tel Aviv: Tel Aviv University; Transaction Books, 1979).

Ginor, Isabella and Remez, Gideon, *Foxbats over Dimona: The Soviet Nuclear Gamble in the Six-Day War* (New Haven, CT: Yale University Press, 2007).

Gorny, Yosef, *From Binational Society to Jewish State. Federal Concepts in Zionist Political Thought, 1920–1990, and the Jewish People* (Leiden and Boston, MA: Brill, 2006).

Jenkins, Roy, *Churchill: A Biography* (New York: Ferrar, Straus and Giroux, 2001).

Judt, Tony, *Post War, A History of Europe since 1945* (New York: Penguin, 2006).

Karsh, Efraim, *Palestine Betrayed* (New Haven, CT: Yale University Press, 2010).

Pean, Pierre, *Les Deux Bombes*, in French (Paris: Fayard, 1982, and new edition, 2002).

Penslar, Derek J., *Zionism and Technocracy: The Engineering of Jewish Settlement in Palestine, 1870–1918* (Bloomington and Indianapolis, IN: Indiana University Press, 1991).

Peres, Shimon, *Battling for Peace, A Memoir*, ed. David Landau (New York: Random House, 1995).

Scharfstetter, Susanna, *Die Dritte Atommacht, Britische Nichtverbreitungspolitik im Dienst von Statussicherung und Deutschlandpolitik 1952–1968* [The Third Atom Power, British Proliferation Policy in Service of Maintaining its Status and its German Policy (1952–1968)] (Munich: DVA, 1999).

Schelling, Thomas C., *The Strategy of Conflict* (Cambridge, MA: Harvard University Press, 1960).

Sheffer, Gabriel, *Moshe Sharett, Biography of a Political Moderate* (Oxford: Clarendon Press, 1996).

Porath, Yehoshua, *The Palestinian-Arab National Movement, 1918–1929* (London: Frank Cass, 1974).

Porath, Yehoshua, *The Palestinian-Arab National Movement, 1929–1939: From Riots to Rebellion*, Volume II (London: Frank Cass, 1977).

Weizmann, Chaim, *Trial and Error: The Autobiography of Chaim Weizmann* (New York: Harper & Bros., 1949).

Weizman, Ezer, *On Eagles' Wings, The Personal Story of the Leading Commander of the Israeli Air Force* (Jerusalem and Tel-Aviv: Steimatzky's Agency 1976).

Wildt, Michael, 'The SD and Palestine: New Evidence from Captured German Documents in Moscow', in Shlomo Aronson (ed.), *New Records – New Perspectives* (Sede Boqer: Ben-Gurion Research Institute, 2002), pp.64–77.

Yakira, Elhanan, *Post-Zionism, Post Holocaust, Three Essays on Denial, Forgetting, and Delegitimation of Israel* (New York: Cambridge University Press, 2009).

Hebrew Sources

Almogi, Yosef, *The Struggle for Ben-Gurion: in the Wake of the Affair* (Jerusalem: Yedioth Ahronoth, 1988).

Aronson, Shlomo, *David Ben-Gurion, Renaissance Leader and the Waning of an Age* (Sede Boqer and Beersheva: Ben-Gurion Research Institute, 1999). An updated English translation is scheduled for publication in September 2010.

Aronson, Shlomo, *The Politics and Strategy of Nuclear Weapons in the Middle East* Vol. A (Jerusalem: Academon, 1994), revised version Vol. B (Jerusalem: Academon, 2006).

Avizohar, Meir, 'Fighting Zionism', in David Ben-Gurion, *Left Behind (Post-Mortem) Memoirs,* Volume VI, January–August 1939, edited and annotated by Meir Avizohar (Tel Aviv: Am Oved, 1987).

Avizohar, Meir, *National and Social Ideals as Reflected in Mapai – The Israeli Labour Party – 1930–1942* (Tel Aviv: Am-Oved, 1990).

Bar-Zohar, Michael, *Ben-Gurion, A Political Biography,* Vol.II and III (Tel Aviv: Am Oved, 1977).

Bareli, Avi, *Mapai in Israel's Early Independence 1948–1953* (Jerusalem: Yad Ben-Zvi, 2007).

Baron, Arie, *Moshe Dayan and the Six-Day War* (Tel Aviv: Ministry of Defence, 1997).

Barnach-Matalon, Naora, *A Good Place on the Side* (no publishing location cited: KIP Publishers, 2009).

Ben-Gurion, David, *Things as They Were* (Tel Aviv: Am Hasefer, 1965).

Ben-Gurion, David, *War Diary, the War of Independence 1948–1949* (Tel Aviv: Ministry of Defence, 1982).

Bloom, Allan, *The Closing of the American Mind*, Hebrew translation (Tel Aviv: Am Oved, 2002).

Cohen, Yeroham, *The Allon Plan* (Tel Aviv: Hakibbutz Hameuchad, 1972).

Dayan, Moshe, *Story of My Life* (Jerusalem: Idanim, 1976).

Elath, Eliahu, *The Struggle for Statehood, Washington: 1945–1948*, Vol. I, 1945–1946 (Tel Aviv: Am Oved, 1979).

Elon, Amos, *The Israelis: Founders and Sons* (New York: Holt, Rinehart and Winston, 1971).

Evron, Yair, *Israel's Nuclear Dilemma* (Tel Aviv: Hakibbutz Hameuchad, 1987).

Eyal, Yigal, *The First Intifada, The Repression of the Arab Revolt by the British Army 1936–1939* (Tel Aviv: Ministry of Defence, 1999).

Feldstein, Ariel L., *Gordian Knot: David Ben-Gurion. The Zionist Organization and American Jewry 1948–1963* (Jerusalem and Sede Boqer: The Hebrew University of Jerusalem, 2005).

Gazit, Shlomo, *The Stick and the Carrot, Israeli Rule in Judea and Samaria* (Tel Aviv: Zemora Bitan, 1985).

Golan, Arnon, *Wartime Spatial Changes, Former Arab Territories within the State of Israel, 1948–1950* (Sede Boqer: Ben-Gurion Research Center, Ben-Gurion University of the Negev Press, 2001).

Golan, Shimon, *A War on Three Fronts, Decision Making by the Supreme Command in the Six Day* War (Tel Aviv: Ministry of Defence, 2007).

Goldstein, Yossi, *Eshkol – A Biography* (Jerusalem: Keter, 2003).

Gorny, Yosef, Bareli, Avi and Greenberg, Yitzhak (eds), *From a Labor Society to a Labor Organization. Articles on the Histadrut during the Yishuv and the Statehood Periods* (Sede Boqer: Ben-Gurion Heritage Center and Tel Aviv University, 2000).

Greenberg, Yitzhak, 'Creation of the Foundations for R&D and Defense Production: Policy and Budgeting Aspects', in *'Iyyunim bi-tequmat Yisrael, Studies in Zionism, the Yishuv and the State of Israel, A Research Annual*, vol. 9 (Sede Boqer: Ben-Gurion Research Center, Ben-Gurion University of the Negev Press, 1999).

Haber, Eitan, *'Today War Will Break Out', The Reminiscences of Brig. Gen. Israel Lior, Aide-de-Camp to Prime Ministers Levi Eshkol and Golda Meir* (Tel Aviv: Edanim, 1987).

Heller, Joseph, *LEHI – Ideology and Politics, 1940–1949*, Vol. I (Jerusalem: Shazar Centre and Keter, 1989).

Heller, Joseph, *The Struggle for the Jewish State, Zionist Politics, 1936–1939* (Jerusalem: The Zalman Shazar Centre for the Furtherance of the Study of Jewish History, 1984).

Horowitz, Dan and Lissak, Moshe, *From Yishuv to State, The Jews of Eretz Yisrael during the British Mandate as a Political Community* (Tel Aviv: Am Oved, 1977).

Horowitz, David, *In the Heart of Events* (Ramat Gan: Massada, 1975).

Israel State Archives, *Levi Eshkol, the Third Prime Minister of Israel, Selected Documents on Chapters in His Life* (Jerusalem: Israel State Archives, 2002).

Kadish, Alon (ed.), *Israel's War of Independence 1948–1949* (Tel Aviv: Ministry of Defence, 2005).

Karpy, Daniel, 'The Mufti of Jerusalem, Amin el Husseini, and His Political Activities during World War II (October 1941–July 1943)', *Ha-tsiyyonut* 9 (1971), pp.285–316.

Karpy, Daniel, 'The Mufti's Plan to Poison the Waters of Tel Aviv', *Ha-umma*, 1, 2 (Summer 2003), pp.37–41.

Keinan, Ofra, 'Immigrants as Implementers of Zionist Ideals: the Impact of Immigrant Settlements on Environmental Change in the Ta'anach Region 1948–1967' (Ph.D. Dissertation, Bar-Ilan University, 1989).

Keinan, Ofra, 'The Kibbutzim and Moshavim Movements and Mass Immigration to Israel during the First Decade of the State', *Cathedra, Quarterly for the History of Eretz-Israel and its Yishuv*, June (2004), pp.113–36.

Keren, Michael, *Ben-Gurion and the Intellectuals* (Sede Boqer: Ben-Gurion University of the Negev, 1988).

Leibowitz, Yeshayahu (ed.), *Hebrew Encyclopaedia* (Jerusalem: Encyclopedia Publishing House, 1967), s.v. 'Ben-Gurion, David', supplement volume, pp.666–77.

Lissak, Moshe, chief editor, *The History of the Jewish Community in Eretz Israel since 1882, Israel, the First Decade* (Jerusalem: The Israel Academy of Sciences and Humanities, 2009).

Margalit, Dan, *I Have Seen Them All* (Tel Aviv: Zmora-Bitan, 1997).

Mishkinski, Moshe, *Studies in Jewish Socialism* (Sede Boqer and Tel Aviv: Ben-Gurion and Tel Aviv University Press, 2004).

Naor, Mordechai (ed.), *The Second Aliya 1903–1914, Sources, Summaries, Selected Issues and Supplementary Material* (Jerusalem: Yad Izhak Ben-Zvi, 1984).

Naor, Mordechai (ed.), *Stockade and Tower 1936–1939* (Jerusalem: Yad Izhak Ben-Zvi, 1987).

Narkiss, Uzi, *Jerusalem the One and Only* (Tel Aviv: Am Oved, 1975).

Narkiss, Uzi, *A Soldier of Jerusalem* (Tel Aviv: Ministry of Defence, 1991).

Near, Henry, *The Kibbutz Movement: A History* (Jerusalem, Tel Aviv and Sede Boqer: Ben-Gurion University Press, 2008).

Ostfeld, Zahava, *An Army is Born* (Tel Aviv: Ministry of Defence, 1994, two volumes).

Paz-Yeshaiahu, Abigail and Gorny, Yosef (eds), *A Historical Achievement and Its Evolution, the Kibbutz and Moshav Settlement Movements, 1910–1990* (Sede Boqer and Tel Aviv: Ben-Gurion University Press, 2006).

Pinkus, Benjamin, *From Ambivalence to an Unofficial Alliance, Israel, France, and the French Jews 1947–1957* (Beersheva: Ben-Gurion University Press, 2005).

Rabin, Yitzhak, *Service Notes* (Tel Aviv: Sifriyat Ma'ariv, 1979).

Rosenthal, Yemima (ed.), *Yitzhak Rabin, Prime Minister of Israel 1974–1977/1992–1995, Selected Documents, Volume I, Early Years and Military Career 1922–1967* (Jerusalem: Israel State Archives, 2005).

Rubin, Joseph (ed.), *Workers' Moshavim, an Anthology,* Vol. 1 (Moshavim + Workers Movement Publishing House, 1969, no further publication data available).

Schweid, Eliezer, *A History of Modern Jewish Religious Philosophy,* Part III, Vol. I, *The Historical Crossroads* (Tel Aviv: Am Oved, 2003).

Shapira, Anita, *From the Dismissal of the Chief of Territorial Defense to the Abolition of the Palmach, Issues in the Struggle for Security Leadership* (Tel Aviv: Hakibbutz Hameuchad, 1985).

Shapira, Anita, *Berl*, Vol. II (Tel Aviv: Sifriyat Ofakim/Am Oved, 1980).

Shapira, Yosef, *Levi Eshkol, on the Steps of the Mission* (Tel Aviv: Massada Publishers, 1969).

Sharett, Moshe, *Sharett's Diaries*, Vol. E (Tel Aviv: Sifriyat Ma'ariv, 1978).

Shiloh, Margalit, *Experiments in Settlements. The Palestine Office 1908–1914* (Jerusalem: Yad Izhak Ben-Zvi, 1988).

Teveth, Shabtai, *David's Zeal, The Burning Ground, The Life of David Ben-Gurion,* Vol. III (Jerusalem and Tel Aviv: Schocken, 1987).

Wallach, Y. *To the Flag: the Establishment of a People's Army in the Midst of Combat* (Tel Aviv: Ministry of Defence, 1997).

Weitz, Yechiam, 'End of the Beginning – Elucidating the Concept of “Genesis of the State”', in Y. Weitz (ed.), *Between Vision and Revision: a Century of Zionist Historiography* (Jerusalem: Yad Izhak Ben-Zvi, 1997), pp.244–7.

Yizhar, Uri, *Between Vision and Power, The History of the Ahdut-ha-'Avoda Po'alei Tsiyyon Party* (Efal: Yad Tabenkin, 2005).

Zameret, Zvi, Halamish, Aviva and Meir-Glitzenstein, Esther (eds), *The Development Towns* (Jerusalem: Yad Izhak Ben-Zvi, 2009).

Zur, Elie (ed.), *'Can't Do Without Us', Mapam's Views on Security and Foreign Policy 1948–1950* (Kibbutz Dalia: Yad Yaari and Yad Tabenkin, 2000).

Index

Page numbers ending in 'n' stand for notes. L.E. stands for Levi Eshkol, where it appears in the index.

A

Acheson, Dean, 215
Acre, 49, 72
actionism, x
Adenauer, Konrad, 98
'Affair', *see* Lavon Affair (Israeli subversive actions in Egypt in 1954; Related inquiries and controversies since 1960)
afforestation campaign (Weitz), 48
Aharonson, Ya'akov, 32n
Ahdut ha-'Avoda (left-wing nationalist party), 33n, 34n, 68, 70, 71, 78, 91, 92, 103, 104, 112–13, 124, 132, 200, 244, 245; coalition with Mapam, 135, 136, 177; *see also* Allon, Yigal; Galili, Yisrael
AID (US Agency for International Development), 164
Air Force, US, 58
All Eshkol's Jokes (booklet), 140
Allen, Roger, 145
Allon, Yigal, 32, 68–70, 77–9, 87n, 90, 101, 112–13, 117, 119, 133, 137, 138, 166, 176, 177, 179, 185, 190, 195, 200, 202–8, 225, 233, 245; *Curtain of Sand*, 218, 240; deterrence-conventional compellence doctrine, 136, 186, 192
Almogi, Yosef, 84, 87–8n
Al-Yaum (Lebanese newspaper), 151
American Civil War, 30, 31
American Manhattan Project, 59
American Skyhawk, 133, 146, 238, 240
Anderson, Robert, 196, 226, 227, 243
Anglo-American Commission, 26
Anglo-Palestine Bank, 12
anti-Nazi boycott campaign, 12
appeasement policy, 16, 19
Al-Aqsa mosque, 13, 200
Arabs: annihilation threats, 57, 58, 123, 207; Israeli, 108, 109; violence among, 4, 7, 16, 48
Arafat, Yasser, 114, 115, 134, 207, 223, 242, 243
Aranne, Zalman, 63, 116

Arendt, Hannah, 96
Arieli, Yehoshua, 139
Arlosoroff, Chaim, 11; murder of (1933), 12
Armistice Agreements (1949), 36, 38, 205
Armistice Demarcation Lines, 78, 120, 203, 221
arms race, containing, 160–70; *see also* nuclear deterrence
Ashdod, 46, 49, 72, 140
Ashqelon, 49, 72
Assad, Hafez, 240
Aswan High Dam, 98, 112, 134, 145, 154
Atatürk, Mustafa Kemal, 38
atom bombs, 58
Atomic Energy Commission, 133
austerity programme of Eshkol, 139
Austria, annexation by Hitler, 16
Avnery, Uri, 76

B

Ba'ath regime, Syria, 113, 114, 166, 190, 204
Badeau, John S., 121
Balfour Declaration (1917), 6, 9n, 15, 19
Bandung conference of 'non-aligned' states (1955), 61
Bank Hapoalim (Workers Bank), 47
Bank of Israel, 138; creation by L.E., 97
Barbour, Walworth, 152, 157–8, 159, 160, 161, 162, 224–5
Bareli, Avi, 9n
Bar-Lev, Chaim, 241
Battle, Lucius D., 128, 152, 163–4, 183
Bauer, Yehuda, 17n
Be'er Toviyya, 15
Beersheba, 46, 49, 73, 121
Begin, Menachem, 13, 95, 109, 118, 129, 195, 202, 203, 205, 206, 220; as commander of IZL, 24, 31–2; far Right nationalist party, 29, 42, 71, 92, 136, 199, 201
Ben Barka, Mehdi, 120, 137, 144, 148n, 153, 178, 179
Ben Bella, Muhammad, 112
Ben-Aharon, Yitzhak, 87n, 112
Beneš, Eduard, 249
Ben-Gurion, David, 17n, 20, 21, 39, 40, 53, 60, 67, 96, 166, 178, 179; and 1965 elections, 115–16, 144; on Bible, 92, 94; as chair of Jewish Agency, 14, 27, 49; conflict with L.E., xi, 93, 107, 144; defence doctrine, 62, 220; Eshkol succeeding as PM, 22, 78, 84; and Kennedy, 90, 131n; L.E. compared *see* Ben-Gurion/Eshkol comparison; and Lavon Affair, 75, 79–80, 81, 116; and Mapai, 8, 23; post-Second World War activities, 25, 27–8; Rafi Party *see* Rafi (Israel Workers List) Party; reforms, 68–9, 71, 135; resignation of, 50, 54, 110, 115; retirement, 106–7; utopianism, 44, 45; West Germany, cooperation with, 67, 81, 90–1, 92, 98; *Yoman-ha-'Milchama* (War Diary), 59, 85n

Ben-Gurion/Eshkol comparison, x, 3, 14, 124; decision-making styles, 28–9, 62, 137, 149–50, 197–8; Dimona issue, 120–1; leadership styles, 141; as prime ministers, 110, 117; thinker (Ben-Gurion) vs doer (Eshkol), 95, 97–8
Ben-Harush, David, 73
Bergmann, Ernst David, 58–9, 60, 61, 133, 143–4, 145; as chair of IAEC, 59, 143
Berlin, 14
Bible, 92, 94–5
bill of obligations, 109
Biltmore Programme (1942), 22, 23, 27
Bismarck, Klaus von, 247
Bitan, Moshe, 162
Black September 1970, 243
Blas, Simcha, 6, 9n
Bloom, Allan, 94–5, 96
Bonds, 44
Bourgès-Maunoury, Morris, 64
Brecher, Michael, 132n
Brezhnev, Leonid, 111, 190, 191
Britain *see* United Kingdom
British Army, 20, 22
British Labour Party, 25
British Proliferation Policy in Service of Maintaining its Status and its German Policy (1952–68), 66
British-Jordanian Defence Treaty, 39
broadcasting, public, 246
Broadcasting Authority, 248
Broadcasting Law, 247
Brody, David, 214–15
Buber, Martin, 39, 51n, 94
Bund, anti-Zionist, 2
Bundy, McGeorge, 104–5, 125, 215–16, 222, 223
Bunker, Ellsworth, 174n
bureaucracy, 95
Burma, 97

C

casus belli, 62, 111, 128, 134, 168, 172, 194, 207, 231
CBS, 246, 247
Central Intelligence Agency (CIA), 121
Chace, James, 218
Chamberlain, Neville, 16, 19
'chosen people', Jews as, 45
Churchill, Winston, 18n, 57, 87n, 187, 249
Cisjordan, 15
'Citizens for Eshkol', 135, 173
coalition, centre-left (Mapai, Mapam and Ahdut ha'Avoda), 135, 136, 177
Cognoscenti, 135
Cohen, Yeroham, 250n
Cohn, Chaim, 77
Cold War, 76, 224
Common Market, 140–1
communes, Jewish, 6
compromiser, L.E. as, 136–7, 149–55, 150, 201
conventional deterrence, 78, 79, 136, 186, 192; *see also* nuclear deterrence
corruption allegations: Lavon affair, 74, 80, 81, 82; *see also* Lavon Affair (Israeli terrorist attacks)
Cuban missile crisis, 111–12
Curtain of Sand (Allon), 218, 240

Czechoslovakia, 16; sacrifice of, 64

D

Dallek, Robert, 186–7, 188
Damascus, pan-Arab regime, 114, 115, 156
Dassault, Marcel, 113
Dayan, Moshe, 61, 64, 66, 69–72, 74, 98, 129, 166, 195, 198, 200, 201, 204, 233, 235, 241, 244, 247; as Chief of General Staff at MOD, 54–5, 56, 62; and Eshkol, 110, 119, 183, 205–9; and Lavon Affair, 75, 82, 117; Rafi Party *see* Rafi (Israel Workers List) Party; Western view of, 98–9
decision-making style of Eshkol, 136–7; Ben-Gurion compared, 28–9, 62, 137, 149–50, 197–8
Degania Bet, Kibbutz, 7, 72
Demilitarized Zone, 166
Depression (1920s), 10n
deterrence: conventional, 78, 79, 136, 186, 192; nuclear *see* nuclear deterrence
development towns, 46, 49, 72
Dimona nuclear reactor project, 65–7, 71, 72, 85, 96, 102; and Egypt, 150–1, 158–9; and US, 89–90, 99, 119–20, 123, 124, 126, 127, 128, 129, 133, 138, 142–3, 151, 158–9, 224, 239; *see also* Israeli-French relations; Lavon Affair; nuclear deterrence
al Din, Zakariyah Muhyi, 228, 229
Displaced Persons (DPs), Jewish, 25–6, 27
Dissenchik, Aryeh, 129, 130
Dobrynin, Anatoly, 153–4
doer, L.E. as, 2, 3, 7, 47, 93
Dome of the Rock, 13, 200
Dostrovsky, Yisrael, 59, 85n, 86n

E

Eban, Abba, 74, 143, 147, 150, 157–61, 174n, 179, 182, 187, 191
Eban-Dulles accord, 183
Egypt, 16, 63; on Dimona, 150–1; Eilat blockade, 182, 202; Israeli-Egyptian peace treaty (1979), 199, 207; missile and unconventional-weapons programme, 91, 98; and Soviet Union, 193–4; and US, 152, 157, 158–9, 163, 182; vulnerability to nuclear attack, 122–3; *see also* Nasser, Gamal Abdel
Egyptian-Syrian-Iraqi federation, 100
Eichmann, Adolf, 95; trial, 91
Eilat, 46, 49, 72; Egyptian blockade on, 182, 202
Eisenhower, D., 89, 188
Eisenstadt, Shmuel Noach, 139
Elad, Avri, 74
electoral reform, Ben-Gurion, 68–9, 71
Elon, Amos, 107, 109, 110
Erhard, Ludwig, 104
Eshed, Haggai, 110, 116

Eshkol, Levi: birth and early life, 1–2; achievements, 251–4; early political career, 2–6; characteristics, 7–8, 41, 149; legacy of, 231–43; as prime minister *see* Prime Minister, L.E. as; *see also* Ben-Gurion/Eshkol comparison
'Eshkol's kids', 98
Etzion Bloc, 209, 222
EURATOM (multinational project), 63
Everett, Mr, 147
Evron, Efraim, 145, 171, 217–18, 221

F

F-4 Phantom, 237–8, 240
Faisal, King of Saudi Arabia, 163, 167
farming settlements, Palestine, 5; First Aliya farmers, 6
Fatah organization, 114, 134, 191, 207, 232, 242
Federation of Jewish Labour in Palestine *see* Histradut (Federation of Jewish Labour in Palestine)
Feinberg, Abe, 164, 168, 239
Final Solution *see* Holocaust
Finance Ministry, 45
Finney, John W., 143, 147
First Aliya (first wave of Zionist immigration to Palestine, early 1880s), 6
First World War, 3–4
Flapan, Simcha, 77
forced-emigration policy (Hitler), 16
Foreign Affairs and Defence Committee (FADC), 75, 80, 82
foreign aid, 44
Forrest, Nathan Bedford, 30
Fortas, Abe, 182
Foster, William, 129
Fourth Aliya (fourth wave of Zionist immigrants to Palestine, mid-1920s), 8
Foxbats over Dimona: The Soviet Nuclear Gamble in the Six-Day War (Ginor and Remez), 189, 191, 192–3, 194, 195
France: military relations with Israel *see* Israeli-French military relations; nuclear deterrence *see* France, nuclear weapons in; Socialist-Radical coalition, 64
France, nuclear weapons in, 61–2, 64–5, 124, 147, 224; A-bomb, 66; cooperation with Israel, 62, 63–4, 65, 85n, 91, 98; intermediate range ballistic missiles, 103, 156, 190; Voutour medium-range bombers, 186
Franco, General Francisco, 64
free-market principles, 140–1
French Atomic Energy Commission (FAEC), 59
FRUS (Foreign Relations of the United States), 9n, 105, 148, 170, 171, 184

G

Galilee, 15, 108, 113, 190
Galili, Yisrael, 32, 33n, 34n, 68,

69, 77–9, 87n, 101, 107, 112–13, 117, 119, 133, 136–8, 166, 176, 179, 190, 195, 206, 225, 245; television, in charge of, 246, 247, 248
Game Theory, 79
garden (development) towns, 46, 49, 72
de Gaulle, General, 59, 65–7, 77, 102, 103, 120, 151, 187, 191, 241
Gavish, Yeshayahu, 181
Gaza Strip, 31, 63, 109, 164, 172, 199, 205, 208, 245, 249; UN peacekeeping forces surrounding, 113–14, 154
Gazit, Mordechai, 99
Gazit, Shlomo, 186
General Assembly Resolution 194 (1948), UN, 38, 39
General Federation of Labour, 45
General Zionist Party, 70–1, 91
German Jews, inflow to Palestine, 13
Germany: 'German scientists affair', 91, 103; Jewish financial institution in, 12; *see also* Nazi Germany
Ginor, Isabella, 189, 190, 191, 192–3, 194, 195
Golan Heights, 166, 190, 198, 204, 205, 206, 212, 230
Goldberg, Arthur, 154, 230n
Goldstein, Yossi, 9n, 38
Gorny, Yosef, 9n
Gorshkov, Sergei, 190
Grazofsky *see* Gur, Shlomo (Grazofsky)
Greater Israel movement, 199, 206
Grechko, Andrei, 112, 125, 131n, 190, 194
Greenburg, Yitzhak, 9n
Gromyko, Andrei, 223–4, 230n, 231
guerrilla operations, 134, 141, 166, 172, 191, 240
Guinness, Walter Edward (1st Baron Moyne), 24
Gur, Shlomo (Grazofsky), 58, 59

H

Ha'avara (Transfer) Agreement (1933), 12, 14
Hadow, Michael, 146, 147
Hagana (semi-legal militia), 7, 21, 25, 28
Haifa, Wadi Salib riots (1959), 73
el Hakim Amer, Abd, 151, 190
'Hanukkah reflections' (Ben-Gurion), 1948, 59, 85n
Haolam Hazeh (magazine), 76
Ha-po'el ha-Tsa'ir (Young Worker) group, 3
Harel, Isser, 190
Harkaby, Yehoshafat, 221
Harman, Avraham, 99, 104, 105
Harriman, W. Averill, 125, 127, 128, 240
al-Husaini, Hajj Amin *see* Mufti of Jerusalem (Hajj Amin al-Husaini)
Ha-Shomer ha-Tsa'ir (Young Guard), 23, 33n, 34n
havlaga (self-restraint), 14
Hazan, Ya'akov, 23
Healey, Denis, 87n

Hebrew University, 98
Hebron, 16, 209, 245
Heikal, Mohammed, 156
Heller, Joseph, 32–3n
Hemed C (division of IDF's Science Corps), 58, 59
Herut (Freedom) Party (far right), 92, 136, 199; *see also* Likud (Unity) Bloc
Herzog, Ya'akov, 230n
Hiroshima, bombing of, 58, 60, 87n
Histradut (Federation of Jewish Labour in Palestine), 8, 9n, 16, 17n, 21, 83, 141, 142, 253; and Alignment, 135; Dayan's attack against, 69; dismissal of Lavon as Secretary General, 83, 84, 107; Executive Council, 24; expansionist economic policy, 6–7; institutions, 47; L.E. as investment expert for, 11–12; Lavon as Secretary General, 74–5; Mapai's control of, 24, 43, 50; and moshav movement, 41; Trade Union Department, 43
Histradut Agricultural Center, L.E. as member and director, 7
Hitler, Adolf, 5, 14, 16–17, 20, 37, 57, 96; *see also* Holocaust; Nazi Germany
Holocaust, 24–6, 37, 44, 56, 58, 91, 95, 96
Holy Land, 13
Horowitz, David, 43, 44, 45, 46; as governor of Bank of Israel, 97, 138
House of Commons, 68
Humphrey, Herbert, 239
Hussein, King of Jordan, 113, 159–61, 163, 167, 171, 187, 195, 198, 217, 222, 242; and Nasser, 202, 204
Husseini, Mussa, 18n
hydrogen bombs, 58

I

IDF *see* Israel Defence Forces (IDF)
immigration, absorbing, 35–42, 44, 46, 51n, 53; *see also* refugees/refugee issue
India, 129
intellectuals, 93, 95, 96, 97, 118
Intelligence Estimate, 167
Interdepartmental Regional Group for Near East and South Asia, 164–5
intermediate range ballistic missiles (IRBMs), 145, 146, 153; France, 103, 156, 190
International Atomic Energy Agency (IAEA), 123, 128, 158, 161, 164
Iraq, 16, 44
IRBMs *see* intermediate range ballistic missiles (IRBMs)
Irgun *see* IZL (Irgun Tsva'i Leummi)
Isaiah, Prophet, 94
Israel: annihilation threats, by Arabs, 57, 58, 123, 207; Armistice Demarcation Lines, 78, 120, 203, 221; Declaration of Independence, 96; domestic reform, under L.E., 110, 136; nuclear deterrence, xii, 31, 60, 121–2, 127, 133, 145, 146,

190, 191, 195; 'nuclear lobby', 162–3; security problem, long-term solution to, 62–3, 78, 171; Six Day War, following, 217–23; television introduced in, 246, 247–8; US, relationship with, 101, 126; wars affecting *see* Six Day War (1967); War of Independence (1948); Yom Kippur War (1973); *see also* Zionism; Zionist Labour Movement
Israel Air Force (IAF), 166, 195
Israel Atomic Energy Commission (IAEC), 59
Israel Defence Forces (IDF), xi, 30, 31, 53, 55, 79, 82, 134; Science Corps, 58, 59
Israel Electric Corporation, 43
Israeli Arabs, 108, 109
Israeli-Egyptian peace treaty (1979), 199, 207
Israeli-French military relations, 62, 63–4, 85n, 91, 98, 120, 144; formal agreement (1957), 65; *see also* Dimona nuclear reactor
Israeli-Palestinian peace negotiations, 39
Ivrit (modern Hebrew), 70
IZL (Irgun Tsva'i Leummi), 20, 24, 25; disbanding of, 31–2; terrorist activities by, 26, 27

J

Jabotinsky, Ze'ev, 12–13, 17n, 20, 21, 82
Jackson, 'Stonewall', 30
Jaffa, return of Arab refugees to, 36
Jarring, Gunnar, 232
Jenkins, Roy, 18n
Jerusalem, 140, 200, 205; Old City, 4, 218; Western Wall, 202, 204
Jewish Agency, 11, 20, 41, 253; Ben-Gurion as chair, 14, 27, 49; Executive Committee, 25; L.E. as treasurer, 42, 103; Political Department, 55; Rural Settlement Department, 41, 46, 72
Jewish Brigade Group, 22
'Jewish Commonwealth' idea, Biltmore conference, 23
Jewish National Fund, 48
Jews, American, 202, 214
Jezreel Valley, 15
Johnson, Lyndon B., xi, 102–6, 124, 150, 157–9, 164, 168, 170, 172, 178, 181, 182, 186–9, 196, 201, 202, 213–17, 224, 226, 229, 232, 234, 252; succeeding of Kennedy, 107, 111
Johnson Library, 127
Jordan, 31; Egyptian struggle with, 114; Hashemite kingdom of, 18n, 233
Jordan River waters, 113, 233, 236
Joseph, Dov (Minister of Justice), 116
Josephtal, Giora, 74
Judea, 235

K

Kamel, Mustafa, 157
Kant, Immanuel, 96
Kaplan, Eliezer, 43, 44, 45, 46

Katchalsky-Katsir, Aharon, 58, 59
Katchalsky-Katsir, Efraim, 58, 59
Katzenbach, Nicholas, 161, 170, 171, 174n
Katznelson, Berl, 8, 23, 56
Kaufman, Ezekiel, 95
Kennedy, John F., 89, 90, 102, 127, 252; Administration, 99–100; assassination, 106–7, 111; and Ben-Gurion, 90, 131n; National Security Action Memorandum 231, 98
Kent, Sherman, 212
Keren, Michael, 93
Khartoum conference (1967), 200, 223, 228
Khrushchev, Nikita, 111, 112, 127
kibbutzim, 4, 21, 40, 51n, 204; Kibbutz Degania Bet, 7, 72; Kibbutz Sede Boqer, 53, 54, 55, 60, 61, 106
Kimche, John, 147
King David Hotel, Jerusalem, 26
Kiryat Malachi, 49
Kiryat Shemona, 49
Knesset, 45, 137; Finance Committee, 64; Foreign Affairs and Defence Committee, 75, 80, 82
Komer, Robert W., 125, 126, 127, 128, 132n, 146, 150, 173n, 240
Kosygin, Alexei, 111, 190

L

L-70 radar-guided anti-aircraft cannon, 101
Labour Party, British, 25
Lafayette Park, Washington, 189
Lavon, Pinchas, 55–6, 60, 69, 74, 82, 218; exoneration of, 116, 117, 118; ousting as Secretary General of Histadrut, 83, 84, 107; and Peres, 77, 82; resignation from Sharett's Government, 61; secessionist group, 107; as Secretary General of Histadrut, 74–5
Lavon Affair (Israeli subversive actions in Egypt in 1954), 67, 92–3, 115, 119, 137, 186; '1954 Affair', 61, 74, 75, 76, 77, 80, 82, 83, 110, 116; '1960 Affair', 61, 74, 75, 81, 82, 84, 93, 117; and Ben-Gurion, 75, 79–80, 81, 116
leadership style of Eshkol, 141
League of Nations, 19
Lee, Robert E., 30
legacy of Eshkol, 231–43
Leibowitz, Yeshayahu, 76, 83, 89, 94, 206, 222, 223
Lenin, Vladimir, ix
Levinson, Larry, 189, 214
Libya, Jewish emigration from, 44
Likud (Unity) Bloc, 42, 199, 252; *see also* Herut (Freedom) Party (far right)
Lincoln, Abraham, 30
Lior, Yisrael, 237, 241
'Little Triangle' (Arab-inhabited region near Tel Aviv), 108
Livne, Eliezer, 76, 89, 206
Lydda, strategic town, 36

M

M48A3 tanks, 105
M60 tanks, 105
Ma'ariv (newspaper), 82, 98
Mah'us, Ibrahim, 156
makher (doer), L.E. as *see* doer, L.E. as
Makleff, Mordechai, 54
mamlakhtiyut (state-worthy behaviour), 135
man of action ('doer'), L.E. as *see* doer, L.E. as
Mandatory Government (British), 6, 7, 11–16, 24, 25
Mapai (Palestine and Israel's Labour party), 23–4, 42, 141, 142, 200, 220, 244; Alignment with, 135; Central Committee, 118, 119, 201; creation (1930), 8; elections of 1944, 77; elections of 1959, 68, 69, 70, 71; fracture (1944), 244; governing institutions, 130n; Histradut, control of, 24, 43, 50; in Knesset, 45, 50; and Palmach, 21, 22; 'Pandora's Box', 82, 84; partitioning of (1944), 22, 23; voting system, 253
Mapam (United Workers Party), 33n, 70, 219; coalition with Ahdut ha-'Avoda, 135, 136, 177; creation (1948), 244
Margalit, Dan, 87n
Marx, Karl, anti-Semitic doctrines, 2
Massa' u-Ma'as, Weizmann memoirs, ix
May 1967 crisis, 169, 170, 182, 189, 190, 219, 251; *see also* Six Day War (1967)
McCloy, John J., 99, 100, 101–2, 125
McNamara, Robert S., 150, 183, 211–12
MD 620 missile, 113
MD 660 missile, 113, 127
medium range ballistic missiles, 127, 134
Meir, Golda, 44, 91, 99, 100, 101, 116, 140
Mekorot water company, 42, 47
Memorandum of Conversation on Nuclear Weapons in the Middle East, 153
Mendès-France, Pierre, 62, 65
'messianic faith', 93, 94
Middle East arms race, 122
MiG 21 jets, 166
MiG 25 jets, 134, 192
Migdal ha-'Emeq, 73
Min Hayesod association, 107
Minister of Agriculture and Development, L.E. as, 46
Minister of Defence, L.E. as, x–xi, 9n, 35, 144
Minister of Finance, L.E. as, 46, 49, 74, 92, 103
Ministry of Defence (MOD), 53, 143, 197–8; Dayan as Chief of General Staff, 54–5, 56
missiles, 106, 112, 122, 134, 167; American Skyhawk, 133, 146, 238, 240; Cuban missile crisis, 111–12; French *see* France, nuclear weapons in; intermediate range ballistic *see* intermediate range ballistic missiles (IRBMs); MD 620 and MD 660, 113, 127;

medium range ballistic, 127, 134; MiG jets, 134, 166, 192; Phantom jets, 237–8, 240; Shavit II, 113; Soviet, 76; surface-to-surface, 104; *see also* nuclear deterrence
Mizrahim (immigrants from Muslim countries), 72, 73, 118, 140, 142, 219–20
Mollet, Guy, 64
Morgenthau, Henry, Jr., 44
Morocco, Jewish emigration from, 44
Morris, W., 145, 147, 148n
moshav movement, 40–1, 48; Nahalal, 72
Mount Carmel, 15
Mufti of Jerusalem (Hajj Amin al-Husaini), 5, 13–14, 15, 35, 38; alliance with Hitler, 14, 27
'Munich reflex', 64

N

Nahalal (first moshav), 72
nakba (Holocaust-like disaster), 40
Narkiss, Uzi, 210n
Nasser, Gamal Abdel, 61–4, 90, 91, 98, 100, 104, 106, 113, 124, 128, 129, 152, 156, 164, 167, 190, 191, 196, 225, 226, 229; Anderson, meeting with, 226–8, 243; conflicts with other Arab states, 114, 171; and Hussein, 202, 204; march into Sinai, 169, 170, 171, 192, 194–5; and Six Day War *see* Six Day War (1967)
National Archive, Kew, 9n
national duty doctrine (Ben-Gurion), 109
National Emergency Government (1967), 13, 31, 202, 221, 252
National Military Organization (NMO) *see* IZL (Irgun Tsva'i Leummi)
National Religious Party (NRP), 135
National Security Action Memorandum, 231 (NSAM), 98
National Security Council, White House, 121
National Unity Government, L.E. presiding over, xi, 198, 199
National Water Carrier programme, 9n, 72, 96, 113, 139
NATO (North Atlantic Treaty Organization), 66
Nazi Germany, 56, 57; negotiating with, 11–13, 14
Ne'eman, Yuval, 86n, 113
Negev, 15, 27, 97; uranium in, 58, 59
New York Times, 130, 143, 146, 147
'1954' affair *see* Lavon Affair (Israeli terrorist attacks)
'1960' affair *see* Lavon Affair (Israeli terrorist attacks)
Nisei, 108
Nixon, Richard, 239
NMO (National Military Organization) *see* IZL (Irgun Tsva'i Leummi)
Nolte, Richard, 195
Non-Proliferation Treaty (NPT), 138, 146, 158, 165, 166, 238; *see also* nuclear anti-proliferation

NPT *see* Non-Proliferation Treaty (NPT)
nuclear anti-proliferation, 111, 112, 126, 129, 138
nuclear deterrence, 57–8, 79, 113; contemporary terminology, 177; Egypt's vulnerability to attack, 122–3; French infrastructure, 61–2; Israel, xii, 31, 60, 121–2, 127, 133, 145, 146, 190, 191, 195; Memorandum of Conversation on Nuclear Weapons in the Middle East, 153; Soviet missiles, 76; submarines, nuclear-capable, 193; *see also* Dimona nuclear reactor project; missiles

O

occupied territories *see* Gaza Strip; West Bank
OECD, 253
open border policy (Dayan), 233
Operation Kadesh, 63
Oratovo, Ukraine (birthplace of L.E.), 1
Oren, Amir, 239
Oren, Elhanan, 30
Origins of Totalitarian Democracy, The (Talmon), 83
Ostfeld, Zahava, 30
Ottomans, Muslim loyalty to, 4

P

Pa'il, Meir, 30
Palestine: arrival/first career steps of L.E., 2–6; mass immigration of European Jews to, 23; *see also* Yishuv (Jewish community in Palestine)
Palestine Liberation Organization (PLO), 113, 145, 154, 242
Palmach (strike forces), 21, 22, 32, 33n, 69, 77
partition resolution, UN (1947), 14, 26, 29, 35, 57, 130n
passivity of European Diaspora Jews, ix
Patinkin, Don-Dan, 83, 96, 97, 98, 139
Pean, Pierre, 64, 65
Peel, Lord Robert/Peel Commission, 15, 16, 21, 23
Peled, Matitiahu, 185
Penslar, Derek J., 5
Peres, Shimon, 55, 56, 60, 61, 64, 66, 68, 71, 77, 113, 119, 126, 129, 136, 147, 244, 245; as Deputy Minister of Defence, 74, 82; under L.E.'s regime, 110, 198; and Lavon Affair, 75, 77, 82, 117; Western view of, 98–9
Phantom jets, 237–8, 240
'Phony War', 20
Pinkus, Benjamin, 85n
Plechanov, Igor Alexandrovich, ix
PLO *see* Palestine Liberation Organization (PLO)
Poland, partitioning of, 20
political messianism, 83–4
pre-emptive counterstrike doctrine, 177, 179, 183
preventive war, 111, 180, 184
Prime Minister, L.E. as, x–xi, 9n, 32; early years, 107–30; succeeding of Ben-Gurion, 22, 78, 84

prophets, Jewish, 94
proportional ballot system, 45
Public Committee for Nuclear Disarmament in Middle East, 75–6, 83
Public Records Office (PRO), 143
Puritanism, 3, 8

Q

Qibbia affair, 1950s, 178, 196n
Qu'ran, 17n

R

Rabin, Yitzhak, 22, 110–11, 125, 126–7, 134, 137, 159, 177–8, 190, 195, 203, 210n, 236, 239–40
Rackah, Joel (Giulio), 59
Rafael, Gideon, 131n, 155–6, 158, 173n
Rafi (Israel Workers List) Party, 134–5, 136, 139, 200, 244, 245–6
Ramle, strategic town, 36
Raphaeli, Nimrod, 210n
rationality theorem, 177
Raziel, David, 21, 24
reactor, nuclear, 61
refugees/refugee issue, 35–42, 44, 46, 51n, 57, 91, 99, 113, 228, 252
Remez, Gideon, 189, 190, 191, 192–3, 194, 195
resettlement activities, 35, 39, 41
resistance policy (Ben-Gurion), 25
'Responsive Leader', L.E. as, 29
restraint policy and Eshkol, 13–14
Revisionist Zionist Movement (Jabotinsky), 12
riots, Arab: in 1920 and 1921, 7; in 1929, 16; in 1936–39, 48
Roosevelt, Franklin D., 215
Rostow, Walt, 162, 164, 165–6, 168, 173n, 188, 189, 202, 211, 212–13, 215
Rotenstreich, Nathan, 82, 83
Rothschild, Baron Edmond de, 5
'rules of the game', 116, 117
Rural Settlement Department, Jewish Agency, 41, 46, 72
Rusk, Dean, 105, 151–5, 157–8, 162, 163, 174n, 183, 213, 238

S

sabras, 70
Sadat, Anwar, 150, 151, 152, 240
Samaria, 235
Samburski, Shmuel, 85n
Samson Option, 186, 202, 253
Samu' village, raid on, 159, 160, 161, 164, 190
Sapir, Pinchas, 47, 49, 71, 72, 98, 116, 118, 137, 140, 233–4; as Minister of Finance L.E.'s dovish colleague and Mapai's 'boss' with L.E., 63, 69; as Minister of Trade and Industry, 46, 64, 73–4
Sarid, Yosef (Yossi), 137–8
Saudi Arabia, Egyptian struggle with, 114
Schelling, Thomas C., 87n, 132n, 177

Schind, Ze'ev, 55
Schmorak, Emil, 47
Schroeder, Gerhard, 104
Schweid, Eliezer, 2, 9n
Science Corps, IDF, 58, 59
Second Aliya (second wave of Zionist immigration to Palestine, 1903–14), 3, 9n
'Second Israel', 42
Second World War, 19, 57; first involvement in military affairs, 21–2; lessons of, 37–8, 56–7
secularization process, 1
Security Council, 231–2
Sede Boqer, Kibbutz, 53, 54, 55, 60, 61, 106
Service Notes, 125, 175n
Shapira, Anita, 33n
Shapira, Moshe, 178
Sharett, Moshe, 39, 44, 56, 60–1, 118; as Prime Minister, 55, 61
Sharm el-Sheikh, 205, 207, 238
Sharon, Arieh, 49, 184
Shavit II missile, 113
Shazar, Zalman, 157
Sheck, Ze'ev, 131–2n
Sherman tanks, 105
Shinui (liberal party), 109
Shkolnik, Deborah (mother of L.E.), 1
Shuqairy, Ahmed, 113, 115, 144–5, 154, 159
Silver, Rabbi Abba Hillel, 26
Sinai, Nasser's march into, 169, 170, 171, 192, 194–5
Six Day War (1967), xi, xii, 28, 29, 76, 109, 147, 170, 189, 202, 207, 234, 241, 252; Israel following, 217–23; and National Emergency Government, 13, 31, 202, 221, 252; Nuclear Dimension, 212; *see also* May 1967 crisis
Skyhawks, 133, 146, 238, 240
Soviet Union, former, 68, 105, 125, 189–96; and Egypt, 193–4; nuclear anti-proliferation agreement, 111, 112, 126, 129; Sputnik, launch of, 76; *see also* superpower relations
Spanish Civil War, 64
Sputnik, launch of, 76
Stalin, Joseph, 20
Stern, Avraham 'Yair', 20–1
Stern Gang/Sternists, 21; Ben-Gurion's campaign against, 25; terrorist activities by, 24, 26, 27
Straits of Tiran, 63, 172, 183, 195, 205, 238, 241; closure, 170, 176, 181, 192
strategic-military seminar (Ben-Gurion), 28
Strauss, Franz-Josef, 104
'stutter speech' of Eshkol, 180, 202
submarines, nuclear-capable, 193
Suez Canal area: crisis of 1956, 63–4, 65, 66; Israeli-French cooperation, 62; Lavon Affair *see* Lavon Affair
Sukarno, Ahmed, 112
superpower relations, 111, 112, 154
surface-to-surface missiles, 104
Symmes, Harrison, 147
Syria: Army, 204; Ba'ath regime, 113, 114, 166, 190, 204

Syrian Heights *see* Golan Heights

T

Tabenkin, Yitzhak, 21, 23, 25, 34n, 68, 77, 90
Tal, Israel, 185
Talbot, Philips, 128, 129
Talmon, Jacob L., 83, 87n
Tel Aviv, American Embassy in, 239
Tel Aviv Workers' Council, 24, 42
television, introduction in Israel, 246, 247–8
Temple Mount, 200
territorial gains, price of, 197–205
terrorist activities, 24, 26
Thant, U., 172
Tiberias, 73
Transfer Committee, 51n
transit camps, 41
Transjordan, 15, 16
treasurer of Jewish Agency, L.E. as, 42, 103
Truman, Harry S., 25–6, 27, 215; Administration, 44
Turkey, eradication of Greek presence in, 38
Turkish-Muslim enmity, First World War, 4
two-state solution, Palestine, 15

U

Ulbricht, Walter, 104
unemployment, 139, 140, 141
United Kingdom: British Proliferation Policy in Service of Maintaining its Status and its German Policy (1952–68), 66; electoral system, and Ben-Gurion's electoral reform, 68, 71; Mandate activities/ Mandatory Government *see* Mandatory Government (British); Peel plan *see* Peel, Lord Robert/Peel Commission; Stern Gang on, 21; White Paper on Palestine (1939), 19, 20, 21, 25, 37
United Nations: General Assembly Resolution 194 (1948), 38, 39; partition resolution *see* partition resolution, UN (1947)
United States: in 1950s, 57–8; American Bill of Rights, 109; American Manhattan Project, 59; American Skyhawk, 133, 146, 238; Atomic Energy Commission, 161; and Dimona reactor, 89–90, 99, 119–20, 123, 124, 126–9, 133, 138, 142–3, 151, 158–9, 224, 239; and Egypt, 152, 157, 158–9, 163, 182; Israeli relationship with, 101, 126; Jews in *see* Jews, American; visits by L.E., 121, 123; *see also* superpower relations
uranium, in Negev, 58, 59
Urbach, Ephraim Elimelech, 83, 94, 96
USS *Liberty*, Israeli attack on, 189, 211
USSR *see* Soviet Union, former
utopianism, of Ben-Gurion, 44, 45

V

Vanunu, Mordechai, 152
Versailles Treaty, 57
Vietnam, 111, 113; American-Jewish criticism of War, 157
Vilensky-Yallan, Emmanuel, 48, 52n
Vilnius, L.E. educated in, 2
violence, among Arabs, 4
vision, and efficiency, 96
Voice of Israel (public radio service), 107, 196n
Voutour medium-range bombers, 186

W

Wadi Salib riots (1959), 73
Wallach, Yehuda, 30
Waqf (Islamic charitable trust organization), 200
War of Independence (1948), 8n, 29–32, 33n, 55, 59, 60, 108, 191, 203
Warneke, Paul C., 238, 239–40
'wars of the Jews', 60
Wattenberg, Ben, 189
weapons of mass destruction (WMDs), 124, 125; *see also* nuclear deterrence
Weber, Max, 95
Weitz, Ra'anan, 47, 48
Weitz, Yechiam, 87n, 107, 109, 110
Weitz, Yosef, 47–8, 51n
Weizman, Ezer, 201, 236
Weizmann, Chaim, 26; memoirs, ix
Weizmann Institute of Science, Rehovoth, 65
West Bank, 31, 36, 39, 40, 90, 160, 205, 208, 209, 237, 249; 'Allon Plan', 200; Etzion Bloc, 209, 222; occupation in 1967, 109, 199, 203
West Germany, Ben-Gurion policy of military cooperation with, 67, 81, 90–1, 92, 98
Western Wall, 202, 204
Wheeler, Earl, 182
White House, xi, 123; National Security Council, 121
White Paper on Palestine (1939), 19, 20, 21, 25, 37
womanizer, L.E. as, 8
women pioneers, Zionist, 4
World Zionist Organization, 5, 17n; Congress, 27; Weizmann president of, ix

X

'X-Committee', 25, 26

Y

Ya'ari, Meir, 23
Yadin, Yigael (IDF Chief of Staff), 46, 54, 74
Yariv, Aharon, 146–7, 153
Yavne, 72
Yemen, 44, 114, 152
Yishuv (Jewish community in Palestine), 12, 14, 19–20, 22, 44; Labour leadership (Ben-Gurion), 20
Yoffe, Avraham, 185
Yom Kippur War (1973), 109, 207, 208, 240, 245
Yoman-ha-'Milchama (War Diary), Ben-Gurion, 59, 85n

Z

Zach, Nathan, 70
Ze'evi, Rehavam, 181, 236, 237, 249n
Zionism: of Eshkol, 118; pre-Zionist and early Zionist efforts, Palestine, 5; public debate on, ix; Social-Democratic, ideology, x
Zionist Labour Movement, 2, 3, 13, 244
Zionization process, DPs, 26